The Struggle for Sovereignty

THE STRUGGLE FOR

Sovereignty

Seventeenth-Century English Political Tracts

VOLUME 2

Edited and with an Introduction by
Joyce Lee Malcolm

LIBERTY FUND
Indianapolis

This book is published by Liberty Fund, Inc., a foundation established to encourage study of the ideal of a society of free and responsible individuals.

𒀔 𒂼𒄄

The cuneiform inscription that serves as our logo
and as the design motif for our endpapers is the earliest-known written
appearance of the word "freedom" (*amagi*), or "liberty."
It is taken from a clay document written about 2300 B.C.
in the Sumerian city-state of Lagash.

Library of Congress Cataloging-in-Publication Data
The struggle for sovereignty: seventeenth-century English political tracts/
edited and with an introduction by Joyce Lee Malcolm.
        p.   cm.
Includes bibliographical references and index.
ISBN 0-86597-187-0 (2-vol. set: hardcover).—ISBN 0-86597-189-7 (2-vol.
set: pbk.).—ISBN 0-86597-152-8 (vol. 1: hardcover).—ISBN 0-86597-153-6
(vol. 1: pbk.).—ISBN 0-86597-186-2 (vol. 2: hardcover).—ISBN 0-86597-
188-9 (vol. 2: pbk.).
        1. Great Britain—Politics and government—1603–1714.   2. Political
science—Great Britain—History—17th century.   3. Civil rights—Great
Britain—History—17th century.   I. Malcolm, Joyce Lee.
JN191.S77   1999
323.5′0941′09032—DC21   97-28248

99 00 01 02 03 C 5 4 3 2 1

99 00 01 02 03 P 5 4 3 2 1

Liberty Fund, Inc.
8335 Allison Pointe Trail, Suite 300
Indianapolis, Indiana 46250-1684

Contents

Parliament and the Succession

The King's Inalienable Prerogative

Introduction

After the clash of ideas and the high drama of the English civil war and Interregnum, the restoration of monarchy in 1660 came as a relief to most Englishmen but seems something of an anticlimax today. The struggle for sovereignty appeared to have swung back to where it had started early in the century. Even when tensions reemerged in the 1670s, the struggle looked a pale copy of the past; fueled by the old frictions, driven by the old fears, bolstered by the same philosophies, the new struggle became a preface to the conservative revolution of 1689. Yet it is the three decades from the Restoration in 1660 through the Glorious Revolution of 1689 whose legacy endured to shape British and American politics and thought. The English Revolution and its republican experiment failed; the Glorious Revolution succeeded. That result and the consensus upon which it depended deserve consideration and explanation. The tracts published during those years, at first few in number, then rising to a flurry from 1678, tell the story of a renewed and revised constitutional conflict that would finally settle the struggle for sovereignty.

The Restoration appears at first a triumph for the royalist cause and the Crown. Charles returned with no new restraints on his own powers, indeed with the leeway a relieved aristocracy and weary public were prepared to grant to ensure stability. His promise of clemency for former enemies and toleration for religious dissenters held out the hope for a more broad-minded polity. But the triumphant royal-

For a summary of the theories and tensions that dominated seventeenth-century England up to 1660, see the introduction to volume 1.

ists were not about to forgive and forget and doubtless felt such clemency unwise if the restoration were to be permanent. Their understandable hostility toward their old enemies was exacerbated when they realized that many of their party would never recover lands confiscated or lost in hardship sales during the civil war and Interregnum.[1] While Charles often disappointed the former royalists, he could not govern without them.

May 1660 marked the restoration not only of the king and his father's party but of the Church of England and of Parliament in its traditional form as well. Neither institution was about to completely subordinate its interests to those of the Crown. In fact, the old relationship between the church and the monarch, formerly so harmonious, was strained by their differing agendas. Those put in charge of the church were not interested in toleration. Once negotiations for a reconciliation with the moderate Presbyterians failed, Anglican leaders insisted upon strict liturgical uniformity and the expulsion of nonconformist ministers from their positions.[2] Nor would they consider easing restrictions on Catholics. This divergence of royal and church interests, coupled with the demise of the Court of High Commission and with it royal power to discipline the clergy, made churchmen look to Parliament rather than the Crown for support whenever the king's policies veered from the narrow path of religious conformity. And Parliament did not disappoint. It gladly passed legislation that mandated religious conformity and ousted Catholics

1. There has been considerable debate about the actual extent of royalist losses. Whatever the damages, there can be no doubt about the resentment of royalists that they were not completely recouped, and that former enemies were often treated better than the royalists would have wished. See Joyce Malcolm, "Charles II and the Restoration of Royal Power," *Historical Journal* 35, no. 2 (1992): 307–30. See also Sir John Habakkuk, "The Land Settlement and the Restoration of Charles II," *Trans. Royal Historical Society*, 5th ser. (1978), 201–22.

2. During the months just after the Restoration moderate Presbyterian leaders negotiated with the Anglican leadership in support of a broader national church. For the best recent book on this subject, see John Spurr, *The Restoration Church of England: 1646–1689* (New Haven, 1991), especially 30–36.

and dissenters from civil and religious posts. Parliament had no intention of becoming a tool of the church, however. It announced its intention to control religious policy when it refused to reinstate the Court of High Commission, rejected Laud's divine right canons of 1640 with their insistence that church government "belongs in chief unto kings," and imposed an oath upon clergymen against all innovations in doctrine.[3] Convocation, the great synod of the Church of England, did not meet from 1664 until 1689.

The restored parliament's relationship with the Crown had been altered by the experience of the republican era as well. True, its treatment of the Crown sometimes bordered on servility. But for many years Charles was dependent upon the two Houses while they were not as compliant as they pretended—witness their refusal to revive those instruments of royal control, the prerogative courts.[4] That refusal settled the competition between common law and royal prerogative in favor of common law. In order to exert legal influence Charles II and especially James II had little option but to place greater pressure on the judiciary.[5] Further, in the key area of finance, Parliament failed to restore the Crown's feudal and historic sources of revenue.

In short, the politics and constitutional views of the 1640s were not identical to those of the 1660s. Even in this different setting, however, it was only a short time before the old quarrels over the powers

3. See An Act for explanation of a clause contained in an Act of Parliament made in the seventeenth year of the late King Charles . . . concerning commissioners for causes ecclesiastical, 1661, 13 Car. II, c. 12, in John Kenyon, *The Stuart Constitution*, 2d ed. (Cambridge, 1986), 350–51.

4. The Triennial Act of 1641 had mandated that Parliament be summoned at least every three years and provided a mechanism to accomplish this should the king refuse. This act was abolished in 1664 on the mistaken assumption that it would force Charles II to dissolve his then parliament. It was replaced by an act that obliged the king to summon a parliament at least every three years, but lacked any mechanism to compel him and laid down no minimum period for a session. 16 Car. II, c. 1, and see John Kenyon, *Stuart Constitution*, 335.

5. See Jennifer Carter, "Law, Courts and Constitution," in *The Restored Monarchy: 1660–1688*, ed. J. R. Jones (Totowa, N.J., 1979), 86.

of king and Parliament, the implications of divine right monarchy, the right of resistance, and fear of standing armies reappeared. Quite different aspects of the constitution became flashpoints, among them Court manipulation of Parliament, the nature of Parliament as a representative institution, the succession to the throne, control of religious policies, and the king's power to dispense with laws. A leitmotif throughout was the subjects' fear that Charles and James might free themselves from dependence on Parliament and the ancient constitution through a standing army. In fact, they did have considerable help in that regard from generous secret pensions granted by Louis XIV. It was a new and in many ways more perilous world for the "ancient constitution," one compelling our attention if we are to understand why, in these unpromising circumstances, Parliament was to emerge the winner of the struggle for sovereignty.

THE RESTORATION OF KING, CHURCH, AND PARLIAMENT

Two main constitutional aspects of the restored parliament demand consideration: its relationship with the king and his government, and its institutional development. The relationship with the king was more complex than it appeared. The long, so-called Cavalier Parliament of 1661, which succeeded the Convention Parliament that recalled Charles, gave—sometimes with imprudent largesse—but took care to preserve its key powers. It began by enacting legislation to protect and strengthen the Crown and solidify royalist political control. The bitter experience of the civil war era and Interregnum that followed shaped these would-be cures. The first measure the Cavalier Parliament passed was a new, broader treason act. This made it treasonable to "compass imagine invent devise or intend" the death or harm of the king or aim to deprive or depose him.[6] Vivid experience

---

6. An Act to Preserve the Person and Government of the King, 1661, 13 Car. II, st. I, c. 1.

with the power of political tracts and polemical preaching to incite the public convinced them to include "any Printing Writing Preaching or Malicious and advised speaking" as potentially treasonable.[7] Further, it was made a punishable offence to "publish or affirm the King to be an Heretick or a Papist" or to assert that he "endeavours to introduce Popery." Parliament took care to ensure the act not "deprive either of the Houses of Parliament or any of theire Members of theire just ancient Freedome and priviledge of debating any matters or busines," that they have "the same freedome of speech and all other Priviledges whatsoever as they had before the making of this Act." An act was passed that prohibited submission of a petition to Parliament or the king by more than ten persons, and another instituted censorship.

The issue that had provoked civil war, the power of the sword, was decided in favor of the Crown. Parliament declared unequivocally "the sole right of the militia to be in the King."[8] On the other hand the act made no provision for using the militia outside England or paying men for longer than a month and prescribed only a mild penalty for disobedience. The militia officers—local aristocrats—had considerable power over its activities. For these reasons many constitutional scholars agree that the act "gave the king the shadow but only a little of the substance of power," and that the actual implication was that "the King's prerogative powers for the regulation of the Militia were minimal."[9]

The Cavalier Parliament that enacted these measures sat in one session after another from 1661 until Charles dissolved it in January

7. Ibid.
8. The Militia Act, 1662, 14 Car. II, c. 3.
9. See J. R. Western, *The English Militia in the Eighteenth Century: The Story of a Political Issue, 1660–1802* (London, 1965), 16; and Mark Thomson, *A Constitutional History of England, 1642–1801* (London, 1938), 160. And see Joseph R. Tanner, *English Constitutional Conflicts of the Seventeenth Century, 1603–1689* (Cambridge, 1928), 224; Anthony Fletcher, *Reform in the Provinces: The Government of Stuart England* (New Haven, 1986), especially 321.

1679—longer than the Long Parliament of the civil war, which sat from 1640 until 1653. During the course of its extraordinary life its constitutional viewpoint went through a metamorphosis, having begun, David Ogg points out, "by removing every shackle from kingship" only to end "in the terrors of a nightmare plot, attacking everything sacred in the prerogative—the king's minister, the king's control of the army, the morality of his consort and the loyalty of the heir presumptive."[10] Before this assault on royal supremacy came a series of internal skirmishes as each house sought to define its own powers before coming to grips with the anomaly of its own longevity as a representative assembly whose term became perpetual.

Behind Parliament's introspection and the competition between the two houses lurked the legacy of the civil war. The Commons, stained by the stigma of its rebellious past, was regarded by the Lords and the Court as not completely reliable. For its part it was especially anxious to reassert its dignity and authority. Tension between the two houses ignited over the Lords' right to original jurisdiction in legal cases. Since the 1620s the Lords had accepted original jurisdiction in cases that were not referred from the House of Commons. With the abolition of Star Chamber in the 1640s the Lords became the judicial wing of Parliament. After the Lords house too was abolished in 1649 the Commons tried to exercise this power, but Cromwell reminded them they lacked the jurisdiction. Nevertheless the House of Commons after the Restoration was unwilling to see the House of Lords resume this authority. Their opportunity for a challenge came when the losing party in a case before the Lords in 1667, *Skinner v. The East India Company*, appealed to the Commons. In the wrangle that followed the Commons challenged the Lords' right of original jurisdiction and effectively won. The case was stricken from both houses' records, and so was technically withdrawn, but the Lords never re-

10. David Ogg, *England in the Reign of Charles II*, 2d ed. (Oxford, 1972), 578–79.

sumed original jurisdiction. The jurisdictional dispute was hotly renewed, however, in a series of cases culminating in *Shirley v. Fagg* in 1675, this time shifting to the Lords' right to decide cases on appeal. Thomas Shirley had appealed to the Lords against a Chancery decree in favor of Sir John Fagg, a member of the Commons. The dispute became so bitter it led to two prorogations or dismissals of Parliament with the Lords ultimately winning the day.[11] In the process each house spelled out what it saw as its distinct place within the constitution.

More fundamental issues were raised by the very longevity of the Cavalier Parliament. In 1675, when it had already been sitting for fifteen years, an anonymous pamphlet appeared calling for its dissolution and new elections.[12] The probable author, Anthony Ashley Cooper, Earl of Shaftesbury, a founder of the future Whig party, hoped new elections would produce members more to his liking. But political interests aside, the tract raised serious constitutional questions about the representative nature of any body of such long duration. Indeed, by 1675 the Earl of Danby, the king's chief minister, had a systematic campaign underway to bribe MPs with cash and posts.[13] This and other evils attributable to the lack of accountability enabled the author to argue that MPs no longer represented their constituents. On 20 November 1675 when one of Shaftesbury's supporters moved in the Lords for a dissolution, the motion lost by only two votes. Two days later Parliament was prorogued for the unprecedented period of fifteen months. When it reconvened Shaftesbury claimed this exceptionally long prorogation was illegal and amounted

11. During a prorogation Parliament was recessed but not dissolved. When the prorogation was ended the same members would reconvene.

12. [Anthony Ashley Cooper, Earl of Shaftesbury], "Two Seasonable Discourses Concerning This Present Parliament" (Oxford, 1675).

13. See for example, Ogg, *Charles II*, 529; J. R. Jones, "Parties and Parliament," in *Restored Monarchy*, ed. Jones, 52–53; and J. R. Jones, *Country and Court: England, 1658–1714* (Cambridge, Mass., 1979), 189–90.

to a dissolution, an assertion that landed him in the Tower of London for a year. More important for political thought than Shaftesbury's machinations is the searching debate over the limits of parliamentary sessions if that body was to be responsive to constituents.

SOVEREIGNTY IN THE CROWN

To protect the regime against rebellion, the king, royalists, and the church attempted to legislate conformity to royalist civil war philosophy, a philosophy that damned all resistance to the king or his servants and recognized no distinction between the king and his office. Strangely, given the marked failure of oaths to enforce the royalists' own loyalty and conformity to Interregnum regimes, they relied upon the same technique to impose their thought-control and purge dissidents. The resulting oaths were included in all sorts of legislation. To ensure that only right-thinking individuals—that is, no supporters of the "good old cause," Presbyterians, other dissenters, or Catholics—served as municipal officials, Parliament imposed loyalty oaths. In addition to the customary oaths of allegiance and supremacy, the 1661 Corporation Act required a declaration that the Solemn League and Covenant of 1644 was unlawful and "against the known laws and liberties of the kingdom," a new oath that proclaimed it "not lawfull upon any pretence whatsoever to take Arms against the King," and finally, denunciation of "that Traiterous Position of taking Arms by His Authority against His Person or against those that are commissioned by Him."[14] Parliament's faith in oaths had its limits however, and the two houses agreed that even if someone were willing to take all these oaths, he could be sacked by special commissioners if they deemed him dangerous to public safety. The Militia Act of 1662 obliged all officers to swear to the same prin-

14. The Corporation Act, 1661, 13 Car. II, st. II, c. 1.

ciples as those in the Corporation Act.[15] These oaths reappeared in
the 1662 Uniformity Act, which obliged all clergymen, college fellows, tutors, and schoolmasters to pledge not only "unfeigned assent
and consent to all and every thing" in the Book of Common Prayer
but to take the nonresistance oath imposed upon town officials and
militia officers.[16] Three years later the Five Mile Act barred nonconformist ministers from approaching within five miles of their former
parishes unless they swore to all oaths in the Uniformity Act and one
more. The ministers had to vow never to "endeavour any alteration of
government either in Church or State."[17] The pledge not to alter the
church harked back to Archbishop Laud's controversial canons of
1640 which imposed an oath upon clergy not to "consent to alter the
government of this Church...as it stands now established."[18] That
oath said nothing about the secular government, nor, to my knowledge, did any other. It thus became a requirement of office to deny
the legitimacy of any resistance to the king or his officials and to reject the ancient distinction, seized upon by the Long Parliament, between the king and his office. For clergy and teachers there was also
a pledge not to alter either church or state.

In February 1675 the bishops suggested that an oath similar to that
in the Five Mile Act be imposed upon members of Parliament and
other officeholders. The king concurred, and in April a bill was duly
introduced in the Lords to require members of Parliament and other
officeholders to swear it was unlawful "on any pretence whatsoever"
to take arms against the king or to endeavor "any alteration in the
government of church or state as it is by law established." Had this
"nonresisting" test bill become law it would have frozen every detail
of church and state government as they then stood and deprived Par-

---

15. The Militia Act, 1662, 14 Car. II, c. 3.
16. An Act for the Uniformity of Public Prayers, 1662, 14 Car. II, c. 4.
17. The Five Mile Act, 1664, 7 Car. II, c. 2.
18. See Archbishop Laud's Canons of 1640, in Kenyon, *Stuart Constitution*, 152.

liament of its most important function. Such was the obsession with the danger of armies, however, that there were suspicions the bill was meant to justify a standing army.

Shaftesbury led the spirited opposition to the bill in the House of Lords. A deservedly famous tract, "A Letter from a Person of Quality to His Friend in the Country," probably penned by him, provides a blow-by-blow account of the stormy debate that raged for almost seventeen days, the Lords often sitting until nine at night, sometimes until midnight, with the king himself in attendance. The bill's supporters managed to win approval for all its clauses although in one instance by a single vote. This crucial legislation would have become law had not the fierce struggle between the two houses over jurisdiction in *Shirley v. Fagg* led to the prorogation of Parliament. Indeed, that jurisdictional dispute may have been exacerbated for just that purpose.

PARLIAMENT AND THE SUCCESSION TO THE THRONE

A few years later a far more serious crisis nearly plunged the realm back into civil war. The issue was the old one of religion, which bore significant constitutional consequences throughout the early modern era. Charles could not erase the deep-seated bigotry and fear his subjects felt toward Catholicism, a faith they equated with absolutism and inquisition. His failed attempts to institute religious toleration stood in marked contrast to triumphs in other spheres and even in contrast to the successes of other English monarchs in setting religious policy. Charles was the first English monarch since the middle ages "successfully defied by his leading churchmen."[19] It was one of his attempts at toleration, his 1672 Declaration of Indulgence, that began the crisis. Parliament's angry response to that unilateral effort

---

19. Ronald Hutton, *The Restoration: A Political and Religious History of England and Wales, 1658–1667* (Oxford, 1985), 181.

to suspend enforcement of the penal laws against Catholics and dissenting Protestants was the Test Act of 1673, designed to do the opposite, to drive Catholics from public office. One can imagine the general dismay of Protestants when one of the victims of the new act was James, Duke of York, heir to the throne, who resigned his posts rather than take the Anglican sacrament and thus revealed that he was a Catholic.[20]

Religious anxiety reached fever pitch in 1678 when unscrupulous informers regaled Parliament and the nation with tales of a supposed popish plot by the queen and her physician to poison Charles and place James upon the throne. As panic swept the kingdom, Charles's negotiations for a French pension to free him from dependence upon Parliament became public. Ministers were blamed, as custom demanded. Shaftesbury and other members of Parliament asked Charles to bar James from his presence and councils. Charles raised the issue of the succession himself, suggesting a scheme to limit the powers of any future Catholic monarch.[21] But that would not do. Shaftesbury and his supporters insisted James be removed from the line of succession.

In January 1679 with his councils in disarray, Charles dissolved the long Cavalier Parliament. But the exclusion controversy preoccupied the three parliaments that succeeded it. The issue created the first real English political parties—Whigs for exclusion of James from the throne because of his Catholicism, Tories for strict succession and absolute obedience to the Crown. Charles refused to consider the exclusion of his brother. His sudden illness in August 1679, however, reminded Englishmen that if the succession were in dispute, his death could plunge them into civil war. The church hierarchy and the

---

20. Charles relied upon his prerogative power in ecclesiastical affairs in issuing the Declaration of Indulgence. It would have suspended the penal laws with the stipulation that Catholics only worship in private, and dissenting Protestant ministers had to be licensed by a magistrate. The reaction to the Declaration was so hostile that Charles withdrew it.

21. See Jones, *Country and Court*, 203.

Tories were prepared to exalt kingship and risk a Catholic monarch rather than face that prospect. Charles adroitly played upon that fear, characterizing the Whigs as dangerous radicals. This tactic and his astute dissolutions of Whig-dominated parliaments enabled the king to break their power, but not before a host of constitutional issues were aired about the relative powers of Parliament and the Crown, in particular Parliament's role in determining the succession. Perhaps no question more closely touched sovereignty itself.

Back came the old civil war arguments with renewed urgency. Had an ancient parliament created the king, or an ancient king created the law and parliament? Theorists argued whichever was more ancient must be sovereign. Strict divine right teaching, as the king's supporters pointed out, meant strict succession. How could Parliament, a mere creature of the Crown, determine the succession? Never mind the awkward fact that Parliament had done just that, most recently during the reign of Henry VIII, albeit by endorsing Henry's own wishes. Back too came the less extreme argument that kings and parliaments had a coordinate, shared power. Everyone agreed the entire realm was present in Parliament in person or by proxy, and only the king in parliament could make or alter law. A few radical thinkers even looked beyond Parliament and argued that the people it represented were sovereign. It was the exclusion controversy that prompted publication of Sir Robert Filmer's manuscript *Patriarcha*, which in its turn provoked Sir Algernon Sidney's powerful refutation, *Discourses Concerning Government*, and John Locke's *First Treatise of Government*. William Petyt, a legal antiquary and Whig polemicist, penned an influential treatise, "The Antient Right of the Commons of England Asserted," in which he stoutly defended the concept of a shared sovereignty against the notion that William, as a conqueror, had created all.[22] Petyt's views were challenged by

22. William Petyt, "The Antient Right of the Commons of England Asserted" (London, 1680).

Robert Brady, physician to Charles and James, in an unblinking defense of the conquest theory with its notion that a vanquished people had only those rights their conqueror chose to grant them. Brady insisted William the Conqueror was the source of English law and even of Magna Carta.[23] At the Glorious Revolution, in an act symbolic of political and philosophical ascendancy, Brady yielded his post as keeper of the records in the Tower to Petyt, and with him divine right theory was supplanted by recognition of the legislative sovereignty of king in parliament.[24]

For the time being, however, the exclusion movement failed. The losing Whigs were hounded from office and treated as potential rebels. Some fled abroad, others like Algernon Sidney and William Lord Russell were executed as traitors for their alleged involvement in the so-called Rye House Plot against Charles. Sidney, condemned by his unpublished manuscript, died as had Sir Henry Vane nearly twenty years before, proclaiming his faith in the "good old cause." Royal power and the necessity for absolute obedience was extolled from pulpit, press, and lecture hall. By 1683 the divine right of monarchy seemed triumphant. Charles would keep a secret promise to Louis XIV, and Parliament would not meet again in his lifetime.

JAMES II AND THE ANCIENT CONSTITUTION

Immediately upon his brother's death in February 1685, James went to the Privy Council, where he promised the councilors that "how-

23. Robert Brady, "The Great Point of Succession Discussed, with a Full and Particular Answer to the Late Pamphlet Entitled a Brief History of the Succession . . ." (London, 1681), B4191. Brady wrote a series of pamphlets during the exclusion controversy including "A Full and Clean Answer to a Book written by William Petit Esquire, Entituled, The Rights of the Commons Asserted . . ." (London, 1681) and "A true and exact history of the succession of the crown" (London, 1681). See for a discussion on Brady's ideas and influence J. G. A. Pocock, *The Ancient Constitution and the Feudal Law* (Cambridge, 1987), especially chap. 8.

24. See Corinne Weston, "England: Ancient Constitution and Common Law," in *The Cambridge History of Political Thought: 1450–1700* (Cambridge, 1991), 410.

ever he had ben misrepresented as affecting arbitrary power, they should find the contrary, for that the laws of England had made the King as greate a monarch as he could desire."[25] To their relief he vowed to "maintain the Government both in Church and State, as by Law establish'd" and to "never depart from the just rights and prerogatives of the Crown . . . and preserve (the nation) in all its lawful rights and liberties." No Stuart, however, had a greater opportunity to become absolute than James. His income was enviable, his army greatly enlarged because of brief rebellions against his succession, and his opportunity to pack parliaments unequalled.[26] As part of Charles's campaign to destroy the Whigs in 1680 he recalled some fifty-eight municipal charters and remodelled them to narrow their electorate and provide more direct Crown control over their officers. In his short reign James would regrant 121 charters to the same end.[27] But it was James's religion that was to cause the greatest outrage, for promises, especially where religion was concerned, could be broken, as Louis XIV proved shortly after James ascended the throne. Louis revoked the Edict of Nantes and with it the promise to French Protestants of perpetual and irrevocable freedom of conscience.

Although he had left the Church of England James did not seek to overthrow it. However, he immediately began placing Catholics in sensitive posts, such as in the army, dispensing with the penal laws

---

25. John Evelyn, *The Diary of John Evelyn*, ed. E. S. deBeer (Oxford, 1955), 4:411–12.

26. James was the first English king since Henry VIII to enjoy financial independence, which John Kenyon reminds us was "a fact of crucial constitutional importance." Kenyon, *Stuart Constitution*, 364. Two rebellions early in his reign, Monmouth's rebellion and Argyll's rebellion, enabled him to boost his regular income. He was also granted proceeds of duties on wine, vinegar, tobacco, and sugar for eight years. The Scots Parliament voted James £260,000 a year for life. As a result he had a yearly revenue of more than £2,000,000. He had an army of forty thousand men. Jennifer Carter judges that he had "made himself so strong militarily that the Revolution of 1688 would not have been possible without outside intervention by armed forces." Carter, "Law, Courts and Constitution," 78. On the other hand James's army itself was split over his policy of introducing Catholics, and during the crisis of 1688 suffered from famous and serious defections.

27. Carter, "Law, Courts and Constitution," 91.

meant to prohibit their service. Adding insult to injury, he then denigrated the Protestant-led militia. Both houses of his otherwise obedient parliament took great exception to what they saw as illegal exercise of the prerogative to place the army in Catholic hands. James prorogued Parliament and dismissed from all their posts those members who had opposed him. The next year he issued batches of dispensations granting Catholics, but not Protestant dissenters, immunity from the penal laws. Just in case his Anglican clergy considered swerving from their unquestioning obedience to the Crown, special "Directions concerning Preaching" were issued in March 1686 against polemical preaching, and a new Court of High Commission was created, renamed the Ecclesiastical Commission, to enforce the ban.

When heavy-handed pressure on town officials and the aristocracy failed to gain sufficient support for his policy of toleration for Catholics, James decided to include Protestant dissenters in his largesse and turned to his old enemies, the Whigs, for support. In April 1687 he used his prerogative to issue a Declaration of Indulgence generally dispensing with penal acts for both Catholics and dissenters. But this would need parliamentary sanction and to ensure a favorable new parliament James used the control the revised municipal charters afforded him to begin a series of mass purges of municipal officials. Hundreds of men who failed to endorse the king's toleration policy were also purged from the commission of the peace and militia offices.[28] James's base of support narrowed with each purge as he alienated hundreds of traditional supporters, only to find dissenters and Whigs reluctant to embrace toleration that included Catholics.[29] Undaunted, he reissued the Declaration of Indulgence in April 1688, this time with the requirement that the bishops order it to

28. More than 250 JPs were discharged. See Jones, *Country and Court*, 232.
29. See Joyce Lee Malcolm, *To Keep and Bear Arms: The Origins of an Anglo-American Right* (Cambridge, Mass., 1994), 110–11.

be read from every Anglican pulpit on two successive Sundays. In response the archbishop of Canterbury and six bishops submitted a petition questioning the legality of this unilateral suspension of all penal laws. The seven clerics were promptly clapped in the Tower to stand trial for seditious libel. While the bishops' protests may have been self-interested, they had a valid constitutional argument. The king's power to dispense with a law in a particular instance was an accepted part of his prerogative. But James's practice of dispensing with a whole batch of laws in order to employ Catholics raised serious questions about royal authority to overturn legislation. This Declaration went further. It sought to suspend all penal laws for all those subject to them. The king's supporters were quick to point out the inconsistency of Anglican clergy who fervently preached absolute obedience to a divine right monarch but ignored this duty when their own interests were at stake.

June 1688 was the turning point in James's reign.[30] On 10 June against expectation the queen gave birth to a son, ensuring a Catholic succession. Twenty days later in an extraordinary trial a jury found the seven bishops not guilty. That same day as Protestants noisily celebrated, six peers and a bishop secretly sent a message to William of Orange, husband of James's daughter Mary, beseeching him to save the realm.

REVOLUTION

William's arrival in November and James's dash to France left the realm without king or Parliament. Indeed, in hopes government would be completely stymied James had even torn up writs for his planned Parliament and as he fled had thrown the Great Seal into the Thames. There were no battles. Thousands of Englishmen of all

---

30. William of Orange had been planning for an invasion at least a year before, however. See J. R. Jones, *The Revolution of 1688 in England* (London, 1972), 209.

persuasions, unanimous "to a wonder," flocked to welcome William, while James's large, leaderless army dissolved.[31] The Glorious Revolution was bloodless but not silent. It sparked a torrent of pamphlets, some quite brilliant, more than thirteen hundred titles in 1689 alone.[32] Tracts assessed recent grievances and future possibilities and plumbed the most basic issues of government—its origins, its proper form, the ultimate sovereign, issues of conquest and abdication, and the nature of allegiance. Some of this soul-searching and political propaganda rose to the level of brilliant political thought. Thousands of copies of "An Enquiry into the Measures of Submission to the supream Authority...," in which Bishop Gilbert Burnet crisply set out Lockean theories of the rights of man and the origins of society, were printed in Holland and distributed upon William's arrival in England.[33] Burnet's tract appeared in at least six separate editions as well as in collections of tracts published in 1688 and 1689.

Much literary energy was expended to justify and clarify a political situation that was profoundly ironic. James's behavior had made a mockery of his divine right pretensions and the divine right theory of monarchy. His flight left his people in a position to reinstate a monarchy if they wished—and on their own terms. Any possibility such a monarch could even pretend to be the exclusive sovereign was ridiculous. James's former Tory supporters found themselves in the embarrassing position, not unlike that of the seven bishops, of having to abandon their passivist and loyalist principles in fact, if not in theory, and to adopt Whig premises in order to reestablish constitu-

31. See below [John Wildman], "Some Remarks upon Government, and Particularly upon the Establishment of the English Monarchy Relating to This Present Juncture" (London, 1689), 870.

32. See Mark Goldie, "The Revolution of 1689 and the Structure of Political Argument," *Bulletin of Research in the Humanities* (winter 1980), 478.

33. Burnet's tract was first published in November 1688 while John Locke's *Two Treatises of Government* was published in 1689 but may have been written some ten years earlier. Both men were at William's court in Holland before the invasion of England. See Richard Ashcraft, *Locke's Two Treatises of Government* (London, 1987).

tional government and fill the throne. Further, both Whigs and Tories struggled mightily to distinguish this revolution from that discredited revolution of mid-century, with its regicide and military rule. In the political vacuum many differences dissolved, exposing the shared concepts that undergirded English constitutional thought. That is not to say there were not real conflicts about what course to take as the members of the Convention Parliament, elected to sort out the situation, began their work. There was also the ticklish business of crafting a settlement that would not alienate William. The result of their efforts was the Declaration of Rights of 12 February 1689, which accused James of endeavoring to "Subvert and extirpate the Protestant Religion, and the Lawes and Liberties of this Kingdome," elevated William and Mary to the throne, and affirmed thirteen of the English people's "ancient and indubitable" rights, nine of which were actually new.[34] The Declaration also contained a specially devised oath of allegiance to William and Mary. Each aspect of the settlement had crucial constitutional ramifications.[35]

There was an important debate, for example, about whether James should be treated as if he had died or had abdicated. A demise would mean the Crown would immediately devolve upon his heir with no interregnum. Since Protestants claimed James's baby son was not his child but had been smuggled into the queen's room in a warming pan, William and Mary could automatically ascend the throne. The problem was that this would omit all reference to James's misdeeds, to violations of the nation's laws, liberties, and religion. Many Englishmen and a majority of the members of the Convention agreed with Anthony Cary, Lord Falkland, that a chance to determine "what Power... [to] give the King, and what not," must not be lost, as it had

34. See Lois Schwoerer, *The Declaration of Rights, 1689* (Baltimore, 1981), 100, 283–84; Joyce Lee Malcolm, "The Creation of a 'True Antient and Indubitable' Right: The English Bill of Rights and the Right to Be Armed," *Journal of British Studies* 32 (July 1993): 226–49.

35. See Howard Nenner, *The Right to Be King: The Succession to the Crown of England, 1603–1714* (Basingstoke, 1995), especially chs. 7, 8, and 9.

in 1660. They must "not only change hands, but things."[36] Sir Robert Howard made a compelling case that this was no demise but an abdication. By his maladministration and flight, James had "de facto" abdicated. According to the original contract government now "devolved into the people, who are here in civil society and constitution to save . . . [their rights]."[37] Howard concluded, "the right is therefore wholly in the people, who are now to new form themselves again, under a governor yet to be chosen." In a situation akin to Hobbes's original state of nature, such radical Whig notions terrified Tories who feared if this interpretation were accepted everything might be altered. Indeed, an anonymous author claimed to have stood for election to the Convention Parliament because of that possibility. As he put it, "the thoughts of being one of the Great Planters of a Government which shall last for Ages, and perhaps till time has run out its last Minutes, is no Ordinary thing."[38] During its debates the Convention agreed there had been an original contract, then sidestepped the prickly question of whether they truly represented the English people. They ultimately agreed that James had abdicated leaving the throne vacant.

Other questions emerged. William insisted that Mary's role as queen be merely ceremonial and that he rule, but on what basis could he claim the throne? Was he a conqueror? Was he to be a king "de jure" or "de facto"? There were frequent comparisons between William's situation and that of the first Tudor king, Henry VII, two centuries earlier. Both men had wives with a better title; neither was the true heir. According to Mark Goldie, William and his entourage chose to base his claim upon "de facto" kingship, which they saw as a

36. For the best record of the proceedings of the Convention Parliament, see "Grey's Debates," in *A Parliamentary History of the Glorious Revolution*, ed. David Lewis Jones (London, 1988), 125–33.

37. Sir Robert Howard is cited in Schwoerer, *Declaration of Rights*, 176–77.

38. A. B., N. T. [John Wildman], "Some Remarks upon Government," reprinted below, 869.

middle ground to make the revolution acceptable to both Whigs and Tories. But while it may have been acceptable to both parties, in fact it was at odds with the basic political philosophy of each. The Whigs wanted an accountable monarch, not one granted obedience because he had seized the throne.[39] The Tories championed strict monarchical succession, which William's elevation clearly violated. But, as Goldie observed, de facto kingship "bolstered the Court and authoritarian monarchy at the expense of classical Whig principles which tended to undermine kingship and classical Tory principles which tended (in some eyes) to undermine this particular king."[40]

The list of thirteen rights affirmed in the Declaration were distilled from a longer list of grievances, many of which required legislative action. The rights proclaimed were those James was charged with threatening or limitations on prerogative powers he was accused of misusing. In the case of the royal prerogative to dispense with a law, the Convention did not remove the power but only took issue with how it "has been assumed and exercised of late." On the other hand, the king's ability to suspend a law or the execution of laws without the consent of Parliament was pronounced illegal. The majority of the supposedly ancient rights, however, had been open to dispute in the past or were, in fact, new rights.[41] Among the latter was the stipulation that there be no standing army in time of peace without

---

39. Quentin Skinner writes of the Whigs' acceptance of the de facto theory as the basis for William's right as monarch: "The irony was complete. Parliamentary right was sustained by an argument which, a generation earlier, might have been used to confute it. The Parliamentarians who had stood for the rights of representative assemblies against absolute power managed to assimilate to themselves the most characteristic argument of the contrary ideology. The Revolutionaries who had denied that the Norman Conquest could ever have interrupted the immemorial rights of Parliament ended up by including a covert attack on the basis of their own claims." See Skinner, "History and Ideology in the English Revolution," *Historical Journal* 8, no. 2 (1965), 176.

40. Mark Goldie, "Revolution of 1689," 519.

41. See Schwoerer, *Declaration of Rights*; Malcolm, *To Keep and Bear Arms*; Jennifer Carter, "The Revolution and the Constitution," in *Britain After the Glorious Revolution*, ed. Geoffrey Holmes (London, 1969), 39–58.

consent of Parliament and that Protestant subjects had a right to keep arms for their defense. These were intended to narrow royal power and give to Parliament and the people control over the sword.

The new oath of allegiance avoided the touchy issue of whether William and Mary were the rightful monarchs and merely asked their subjects to swear to "bee faithfull and beare true Allegiance to their Majesties King William and Queen Mary." Despite its undemanding language, the new oath failed to end the argument over allegiance. A vigorous dispute about whether an honorable man could swear allegiance to the new rulers continued for some years. Many of the arguments echoed those of the allegiance debate of the early 1650s, although this time there was consensus that however one justified the switch of monarchs, the nation meant to have William and Mary as king and queen. The nonjurors, those who refused to take the new oath, were nearly all Anglican clergy who stuck at violating their oath of allegiance to James as long as he lived and claimed the throne. To persuade them to accept the new monarchs the argument that James had abdicated was bolstered by reference to William as the instrument of God's will, a will that the faithful had to obey. Appeals were made to their civic-mindedness. Surely, it was better to obey the ruler, especially such a selfless ruler as William, than to risk civil war? A "de facto" king had a claim on the obedience of his subjects, especially if he kept order and behaved in a legal manner. Allegiance was loyalty to the community, not merely to a particular monarch. Nonjurors were reminded of earlier English kings with dubious claims to the throne. Over time obedience itself had bestowed legitimacy. An effort was made to avoid resort to Hobbes's arguments in favor of absolute obedience to any ruler or conqueror who provided security and order.[42] This took some doing because the argument for obedience to a de facto monarch was close to the rationale

---

42. Thomas Hobbes, *Leviathan, or the Matter, Forme, and Power of a Commonwealth Ecclesiastical and Civil* (London, 1651).

used by Hobbes. William Sherlock, a nonjuror turned loyalist, accomplished the feat when he pointed out that legitimate authority rested on the consent of the governed, and the Convention Parliament had granted William and Mary that consent.[43]

The work of the Convention Parliament was imperfect. The articles in the Declaration of Rights now seem vague and hesitant. They had been drafted in haste as it was dangerous to leave the kingdom for long without a king and settled government. Many important reforms awaited resolution. Since innovation was regarded with such suspicion, it was in the interests of the revolutionaries that they characterize their deeds as supremely conservative. For two centuries historians accepted that claim. Indeed, many still do. In a famous passage on the Glorious Revolution written in the nineteenth century, the great Whig historian Thomas Macaulay rejoiced, "not a single flower of the crown was touched. Not a single new right was given to the people. The whole English law, substantive and adjective, was . . . almost exactly the same after the Revolution as before it."[44] He

43. See [William Sherlock], "Their Present Majesties Government Proved to be Throughly Settled, and That We May Submit to It, without Asserting the Principles of Mr. Hobbs" (London, 1691), reprinted below, 1005–37. Far from being persuaded by these arguments many nonjurors not only refused to take the oath of allegiance to William and Mary or the Abjuration Oath of 1701 but the oath of allegiance to George I in 1714. In fact, the nonjuror movement continued well into the eighteenth century. See J. C. D. Clark, *The Language of Liberty, 1660–1832: Political Discourse and Social Dynamics in the Anglo-American World* (Cambridge, 1994), 191.

44. Thomas Macaulay, *The History of England from the Accession of James II*, ed. C. H. Firth (London, 1913–1915), 3:1308–10. A number of fine studies have now been done on the constitutional, philosophical, and political results of the revolution settlement. See, for example, John Kenyon, *Revolution Principles: The Politics of Party, 1689–1720* (Cambridge, 1977); J. R. Jones, ed., *Liberty Secured? Britain Before and After 1688* (Stanford, 1992); and H. T. Dickinson, "The Eighteenth-Century Debate on the Sovereignty of Parliament," *Trans. Royal Historical Society*, 5th ser., vol. 26 (London, 1976). For modern historians who see the Glorious Revolution as conservative, see, for example, John Miller, *The Glorious Revolution* (London, 1983); and Stuart Prall, *The Bloodless Revolution: England 1688* (Madison, Wis., 1985). Howard Nenner emphasizes the timidity of the Convention in "Constitutional Uncertainty and the Declaration of Rights," in *After the Reformation: Essays in Honor of J. H. Hexter*, ed. Barbara Malament (Philadelphia, 1980), 291–308.

conceded that some "controverted points had been decided according to the sense of the best jurists; and there had been a slight deviation from the ordinary course of succession" and judged, "This was all; and this was enough." But Macaulay's ringing phrases have perpetuated a subterfuge. The Glorious Revolution was indeed a revolution; however, it tried to disguise the fact. Parliament had made a king, had defined his powers, and had set the stage for its own supremacy. Parliament was about to win the struggle for sovereignty. But in its great moment of triumph, its work was couched in the time-honored language of the ancient constitution, as indeed it should have been.

Chronology

1603   Accession of James I (King James VI of Scotland).

1604   Hampton Court Conference.

1605   Gunpowder Plot.

1618   Outbreak of Thirty Years War.

1625   Death of James I; accession of Charles I.

1627   Five Knights' Case.

1628   Parliament meets. Petition of Right.

1629   England begins eleven-year period without a parliament.

1633   Appointment of Archbishop Laud.

1634   First levy of ship money.

1637   King wins Ship Money Case, 7 judges for, 5 against.

1638   Scottish National Covenant.

1639   First Bishops' War.

1640   Short Parliament meets in April. Long Parliament meets in November.

1641   Uprising in Ireland, massacre of Protestants.

1642   Outbreak of civil war.

1643   Solemn League and Covenant. Scots enter war in England.

1645   New Model Army created.

1646   Charles surrenders.

1647   Charles captured by army. Army debates at Putney.

1648   Second civil war. Pride's Purge.

1649   Charles tried and executed. Monarchy and House of Lords abolished. England declared a commonwealth.

1650   Engagement Oath required. Charles II and Scots defeated at Dunbar.

1651   Charles II and Scots defeated at Worcester. Charles flees to France.

1653   Cromwell expels the Rump Parliament. Instrument of Government drawn up. Cromwell becomes Lord Protector.

1654   First Protectorate Parliament.

1655   Penruddock's uprising.

1656   Rule of Major Generals. Second Protectorate Parliament.

1657   Cromwell refuses crown.

1658   Cromwell dies. Richard Cromwell becomes Protector.

1659   Richard Cromwell resigns. Rump Parliament recalled. George Monck marches with army to London.

1660   Long Parliament recalled. Convention Parliament summoned. Charles II invited back. Monarchy restored. Trial of regicides.

1661   Cavalier Parliament meets. Passage Militia Act, Corporation Act.

1662   Passage Uniformity Act. Trial of Sir Henry Vane.

1670   Secret Treaty between Charles II and Louis XIV.

1672   Charles issues Declaration of Indulgence.

1673   Test Act.

1678   Second Test Act.

1680   Exclusion Bill introduced.

1683   Rye House Plot. Trial of William Lord Russell, Algernon Sidney. Oxford decrees condemn all resistance.

1685   Charles II dies. Accession of James II.

1687   James II issues Declaration of Indulgence.

1688   Seven Bishops Trial. Arrival of William of Orange. Glorious Revolution.

1689   Convention Parliament meets. Bill of Rights. Accession of William and Mary.

Of Parliament

Sir Henry Vane, 1613–1662

THE

TRYAL

OF

Sir Henry Vane, Kt.

AT

The KINGS BENCH, *Westminster,*
June the 2d. and 6th. 1662.

Together

With what he intended to have Spoken the Day of his
Sentence, (*June* 11.) for *Arrest of Judgment,* (had
he not been interrupted and over-ruled by the
Court) and his *Bill of Exceptions.*

With other Occasional SPEECHES, &c.

Also his SPEECH and PRAYER, &c. on the *Scaffold.*

Printed in the Year, 1662.

*W*ith the exception of the regicides, Sir Henry Vane was one of only two parliamentarians specifically excluded by the Convention Parliament from pardon after the Restoration.

Vane began his political career when he served briefly as governor of the Massachusetts Bay colony. Back in England he became joint treasurer of the navy and was actually employed in the expenditure of ship money. He sat for Hull in the Commons of the Short and Long Parliaments where he joined those working to abolish episcopacy. He was a vigorous, lifelong proponent of religious toleration. It was he who discovered the council notes of his father that sealed the fate of the Earl of Strafford.

During the civil war, Vane was one of the leaders of Parliament and a close ally of Oliver Cromwell. He believed the people were the source of all just power, but after the king's surrender he hoped for some accommodation with him. Vane was so offended by Pride's Purge that he abandoned the Commons until after Charles's trial and execution. Nor would he sit on the new Council of State until the stipulation that he take an oath approving the king's execution and the abolition of monarchy was dropped. He was very active in Commonwealth affairs but left government again in 1653 upon Cromwell's eviction of the Rump. He regarded this as a betrayal of the cause. In 1656 he made his feelings public in a tract, "Healing Question propounded and resolved," which blamed the imposition of the protectorate for the divisions that had arisen among the supporters of the Rump. He openly called for a convention to devise a new constitution, one that would provide for liberty and the common good of all adherents of the old cause. Not surprisingly, Vane was summoned before the Council. He was ordered to give a bond that he would do nothing against the government. His refusal earned him several months of imprisonment.

In 1659 Vane returned to government to sit in Richard Cromwell's parliament and in the restored Long Parliament that followed, apparently hoping to curb the power of protectors on the one hand, and to prevent the return of monarchy on the other. But his reputation was destroyed when he continued at his post as commissioner of the admiralty after 13 October when General John Lambert turned out the Long Parliament and then attempted to reconcile the army and the Parliament. Once the Long Parliament was restored by Monck, its members expelled Vane to general rejoicing. After the Restoration the Convention Parliament excluded him from pardon as a "person of mischievous activity." Most of Vane's former colleagues chose to flee or made their peace with the Crown. Vane remained to face a charge of high treason, prepared to die an unrepentant martyr to the "good old cause."

To his surprise Vane was charged with crimes against Charles II, not Charles I. He was no lawyer but defended himself ably, despite the prohibition against his consulting with anyone or summoning any witnesses—typical liabilities under which those charged with treason labored. Even then he might have been pardoned, but his tenacious adherence to the sovereignty of people and Parliament and his plea that, along with the great majority of Englishmen, he had merely obeyed the "de facto" government, precluded any hope of clemency. His execution was set for the anniversary of the battle of Naseby. Vane's speech on the scaffold was purposely drowned out by the beat of drums. Fortunately the account of his trial and his scaffold speech were published, albeit anonymously. His scaffold speech alone appeared in two other editions. Vane's comportment at the end and adherence to his principles earned him much respect. Pepys reckoned the king had lost more than he had gained by the execution.

The Tryal of Sir *Henry Vane* Knight, at the Kings Bench, *Westminster,* June the 2d. and 6th. 1662.

READER,

Thou shalt not be detained with any flourishing Preface. 'Tis true; whether we consider the Person or Cause, so much might pertinently be said, as (were the Pen of some ready Writer imployed therein) a large Preamble might seem to need but a very short Apology, if any at all. Yet, by that time we have well weighed what this Sufferer hath said for himself, and left behind him in writing, it will appear, that there needed not any tongue of the Learned, to form up an Introduction thereunto, but meerly the hand of a faithful Transcriber of his own Observations, in defence of himself and his Cause. Rest assured of this, thou hast them here fully and clearly represented.

The necessity of this course for thy information, as to the truth of his Case, be pleased to consider on these following accounts. He was much overruled, diverted, interrupted, and cut short in his Plea (as to a free and full delivery of his mind upon the whole matter at the Bar) by the Judges of the King's-Bench, and by the King's Counsel. He was also denied the benefit of any Counsel to speak on his behalf.[1]

And what he did speak at the Bar and on the Scaffold, was so disgustful to some, that the Books of those that took Notes of what passed all along in both places, were carefully called in and suppressed. It is therefore altogether unpossible to give thee a full Narrative of all he said, or was said to him, either in Westminster-Hall, *or on* Tower-Hill.

The Defendant foreseeing this, did most carefully set down in writing, the substance of what he intended to enlarge upon, the three dayes of his appearance at the King's-Bench Bar, and the day of his Execution. Monday June 2. 1662, was the day of his Arraignment. Friday June 6.

---

1. The defendant in a treason trial of this period was typically not permitted counsel, although Vane should have been allowed to make a full plea on his own behalf.

was the day of his Trial, and the Jurors' Verdict. Wednesday June 11. *was the day of his Sentence. Saturday* June 14. *was the day of his Execution on* Tower-Hill, *where limitations were put upon him, and the interruptions of him by many hard speeches and disturbing carriages of some that compassed him about upon the Scaffold, as also by the sounding of Trumpets in his face to prevent his being heard, had many eye and ear witnesses.*

Upon these considerations, I doubt not, it will appear indispensably necessary, to have given this faithful Transcript of such Papers of his, as do contain the most substantial and pleadable grounds of his publick actings, any time this twenty years and more, as the only means left of giving any tolerable account of the whole matter, to thy satisfaction. Yet such Information as could be picked up from those that did preserve any Notes, taken in Court or at the Scaffold, are here also recorded for thy use, and that, faithfully, word for word.

Chancellor Fortescue[2] *doth right worthily commend the Laws of* England, *as the best now extant and in force, in any Nation of the world, affording (if duely administered) just outward liberty to the People, and securing the meanest from any oppressive and injurious practices of Superiours against them. They give also that just Prerogative to Princes, that is convenient or truly useful and advantagious for them to have; that is to say, such as doth not enterfere with the People's just Rights, the intire and most wary preservation of which, as it is the Covenant-duty of the Prince, so is it his best security and greatest honour. 'Tis safer and better for him to be loved and rightly feared by free Subjects, than to be feared and hated by injured slaves.*

The main fundamental Liberties of the free People of England, *are summed up and comprehended in the 29th Chapter of* Magna Charta. *These words;*

2. Sir John Fortescue, lord chief justice of the King's Bench in the fifteenth century, was known in the seventeenth century for his treatise *De Laudibus Legum Angliae*, first printed in 1537.

No freeman shall be taken or imprisoned, or be disseized of his Freehold, or Liberties, or free-customs, or be outlawed or exiled, or any otherwise destroyed. Nor will we pass upon him, or condemn him, but by lawful Judgement of his Peers, or by the Law of the Land. We will sell to no man, we will not deny or defer to any man, either Justice or Right.

Lord Chief Justice Cook *observes here nine famous branches of the Law of* England, *couched in this short Chapter, and discourses upon them to good purpose.*[3] *He saith also, that from this Chapter, as out of a root, many fruitful branches of the Law of* England *have sprung.*

As for the very leading injury to other wrongings of the Subject, (to wit, the restraint or imprisonment of his person) so curious and tender is the Law in this point, that (sayes Cook*) no man is to be attached, arrested, taken, or restrained of his liberty, by petition or suggestion to the King or to his Council, unless it be by Indictment or Presentment of good and lawful men (of the neighbourhood) where such deeds be done.*

This great Charter of England's *Liberties, made* 9 Hen. 3. *and set in the front of all succeeding Statute-Laws or Acts of Parliament, (as the Standard, Touch-stone or Jury for them to be tried by) hath been ratified by about two and thirty Parliaments, and the Petition of Right,* 3. Caroli.

The two most famous Ratifications hereof, entituled, Confirmationes Chartarum, & Articuli super Chartas, *were made* 25 *and* 28 *of* Edw. I.

All this stir about the great Charter, some conceive very needless, seeing that therein are contained those fundamental Laws or Liberties of the Nation, which are so undeniably consonant to the Law of Nature, or Light of Reason, that Parliaments themselves ought not to abrogate, but preserve them. Even Parliaments may seem to be bounded in their Legislative Power and Jurisdiction, by divine Equity and Reason, which is an eternal and therefore unalterable Law. Hence is it, that an Act of Parliament that is evidently against common Right or Reason, is null and

3. This is a reference to Sir Edward Coke's *Second Institute,* "Commentary on Magna Carta," which was published in 1642 by order of the House of Commons.

void in itself, without more ado. Suppose a Parliament by their Act should constitute a man Judge in his own cause, give him a meer Arbitrary power; such Act would be in itself void.

This is declared to be the ground of that exemplary Justice done upon Empson *and* Dudley,[4] (*as acting contrary to the People's Liberties in* Magna Charta) *whose Case is very memorable in this point. For, though they gratified* Henry 7th *in what they did, and had an Act of Parliament for their Warrant, made the* 11th *of his Reign, yet met they with their due reward from the hands of Justice, that Act being against Equity and common Reason, and so, no justifiable ground or apology for those infinit Abuses and Oppressions of the People, they were found guilty of.*

The Statute, under colour whereof they acted, ran to this effect. Be it enacted, that the Justices of the Assizes, and Justices of the Peace upon Information for the King, before them to be made, have full power and authority by their discretion, to hear and determine all offences and contempts. *Having this ground, they proceeded against the People, upon meer Information, in the execution of Penal Laws, without any Indictment or Presentment by good and lawful men, but only by their own Promoters or Informers, contrary to the 29th of* Magna Charta, *which requires, That no free-man be proceeded against, but by lawful Judgement of his Peers, or by the Law of the Land.*

Secondly, This Act allowed them to hear and determine arbitrarily, by their own discretion, which is not according to the Law and Custom of England. *And* Cook *sayes, 'Tis the worst (and most aggravated) oppression of all, that is done under the colour of Law, or disguise of Justice.*

Such a Statute or Act of Parliament, is, not only against the light of Reason, but against the express letter of unrepealed Statute-Law; 42. Edw. 3. 1. *It is assented and accorded,* That the great Charter, and

---

4. Sir Richard Empson and Edmund Dudley, financial advisors to Henry VII, were bitterly hated for the manner in which they carried out a system of extortions intended to enrich the Crown. Both were executed in 1510 on a charge of constructive treason for having urged friends to arm themselves during Henry VII's last illness.

the Charter of Forest be holden and kept in all points, and if any Statute be made to the contrary, that shall be holden for none.

This also is consonant to the first chapter of the great Charter itselfe, made 9. Hen. 3. We have granted to all the free men of our Realm, these Liberties underwritten, to have and to hold to them and their heirs, of Us and our Heirs, forever.

But what if this great Charter itself had never been made? had England *been to seek for righteous Laws and just Liberties? nothing lesse. The same Liberties and Laws were ratified before that, in the great Charter made the seventeenth year of King* John, *and mentioned (among others) by* Matthew Paris.

And to what yet amounted the matter of all these Grants, but what the Kings themselves were bound before to observe, by the Coronation Oaths, as the antient fundamental Laws or Customs of this Land? This we may find in Mr. Lambard's *Translation of the Saxon Laws,*[5] *from the time of King* Ina, *who began* anno 712; *to* Hen. 1. *who began* 1100. *Amongst the Saxons, King* Alfred *is reputed the most famous and learned Compiler of our Laws, which were still handed along from one King to another, as the unalterable Customs of the Kingdom. In the 17th chapter of* Edward *the Confessor's Laws, The mention of the duty of a King (which, if not performed,* nec nomen Regis in eo constabit)[6] *is remarkable. And Mr.* Lambard *tells us, that even* William *the* Conqueror, *did ratifie and observe the same Laws that his kinsman* Edward *the* Confessor *did, as obliged by his Coronation Oath.*

So then, neither the great Charter in King John's *time, nor that of* 9. Hen. 3. *were properly a new Body of Law, but a Declaration of the antient fundamental Laws, Rights and Liberties of this Nation, in Brittish, Saxon, Danish and Norman times, before. This,* Cook *in his Proem*

---

5. William Lambarde's work *Archaionomia*, first printed in 1568, was a collection and paraphrase of the Anglo-Saxon laws. A second edition of this work was published by Whelock in Cambridge, 1644.

6. The name of the King agreeth not unto him.

to the second part of his Institutes, observes; where he notes also, that this Charter is not called great, for quantity of words, (a sheet of Paper will contain it) but for the great importance and weight of its matter.

Through the advice of Hubert de Burgo *Chief Justice of* England, Edward *the first, in the eleventh year of his Reign, did, in a Council held at* Oxford, *unjustly cancel this great Charter, and that of Forest:* Hubert *therefore was justly sentenced according to Law, by his Peers, in open Parliament. Then,* 25 Ed. 1. *The Statute, called,* Confirmationes Chartarum *was made, in the first chapter whereof, the* Magna Charta *is peculiarly called the Common Law.* 25. Ed. 1. *cap.* 2. Any Judgment given contrary to the said Charter, is to be undone and holden for naught. *And cap.* 4. Any that by word, deed, or counsel, go contrary to the said Charter, are to be excommunicated by the Bishops; and the Arch-Bishops of *Canterbury* and *York* are bound to compel the other Bishops to denounce sentence accordingly, in case of their remisness or neglect.

The next famous sticklers to Hubert de Burgo, *for Arbitrary Domination, were the two* Spencers, *father and son,*[7] *by whose rash and evil counsel (sayes* Cook) Edward *the second was seduced to break the Great Charter, and they were banished for their pains.*

By these passages we may observe, how the People would still be struling (in and by their Representatives) for their Legal Rights and Just Liberties; to obviate the Encroachers whereof, they procured several new Ratifications of their old Laws, which were indeed in themselves unrepealable, even by Parliaments, if they will act as men, and not contradict the Law of their own Reason, and of the common Reason of all mankind.

By 25 Ed. I. *cap 1. Justices, Sheriffs, Mayors, and other Ministers, that*

---

7. Hugh Despenser, a royal official, and his son Hugh the younger, the favorite of Edward II, held great power, even over the king. After Edward was captured in a general uprising of English magnates, Despenser the younger was executed and Edward forced to abdicate in favor of his heir Edward III.

have the Laws of the Land to guide them, are required to allow the said Charter to be pleaded in all its points, and in all causes that shall come before them in Judgment.

This is a clause (says Cook) *worthy to be written in letters of gold;* That the Laws are to be the Judges' guides, *(and therefore not the Judges, the guides of the Laws, by their arbitrary glosses) which never yet misguided any that certainly knew and truly followed them. In conso-nancy herewith, the Spaniard says, Of all the three learned Professions, The Lawyer is the only lettered man, his business and duty being to follow the plain literal construction of the Law, as his guide, in giving Judg-ment. Pretence of mystery here, carries in the bowels of it, intents, or at least a deep suspition of arbitrary domination. The mind of the Law is not subject to be clouded, disturbed or perverted by passion or interest. 'Tis far otherwise with Judges; therefore 'tis fitter and safer the Law should guide them, than they the Law.* Cook *on the last mentioned Statute affirms, That this great Charter, and the Charter of Forest, are properly the Common Law of this Land, or the Law that is common to all the Peo-ple thereof.*

2 Ed. 3. *cap.* 8. Exact care is taken, that no Commands by the Great or Little Seal, shall come to disturb or delay Common Right. Or, if such Commands come, the Justices are not thereby to leave to do Right, in any point. *So* 14 Ed. 3. 14. 11 Ric. 2. 10. *The Judges' Oath,* 18 Ed. 3. 7. *runs thus:*

If any force come to disturb the execution of the Common Law, ye shall cause their bodies to be arrested and put into Prison. Ye shall deny no man Right by the King's Letters, nor counsel the King any-thing that may turn to his dammage or disherison.[8]

The late King in his Declaration at Newmarket, 1641, *acknowledged the Law to be the Rule of his Power. And his Majesty that now is, in his*

8. To disinherit or deprive of his rightful position.

Speech to both Houses, the 19th of May *last, said excellently,* The good old Rules of Law are our best security.

The Common Law then, or Liberties of England, *comprized in the* Magna Charta *and the Charter of Forest, are rendered as secure, as authentick words can set them, from all Judgments or Precedents to the contrary in any Courts, all corrupting advice or evil counsel of any Judges, all Letters or Countermands from the King's Person, under the Great or Privy Seals; yea, and from any Acts of Parliament itself, that are contrary thereunto. As to the Judges, no question, they well know the story of the 44 corrupt Judges, executed by* King Alfred, *as also of* Tresillian, Belknap, *and many others since.*

By 11 Hen. 7. *cap.* 1. They that serve the King in his Wars, according to their duty of Allegiance, for defence of the King and the Land, are indempnified; If against the Land, and so not according to their Allegiance, the last clause of that chapter seems to exclude them from the benefit of this Act.

6. Hen. 8. 16. Knights and Burgesses of Parliament are required not to depart from the Parliament, till it be fully finished, ended or prorogued.

28 Ed. 3. *cap.* 3. No man is to be imprisoned, disherited, or put to death, without being heard what he can say for himself.

4 Ed. 3. 14. *and* 36 Ed. 3. 10. A Parliament is to be holden every year, or oftener if need be.

1 Ric. 3. *cap.* 2. The subjects of this Realm are not to be charged with any new imposition, called a *Benevolence.*

37 Ed. 3. c. 18. All those that make suggestions against any man to the King, are to be sent with their suggestions before the Chancellor, Treasurer, and his grand Council, and there to find surety that they will pursue their suggestions; and are to incur the same pain, the party by them accused should have had, if attained, in case the suggestion be found evil, or false.

21 Jacobi, *cap.* 3. All Monopolies and Dispensations, with Penal Laws, are made void, as contrary to the great Charters.

These quotations of several Statutes, as Ratifications and Restorers of the Laws of the Land, are prefixed to the following Discourses and Pleas of this Sufferer, as certain, steady, unmovable Landmarks, to which he oft relates. The rouling Seas have other Laws, peculiar to themselves, as Cook *observes (on that expression,* Law of the Land*) in his Comment on the 29th Chapter of* Magna Charta. *Offences done upon the High Sea, the Admiral takes conusance of, and proceeds by the Marine Law.*

But have those steady Land-marks, though exactly observed and never so pertinently quoted and urged by this Sufferer, failed him, as to the securing of his Life? 'Tis because we have had Land-floods *of late; Tumults of the People, that are compared to the* raging Seas, *Psal. 65. 7.*

The first Paper of this deceased Sufferer, towards the defence of his Cause and Life, preparatory to the Trial, (as the foundation of all that follows) before he could know how the Indictment was laid, (and which also a glance back to any crime of Treason since the beginning of the late War, that the Attorney General reckoned him chargeable with, shews to be very requisit) take as followeth.

Memorandums touching my Defence.

The Offence objected against me, is *levying War,* within the Statute 25 *Ed.* 3.[9] and by consequence, a most high and great failure in the duty which the Subject, according to the Laws of *England,* stands obliged to perform, in relation to the Imperial Crown and Soveraign Power of *England.*

9. The statute of 25 Edward III. cap. 2 (1352) contained the stipulation that to "levy war against our lord the king in his realm" is treason. Pollock and Maitland find that Edward III was the first English king since the Conquest "who could afford to make such a declaration." See Frederick Pollock and Frederic Maitland, *The History of English Law,* 2d ed. (Cambridge, 1968), 2:505.

The crime, if it prove any, must needs be very great, considering the circumstances with which it hath been accompanied: For it relates to, and takes in a series of publick action, of above twenty years continuance. It took its rise and had its root in the Being, Authority, Judgment, Resolutions, Votes and Orders of a Parliament, and that, a Parliament not only authorized and commissionated in the ordinary and customary way, by his Majestie's Writ of Summons, and the People's Election and Deputation, subject to Adjournment, Discontinuance, and Dissolution, at the King's will; but which by express Act of Parliament, was constituted in its continuance and exercise of its Power, free from that subjection, and made therein wholly to depend upon their own will, to be declared in an Act of Parliament, to be passed for that purpose, when they should see cause. To speak plainly and clearly in this matter; That which is endeavoured to be made a Crime and an Offence of such an high nature in my person, is no other than the necessary and unavoidable Actings of the Representative Body of the Kingdom, for the preservation of the good People thereof, in their allegiance and duty to God and his Law, as also from the imminent dangers and destruction threatened them, from God's and their own Enemies.

This made both Houses in their *Remonstrance (May 26. 1642.)* protest; *If the Malignant spirits about the King, should ever force or necessitate them to defend their Religion, the Kingdom, the Priviledges of Parliament, and the Rights and Liberties of the Subjects, with their Swords; The Blood and Destruction that should ensue therupon, must be wholly cast upon their account, God and their own consciences telling them, that they were clear; and would not doubt, but that God and the whole world would clear them therein.*

In his Majestie's *Answer* to the *Declaration* of the two Houses, *(May 19. 1642.)* he acknowledgeth his going into the House of Commons to demand the five Members, was an errour: And that was it, which gave the Parliament the first cause to put themselves in a posture of defence, by their own Power and Authority, in commanding the Trained-Bands of the City of *London*, to guard and secure them from Violence, in the discharge of their Trust and Duty, as the two Houses of Parliament, appointed by Act, to continue, as above-mentioned.[10]

The next cause was, his Majestie's raising Forces at *York*, (under pretence of a Guard) expressed in the humble Petition of the Lords and Commons *(May 23. 1642.)* wherein they beseech his Majesty to disband all such Forces, and desist from any further designs of that nature, otherwise they should hold themselves bound in duty towards God, and the Trust reposed in them by the People, and the Fundamental Laws and Constitutions of this Kingdom, to employ their care and utmost power, to secure the Parliament, and preserve the peace and quiet of the Kingdom.

May 20. 1642, The two Houses of Parliament gave their Judgment, in these Votes.

First, *That it appears that the King (seduced by wicked Counsel) intends to make War against the Parliament, who in all their Consultations and Actions have proposed no other end to themselves, but the Care of his Kingdoms, and the performance of all Duty and Loyalty to his Person.*

Secondly, *That whensoever the King maketh War upon the Parliament, it is a breach of Trust reposed in him by his People, contrary to his Oath, and tending to the dissolution of this Government.*

Thirdly, *That whosoever shall serve or assist him in such Wars, are Traitors by the fundamental Laws of this Kingdom, and have been so adjudged by two Acts of Parliament, and ought to suffer as Traitors.*

Die Jovis, Octob. 8. 1642, In the Instructions agreed upon by the Lords and Commons about the Militia, They declare, *That the King (seduced by wicked Counsel) hath raised War against the Parliament, and other his good Subjects.*

And by the Judgment and Resolution of both Houses, bearing

---

10. The king's answer is reprinted in volume 1, 145–77.

date *Aug. 13. 1642,* upon occasion of his Majestie's *Proclamation* for suppressing the present Rebellion under the Command of *Robert* Earl of *Essex,* They do unanimously publish and declare, *That all they who have advised, declared, abetted, or countenanced, or hereafter shall abet and countenance the said* Proclamation, *are Traitors and Enemies to God, the King and Kingdom, and guilty of the highest degree of Treason that can be committed against the King and Kingdom, as that which invites his Majestie's Subjects to destroy his Parliament, and good People, by a Civil War; and by that means, to bring ruine, confusion and perpetual slavery upon the surviving part of a then wretched Kingdom.*

The Law is acknowledged by the King, to be the *only Rule,* by which the People can be justly governed; and that, as it is his duty, so it shall be his perpetual, vigilant care, to see to it. Therefore he will not suffer either or both Houses by their Votes, without or against his Consent, to enjoin anything that is forbidden by the Law, or to forbid anything that is enjoined by the Law.

The King does assert in his Answer to the House's Petition, *(May 23. 1642.) That He is a part of the Parliament, which they take upon them to defend and secure; and that his Prerogative is a part of, and a defence to the Laws of the Land.*

In the Remonstrance of both Houses, *(May 26. 1642.)* They do assert; *That if they have made any Precedents this Parliament, they have made them for posterity, upon the same or better grounds of Reason and Law, than those were, upon which their Predecessors made any for them;* and do say, *That as some Precedents ought not to be Rules for them to follow, so none can be limits to bound their Proceedings, which may and must vary, according to the different condition of times.*

And for the particular, with which they were charged, of setting forth Declarations to the People who have chosen and entrusted them with all that is dearest to them, if there be no example for it in former times; They say, *it is because there never were such Monsters before, that attempted to disaffect the People towards a Parliament.*

They further say; *His Majestie's Towns are no more his care than his*

Kingdom, nor his Kingdom than his People, who are not so his own, that he hath absolute power over them, or in them, as in his proper Goods and Estate; but fiduciary, for the Kingdom, and in the paramount right of the Kingdom. They also acknowledge the Law, to be the safeguard and custody of all publick and private Interests. They also hold it fit, to declare unto the Kingdom, (whose Honour and Interest is so much concerned in it) what is the Priviledge of the great Council of Parliament, herein; and what is the Obligation that lies upon the Kings of this Realm, as to the passing such Bills as are offered to them by both Houses, in the name, and for the good of the whole Kingdom, whereunto they stand engaged, both in Conscience and Justice, to give their Royal Assent.

First, *In Conscience;* in respect of the Oath that is, or ought to be taken by them, at their Coronation, as well to confirm by their Royal Assent, all such good Laws as the People shall chuse, (whereby to remedy such inconveniencies as the Kingdom may suffer) as to keep and protect the Laws already in being.

The form of the *Oath* is upon Record, and asserted by Books of good authority. Unto it relation is had, 25 *Ed.* 3. entituled, *The Statute of Provisors of Benefices.*

Hereupon, The said Commons prayed our said Lord the King, (since the Right of the Crown of *England,* and the Law of the said Realm, is such, that upon the mischiefs and dammages which happen to this Realm, he ought and is bound by his Oath, with the accord of his People in Parliament, to make Remedy and Law, for the removing thereof) That it may please him to ordain Remedy.

This Right, thus claimed by the Lords and Commons, The King doth not deny, in his Answer thereunto.

Secondly, *In Justice* the Kings are obliged as well as in *Conscience,* in respect of the Trust reposed in them, to preserve the Kingdom by the making of new Laws, where there shall be need, as well as by observing of Laws already made; a Kingdom being many times as much exposed to ruine for want of a new Law, as by the violation of those that are in being.

This is a most clear Right, not to be denied, but to be as due from his Majesty to his People, as his Protection. In all Laws framed by both houses, as *Petitions of Right*, they have taken themselves to be so far Judges of the Rights claimed by them, That when the King's Answer hath not been in every point, fully according to their desire, they have still insisted upon their Claim, and never given it over, till the Answer hath been according to their demand, as was done in the late *Petition of Right*, 3. Caroli.

This shews, the two Houses of Parliament are *Judge* between the King and the People in question of Right, as in the Case also of *Ship-money* and other illegal Taxes; and if so, why should they not also be Judge in the Cases of the Common Good and Necessity of the Kingdom, wherein the Kingdom hath as clear a Right to have the benefit and remedy of the Law, as in any other matter, saving Pardon and Grants of Favour?

The Malignant Party are they, that not only neglect and despise, but labour to undermine the Law, under colour of maintaining it. They endeavour to destroy the Fountain and Conservators of the Law, the *Parliament*. They make other Judges of the Law, than what the Law hath appointed. They set up other Rules for themselves to walk by, than such as are according to Law; and dispence with the Subjects' obedience, to that which the Law calls Authority, and to their Determinations and Resolutions, to whom the Judgment doth appertain by Law: Yea, though but private persons, they make the Law to be their Rule, according to their own understanding only, contrary to the Judgment of those that are the competent Judges thereof.

The King asserts, That the Act of Sir *John Hotham*[11] was *levying War against the King*, by the letter of the Statute, *25 Ed.* 3. cap. 2.

---

11. In the summer of 1642 Hotham was sent by Parliament to Hull where the major English arsenal outside London was located, and there refused entrance to the King and his retinue.

The Houses state the Case, and deny it to be within that Statute; saying, If the letter of that Statute be thought to import this; That no War can be levied against the King, but what is directed and intended against his Person; Or, that every levying of Forces for the defence of the King's Authority, and of his Kingdom, against the personal Commands of the King, opposed thereunto, (though accompanied with his presence) is Treason, or levying War against the King. Such Interpretation is very far from the sense of that Statute, and so much the Statute itself speaks, beside the authority of Book-cases. For if the clause of levying War had been meant only against the King's Person, what need had there been thereof, after the other branch in the same Statute, of compassing the King's death, which would necessarily have implied this? And because the former doth imply this, it seems not at all to be intended, at least, not chiefly, in the latter branch, but the levying War against his Laws and Authority; and such a levying War, though not against his Person, is a levying War against the King; whereas the levying of Force against his personal Commands, though accompanied with his Presence, and not against his Laws and Authority, but in the maintenance thereof, is no levying of War against the King, but for him, especially in a time of so many successive plots and designs of Force against the Parliament and Kingdom, of probable Invasion from abroad, and of so great distance and alienation of his Majestie's affections from his Parliament and People, and of the particular danger of the Place and Magazine of *Hull*, of which the two Houses sitting, are the most proper Judges.

In proclaiming Sir *John Hotham* Traitor, they say, The breach of the Priviledge of Parliament was very clear, and the subversion of the Subject's common Right. For though the Priviledges of Parliament extend not to these cases, mentioned in the Declaration of Treason, Felony, and breach of the Peace, so as to exempt the Member of Parliament from Punishment, or from all manner of Process and Trial, yet it doth priviledge them in the way and method of their Trial and Punishment, and that the Parliament should first have the Cause brought before them, that they may judge of the Fact, and of the grounds of their Accusation, and how far forth the manner of their Trial may or may not concern the Priviledge of Parliament: Otherwise, under this pretext, the Priviledge of Parliament in this matter, may be so essentially broken, as thereby the very Being of Parliaments may be destroyed. Neither doth the sitting of a Parliament suspend all or any Law, in maintaining that Law, which upholds the Priviledge of Parliament, which upholds the Parliament, which upholds the Kingdom.

They further assert; That in some sense, they acknowledge the *King* to be the only person, against whom Treason can be committed, that is, as he is *King,* and that Treason which is against the Kingdom, is more against the *King,* than that which is against his Person; because he *is King:* For Treason is not Treason, as it is against him *as a man,* but *as a man that is a King,* and as he hath, and stands in that relation to the Kingdom, entrusted with the Kingdom, and discharging that Trust.

They also avow, That there can be no competent Judge of this or any the like case, but a *Parliament;* and do say, that if the wicked Counsel about the King could master this Parliament by force, they would hold up the same power to deprive us of all Parliaments, which are the ground and pillar of the Subject's Liberty, and that which only maketh *England* a free Monarchy.

The Orders of the two Houses carry in them *Law for their limits, and the Safety of the Land for their end.* This makes them not doubt but all his Majestie's good Subjects will yeeld obedience to his Majestie's Authority, signified therein by both Houses of Parliament: for whose encouragement, and that they may know their Duty in

matters of that nature, and upon how sure a ground they go, that follow the Judgment of Parliament for their guide. They alledge the true
meaning and ground of that Statute, 11. *Hen. 7. cap.* 1.[12] printed at
large in his Majestie's Message, *May* 4; This Statute provides, that
none that shall attend upon the King and do him true service, shall be
attainted, or forfeit anything.

What was the scope of this Statute?

Answer. To provide, that men should not suffer as Traitors for serving the King in his Wars, according to the duty of their Allegiance.
But if this had been all, it had been a very needless and ridiculous
Statute. Was it then intended (as they seem to make it, that print it
with his Majestie's Message) that those should be free from all crime
and penalty, that should follow the King and serve him in War, in
any case whatsoever, whether it were for or against the Kingdom or
the Laws thereof? That cannot be: for that could not stand with the
duty of their Allegiance, which, in the beginning of this Statute, is
expressed to be, *to serve the King for the time being in his Wars, for the
defence of him and the Land.* If therefore it be against the Land, (as it
must be, if it be against the Parliament, the Representative Body of
the Kingdom) it is a declining from the duty of Allegiance, which
this Statute supposes may be done, though men should follow the
King's Person in the War. Otherwise, there had been no need of such
a *Proviso* in the end of the Statute, that none should take benefit
thereby, that should decline from their Allegiance.

That therefore which is the Principal Verb in this, is *the serving of
the King for the time being,* which cannot be meant of a *Perkin Warbeck,*[13] or any that should call himself *King,* but such a one, as (what-

---

12. 11 Henry VII, cap. 1 (1495), An Act that no person going with the King to the wars shall
be attaint of treason, known as the De facto Act. This act ensured that no one could be accused of treason for obeying the king at the time in question. See Geoffrey Elton, *The Tudor
Constitution,* 2d ed. (Cambridge, 1982), 2.

13. Perkin Warbeck was a notorious pretender to the throne in the late fifteenth century.
He claimed he was Richard, Duke of York, son of Edward IV. He was banished by Henry VII

ever his Title might prove, either in himself or in his Ancestors) should be received and acknowledged for such, by the Kingdom, the Consent whereof cannot be discerned but by Parliament; the Act whereof, is the Act of the whole Kingdom, by the personal Suffrage of the Peers, and the Delegate Consent of the Commons of *England*. *Henry* 7th therefore, a wise Prince, to clear this matter of contest, happening between Kings *de facto* and Kings *de jure*, procured this Statute to be made, *That none shall be accounted a Traitor for serving in his Wars, the King for the time being;* that is, him that is for the present allowed and received by the Parliament in behalf of the Kingdom. And as it is truly suggested in the Preamble of the Statute; It is not agreeable to reason or conscience, that it should be otherwise, seeing men should be put upon an impossibility of knowing their duty, if the Judgment of the highest Court should not be a Rule to guide them. And if the Judgment thereof is to be followed, when the question is, *who is King?* much more, when the question is, *what is the best service of the King and Kingdom?* Those therefore that shall guide themselves by the Judgment of Parliament, ought (whatever happen) to be secure and free from all account and penalties, upon the ground and equity of this Statute.

To make the Parliament countenancers of Treason, they say, is enough to have dissolved all the bands of service and confidence between his Majesty and his Parliament, of whom the Law sayes, a dishonourable thing ought not to be imagined.

This Conclusion then is a clear Result from what hath been argued; That in all Cases of such difficulty and unusualness, happening by the over-ruling Providence of God, as render it impossible for the Subject to know his duty, by any known Law or certain Rule extant, his relying then, upon the Judgment and Reason of the whole Realm,

---

but welcomed by James IV of Scotland. Warbeck proclaimed himself Richard IV in 1496 and was captured as he led an uprising to seize the crown.

declared by their Representative Body in *Parliament*, then sitting, and adhering thereto, and pursuing thereof, (though the same afterwards be by succeeding Parliaments, judged erroneous, factious and unjust) is most agreeable to right Reason and good Conscience; and in so doing, all persons are to be free and secure from all Account and Penalties, not only upon the ground and equity of that Statute, 11 *Hen. 7.* but according to all Rules of Justice, natural or moral.

*   *   *

The Valley of Jehoshaphat, *considered and opened,*
by comparing 2. Chron. 20. *with* Joel 3.

It was the saying of *Austine;* Nothing falls under our senses, or happens in this visible World, but is either commanded or permitted from the invisible and unintelligible Court and Pallace of the highest Emperor and universal King, who is the chief over all the kings of the earth. For although he hath both commanded and permitted a subordinate external Government over Men, administered by man, for the upholding of Justice in human Societies, and for the peace, welfare, and safety of men that are made in God's Image; yet, he hath not so entirely put the Rule of the whole earth out of his own hands, but that in cases of eminent injustice and oppression (committed in Provinces, States and Kingdomes, contrary to his Lawes, to their own, and the very end of Magistracy, which is the conservation of the People's just Rights and Liberties) *He that is higher than the highest amongst men, doth regard,* and will shew by some extraordinary interposition of his, that *there are higher than they.*

Such a seasonable and signal appearance of God, for the Succor and Relief of his People, in their greatest Straits and Exigencies, (when they have no might, visible Power, or armed Force, to undertake the great company and multitude that comes against them, nor know what to do, save only to have their eyes towards him) is called in Scripture, *The day of the Lord's Judgment.* Then the Battel and cause of the Quarrel, will appear to be not so much theirs, as the Lord's: and the frame of their heart will be humble before the Lord, believing in the Lord, and believing his Prophets, for their good success and establishment.

This Dispensation is very lively described under the Type, and by the Name of *The Valley of Jehoshaphat*, as to the Season and Place wherein God will give forth a signal appearance of himself in Judgement, on the behalf of his People, for a final decision of the Controversie between them and their enemies. It Litterally and Typically fell out thus, as is at large recorded, 2 *Chron.* 20.

By way of allusion to this, and upon occasion of the like, yea, and far greater Extreamities, which God's People in the last dayes, are to be brought into, is that Prophesie, *Joel* 3. for a like, yea, a far greater and more signal appearance of God for their Deliverance and Rescue, in order to a final Decision of the Controversie, between his People and the Inhabitants of the earth, by his own Judgement. This is there called, *The Valley of Jehoshaphat*, in which the Lord will sit to Judge all his enemies round about. In this Battel and great Decision of his People's Controversie, he will cause his Mighty Ones to come down from Heaven, to put in their sickle as reapers in this Vintage and Harvest, when the wickedness is great. Unto this, *Revel.* 14. 14, 20. refers, which doth plainly evidence, that this grand Decision is to fall out in the very last of times, and probably, is that, which will make way to the Rising of the Witnesses, and will be accompanied with that *Earthquake, in which shall be slain, of men seven thousand, and the tenth part of the City will* thereupon *fall, Rev.* 11.

It is expressed, *Joel 3.* That in this day of the Lord, wherein he will *near, in the Valley of Decision, the Heavens and the Earth shall shake, by the Lord's own roaring out of Sion; and he himself will be the Harbour, Hope and Strength of his People. The Sun and Moon* of earthly Churches and Thrones of Judicature, that contest with them, *shall be darkened, and the Stars,* (even the choicest and most illuminated

gifted Pastors & Leaders, in the earthly *Jerusalem* Churches, with
their most refined Forms of Worship, resisting the power of true spiritual Godliness) *shall withdraw their shining.* Even their holy flesh
will pass off from them and consume away upon their spiritual lewd-
ness, and confident opposing the Faith of God's Elect, *Jer.* 11. 17.
*Their very Eyes will consume away in their holes, with which they say,
we see;* and for which, Christ tells the *Pharisees,* in like case, that
therefore their sin remaineth. (John 9. 41). Or, *there remaineth no more
benefit from Christ's Sacrifice, for their sin;* and therefore *only a fearful
looking for of the fiery and devouring indignation,* Heb. 10. 26, 27.

Here's that, the great confidence and boast of many professing
Churches and eminent Pastors in the earthly *Jerusalem* Fabrick, or
House on the sand, will come to, *Ezek.* 13. and *Mat.* 7. Their very
Eyes, their high enlightenings and excellent spiritual Gifts, their su-
pernatural or infused human Learning, that's admitted only as an
adorning and accomplishment of the natural man, (unaccompanied
with that Fire-Baptisme, that's performed by the unspeakable gift of
the Spirit itself, for the transforming of the natural man into spiritual) even these Eyes becoming evil, (*Mat.* 6.23.) and this light, opposing and preferring itself to the more excellent discerning and
marvellous light in spiritual Believers, are turned by the just Judgement of God, into the greatest and most fatal blindness and darkness of all. Their tongues also, though the tongues of men and angels,
for excellency and dexterity of expressing what they see, with the formentioned eyes, will consume away in their mouth, (*Zech.* 14.12.) and
leave them exposed to become, and accordingly be dealt with, as meer
sounding brass and tinckling Cymbals, (1 *Cor.* 12.31. and 13. 1.) *giving
no certain sound,* and right warning to the Battels of the Lord, *the good
fight of Faith.*

This comes to pass through their confidence in those attainments,
which may be, and oft are turned into an Idol of jealousie, and spiritual whoredom, *Ezek.* 16. 1, 15.

All these considerations of Church and State, put together, afford great ground of enquiry, as to the Condition of the times in which we live, how far the face which they bear, (and which God hath put upon them, in the course of his Providences, for some years now past) doth speak or signifie the near approach of any such extraordinary and signal appearance or day of God's Judgement, for the Decision of his own or his People's quarrel and controversie with the prophane Heathen that are round about them, waiting for an advantage, utterly and universally to remove and root them out from off the face of the whole earth?

That which hath been acted upon the Theater of these Nations, amongst us, in the true state of our Controversie, seems to be reducible to this following Querie;

Whether the Representative Body of the Kingdom of England, *in Parliament assembled, and in their Supream Power and Trust made indissolvable, unless by their own Consent and free Vote, and this by particular and express Statute, have not had a just and righteous Cause? A Quarrel more God's, than their own?*

1. It may appear they had; *First,* from the Ground of their undertaking the War; Was it not in their own and the Kingdom's just and necessary defence, and for the maintaining of the publick Rights and Liberties of both?

2. *Secondly,* Was it not undertaken upon mutual Appeals of both Parties to God, desiring him to judge between them, to give the Decision and Issue by the Law of War, (when no other Law could be heard) as the definitive Sentence in this Controversie, from the Court of Heaven?

3. *Thirdly,* Pursuant to such Decision, did they not recover and repossess the Kingdom's original and primitive freedom? Did they not endeavour to conserve and secure it, as due to them by the Law of God and of Nature? For man was made in God's Image, and all *Adam's* Posterity are properly one Universal Kingdom on earth, under

the Rule and Government of the Son of God, both as Creator and Redeemer.

By virtue of this original and primitive Freedom so recovered, they were at their own choice, whether to remain in, and retain this their true freedom (unresigned and unsubjected to the Will of any Man) under the Rule of the Son of God and his Lawes, or else to set up a King or any other Form of Government over them, after the manner of other Nations. In this latter case, it is acknowledged, that when a Commonwealth or People, do choose their first King, upon condition to obey him and his Successors, Ruling justly; they ought to remain subject to him, according to the Law, and tenor of the Fundamental Compact with him, on whom they have transferred their Authority. No Jurisdiction remaineth in them (after that free and voluntary Act of theirs) either to Judge the Realm, or determine who is the true Successor, otherwise than is by them reserved and stipulated, by their Fundamental Laws and Constitutions of Government.

And though the righteousness of this Cause (contained in the forementioned particulars) be such, as carries in it its own evidence; yet, as (as things have fallen out) it is come to be oppressed and buried in the grave of Malefactors; in the room of which, a contrary Judgement and Way, is visibly owned, upheld, and intended to be prosecuted to the utmost, for its own fast-rooting and establishment; and this, by the common Consent and Association of Multitudes. What then remains for the recovery and restitution of that good old Cause and Way, but such a seasonable and signal appearance of God, (as aforesaid) in the Valley of *Jehoshaphat?* What but the taking things immediately into his own hands, for administration of Judgement, and giving the last and final decision? Especially, since what was foretold by *Daniel,* is remarkably accomplished amongst us, to wit, that the visible Power of God's People should be broken and scattered, so as that they should have no might remaining in and with them, to go against the Multitudes, that design and resolve their Ruine.

There is not any remedy left to them, wherein they may expect success, but from such a signal day of the Lord's immediate appearance in Judgement on their behalf. *For their sakes therefore, O Lord, return thou on high,* (Psal. 7.7.) *take thy Throne of Judicature over men, from which thou hast seemed to have departed, and execute that righteous Judgement, which thou hast seemed for a season to have suspended, upon wise and holy ends best known to thy self.*

In such a dark and gloomy day, those that truely fear the Lord, are directed and required by him, not to fear or be dismayed, because he will be with them. They are encouraged in the way of Faith only, to expect this deliverance; even to *stand still,* as having no need to fight in this Battel, but only *to see the Salvation of the Lord,* through believing.

Antient Foundations, when once become destructive to those very ends for which they were first ordained, and prove hinderances, to the good and enjoyment of human Societies, to the true Worship of God, and the Safety of the People, are for their sakes, and upon the same Reasons to be altered, for which they were first laid. In the way of God's Justice they may be shaken and removed, in order to accomplish the Counsels of his Will, upon such a State, Nation, or Kingdom, in order to his introducing a righteous Government, of his own framing.

This may have been the cause of our Wanderings as it were in a Wilderness, and of God's bringing us back again into *Egypt,* after our near approach to the Land of Rest; that we have no better known, and had no more care to prosecute, what he principally intended in and by all our Changes and Removes, in the course of his

Providence. Yea we have added this also, to the rest of our sins, that we have improved the Gifts and Deliverances that God bestowed upon us, another way, and to another end than was by him intended, as well as Providentially intimated, by that holy Decree of his, in the Decision, declared at the Trial in his Martial Court, with points of Swords.

Here the great Controversie that had been depending many Ages between Rulers and the Ruled, (as to the Claimes of the one in point of Prerogative; and of the other in their Spiritual and Temporal Freedoms) was after many heats & colds, many skirmishings and battels, at last decided by the Sword. This is a way of Trial allowed by the known common Law of *England,* and the Law in force throughout all Nations. By this, the Verdict is given forth from a Court of such a Nature, as from whence there is no further appeal; Especially since after the Trial past, quiet possession was given to the Conquerors, and continued some years. Upon this, Reason and Gratitude to God, obliged us to such a prosecution as might answer the true end of Government; and in especial after that manner, as might be most to God's well-pleasing.

The Powerful Being which by success of Armes, as given to the People's Representative Body in Parliament, did communicate to it essentiallity, according to the nature of that Being, for which it was ordained. For that Being, with Power of continuing together at their own pleasure, were as the Soul and Body, unseperated, and they might have performed things necessary at present, for the safety and preservation of the Body they represented. They might have been a good help to settle righteous Government, in a constitution most acceptable to God, and beneficial to the Governed, on the Foundation of God's Institution, and the People's Ordination, in consent together, laid by the Power of God and the People's own Swords, in the hands of their faithful Trustees.

It would imply a high contempt of God and his Dispensations, so

signal amongst us, to communicate the benefit of them to his opposers. The right of choosing and being chosen into places of Trust
in the Government, was returned by the Law of the Sword (which is
paramount to all human Laws) into its primitive exercise, which is
warranted by the Law of God and of Nature. By that Law the most
famous Monarchies of the World in all Ages were first constituted
and setled; and by it God decided our Cause, looking for an event
and fruit answerable to the benefit by him given; even such a Government, as God would have given us the Pattern of (had we sought
it, as was our duty) whereby Justice and Mercy should have been daily
administered according to his will, to the bringing on the *new Heavens and new Earth, wherein Righteousness might dwell.*

The Vessel of this Commonwealth now weather-beaten and torn,
seems to be more in danger, than that wherein *Jonah* would have fled
to *Tarus:* For though we have cast forth a great part of our goods to
secure it, this has done us but small good. That Ship had but one
Delinquint aboard, which occasioned the Storm; and his being
thrown into the Sea, brought immediate safety. They had also many
skilful Seamen to guide it, but all our Pilots are cast over-board, and
none left in appearance, but guilty Passengers. Nay, admit with
Jonah, both the Commonwealth and Cause be brought into most
desperate Exigents and Extreamities, from whence there is no more
appearing redemption for them, than such as they have, that go down
quick into the grave and belly of the Whale; yet they may be preserved, even by that which naturally of itself is irrecoverably destructive to them, and be employed again in service by him against
whom they have been so ungratefully rebellious after former great
deliverances. So infinite are God's Mercies, yea, so exceeding Merciful are the severest of his Judgements and Dispensations towards his
People.

Thus may both People and Army be deprived of their Power, and
another party let in to plague and root out from amongst us, such as

are more wicked than themselves, and so make room for a more righteous Generation, which will begin all things anew.

By the course of things acted amongst us, God's sentence on our behalf is made void, and that seems given away forever, which was recovered by the Sword. Our troubles are only prorogued. No Faith or Contract is thought meet to be kept with Rebels and Hereticks, when by acquired Power it may be broken. 'Twas the great folly and self-flattery of some, to think it would be otherwise. It is most certainly true, that no Time or Prescription, is a just Bar to God's and the People's Right.

To murmure against God's Verdict, and resist his Doom, so solemnly given and executed amongst us, in the sight and concurring acknowledgement of the Nations round about, is to become adversaries to God, and to betray our Countrey. If God then do think fit to permit such a dispensation to pass upon us, it is for the punishement of our sins, and for a plague to those that are the Actors therein; to bring more swift exemplary vengeance upon them. Such as have discharged a good Conscience in what may most offend the higher Powers, are not to fear, though they be admitted to the exercise of their Rule, with an unrestrained Power, and revengeful mind.

Though from that Mountain, the Storm that comes, will be very terrible, yet some are safest in Storms, as experience shews. Yea best therein by God's Mercies, when their greatest enemies think most irrecoverably to undo them.

Our late Condition held much resemblance with that of the *Jewes,* and we deserve as well to be rejected as they were. If Christ were in the flesh amongst us, as he was with them, we are as likely to prefer theeves and murtherers before him, and crucifie him.

The present necessity in a righteous Cause is to be submitted to, and we are not to be discouraged by the danger, which to some seems threatened us, from former or present Laws. For no man that acts for common safety, when the Sword hath absolute power, and shall also command it, can justly be questioned afterwards for acting contrary to some former Laws, which could be binding no longer than whilst the Civil Sword had Soveraignty.

What People under Heaven have had more Experiments of God's timely assistance in all their Extreamities, than *Englishmen*, as well with respect to times past, as within our remembrance? Are the like Mercies recorded of any Nation? In their times of greatest Confusion they were preserved. They were a living active Body without a Head: A Bush burning in the Flames of a Civil War, yet not consumed: A People when without a Government, not embued with one another's Blood. A wonder to all Neighbours round about, and many signal Changes brought about without Blood, which indubitably evidences that God is in the Bush: and would gather us together as Chickens under a Hen, to be brooded by him, if we were not most stubbornly hardened.

Our sins have been the cause, that our Counsels, our Forces, our Wit, our Conquests, and our-Selves have been destructive to ourselves, to each other, and to a happy advancement towards our long expected and desired Settlement. Until these sins of ours be repented truly and throughly, all the Wisdom and Power upon Earth shall not avail us, but every day, every attempt, will encrease our Troubles, until there be a final extirpation of all that hinders God's Work; When this once is, nothing shall harm us, God being a sure refuge against all evils, if we reconcile ourselves to him by Faith and Repentance. Then, even those things that are most mischievous in their own natures, shall be made our advantage and security.

The People's Cause whom God after trial hath declared free, is a righteous one, though not so prudently and righteously managed as it might and ought to have been. God's doom therefore is justly executed upon us, with what intent and jugglings soever it was prosecuted by men.

Man's corruption makes him more firmly to adhere to that which is good: in which case, it is not many times, Virtue so much as Necessity that keeps men Constant; having no other means of safety and subsistance for the most part.

The goodness of any Cause is not meerly to be judged by the Events, whether visibly prosperous or unprosperous, but by the righteousness of its Principles: nor is our Faith and Patience to fail under the many fears, doubts, wants, troubles, and Power of Adversaries, in the passage to the recovery of our long lost Freedom. For it is the same Cause with that of the *Israelites* of old, of which we ought not to be ashamed or distrustful.

How hath it fared with the Cause of Christ generally, for more now than 1600 years, being made the common object of scorn and persecution, not from the base and foolish only, but from the noblest and wisest persons in the World's esteem? Yet, though our Sufferings and the time of our warfare seems long, it is very short, considering the perpetuity of the Kingdom which at last we shall obtain, & wherein we shall individually reign with the chief Soveraign thereof. For whereas all the Kingdoms of the World have not yet lasted 6000 years, this is everlasting and without end. They that overcome by not loving their lives unto the death, (*Rev.* 12.11.) shall be Pillars in the House of this everlasting Kingdom, never to be removed. They shall be Kings and Priests to God, sitting with him upon his Throne, subjecting the Nations, and reigning with him for ever and ever. This is a Kingdom that consists with the Divinity of Christ, and humanity of men. Such a reign of Christ upon earth, as will not be without Laws agreeable to human Nature, nor without Magistrates appointed as Officers under him; in which Election, God and the People shall have a joint concurrence. God's Throne in men's Consciences must then be resigned, and his People permitted to enjoy the Liberties, due to them by the Laws of Grace and Nature. Into this, God's own immediate hand can now only lead us, by his own coming to Judgement in the Valley of *Jehoshaphat.*

Anthony Ashley Cooper,
Earl of Shaftesbury, 1621–1683

Two Speeches.

I. The Earl of *Shaftsbury's* Speech in the House of Lords the 20*th.* of *October,* 1675.

II. The D. of *Buckingham's* Speech in the House of Lords the 16*th.* of *November* 1675.

Together with the Protestation, and Reasons of several Lords for the Dissolution of this Parliament; Entred in the Lords Journal the day the Parliament was Prorogued, *Nov.* 22*d.* 1675.

AMSTERDAM,
Printed *Anno Domini.* 1675.

*P*rior to the civil war the constitutional energies of the two houses were devoted to defining the balance between themselves and the Crown. After the Restoration much of their focus was directed toward defending their roles vis-à-vis each other. A dispute over their judicial roles in the case of Shirley v. Fagg *provoked Shaftesbury's speech reprinted below. The speech is of particular interest because in it Shaftesbury explains the key role the House of Lords was believed to play within English government. The views and speeches of the members of Parliament were supposed to be confidential, which is presumably the reason the publisher claimed "Two Speeches" was printed in Amsterdam.*

Shaftesbury had been a notorious, albeit probably principled, side-changer during the civil war, joining the royal cause in mid-1643 only to desert it within the year as he became fearful of the king's aims. He was active in Interregnum governments and urged Cromwell to accept the crown. When Cromwell refused Shaftesbury resigned from the Council of State. Like Vane he sat in Richard Cromwell's parliament, but unlike Vane he supported the return of monarchy. Shaftesbury joined Charles's "cabinet council" in 1670 and two years later became lord chancellor. As chancellor he fought for religious toleration in the form of Charles's unpopular declaration of indulgence. He abruptly switched, however, and vehemently supported the Test Act against Catholics, perhaps because he had learned of the king's secret promise to Louis XIV to convert. In November 1673 Shaftesbury was dismissed from office and became a leader of the opposition and creator of the group that was to become the Whig party. It was as leader of the opposition that he spoke on behalf of the jurisdiction of the Lords.

The case of Shirley v. Fagg *arose when the plaintiff, Dr. Shirley, lost a case in Chancery and appealed to the Lords against Sir John Fagg, an MP for Steyning. In an earlier dispute,* Skinner v. The East India Company, *the Commons had challenged the Lords' right to original jurisdiction and won. Now they claimed this appeal was also a breach of privilege that infringed upon their role as a court. To demonstrate the seriousness with which they regarded the matter they sent Fagg to the Tower as punishment for appearing before the Lords and arrested four barristers due to appear in a similar case. Shaftesbury and the opponents of the nonresisting test bill have been accused of goading the Commons into immoderate actions in this case in order to block consideration of that bill. Even if the accusation were true, such a scheme would have failed if the case had not raised a serious constitutional issue. With Shaftesbury's urging the Lords stood upon their right to hear appeals, even when a member of the Commons was involved. All other business came to a halt, and the king felt obliged to prorogue Parliament. The Lords' view ultimately prevailed, for the Commons dropped its objections to the supreme appellate jurisdiction of the Lords.*

"The Duke of Buckingham's Speech," also listed on the title page, is not included in this volume. A list of errata that had been called for by the printer and had "escaped the Press through hast" has been incorporated.

The Earl of Shaftsbury's *Speech in the House of Lords, upon the Debate of Appointing a Day for the Hearing Dr.* Shirley's *Cause,*[1] *the* 20th *of* October, 1675.

My *Lords,*

Our All is at Stake, and therefore You must give me leave to speak freely before We part with it. My Lord Bishop of *Salisbury* is of Opinion, *that we should rather appoint a day to consider what to do upon the Petition; than to appoint a day of hearing:* And my *Lord Keeper,* for I may name them at a Committee of the whole House tells Us in very Eloquent and Studied Language, *That he will Propose Us a way far less liable to Exception, and much less Offensive and Injurious to our own Priviledges, than that of appointing a day of Hearing.* And I beseech Your Lordships, did you not after all these fine Words expect some Admirable Proposal! But it ended in this. *That Your Lordships should appoint a day, nay very long day to Consider what You would do in it.* And my Lord hath undertaken to convince you, that this is Your only Course by several undeniable Reasons; the first of which is: *That 'tis against your Judicature to heer this Cause which is not proper before Us, nor ought to be relieved by Us.* To this my Lords give me leave to Answer, that I did not expect from a man Professing the Law; that after an Answer by Orders of the Court was put in, and a day had been appointed for Hearing, which by some Accident was set aside, and the Plaintiffe moving for a second day to be assigned that ever without hearing Counsel on both sides; the Court did enter into the Merits of the Cause. And if your Lordships should do it here in a Cause attended with the Circumstances this is, it would not only

1. The functions of the House of Lords included serving as a supreme court and also trying persons impeached by the House of Commons. When Dr. Shirley appealed to the House of Lords against Sir John Fagg, a member of the Commons, however, the Commons refused to allow Fagg to answer while Parliament was sitting and voted the suit a breach of their privilege. See David Ogg, *England in the Reign of Charles II* (London, 1972), 470–71.

be an apparent Injustice, but a plain *Subterfuge* to avoid a Point you durst not maintain.

But my Lord's second Reason speaks the Matter more clearly, for that is: *Because 'tis a doubtful case, whether the Commons have not Priviledge,* and therefore my Lord would have You, *To appoint a farther and a very long day to consider of it,* which in plain English is, that Your Lordships should confess upon Your Books, that you conceive it on second Thoughts a doubtful Case, for so Your *Appointing a day to Consider* will do, and that for no other Reason, but because my Lord *Keeper* thinks it so, which I hope will not be a Reason to prevail with Your Lordships; since we cannot yet by experience tell that his Lordship is capable of thinking Your Lordships in the Right, in any Matter against the *Judgement* of the *House of Commons;* 'tis so hard a thing even for the ablest of men to change ill Habits.

But my Lord's third Reason, is the most Admirable of all which he Styles *Unanswerable,* viz. *That Your Lordships are all convinced in Your Consciences that this (if prosecuted) will cause a Breach.* I beseech Your Lordships, consider whether this Argument thus applied would not overthrow the Law of Nature, and all the Laws of Right and Property in the World: For 'tis an Argument, and a very good one, that You should not stand or insist on Claims, where You have not a clear Right; or where the Question is not of Consequence and of Moment, in a Matter that may produce a Dangerous Pernitious Breach between Relations, Persons, Bodies politick joined in Interest, and High Concerns together. So on the other hand, if the Obstinancy of the Party in the wrong, shall be made an unanswerable Argument for the other Party to recede and give up his just Rights, How long shall the People keep their Liberties, or the Princes or Governours of the World their Prerogatives! How long shall the Husband maintain his dominion, or any man his Property from his Friend, or his Neighbour's Obstinancy? But my Lords when I hear my Lord *Keeper* open so Eloquently *the Fatal Consequences of a*

Breach: I cannot forbear to fall into some admiration how it comes to pass: That (if the *Consequences be so fatall*) the King's Ministers in the House of *Commons*, of which there are several that are of the *Cabinet*, and have daily resort to His *Majesty* and have the Direction and Trust of his Affaires: I say that none of these should press these Consequences there, or give the least stop to the Carreer of that House in this Business; but that all the Votes concerning this Affair, nay even that very Vote, *That no Appeal from any Court of Equity is cognisable by the House of Lords*, should pass *nemine contradicente*.[2] And yet all the great Ministers with us here, the *Bishops* and other *Lords* of greatest dependance on the Court contend this point, as if it were *pro Aris & focis*.[3] I hear his *Majesty* in *Scotland* hath been pleased to declare against *Appeals in Parliament*, I cannot much blame the Court if they think (the *Lord Keeper*, and the *Judges* being of the *King's* Naming, and in His Power to change) that the Justice of the Nation is safe enough, and I my *Lords* may think so too, during this *King's* time, though I hear *Scotland* not without reason complain already. Yet how future *Princes* may use this Power, and how *Judges* may be made not men of Ability or Integrity, but men of Relation and Dependance, and who will do what they are commanded; and all men's Causes come to be Judged, and Estates disposed of as Great Men at Court please.

My *Lords*, the Constitution of our Government hath provided better for Us, and I can never believe so Wise a Body as the *House of Commons*, will prove that Foolish woman, which plucks down her House with her hands.

My *Lords*, I must presume in the next place to say something to what was offered by my *Lord Bishop of Salsbury*, a man of Great Learning and Abilities, and always versed in a stronger and closer way of Reasoning, than the Business of that Noble *Lord* I answered

2. With no one contradicting.
3. For [in favor of] altars and hearths.

before did accustome him too, and that Reverend *Prelate* hath stated the matter very fair upon two Heads.

The first, *whether the hearing of Causes and Appeals, and especially in this Point where the Members have priviledge, be so Material to us, that it ought not to give way to the Reason of State, of greater Affairs that pressed us at the time.*

The second was, *If this Business be of that Moment, yet whether the appointing a day to consider of this Petition; would prove of that consequence, and prejudice to your Cause.*

My *Lords*, to these give me leave in the first place to say, that this Matter is no less than Your whole *Judicature*, and Your *Judicature* is the life and soul of the Dignity of the *Peerage of England*, you will quickly grow burdensome, if you grow useless, you have now the greatest and most useful end of *Parliament* principally in you, which is not to make new Laws but to redress Grievances, and to Maintain the Old Land-Marks. The *House of Commons'* Business is to complain, Your *Lordships'* to redress, not only the Complaints from them that are the Eyes of the Nation, but all other particular persons that address to You. A Land may Groan under a Multitude of Laws I believe Ours does, and when Laws grow so multiplied, they prove oftener Snares, than Directions and Security to the People. I look upon it as the ignorance and weakness of the latter Age, if not worse, the effect of the Designes of ill men; that it is grown a general opinion, that where there is not a particular direction in some *Act of Parliament* the Law is defective, as if the *Common Law* had not provided much better, Shorter, and Plainer for the Peace and Quiet of the Nation than intricate, long, and perplexed *Statutes* do: which has made Work for the *Lawyers*, given power to the *Judges*, lessened Your Lordships' Power, and in a good measure unhinged the security of the People.

My *Lord Bishop* tells You, *That Your whole Judicature is not in question, but only the priviledge of the House of Commons, of their Members not appearing at Your Barr.* My Lords, were it no more, yet *that* for Justice and the People's sake You ought not to part with. How far a Priviledge of a *House of Commons,* their Servants, and those they own, doth extend *Westminster Hall,* may with Griefe tell Your *Lordships.* And the same Priviledge of their Members being not sued, must be allowed by Your *Lordships,* as well, and what a failer of Justice this would prove whilst they are *Lords* for life, and you for Inheritance, let the World Judge; for my part I am willing to come to Conference whenever the Dispute shall begin again, and dare undertake to your *Lordships,* that they have neither Precedent, Reason, nor any Justifiable pretence to show against us; and therefore my *Lords,* if you part with this undoubted Right meerly for the asking, where will the asking stop! And my *Lords,* we are sure it doth not stop here, for they have already *nemine Contradicente!* Voted against *Your Lordships' power of Appeals from any Court of Equity!* So that you may plainly see where this Caution and reason of State means to stop, not one jot short of laying your whole Judicature aside, for the same reason of passing the King's Money, of not interrupting good Laws, or whatever else must of necessity avoid all Breach upon what score soever. And your *Lordships* plainly see the Breach will be as well made upon your Judicature in general as upon this, so that when your *Lordships* have appointed a day; a very long day, or to consider whether Dr. *Shirley's* Cause be not too hot to handle. And when you have done the same for Sir *Nicholas Stoughton* whose Petition I hear is coming in, your *Lordships* must proceed to a Vote *to lay all private Business aside for six Weeks,* for that Phrase of private Business hath obtained upon this last Age, upon that which is your most publique Duty and Business; namely the Administration of Justice. And I can tell your *Lordships,* besides the reason that leads to it, that I have some intelligence of the designing such a Vote: For on the second day of your sitting, at the rising of the *Lords House* there came a Gentleman into the Lobby belonging to a very great Person, and askt in great haste *are the Lords up? have they passed the Vote?* And being asked what Vote? He answered *the Vote of no Private Business for six Weeks.*

My *Lords,* if this be your Business, see where you are, if ye are to Postpone our Judicature for fear of offending the *House of Commons* for six Weeks: that they in the *interim* may passe the *Money,* and other acceptable Bills that His *Majesty* thinks of Importance; are so many wise men in the *House* of *Commons* to be laid asleep, and to pass all these acceptable things; and when they have done, to let us to be let loose upon them.

Will they not remember this next time there is want of *Money?* Or may not they rather be assured by those Ministers that are amongst them, and go on so unanimously with them, that the *King* is on their side in this Controversie, and when the publique Businesses are over, our time shall be too short to make a Breach or vindicate ourselves in the Matter? And then I beg your *Lordships* where are you; after you have asserted but the last *Session* your right of Judicature, so highly even in this Point, and after the *House of Commons* had gone so high against you on the other hand, as to post up their *Declaration* and *Remonstrances* on *Westminster Hall Doors,* the very next *Session* after you postpone the very same Causes, and not only those, but all Judicatures whatever. I beseech your *Lordships,* will not this prove a fatal precident and confession against yourselves? 'Tis a Maxim, and a rational one amongst Lawyers, *that one Precedent where the Case hath been Contested, is worth a 1000 where there hath been no Contest.* My Lords, in saying this I humbly suppose I have given a sufficient answer to my *Lord Bishop's* second Question; *Whether the appointing a day to consider what you will do with this Petition of that consequence to your right,* for it is a plain confession, that it is a doubtful Case, and that infinitely stronger than if it were a new thing to you never heard of before; For it is the very same *Case,* and the very same thing desired in that *Case,* that you formerly ordered and so strongly asserted; so that upon time, and all the deliberation imaginable, you declared yourselves to become doubtful, and you put yourselves out of your own hands, into that power that you have no reason to believe on your side in this Question.

My Lords, I have all the duty imaginable to his *Majesty*, and should with all submission give way to anything that he should think of Importance to his affairs: But in this Point it is to alter the constitution of the *Government*, if you are asked to lay this aside; And there is no reason of State can be an Argument to your *Lordships* to turn yourselves out of that Interest you have in the constitution of the *Government*, 'tis not only your concern that you maintain yourselves in it, but 'tis the concern of the Poorest man in *England* that you keep your Station. 'Tis your *Lordships'* concern, and that so highly, that I will be bold to say the *King* can give none of you a requital or recompence for it, what are empty Titles? What is present Power, or Riches and a great Estate, wherein I have no firme nor fixed property? 'Tis the constitution of the *Government* and Maintaining it that secures your *Lordships* and every man else in what he hath. The Poorest Lord, if the Birthright of the *Peerage* be maintained, has a Fair Prospect before him for himself or his Posterity: But the greatest Title with the greatest present Power and Riches, is but a mean creature, and maintains those absolute *Monarchies* no otherwise than by servile low flatteries and upon uncertain terms.

My Lords, 'Tis not only your Interest, but the Interest of the Nation that you Maintain your Rights, for let the *House of Commons* and *Gentry* of *England* think what they please, there is no *Prince* that ever governed without *Nobility* or an *Army:* if you will not have one; you must have t'other, or the *Monarchy* cannot long support, or keep itself from tumbling into a *Democratical Republique*. Your *Lordships* and the people have the same cause, and the same Enemies. My Lords, would you be in favour with the King? 'Tis a very ill way to it, to put yourselves out of a future capacity, to be considerable in his service. I do not find in Story, or in Modern Experience, but that 'tis better, and a man is much more regarded that is in a capacity and opportunity to serve, than he that hath wholly deprived himself of all for his *Prince's* service. And I therefore declare that I will serve my *Prince* as a *Peer*, but will not destroy the *Peerage* to serve him.

My *Lords*, I have heard of 20 foolish Modells and Expedients to secure the Justice of the Nation, and yet to take this Right from your *Lordships* as the *King* by his *Commission* appointing *Commoners* to hear *Appeals;* or that the twelve *Judges* should be the persons, or that persons should be appointed by Act of Parliament, which are all not only to take away your *Lordships'* just Right, that ought not to be altered any more than any other part of the *Government*, but are in themselves when well weighed Ridiculous. I must deal freely with your *Lordships*, these things could never have risen in men's minds, but that there has been some kind of Provocation that has given the first rise of it. Pray my Lords forgive me, if on this occasion I put you in mind of *Committee Dinners*, and the Scandal of it, those Droves of Ladies that attended all Causes; 'twas come to that pass, that men even Hired or Borrowed of their Friends' handsom Sisters or Daughters to deliver their Petitions. But yet for all this I must say, that your Judgments have been Sacred, unless in one or two Causes, and those we owe most to that Bench; from whence we now apprehend most danger.

There is one thing I had almost forgot to speak to, *Which is the Conjuncture of time, the Hinge upon which your reason of State turns;* and to that my Lords give me leave to say, if this be not a time of Leisure for you to vindicate your Priviledges, you must never expect one. I could almost say that the Harmony, good Agreement, and Concord that is to be prayed for at most other times, may be fatall to us now, we owe the Peace of this last two years and the disingagement from the *French* interest to the two Houses differing from the Sense and Opinion of *Whitehall*, so at this time, the thing in the World this Nation hath most reason to apprehend, is a General

Peace, which cannot now happen without very advantagious Terms to the *French*, and Disadvantagious to the House of *Austria*. We are the King's great Counsellors and if so, have Right to differ, and give contrary Councels to these few are nearest about him, I fear they would advance a General Peace, I'm sure I would advise against it, and hinder it at this time by all the ways imaginable. I heartily wish nothing from you may add weight and reputation to those Councels would assist the *French*. No Money for Ships, nor Preparation you can make, nor Personal assurances our Prince can have, can secure us from the *French* if they are at leisure, he is grown the most Potent of us all at *Sea*. He has Built 24 Ships this last year; and has 30 more in number than we besides the advantage that our Ships are all out of Order, and his so exquisitely provided for, that every Ship has his particular Store-house. 'Tis incredible the Money he hath, and is bestowing in making Harbors, he makes nature itself give way to the vastness of his Expence. And after all this shall a Prince so Wise, so intent upon his affairs, be thought to make all these preparations to Saile over Land, and fall on the back of *Hungary*, and Batter the walls of *Kaminit'z*, or is it possible he should oversee his Interest in seizing of *Ireland*, a thing so feasible to him, if he be master of the Seas, as he certainly now is; and which when attained gives him all the *Southern*, *Mediteranian*, *East and West India Trade*, and renders him both by Scituation and excellent Harbors, perpetual Master of the Seas without Dispute.

My Lords, to conclude this point, I fear the Court of *England* is greatly mistaken in it, and I do not wish them the reputation of the concurrance of the Kingdom: And this out of the most sincere Loyalty to his Majesty, and love to my Nation.

My Lords, I have but one thing more to trouble you with, and that peradventure is a consideration of the greatest weight and concern, both to your Lordships, and the whole Nation. I have often seen in this House, that the Arguments, with strongest reason, and most convincing to the Lay Lords in General have not had the same effect upon the Bishops' Bench; but that they have unanimously gone against us in matters, that many of us have thought Essential and undoubted Rights; And I consider, that 'tis not possible, that Men of great Learning, Piety, and Reason, as their Lordships are, should not have the same care of doing right, and the same conviction, what is right upon clear reason offered, that other your Lordships have. And therefore, my Lords, I must necessarily think, we differ in principles; And then 'tis very easie to apprehend what is the clearest sense to men of my principle, may not at all perswade or affect the Conscience of the best man of a different one. I put your Lordships the case plainly, as 'tis now before us. My principle is, *That the King is King by Law, and by the same Law that the poor Man enjoys his Cottage;* and so it becomes the concern of every man in *England,* that has but his liberty, to maintain and defend, to his utmost, the King in all his Rights and Prerogatives. My Principle is also, *That the Lords House, and the Judicature and Rights belonging to it, are an Essential part of the Government,* and Established by the same Law; The King governing and administering Justice by His House of Lords, and advising with both His Houses of Parliament in all important matters, is the Government I own, am born under, and am obliged to. If ever there should happen in future ages (which God forbid) a King governing by an Army, without His Parliament, 'tis a Government I own not, am not obliged to, nor was born under. According to this Principle, every honest man that holds it, must endeavour equally to preserve the frame of the Government, in all the parts of it, and cannot satisfie his Conscience to give up the Lords House for the Service of the Crown, or to take away the just rights and priviledges of the House of Commons to please the Lords. But there is another Principle got into the World, my Lords, that hath not been long there; for Arch-Bishop *Laud* was the first Author that I remember of it: And I cannot find, that the Jesuites, or indeed the Popish Clergy hath ever owned it, but some of the Episcopal Clergy of our *British Isles:* and 'tis withal, as 'tis new, so the most dangerous destructive Doctrine to our Government and Law, that ever was. 'Tis the first of the Cannons published by the Convocation, 1640. *That Monarchy is of Divine Right.* This Doctrine was then preached up, and maintained by *Sibthorp, Manwaring,*[4] and others, and of later years, by a Book published by Dr. *Sanderson, Bishop of Lincoln,* under the name of *Arch-Bishop Usher,*[5] and how much it is spread amongst our Dignified Clergy, is very easily known. We all agree, *That the King and His Government, is to be obeyed for Conscience' sake;* and that the Divine Precepts, require not only here, but in all parts of the World, *Obedience to Lawful Governours.* But that this Family are our Kings, and this particular frame of Government, is our lawful Constitution, and obliges us, is owing only to the particular Laws of our Country. This *Laudean* Doctrine was the root that produced the *Bill of Test*[6] last *Session,* and some very perplexed Oaths[7] that are of the same nature with that, and yet imposed by several *Acts of this Parliament.*

In a word, if this Doctrine be true, our *Magna Charta* is of no force, our Laws are but Rules amongst ourselves during the King's pleasure. Monarchy, if of Divine Right, cannot be bounded or limited by human Laws, nay, what's more, cannot bind itself; and All our Claims of right by the Law, or Constitution of the Government, All the Jurisdiction and Priviledge of this House, All the Rights and

---

4. See, for example, Robert Sibthorpe, "Apostolike Obedience. Shewing the Duty of Subjects to pay Tribute and Taxes to their Princes, according to the Word of God" (London, 1627) and Maynwaring, vol. 1, 56–71.

5. Robert Sanderson, an Anglican theologian and chaplain to Charles I and later Bishop of Lincoln, wrote a preface to a book written by James Ussher, Archbishop of Armagh, at the command of Charles I and published by Sanderson, entitled "The Power communicated by God to the Prince, and the Obedience required of the Subject" (London, 1661).

6. 25 Car. II, cap. 2, An Act for preventing dangers which may happen from Popish recusants, 1673.

7. Acts passed by the Cavalier Parliament that imposed special oaths were the Corporation Act, 13 Car. II, st. 2, cap. 1 (1661); the Militia Act of 1662, 14 Car. II, cap. 3; the Uniformity Act, 14 Car. II, cap. 4 (1662); the Five Mile Act, 7 Car. II, cap. 2 (1665).

Priviledges of the House of Commons, All the Properties and Liberties of the People, are to give way, not only to the interest, but the will and pleasure of the Crown. And the best and worthiest of Men, holding this principle, must Vote to deliver up all we have, not only when reason of State, and the separate Interest of the Crown require it, but when the will and pleasure of the King is known, would have it so. For that must be, to a man of that principle, the only rule and measure of Right and Justice. Therefore, my Lords, you see how necessary it is, that our Principles be known, and how fatal to us all it is, that this Principle should be suffered to spread any further.

My Lords, to conclude, your Lordships have seen of what consequence this matter is to you, and that the appointing a day to consider, is no less than declaring yourselves doubtful, upon second and deliberate thoughts, that you put yourselves out of your own hands, into a more than a moral probability, of having this Session made a precedent against you. You see your Duty to yourselves and the People; and that 'tis really not the interest of the *House of Commons,* but may be the inclination of the Court, that you loose the Power of Appeals; but I beg our House may not be *Felo de se,*[8] but that your Lordships would take in this affair, the only course to preserve yourselves, and appoint a day, this day 3 weeks, for the hearing Dr. *Shirley's* Cause, which is my humble motion.

FINIS.

8. May not kill itself.

H. S. [Henry Scobell, d. 1660]

POWER

OF THE

LORDS

AND

COMMONS

IN

PARLIAMENT

In point of

JUDICATURE

briefly discours'd.

At the Request of a Worthy Member of the House of Commons.

LONDON, Printed in the Year, 1680.

*T*his short history of the power of Parliament from the time of the
Norman Conquest and, in particular, the role of the Commons as
a court is customarily attributed to Henry Scobell, clerk of Parliament during the Interregnum.

Scobell died twenty years before its publication. But if the attribu-
tion is correct in 1648 its author had been granted the clerkship of the
Parliament for life. Scobell also served as censor and was therefore
responsible for licensing newspapers and political pamphlets. With
Oliver Cromwell's eviction of the Rump Parliament in 1653 Scobell
became assistant secretary to the Council of State and, when Oliver's
first parliament convened, he was reappointed clerk. However, he
was less popular with subsequent parliaments. In 1656/57 he was replaced as clerk, and the following year the restored Rump Parliament
took exception to some of his past actions. Its members ordered a bill
brought in to repeal the act granting Scobell his lifetime appointment

as clerk and began to investigate his behavior during the 1650s. Sco-bell died in 1660.

During the 1650s Scobell had written and published a series of tracts on parliamentary methods, proceedings, and acts, some of which were republished after his death. The tract reprinted here fits into this genre. Scobell had, at least once before, signed a tract with his initials. There is no record this tract appeared during Scobell's lifetime. It may have been a report he had composed that remained many years in manuscript. The motive of its publication in 1680 was to enhance the prestige of Parliament and the House of Commons as a court at a crucial time. Its publication coincided with the campaign to boost the status of Parliament as part of the effort to exclude the Catholic Duke of York from the succession. Two further editions of the tract appeared after the Glorious Revolution.

SIR,

To give you as short an account of your Desires as I can; I must crave leave to lay you, as a Foundation, the *Frame* or *First Model* of this *State.*

When, after the *Period* of the *Saxon Time, Harald* had advanced himself into the Royal Seat; the *Great* men, (to whom but lately he was no more than *Equal* either in *Fortune* or *Power*) disdaining this Act of Arrogancy and Ambition, called in *William* Duke of *Normandy,* (the most Active Prince of any in these *Western* Parts, and renowned for the Victories that he had successfully Atchieved against the *French* King, then the most Potent *Monarch* in *Europe*).

This *Duke* led along with him to this work of *Glory* many of the *Younger* Sons of the best *Families* of *Normandy, Picardy* and *Flanders;* who, as *Voluntiers,* accompanied the undertaking of this *Fortunate* Man.

The *Usurper* being Slain, and the *Crown,* by *War,* gained; to secure *Certain* to his *Posterity* what he had so *Suddenly* gotten, he shared out his *Purchase* retaining in Each *County* a *Portion,* to support the Soveraign *Dignity,* which was styled *Demenia Regni;* (now the *Ancient Demesnes*) and assigning to others his *Adventurers* such *Proportions,* as engaged to himself the *Dependency* of their *Personal Service* (such Lands only excepted, as, in *Free Alms,* were allotted to the *Church*). *These* were termed *Barones Regis,* or the *King's Immediate Free-holders;* for the word *Baro* imported then no more.

As the *King* to *These,* so *These* to their *Followers,* Subdivided part of their *Shares* into *Knights-Fees,* and their *Tenants* were called, *Barones Comitis,* or the like; for we find, as in the *King's Writ,* so in *Theirs, Baronibus suis al François & Anglois,* to their *Barons,* as well *French* as *English;* the Royal Gifts, for the most part, extending to whole *Counties* or *Hundreds;* an *Earl* being Lord of the *One,* and a *Baron* of the *Inferiour* Donations to Lords of *Townships* or *Mannours.*

And as the *Land,* so was also the *Course* of *Judicature* divided, even from the *Meanest* to the *Highest* Portion; each *Several* had his *Court* of *Law,* preserving still the Custom of our Ancestors the *Saxons,* who *jura per Pagos reddebant,* distributed Justice throughout each Village. And these were termed *Court Barons,* or the *Freeholders' Court,* (*twelve* usually in number) who with the *Thame,* or Chief Lord, were *Judges.*

The *Hundred-Court* was next, where the *Hundredis,* or *Alderman-nus* (Lord of the *Hundred*) with the *chief* Lord of each *Township* within their Limits, judged. God's People observed *This* form; in the Publick *Centureonis & Decam Judicabant Plebem omni tempore,* Hundreds and Decennaries administering Justice to the People at all times.

The *County-Court,* or *Generale Placitum,* was the next. *This* was to supply the Defect, or remedy the Corruption of the *Inferiour:* For *Ubi Curiae* Dominorum *probantur defecisse, pertinet ad* Vice Comitem Provinciarum; where the *Hundred-Court* was found *Defective,* matters were referred to the Lord of the *County.* The *Judges* here were *Comites & Barones Comitatus, qui Liberas, in hoc. Terras habeant; Earls* and *Barons* of the *County,* that were Free-holders in the same.

The *last* and *Supreme* Court, and *proper to our Question,* was *Generale Placitum apud London,* the *General Council* at London; *Universalis Synodus,* the *Universal Synod,* in *Charters* of the Conquerour, *Capitalis Curiae,* the *Capital Court;* by *Glanvil, Magnum & Commune Concilium coram Rege, & Magnatibus suis;* the Great and Common Council before the *King* and his *Nobles.*

In the *Rolls* of *Henry* the Third, *It* is not *Stative,* but *summoned* by *Proclamation. Edicture Generale Placitum apud* London (says the Book of *Abingdon*) whither *Duces, Principes, Satrapre, Rectores, & Causidici ex omni parte confluxerunt ad istam Curiam,* saith *Glanvil,* the *General Assembly* was called at *London;* whither Dukes, Princes, Peers, Rectors, and Lawyers resorted from all Quarters: And Causes were referred *propter aliquam dubitationem quae emergit in Comitatu cum Comitatus nescit dijudicare;* upon any Question or Difficulty which the County Court was not able to solve. Thus did *Ethelweld,* Bishop of *Winchester,* transfer his Suit against *Leostine* from the County *ad Generale Placitum,* or the *General Assembly.* In the time of King *Etheldred,* Queen *Edgine* against *Goda,* from the County appealed to King *Etheldred* at *London, Congregatis Principibus & Sapientibus Angliae,* where the Princes and Wise Men of the Land were met together. A Suit between the Bishops of *Winchester* and *Durham,* in the time of S. *Edward, Coram Episcopis & Principibus Regni in praesentia Regis ventilata & finita;* was handled and determined by the Bishops and Princes of the Realm in the presence of the King. In the 10th year of the Conquerour, *Episcopi, Comites & Barones Regni potestate adversis Provinciis, ad Universalem Synodum, pro causis audiendis & tractandis, convocati;* the Bishops, Earls and Barons of the Realm, &c. being assembled at the Universal Council to hear and determine Controversies, (says the Book of *Westminster*). And *This* continued all along in the succeeding King's Reign, until toward the end of *Henry* the Third.

As this Great *Court* or *Council,* (consisting of the *King* and *Barons*) ruled the important Affairs of *State,* and controlled all Inferiour *Courts;* so were there certain *Officers,* whose transcendant Power seemed to be set for the circumscribing the Execution of the *Prince's Will;* as the *Steward, Constable,* and *Marshal,* fixed upon *Families* in *Fee,* for many Ages. They (as *Tribunes* of the *People,* or *Ephori* among the *Lacedemonians*) growing by unmanly Courage terrible to *Monarchy,* fell at the feet and mercy of the King, when the daring Earl of *Leicester* was slain at *Evesham.*

This *Chance*, and the dear *Experience Henry* the Third himself had made at the *Parliament* at *Oxford*, in the fortieth year of his Reign; together with the *Memory* of the many straits his *Father*[1] was driven unto, especially at *Runny-Mead* near *Stanes;* brought *this* King to *begin* what his *Successors* fortunately *finished;* in *lessening* the Strength and Power of his Great *Lords*. And this was effected by searching into the *Regality* they had usurped over their *peculiar Soveraigns*, whereby they were found to be (as the Book of St. *Albans* termeth them) *quot Domini, tot Tyranni*, how many *Lords*, so many *Tyrants;* and by weakening that *Influence* and *Sway* which they carried in the *Parliaments*, by commanding the *Service* of many *Knights, Citizens*, and *Burgesses*, to the *Great Council*.

Now began the frequent sending of *Writs* to the *Commons;* Their assent not only used in *Money, Charge*, and making *Laws*, (for, before, all *Ordinances* passed by the *King* and *Peers*) but their Consent also in *Judgements* of all Qualities whether *Civil* or *Criminal*. In proof whereof I will produce some few succeeding *Precedents* out of *Record*.

When *Adamor* (that proud *Prelate* of *Winchester*, the King's *Half Brother*) had aggrieved the State by his formidable *Insolence;* he was banished by the joint sentence of the *King*, the *Lords*, and *Commons*. And this appeareth expressly, by the *Letter* sent to *Pope Alexander* the Fourth, who expostulated a *Revocation* of him from Exile because he was a *Church-man*, and so not Subject to any Censure. In *This* the answer is *Si Dominus Rex aut Majores Regni hoc vellent* (meaning his *Revocation*) *Communitas tamen, Ipsius Ingressum in Angliam iam Nulla tenus sustineret;* though the *King* and *Lords* should consent to his *Revocation*, yet would the *Commons* never allow of it. The *Peers* Subscribe this *Answer* with their Names, and *Petrus de Mountford vice Locius Communitatis*, as *Speaker*, or *Proctor* of the *Commons*.

1. Henry III was the son of King John.

For by *that Style* Sir *John Tiptoft (Prolocutor)* affirmeth under his *Arms* the *Deed* of *Entail* of the *Crowns* by *King Henry* the fourth, in the eighth year of his Reign, for *all* the *Commons.*

The Banishment of the two *Spencers* in the fifteenth of *Edward 2d. Prelates, Comites, & Barones, & les autres Peeres de la Terre, & Communes de Royaulme,* the Prelates, Earles, and Barons, and the rest of the Peers of the Realm, and Commons of the Land, do give Consent and Sentence to the Revocation and Reversement of the *Former* Sentence; *the Lords and Commons accord;* and so it is expressed in the *Roll.*

In the first of *Edward* the 3d. when *Elizabeth* the Widdow of *Sir John de Burgo,* complained in *Parliament,* that *Hugh Spencer* the Younger, *Robert Boldock,* and *William Cliffe* his Instruments had by *Duresse* forced her to make a Writing to the King, whereby she was despoiled of all her Inheritance; Sentence is given for her in these words; *Pur ceo que avis est al Evesques, Counts, & Barons, & autres Grandes, & a tout* Cominalte *de la Terre, que le dit script est fait contre Ley & tout manere de Raison, si faist le dit Escript per agard del Parliament dampue alloquens al livre a la dit* Elizabeth, Forasmuch as it appeareth unto the Bishops, Earls, and Barons, and all the Commonalty of the Land, that the said Writing was made against all Law and Reason, it is adjudged by Parliament, &c.

In *An. 4. Edward 3.* it appeareth by a Letter to the *Pope,* that to the Sentence given against the Earl of *Kent* the Commons were Parties, as well as the Lords and Peers; for the King directed their Proceedings in these words, *Comitibus Magnatibus, Baronibus, & aliis de* Communitate *dicti Regni ad Parliamentum illud congregatis iniunximus; ut super his discernerent & judicarent, quod Rationi & Justitiae conveniret, habere prae Oculis solum Deum, qui eum concordi unanimi sententia tanquam Reum criminis laesae Majestatis morti adjudicarent eius sententia, &c.* We have commanded the Earls, Peers, Barons, and others of the Commonalty of the said Realm assembled in Parliament, to determine in this matter according to Reason and Justice, having only God before their Eyes; and by an unanimous consent they have sentenced him to death, as guilty of *High-Treason.*

When in the 50th year of *Edward 3.* the Lords had pronounced the Sentence against *Richard Lions* otherwise than the Commons agreed, they appealed to the King, and had Redress, and the Sentence entered to their Desires.

When, in the first Year of *Richard* the Second, *William Weston,* and *John Jennings,* were Arraigned in Parliament for surrendering certain *Forts* of the King's; the *Commons* were *Parties* to the Sentence against them given, as appeareth by a *Memorandum* annexed to That *Record.* In the first of *Henry* the Fourth, although the *Commons* referre, by *Protestation,* the pronouncing of the Sentence of Deposition against King *Richard* the Second unto the Lords; yet are they equally Interressed in it; as appeareth by the *Record:* For there are made *Proctors,* or *Commissioners,* for the *whole Parliament,* one *Bishop,* one *Abbott,* one *Earl,* one *Baron,* and two *Knights* (*Gray* and *Erpingham*) for the *Commons.* And to infer that because the *Lords* pronounced the Sentence, the point of *Judgment* should be only *Theirs,* were as absurd, as to conclude that no *Authority* was vested in any other *Commissioner* of *Oyer* and *Terminer,* than in the Person of that Man only that speaketh the Sentence.

In the *2d.* of *Henry 5.* The Petition of the *Commons* importeth no less than a *Right* they had to *Act* and *Assent* to all things in *Parliament;* and so it is answered by the *King.* And had not the *adjourned-Roll* of the *Higher-House* been left to the *sole* Entry of the *Clerk* of the *Upper-House,* (who, either out of neglect to observe due *Form,* or on set purpose to obscure the *Commons-Right,* and to flatter the *Power* of those who he, *immediately* served, omitted them), there would have been frequent *Examples* of *all Times* to clear This *doubt,* and to preserve a just *Interest* to the *Commonwealth.* And how conveniently it suits with *Monarchy* to maintain This *Form*, lest others of that well-framed *Body* knit under one *Head*, should swell too Great and Monstrous, may be seen with half an Eye; *it* being (in my Opinion) at least equally Liable to suffer a-fresh under an *Aristocracy*, as a *Democracy*.

SIR, I am Your most humble Servant. H. S.

FINIS.

[Anthony Ashley Cooper,
Earl of Shaftesbury, 1621–1683]

TWO
SEASONABLE
DISCOURSES

Concerning this present

Parliament.

OXFORD,
Printed in the Year, 1675.

This tract has been attributed to the Earl of Shaftesbury, then leader of the opposition and a staunch critic of both Court policy and the long, Cavalier Parliament.

Shaftesbury was intent upon getting the Cavalier Parliament, sitting since 1661, finally dissolved. Many of its members were in the pay of the Court and clearly it was no longer representative of the country. Shaftesbury was not disinterested in the matter. He had been dismissed from the Privy Council in May 1674 and promptly became a leader of the opposition in Parliament. He hoped fresh elections would give his side a majority. When Parliament reconvened in October 1675, he made dissolution a priority. Shaftesbury had a penchant for summoning up serious constitutional issues to achieve political ends.

In this instance legitimate and probing questions were raised about the ability of a parliament sitting for a great many years to carry out its constitutional function. On 20 November 1675 Lord Mohun, one of Shaftesbury's opposition group, moved in the Lords for a dissolution. After a heated debate the motion was defeated by two votes. Two days later Parliament was prorogued although for the unprecedented period of fifteen months. In 1677 when it reconvened, Shaftesbury would claim this long prorogation made it unlawful and attempted once again to force a dissolution. His assertion of illegality landed him in the Tower of London, where he was held for a year.

The tract reprinted here appeared in two editions. Again the tactic was used of publishing and publicizing parliamentary debate.

The Debate or Arguments for Dissolving This Present Parliament, and the Calling Frequent and New Parliaments.

As they were delivered in the House of Lords, *November the 20th. 1675.*

That it is according to the Constitution of the *Government,* the ancient Laws and Statutes of this *Realm,* that there should be frequent and new *Parliaments,* and the practice of all Ages, till this last, hath been accordingly; *Parliaments,* both long before and after the Conquest, were held *three times a year,* viz. *Easter, Whitsontide,* and *Christmas,* during the space of *Eight Days* for each time, and so continued with some variations, as to the times of Calling, and length of Holding; but always very short untill the Reign of *Edward 3* in the *fourth year* of whose Reign there was a Law made, *That Parliaments should be holden every year once, or more often,* and how this Law is to be understood, whether of a New Parliament every Year, or calling the Old, is most manifest, by the practice, not only of all the Ages before, but of some Hundred of Years since that Law: Prorogations or Long Adjournments, being a thing never heard of untill latter Years.

And it is most unreasonable, that any particular number of Men should for many Years ingross so great a Trust of the People, as to be their Representatives in the *House of Commons;* And that all other the Gentry; and the Members of *Corporations* of the same Degree and Quality with them, should be so long excluded. Neither is it agreeable with the nature of Representatives to be continued for so long a time; and those that *choose* them, not to be allowed frequent opportunity of changing the hands; in which they are obliged to put so great a trust. The mutual correspondence and Interests of those who *choose* and are *chosen;* admitting of great variations in length of time. How many in this present *House* of *Commons* are there, whose business and acquaintance has not given them the occasion of the correspondence of one Letter, (for these many Years) with any *Person* of those places for whom they serve? How many may there be in future Parliaments, if continued as long as This, that may be *Protestants* when they are *chosen*, and yet may come in so many Years justly to be suspected to have changed their *Religion?* Nay, How many in this present Parliament are there, who were by the *People* when they were of the same adequate Interest with them, and in length of time, by the Favour and Goodness of the *Prince*, and their own great Merits, are become Officers in the *Court*, and about the *Revenue?* This is not spoken to reflect on *them*, for many of *them* have behaved themselves very worthy of those *places;* but yet themselves cannot say, that they are equally as free to act for those that *choose them*, as they were before: Nor are they of the same *Interest*, as when they were *chosen;* for now they gain, and have the advantage by the *People's payments*. And if they should say, *They are the same Men they were*, We may call their *Fellow Members* that have sat with them to Witness, whether the *Proverb* be not true, that *Honores mutant mores*,[1] whether they have the same *Opinion*, and the same *Freedom* they had before. Nay, may it not be said without offence, that even in this *House* of *Commons*, there are not a few, who, when they were *chosen*, were lookt upon as *Men of Estates;* and are either since grown or discovered to be of that *indigent condition*, that they are much fitter to receive the *publick maintenance*, than give the *publick money;* and it may be charitably supposed, that those *Gentlemen* are so modest, as to be willing to lay down, if they could, the *publick Trust*. But 'tis most certain, that those *places* they *serve* for, would not be willing to continue them in it. There is no question, but 'tis the *King's* undisputed *Prerogative* to call and end *Parliaments* when he please, and no man, nor number of men can limit him a time; but the greatest *Prince* cannot avoid the being limited by the nature of things; Representatives of the *People* are nec-

---

1. Honors change customs.

essary to the making Laws, and there is a time when it is morally demonstrable, that men cease to be Representatives, there being Circumstances and Proprieties that distinguish everything as well as *Person* in the *World*. So that to conclude this head, We Owe the *Prince* the observance of his *time* and *place* both for *calling* and *duration* of *Parliaments*, and the *Prince* owes us, not only the frequencies of *Parliaments*, but that our Representations should be preserved to us in *them*.

And further, if you consider the constitution of our *Government*, where the *King* as *Head* (from whom all the vital and animal Spirits are diffused through the Body) has the care of *all*, whose Interest is to seek the welfare of the whole; all being his, the *strength* of the Nation being his *strength*, the *riches* his *riches*, the *glory* and *honour*, his *glory* and *honour*, and so on the contrary. But least passion mistake flattery, or the ill designs of those about the *Prince*, should make him grow cross to his Real, and follow a destructive imaginary Interest: There is an Estate of Hereditary *Nobility*, who are by Birth-right the *Councellors* of the *Kingdom*, and whose Interest and Business it is, to keep the Ballance of the *Government* steady, that the Favourites and great Officers, exceed not their bounds, and oppress the People, that Justice be duely Adminstered, and that all parts of the *Government* be preserved entire. Yet even These may grow insolent (a Disease *Greatness* is liable to) or may by *Offices, Dependencies, hopes* of *Preferment*, and other accidents, become, as to the major part of them, rather the obsequious flatterers of the Court, than true supporters of the publick and *English Interest*, and therefore the Excellence of our *Government*, affords us another Estate of Men, which are the *Representatives* of the Free-holders, Cities, principal Burroughs, and Corporations of *England*, who by the Old Law, were to be new chosen once a year, if not oftener, so that they perfectly gave the sence of those that *chose* them, and were the same thing as if *those* were present that *chose*, they so newly coming from *them*, and so quickly returning to give an account of their Fidelity, under the penalty of shame, and no further Trust.

Thus you have in our *English Government*, the *House of Commons* affording the *Sence*, the *Mind*, the *Information*, the *Complaints*, the *Grievances*, and the *desires* of all those People for whom they serve, throughout the whole Nation. The People are thus secure, no Laws can be made, nor Money given, but what themselves, though at home, fully consent and agree to. The *Second Estate* in this *Government*, is the *Lords*, who are the *Councill*, the *Wisdom*, and *Judgment* of the *Nation*, to which their Birth, Education, and constant imployment, being the same in every Parliament, prepares and fits them. The last, and supream of all, is the *King*, One who gives Life and Vigour to the proceedings of the other Two; The Will and Desires of the People, though approved by the Wisdom and Judgment of the *Lords*, are Abortive, unless he bids them be an Act.

Human reason can hardly contrive a more excellent Government. But if you will alter this Government, in any of the Three Parts of it, the disorders and Inconveniencies incident to the nature of such alteration, must necessarily follow; As for instance, the long continuance of any such as are entrusted for others, especially of such as have so great a power over the Purse of the Nation, must necessarily produce *Caballs*, and *Parties*, and the carrying on of private *Interests* and *Court-Factions*, rather than the *publick good*, or the true *Interest* either of the *King* or *Kingdom*. How vastly is the priviledge of a *Parliament man* encreased since the middle of the Reign of Henry 8.? Before, it was several times agreed by all the *Judges*, and observed as the Law, That a Member and his Servants, were exempted only from *Arrests* and *Outlawries*, but might be *impleaded*, *sued*, and *Attached* by his *Land* and *Goods*; yet now they must not be *sued* in any *Case*, nor dispossessed of anything during the time of *Priviledge*; nay, these two last *Sessions* the *Priviledge* must extend to exempt them even from the *Judicature of Parliament* itself: As also before the same *King's Reign* the House of *Commons* never thought of *Judicature*, as being in the nature of their Constitution uncapable of it. But since they are not only become *Judges* of their own *Priviledges*, condemning and imprisoning their fellow-*Subjects* at pleasure, and without an *Oath*, and also *Judges* of all *Elections*, by which very often *they*, and not the *places*, chuse their *fellow-members*: But now 'tis come to that, that the *House of Commons* pass sentence on the *Lords'* proceedings, make new crimes, and add Preinstruments to them by their own Authority. If you will ask the reason of this change, 'tis plain that *Parliaments* began in *Henry 8's* time to be longer than they ought, That Prince knowing that *long Parliaments* were fitted to make great Changes, *they* have been too frequent since, but never of that length as *this*. Besides all this, the long continuance of *Representatives* renders them liable to be *corrupted* and won off from the *Publique-Interest;* it gives them time to settle their *Cabals* and *Interest* at *Court*, and takes away the great Security the *Nation* has; that if it be possible to happen that the *Spiritual Lords* because of their great dependence on the *Crown*, the *Popish Lords* being under the pressure of so severe Laws, together with the *Court Lords* and great *Officers* should in any future Age make up a greater number of the *House of Lords*, and should pass things very prejudicial to the *Publick*, yet all should prove ineffectual, and the *Nation* remain safe in an *House of Commons* lately chosen that have not had time to learn new *Sentiments*, or to put off their old *Principles* at a good Market. How great has been the modesty of this present *House of Commons*, that having had the *Purse* of the *Nation* thus long in their hands, as being those that first begun the Grants of *Subsidies and Aids* to the *King*, and so by consequence have all the Addresses made to *them*, whenever the wants of the *Crown* (which in this active *Age* are very often) require it, that they have not made use of it to the prejudice of the *Publick*, or to their own advantage. It was a very high Temptation, and might easily have rendered them in their own Opinion more than *Lords*, and they are rather to be commended that they insisted on no higher Terms with the *Lords House*, than wondered at for what they did. Considering the matter, ground and the circumstances wherein they stood, and yet they were certainly mistaken, and not a little forgot themselves, when they would not allow the *Lords House* a power of lessening the *Summs* in any *Bill* of *Subsidie* or *Aid* that they had once set;[2] which was not only directly contrary to the *Interest* of the *People* that chose them, but against the *ancient* and express *Rule* and *Custom* of *Parliament*, whereby it is clear if the *Commons* grant five *Subsidies*, and the *Lords* agree but to *four*, that *Bill* of *Subsidie* need not be sent down to the *Commons* for their consent to such an alteration. And they certainly were grown very high in their own Opinion, and had a very low esteem for the *Lords*, when they neglected the safety of their best Friends in that House, and did almost with scorn refuse the passing of the *Bill* for the more fair and equal *Trial of Peers*, which in several *Sessions* was sent down to them. How great were the apprehensions of all sober and wise Men at every meeting of this present *Parliament* during these late *years*, and how much is to be ascribed to the goodness of our *Prince*, and to the vertue of the *Members* of this present *House of Commons*, that *Honours, Offices, Pensions, Money, Imployments* and *Gifts* had not been bestowed and accepted, and the *Government*, as in *France, Denmark* and other Countries, made *absolute* and at the *will* of the *Prince?* How easie this may be done in future Ages under such Princes, and such an House of Commons as may happen, if long and continued *Parliaments* be allowed for *Law*, may be made some measure of by this, where though the *Prince* had no design, and the Members of the *House of Commons* have shewed so great Candor and Self-denial, yet the best Observers are apt to think that we owe it to the strong and opposite *Factions* at *Court*, that many things of great Alterations have not passed.

2. See House of Commons, 13 April 1671, *CJ*, IX, 235, 239, 509.

And moreover, it cannot be passed over with silence, nor considered without great thoughts of heart, to what a price a Member of the House of Commons place is come. In former times when *Parliaments* were short and frequent, The *Members* constantly received their *wages* both of their *Counties* and *Burroughs;* many of the poorer *Burroughs* petitioned to be excused from sending Members, as not being able to bear their charge; and were so. Laws were made in favour of the Gentry, that *Corporations* should compel none but their *Freemen* of their own *Town* to serve for them; Nay you shall find in all the ancient *Returns* of *Writs* for *Knights* of the *Shires,* their Sureties for their appearance returned with them. But now the case is altered, £.1500 and £.2000 and lately £.7000 is a price Men pay to be intrusted: 'Tis to be hoped the Charity of those worthy Persons, and their Zeal for the Publique Interest has induced them to be at this Expence; But it were better to be otherwise, and there is a scurvy English Proverb, *That Men that buy dear, cannot live by selling cheap.* And besides all these, the very *priviledge* of the Members, and of those they protect in a Parliament of so long duration, is a pressure that the Nation cannot well support itself under; So many thousand *Suits of Law* stopt, so vast a *Sum of Money* withheld from the right owners, so great a quantity of *Land* unjustly *possessed,* and in many Cases the length of time securing the *possession,* and creating a *Title.* And 'tis an Observation not unworthy the making, that all this extent of *Priviledge* beyond its due bounds has first risen from the Members of the *House of Commons;* That *House* to this day pretends to *forty days' priviledge* before and after *Parliament,* the *House of Lords* but *twenty,* and yet the *priviledge of Parliament* is the same to both: and if the *House of Commons* obtain their *forty days* to become *Law* and *Custom,* the *Lords* will certainly enjoy the same *priviledge.* But the cure of this Evil is very easy in *frequent* and *short Parliaments,* The Members will affect no larger *priviledges* than are necessary and useful to them, for such as oppress and injure others cannot expect a *second choice*, and the present time is but short.

To all this there are *two Objections* that make a great sound, but have really nothing of weight in them; The *first Objection* is, *That the Crown is in danger if you call a new Parliament*. If those men be in earnest that urge this, it were to be wished they would consider well what are the Men are likely to be chosen; and they are not difficult to be guest at through the whole Kingdom, Men of *Quality*, of *Estates*, and of the *best Understanding*. Such will never affect *change*, or disturb the *King's Government*. A *New Parliament* will be the *Nation*, and that will never stick at finall matters to render themselves acceptable to their *Prince*. Would the *King* have acquaintance with his *People? This is his way*. Would he have yet more the love of his People? *Thus he is sure to have it*. Would the *King* have a considerable sum of *Money* to pay his *Debts* and put him at ease? *Thus he cannot fail of it*, nay he shall have it as a pledge of endearment between *him* and his *people*, they give it themselves, and they know the *King* receives it as from them. The *English Nation* are a generous *people*, and have at all times exprest themselves ready to *supply* even the *Humours*, and *Excesses* of their *Princes*, and some of the best beloved *Princes* we have had were such as by *Warr*, or otherwise put us to most *Expence:* Witness *Edward* the 1st, *Edward* the 3d, and *Henry* the 5th; but then always they were satisfied that the *Honour* of the *Nation* was preserved, and whatever private or personal *Excesses* the *Prince* had, yet the *Nation* was secure, there was no design upon them, neither should their *money* or their *strength* be used against them. *All this is the happiness of our present state under our most gracious King*. But how shall the People know and be secure it is so, but by those they annually send up to *Parliament* from amongst themselves; Whereas if the *King* should have a great *Sum of Money* given by this *Parliament*, it would be lookt upon as *theirs*, not as the *People's* gift, and the best of Men with their

Circumstances cannot avoid the suspicion, when they give much to have received some; and men will not so chearfully undergo the Burthen of a *Tax*, and their own Wants in the time of this general Poverty, when they apprehend others have the Thanks, and perhaps the Reward of their Sufferings.

The *second Objection* is with great apprehensions and passion urged by the *Bishops; That the Church and this Parliament fall together.* Which Objection how vain it is you will easily confess, if (as was said before) the persons that are like to be chosen be considered, The dissenting *Protestants* may very probably find more Favour and ease, but the *Church* can never suffer, either in her *Lands* or *Dignities* she now enjoys, by an *House of Commons* consisting of Men of the best Quality and Estates in *England*, as the next certainly will do. But, on the other side, what do the *Bishops* mean by this Assertion? Most certainly it is not their intent to make the *Interest* of the *Church* and the *Nation* direct opposit and inconsistent one with the other; and yet in saying this they confess, that this *House of Commons* are not the true *Representatives* of those they serve for; that the People and they are of different minds; that if they were to choose again, they would choose other men of other sentiments. And it must be confessed that whatever is not natural is by force, and must be maintained by force. A *standing Parliament* and a *standing Army* are like those *Twins* that have their lower parts united, and are divided only above the *Navel;* they were born together, and cannot long outlive each other. Certainly that man is no friend to the *Church* that wishes it a *third* incorporated with those two.

To conclude this Debate, the continuance of this *present Parliament* any longer is unpracticable; the breach this *House of Commons* has made upon the *Lords* is as unlikely to be repaired with these present Men, as it is to be renewed by another *House of Commons* of a *new Election.* If you consider the *Power*, the *Courtship*, and the *Addresses* that these Men have for so many years enjoyed and received, they may almost be forgiven if they think themselves greater Men than the *Lords* in the higher House; besides it is very well known that many of the ablest and most worthy Patriots amongst them have carried this Difference to the greatest height with this only design, that by this means they might deliver the Nation from the danger and pressure of a long continued Parliament: Whereas a new chosen *House of Commons*, especially if it were fixt, and known that it could not remain long, could not be apprehended to have any affectation to exceed their just bounds, nor to renew a Contest, where the *Interest* of the *People* is manifestly on the *Lords'* side; for besides the undoubted Right and constant Practice that the *Lords* enjoy in the Case of *Appeals* from *Courts of Equity*, all other Expedients when well considered, give the *Crown*, the *Favourites* and *Ministers* the power over every man's *Estate* in *England*.

Thus you see 'tis the *Interest* of all sorts of men to have a *New Parliament*; This will give the *King* constant and never-failing *Supplies* with the hearts and good-will of his People: This will not only preserve the *Church* in the Honours, Dignities and Revenues she now enjoys, and make her the *Protectrix* and *Asylum* of all the *Protestants* through *Europe*, but will also encrease the Maintenance of the *Ministry* in *Corporations* and great *Towns*, which is now much wanting, and of great concern to the *Church*. This will procure the dissenting *Protestants* Ease, Liberty, and Protection. The *Papists* may justly expect by this to be delivered from that grievous pressure of *penal Laws* they lie under, if they can be contented with being deprived of access to *Court*, bearing *Offices* or *Arms*. The great *Officers* and *Ministers* may under this enjoy their *places* undisturbed and in quiet, and be secure with a moderate Conduct, and reasonable Condescentions to attain that in a *new Parliament* which they have by experience found is impossible in the *old*. In a word, there is not to be imagined an *Interest* against this, unless there be an inveterate *party* still remaining in our World, who to compass their Revenge, and repair their broken Fortunes, would hope to see the *Act of Oblivion* set aside, and this happy *Monarchy* turned into an *absolute, Arbitrary, Military Government*; But Charity bids us hope there are no such Men.

FINIS.

[Anthony Ashley Cooper,
Earl of Shaftesbury, 1621–1683]

A
LETTER
From a Person of
QUALITY,
To His
FRIEND
In The
COUNTRY.

Printed in Year, 1 6 7 5 .

*T*his anonymous pamphlet records the extraordinary debate that took place in the House of Lords in April 1675 over the nonresisting test bill. It provides a rare opportunity to eavesdrop on discussion in the Lords on a matter of great constitutional importance. According to the bill's opponents, had the proposed oath been instituted it would have frozen the government of both church and state and made the civil government far more authoritarian. The tract was published early in the following session and caused an uproar. It is usually attributed to Shaftesbury although on occasion to his secretary John Locke instead. Locke denied authorship. If not personally written by Shaftesbury, it was most likely dictated by him to Locke or written under his direction and scrutiny.

The wrangle treated in the tract began on 15 April 1675 when a bill was introduced into the House of Lords that would have required all members of Parliament and other officeholders to swear that it was unlawful "on any pretence whatsoever" to take arms against the king or those commissioned by him or to endeavor "any alteration in the government in church or state as it is by law established." The bishops had suggested the imposition of such a loyalty oath the previous February. Had it become law it would have restricted legislative initiatives and prevented fundamental change or reform in church or state. Moreover, there were well-founded suspicions that the bill was meant to justify a standing army.

The nonresisting test bill was vigorously opposed by a substantial group of lords led by the Earl of Shaftesbury. The passionate debate in the House of Lords continued for seventeen days—the Lords often *sitting until nine at night, sometimes until midnight. The king regarded the bill of such moment that he was personally present during the discussions. Despite the bitter opposition to it, a group of peers and bishops managed to win approval for all the main clauses in the bill although in one instance only by a single vote.*

Unable to defeat the bill in the Lords, its opponents' attention turned to the Commons. There the bill would probably have passed had it not been overshadowed by the dispute between the two houses over their respective jurisdiction in the case of Shirley v. Fagg. *In fact, opposition politicians are believed to have exacerbated that quarrel chiefly to block the Commons' consideration of the test bill. If that was the intent they succeeded. The jurisdictional dispute reached such a pitch that all business ground to a halt, and on 9 June the king felt constrained to prorogue Parliament. The attempt to pass the nonresisting test was dropped.*

The "Letter from a Person of Quality, to His Friend in the Country" appeared in a single edition early in November 1675. It was enormously effective in galvanizing public opinion but outraged many members of Parliament because it violated the confidentiality of parliamentary debate. On 8 November a complaint was lodged against the tract in the House of Lords. On that House's orders it was publicly burnt two days later and a committee established to enquire into its author, publisher, and printer. Its author was never determined. A single answer to the tract appeared in 1676 written by Marchamont Nedham, a journalist employed by the Court to aim literary darts at the opposition.

A Letter from a Person of Quality, to His Friend in the Country.

SIR,

This Session being ended, and the Bill of the *Test*[1] neer finished at the Committee of the whole House; I can now give you a perfect Account of this STATE MASTERPIECE. It was first hatcht (as almost all the Mischiefs of the World have hitherto been) amongst the *Great Church Men,* and is a Project of several Years' standing, but found not Ministers bold enough to go through with it, until these *new ones,* who wanting a better Bottom to support them, betook themselves wholly to this, which is no small Undertaking if you consider it in its whole Extent.

First, to *make a distinct Party* from the rest of the Nation of the High Episcopal Man, and the Old Cavalier, who are to swallow the hopes of enjoying all the Power and Office of the Kingdom, being also tempted by the advantage they may receive from overthrowing the *Act of Oblivion,*[2] and not a little rejoicing to think how valiant they should prove, if they could get any to fight the Old Quarrel over again; Now they are possest of the Arms, Forts, and Ammunition of the Nation.

Next they design to *have the Government of the Church Sworne to as Unalterable,* and so Tacitely owned to be of Divine Right, which though inconsistent with the Oath of Supremacy;[3] yet the Church

1. The "test" here referred to should not be confused with the Test Act of 1673, which aimed to keep Catholics from holding public office.

2. The Act of Oblivion, 12 Car. II, cap. 11, An Act of free and general pardon, indemnity and oblivion, 1660 pardoned those who had opposed the royal cause during the "late distractions" with some few exceptions.

3. The Act of Supremacy, 1 Eliz. I, cap. 1 (1559) contained the Oath of Supremacy, which acknowledged the English monarch as "the only supreme governor" of the realm "as well in all spiritual or ecclesiastical things or causes as temporal, and that no foreign prince, person, prelate, state or potentate hath or ought to have any jurisdiction, power, superiority, preeminence or authority ecclesiastical or spiritual within this realm." Anyone refusing to take the oath suffered loss of ecclesiastical or temporal and lay promotion and office and was disabled thereafter from retaining or exercising any such office.

Men easily break through all Obligations whatsoever, to attain this Station, the advantage of which, the Prelate of *Rome* hath sufficiently taught the World.

Then in requital to the Crown, they declare the Government *absolute* and *Arbitrary*, and allow Monarchy as well as Episcopacy to be *Jure Divino*, and not to be bounded, or limited by human Laws.

And to secure all this they resolve to take away the Power, and opportunity of *Parliaments* to alter anything in Church or State, only leave them as an *instrument* to raise Money, and to pass such Laws, as the Court, and Church shall have a mind to. The Attempt of any other, how necessary soever, must be no less a Crime than Perjury.

And as the topstone of the whole Fabrique, a pretence shall be taken from the Jealousies they themselves have raised, and a real necessity from the smallness of their Partie to encrease, and keep up a standing Army, and then in due time the Cavalier and Church man, will be made greater *fools*, but as errant *Slaves* as the rest of the Nation.

In order to this, The *first step* was made in the *Act for Regulating Corporations*,[4] wisely beginning, that in those lesser Governments which they meant afterwards to introduce upon the Government of the Nation, and making them Swear to a Declaration, and belief of such propositions as themselves afterwards upon debate, were enforced to alter, and could not justifie in those words; so that many of the Wealthiest, Worthiest, and Soberest Men, are still kept out of the Magistracy of those places.

The *next step* was in the *Act of the Militia*,[5] which went for most of the chiefest Nobility and Gentry, being obliged as Lord-Lieutenants,

4. The Corporation Act, 13 Car. II, st. 2, cap. 1 (1661) required town officials to take an oath declaring "it is not lawful upon any pretence whatsoever to take arms against the king.... I do abhor the traitorous position of taking arms by his authority against his person or against those that are commissioned by him."

5. The Militia Act of 1662, 14 Car. II, cap. 3, An Act declaring the sole right of the Militia to be in the King, and for the present ordering and disposing the same required that no peer would be capable of serving as a lieutenant or deputy lieutenant unless he swore "that it is not lawful upon any pretence whatsoever to take arms against the king, and that I do abhor that

Deputy-Lieutenants, &c. to Swear to the same Declaration, and Belief, with the addition only of these words *In pursuance of such Military Commissions,* which makes the Matter rather worse than better. Yet this went down smoothly as an Oath in fashion, a testimony of Loyalty, and none adventuring freely to debate the matter, the humor of the Age like a strong Tide, carries Wise and good Men down before it. This Act is of a piece, for it establisheth a *standing Army* by a Law, and swears Us into a *Military Government.*

Immediately after this, Followeth the *Act of Uniformity,*[6] by which all the Clergy of *England* are obliged to subscribe, and declare what the Corporations, Nobility, and Gentry, had before Sworn, but with this additional clause of the Militia Act omitted. This the Clergy readily complied with; for you know That sort of Men are taught rather to obey, than understand, and to use that *Learning* they have, to *justify,* not to *examine* what their Superiors command. And yet that *Bartholomew day*[7] was fatal to our Church, and Religion, in throwing out a very great Number of *Worthy, Learned, Pious, and Orthodox Divines,* who could not come up to this, and other things in that Act. And it is an Oath upon this occasion worth your knowledg, that so great was the Zeal in carrying on this Church affair, and so blind was the Obedience required, that if you compute the time of

---

traitorous position that arms may be taken by his authority against his person or against those that are commissioned by him in pursuance of such military commissions."

6. The Uniformity Act, 14 Car. II, cap. 4 (1662) included an oath swearing "unfeigned assent and consent to all and every thing contained and prescribed in and by the book entitled the Book of Common Prayer" and a second oath similar to that required of militia officers foreswearing taking arms against the king and including a declaration to "conform to the liturgy of the Church of England as it is now by law established; and I do declare that I do hold there lies no obligation upon me or any other person from the oath commonly called the Solemn League and Covenant to endeavour any change or alteration of government either in Church or State...."

7. The Act of Uniformity was to take effect on St. Bartholomew's Day 1662. The choice of day seems unpolitic as it doubtless reminded the aggrieved nonconformists of the notorious St. Bartholomew's Day massacre, 23–24 August 1572, a massacre of Protestants in Paris and the French provinces.

the passing this Act, with the time allowed for the Clergy to subscribe the Book of *Common Prayer* thereby established; you shall
plainly find it could not be Printed, and distributed so, as one Man in
forty could have seen and read the Book they did so perfectly Assent
and Consent to.

But this Matter was not compleat until *the Five Mile Act*[8] passed at
Oxford, wherein they take an opportunity to introduce the Oath in
the terms they would have it. This was then strongly opposed by the
Lord Treasurer *Southampton*, Lord *Wharton*, Lord *Ashley*, and others
not only in the Concern of those poor Ministers that were so severely
handled, but as it was in itself, a most Unlawful, and Unjustifiable
Oath; however, the Zeal of that time against All *Nonconformists*, easily passed the Act.

This Act was seconded the same Sessions at *Oxford* by another Bill
in the House of Commons, to have imposed that Oath on the *whole
Nation;* and the Providence by which it was thrown out, was very remarkable; for Mr. *Peregrine Bertie*, being newly chosen, was that
morning introduced into the House by his Brother the now Earl of
Lindsey, and Sir *Thomas Osborn* now Lord Treasurer, who all Three
gave their Votes against that Bill; and the Numbers were so even
upon the division, that their three Votes carried the Question against
it. But we owe that Right to the Earl of *Lindsey*, and the Lord Treasurer, as to acknowledg that they have since made ample Satisfaction
for whatever offence they gave either the Church or Court in that
Vote.

Thus our *Church* became *Triumphant*, and continued so for divers

---

8. The Five Mile Act, 7 Car. II, cap. 2 (1665) forbids nonconformist ministers and unli-
censed preachers from coming within five miles of the parish where they had been the incumbent unless they first consented to "the use of all things contained in the Book of Common
Prayer," or subscribed to the declaration contained in the Uniformity Act and, in addition,
swore an oath identical to that in the Militia Act and Uniformity Act with the additional requirement "that I will not at any time endeavour any alteration of government either in Church
or State."

years, the dissenting *Protestant* being the only *Enemy,* and therefore only persecuted, whilest the Papists remained undisturbed being by the Court thought Loyal, and by our Great Bishops not dangerous, they differing only in Doctrine, and Fundamentalls; but, as to the Government of the Church, that was in their Religion in its highest Exaltation.

This Dominion continued unto them, untill the Lord *Clifford,* a Man of a *daring* and *ambitious spirit,* made his way to the chief Ministery of Affairs by other, and far different measures, and took the opportunity of the War with *Holland,* the *King* was then engaged in, to propose *the Declaration of Indulgence,* that the Dissenters of all sorts, as well Protestants as Papists, might be at rest, and so vast a number of People, not be made desperate, at Home, while the *King* was engaged with so potent an Enemy abroad. This was no sooner proposed, but the Earl of *Shaftsbury* a Man as daring but more Able, (though of principles and interest, Diametrically opposite to the other) presently closed with it, and perhaps the opportunity I have had by my conversation with them both, who were Men of diversion, and of free and open Discourses where they had a confidence; may give you more light into both their Designs, and so by consequence the aimes of their Parties, than you will have from any other hand. My *Lord Clifford* did in express Terms, tell me one day in private Discourse; *That the King, if He would be firm to Himself, might settle what Religion He pleased, and carry the Government to what height He would; for if Men were assured in the Liberty of their Conscience, and undisturbed in their Properties, able and upright Judges made in* Westminster-Hall *to judg the Causes of* Meum *and* Tuum, *and if on the Other hand the Fort of* Tilbury *was finished to bridle the City, the Fort of* Plymouth *to secure the West, and Armes for 20,000 in each of these, and in* Hull *for the Northern parts, with some addition, which might be easily and undiscernedly made to the Forces now on foot, there were none that would have either Will, Opportunity, or Power to resist.*

But he added withall, he was so sincere in the maintenance of Propriety, and Liberty of Conscience, that if he had his Will, though he should introduce a Bishop of Durham, *(which was the Instance he then made, that See being then vacant) of another Religion, yet he would not disturb any of the Church beside, but suffer them to dye away, and not let his change (how hasty soever he was in it) overthrow either of those principles, and therefore, desired he might be thought an honest Man as to his part of the Declaration,*[9] *for he meant it really.* The Lord *Shaftsbury* (with whom I had more freedom) I with great assurance, asked what he meant by the *Declaration,* for it seemed to me (as I then told him) that it assumed *a Power to repeal and suspend all our Laws, to destroy the Church, to overthrow the Protestant Religion, and to tolerate Popery.* He replied half angry, *That he wondered at my Objection, there being not one of these in the Case: For the King assumed no power of repealing Laws, or suspending them, contrary to the will of his Parliament, or People, and not to argue with me at that time the power of the King's Supremacy, which was of another nature than that he had in Civills, and had been exercised without exception in this very case by His Father, Grandfather, and* Queen Elizabeth, *under the Great Seal to Forreign* Protestants, *become subjects of* England, *nor to instance in the suspending the Execution of the two Acts of* Navigation *and* Trade, *during both this, and the last* Dutch War *in the same words, and upon the same necessity, and as yet, without Clamour that ever we heard. But, to pass by all that, this is certain, a Government could not be supposed whether* Monarchical, *or other of any sort, without a standing Supream Executive power, fully enabled to Mitigate, or wholly to suspend the Execution of any penal Law, in the Intervalls of the* Legislative *power, which when assembled, there was no doubt but wherever there lies a* Negative *in passing of a Law, there the address or sense known of either of them to the*

9. References to the "Declaration" here and on the following pages are to Charles II's Declaration of Indulgence of 15 March 1672. The king bowed to pressure and cancelled the Declaration on 8 March 1673.

contrary, (as for instance of either of our two Houses of Parliament *in* England*) ought to determine that Indulgence, and restore the Law to its full execution: For without this, the Laws were to no purpose made, if the Prince could annull them at pleasure; and so on the other hand, without a Power always in being of dispensing upon occasion, was to suppose a constitution extreamly imperfect and unpracticable, and to sure those with a* Legislative *power always in being, is, when considered, no other than a perfect Tyranny. As to the Church, he conceived the Declaration was extreamly their Interest; for the narrow bottom they had placed themselves upon, and the Measures they had proceeded by, so contrary to the Properties, and Liberties of the Nation, must needs in short time, prove fatall to them, whereas this led them into another way to live peaceably with the dissenting and differing* Protestants, *both at home and abroad, and so by necessary and unavoidable Consequences, to become the Head of them all; For that place is due to the Church of* England, *being in favor, and of neerest approach to the Most powerful Prince of that* Religion, *and so always had it in their hands to be the Intercessors and Procurers of the greatest Good and Protection, that party throughout all* Christendom, *can receive. And thus the Arch Bishop of* Canterbury *might become, not only* Alterius Orbis, *but* Alterius Religionis Papa,[10] *and all this addition of Honor and Power attained without the least loss or diminution of the Church; It not being intended that one living Dignity, or Preferment should be given to Any but those, that were strictly Conformable. As to the* Protestant *Religion, he told me plainly, It was for the preserving of That and that only that he heartily joined in the* Declaration; *for besides that, he thought it his Duty to have care in his Place and Station, of those he was convinced, were the People of* God *and feared Him, though of different persuasions; he also knew nothing else but Liberty, and Indulgence that could possibly (as our case stood) secure the* Protestant *Religion in* England; *and he begged me to consider, if the Church of* England

---

10. Thus the Archbishop of Canterbury might become Pope not only of another world, but also of another religion.

should attain to a rigid, blind, and undisputed Conformity, and that power of our Church should come into the hands of a Popish Prince, *which was not a thing so impossible, or remote, as not to be apprehended, whether in such a case, would not all the Armes and Artillery of the Government of the Church, be turned against the present Religion of it, and should not all good* Protestants *tremble to think what Bishops such a Prince was like to make, And whom those Bishops would condemn for Hereticks, and that Prince might burn; Whereas if this which is now but a* Declaration, *might ever by the Experience of it, gain the Advantage of becoming an Established Law, the true* Protestant *Religion would still be kept up amongst the Cities, Towns, and Trading places, and the Worthiest, and Soberest (if not the greatest) part of the Nobility, and Gentry, and People. As for the toleration of Popery* he said, *It was a pleasant Objection, since he could confidently say that the* Papists *had no advantage in the least by the* Declaration, *that they did not as fully enjoy, and with less noise, by the favor of all the Bishops before. It was the Vivacity of the* Lord Keeper, *that they were named at all, for the whole advantage was to the dissenting Protestants, which were the only Men disturbed before; and yet he confest to me, that it was his opinion, and always had been, that the* Papists *ought to have no other pressure laid upon them, but to be made uncapable of Office, Court, or Armes, and to pay so much as might bring them at least to a ballance with the Protestants, for those chargable Offices they are liable unto; and concluded with this that he desired me seriously to weigh, whether Liberty and Propriety were likely to be maintained long in a Countrey like Ours, where Trade is so absolutely necessary to the very being, as well as prosperity of it, and in this Age of the World, if Articles of Faith and Matters of Religion should become the only accessible ways to our Civil Rights.*

Thus Sir, You have perhaps a better acount of the *Declaration,* than you can receive from any other hand, and I could have wisht it a longer continuance, and better Reception than it had: for the Bishops took so great Offence at it, that they gave the Alarum of *Popery* through the whole Nation, and by their Emissaries the Clergy (who by the Connexture and Subordination of their Government, and their being posted in every Parish, have the Advantage of a quick dispersing their Orders, and a sudden and universal Insinuation of whatever they please) raised such a cry, that those good and sober Men, who had really long feared the Encrease and continuance of *Popery*, had hitherto received, began to believe the Bishops were in earnest; their Eyes opened, though late, and therefore joined in heartily with them; so that at the next meeting of Parliament, the *Protestants'* Interest was run so high, as an Act came up from the *Commons* to the *House of Lords* in favor of the dissenting Protestants, and had passed the Royal Assent for the *Excluding all Papists from Office*, in the Opposition the *Lords*, but for want of time, Besides, another excellent *Act* passed of which, the Lord Treasurer *Clifford* fell, and yet to prevent his ruine, this Sessions had the speedier End. Notwithstanding, the Bishops attained their Ends fully, the *Declaration* being *Cancelled*, and the great Seal being broken off from it, The Parliament having passed an Act in favor of the Dissenters, and yet the sense of both Houses sufficiently declared against all Indulgence but by *Act of Parliament*. Having got this Point, they used it at first with seeming Moderation, there were no general Directions given for prosecuting the *Nonconformists*, but here and there some of the most Confiding Justices, were made use of to try how they could receive the Old Persecution; for as yet the Zeal raised against the *Papists*, was so great, that the worthiest, and soberest, of the Episcopal party, thought it necessary to unite with the dissenting *Protestants*, and not to divide their Party, when all their Forces were little enough. In this posture the *Sessions of Parliament* that began *Oct. 27. 1673.* found Matters, which being suddenly broken up, did nothing.

The next Sessions which began *Jan 7.* following, the *Bishops* continued their *Zeal against Papists*, and seemed to carry on in joining with the Countrey Lords, many excellent Votes in order to a Bill, as in particular, *That the Princes of the Blood-Royal should all Marry Protestants*, and many others, but their favor to dissenting *Protestants* was gone, and they attempted a Bargain with the Countrey Lords, with whom they then joined not to promote anything of that nature, except *the bill for taking away Assent and Consent; and renouncing the Covenant.*[11]

This Session was no sooner ended without doing anything, but the whole Clergy were instructed to declare that there was now no more danger of the *Papists*. The *Fanatic* (for so they call the dissenting *Protestant*) is again become the *only dangerous Enemy,* and the Bishops had found a *Scotch* Lord, and two new Ministers,[12] or rather Great Officers of *England,* who were desperate and rash enough, to put their Master's business upon so narrow and weak a bottom; And that *old Covenanter Lauderdale,* is become the *Patron of the Church,* and has his Coach and table filled with Bishops. The Keeper and the Treasurer are of a just size to this affair, for it is a certain rule with the Church Men, to endure (as seldom as they can) in business, Men abler than themselves. But his Grace of *Scotland* was least to be executed of the Three, for having fallen from *Presbitery, Protestant* Religion, and all principles of Publick good and private friendship, and become the Slave of *Clifford* to carry on the Ruine of all that he had professed to support, does now also quit even *Clifford's* generous Principles, and betake himself to a sort of Men, that *never forgive any Man the having once been in the right;* and such Men, who would do the worst of things by the worst of means, enslave their country, and betray them, under the mask of Religion, which they have the

11. In February 1675 an Order in Council and royal Declaration were issued insisting upon enforcement of the laws against nonconformists.

12. The reference is to the "Scotch Lord," James Maitland, Duke of Lauderdale. The two new ministers are Sir Thomas Osborne, Earl of Danby, appointed Lord Treasurer in October 1673 and Heneage Finch, Earl of Nottingham, appointed Lord Keeper of the Seals the same year.

publick Pay for, and charge off; so seething the Kid in the Mother's milk. Our Statesmen and Bishops being now as well agreed, as in Old *Laud's* time, on the same principles; with the same passion to attain their end, they in the first place give orders to the Judges in all their Circuits to quicken the Execution of the Laws against Dissenters; a *new Declaration*[13] is published directly contrary to the former, most in words against the *Papists,* but in the Sense, and in the close, did fully serve against both, and in the Execution, it was plain who were meant. A *Commission* besides, comes down directed to the principal Gentlemen of each country, *to seize the Estates of* both *Papists* and *Fanatics,* mentioned in a List annexed, wherein by great misfortune, or skill, the Names of the *Papists* of best quality and fortune (and so best known) were mistaken, and the Commission rendered ineffectual as to them.

Besides this, the great Ministers of State did in their common publick assure the party, that all the places of Profit, Command, and Trust, should only be given to the old *Cavalier;* no Man that had served, or been of the contrary Party, should be left in any of them; And a direction is issued to the Great Ministers before mentioned, and Six or seven of the Bishops to meet at *Lambeth-House,* who were like the Lords of the Articles in *Scotland,* to prepare their compleat Modell for the ensuing *Session of Parliament.*

And now comes this *memorable Session of Aprill* 13.75 then, which never any came with more expectation of the Court, or dread and apprehension of the People; the Officers, Court Lords, and Bishops, were clearly the major Vote in the *Lords House,* and they assured themselves to have the Commons as much at their dispose when they reckoned the number of the Courtiers, Officers, Pensioners encreased by the addition of the Church and Cavalier party, besides the Address they had made to Men of the best quality there by hopes of

13. Charles had issued orders in January 1675 calling for the enforcement of the laws against Nonconformists and Catholics.

Honor, great employment, and such things as would take. In a word, the *French* King's Ministers, who are the great Chapmen of the World,[14] did not out-doe ours at this time, and yet the *overruling hand of God* has blown upon their Politicks, and the Nation is escaped this Session, like *a Bird out of the Snare* of the Fowler.

In this Sessions the Bishops wholly laid aside their Zeal against *Popery*. The Committee of the whole House for Religion, which the Country Lords had caused to be set up again by the example of the former Sessions, could hardly get, at any time, a day appointed for their Sitting, and the main thing designed for a Bill voted in the former Session, *viz. the marrying our Princes to none but Protestants*, was *rejected* and carried in the Negative by the unanimous Votes of the *Bishop's Bench;* for I must acquaint you that our great Prelates were so neer an Infallibility, that they were always found in this Session of one mind in the *Lords House;* yet the Lay Lords, not understanding from how excellent a Principle this proceeded, commonly called them for that reason *the dead Weight,* and they really proved so in the following business, for the third day of this Session this *Bill of Test* was brought into the Lords House by the Earl of *Lindsey*. Lord High Chamberlain, a person of great quality, but in this imposed upon, and received its first reading and appointment for the second without much opposition; the Country Lords being desirous to observe what weight they put upon it, or how they designed to manage it.

At the second reading, the Lord Keeper, and some other of the Court Lords, recommended the Bill to the House in Set and Elaborate *Speeches*, the *Keeper* calling it *A moderate Security to the Church and Crown,* and that no honest Man could refuse it, and whosoever did, gave great suspicion of Dangerous, and *Anti-Monarchicall* Principles, the other Lords declaime very much upon the Rebellion of the late Times, the great number of *Fanatics*, the dangerous princi-

---

14. Chapmen were traders or peddlers.

ples of rebellion still remaining, carrying the Discourse on as if they meant to trample down the *Act of Oblivion*, and all those whose Securities depended on it, But the Earl of *Shaftsbury* and some other of the Country Lords, earnestly prest that the Bill might be laid aside, and that they might not be engaged in the debate of it; or else that that Freedom they should be forced to use in the necessary defence of their Opinion, and the preserving of their Laws, Rights, and Liberties, which this Bill would overthrow, might not be misconstrued: For there are many things that must be spoken upon the debate, both concerning Church and State, that it was well known they had no mind to hear. Notwithstanding, this the great Officers and Bishops called out for the Question of referring the Bill to a Committee; but the Earl of *Shaftsbury*, a Man of great Abilities, and knowledg in Affairs, and one that, in all these variety of changes of this last Age, was never known to be either bought or frighted out of his publick Principles, at Large opened the mischievous, and ill designs, and consequences of the Bill, which as it was brought in required all Officers of Church and State, and all Members of both Houses of *Parliament*, to take this Oath following.

I, A. B. *do declare that it is not Lawful upon any pretence whatsoever, to take up Armes against the King, and that I do abhorr that Traiterous position of taking Armes by His authority, against His Person, or against those that are commissioned by Him in pursuance of such Commission; And I do swear that I will not at any time endeavor the Alteration of the Government, either in Church or State, so help me God.* The Earl of *Shaftsbury* and other Lords, spake with such convincing Reason, that all the Lords, who were at liberty from Court-Engagements, resolved to *oppose* to the uttermost, *a Bill of so dangerous consequence;* and the debate lasted Five several days before it was committed to a Committee of the whole House, which hardly ever happened to any Bill before. All this and the following debates were managed chiefly by the Lords, whose Names you will find to the following *Protestations;* the *First* whereof, was as followeth.

We whose Names are under Written being Peers of this Realm, do according to our Rights and the ancient Usage of Parliaments, *declare that the Question having been put whether the Bill (entitled an Act to prevent the danger which may arise from Persons disaffected to the Government) doth so far intrench upon the Priviledges of This House; that it ought therefore to be cast out. It being resolved in the Negative, We do humbly conceive that any Bill which imposeth an Oath upon the* Peers *with a Penalty, as this doth, that upon the refusal of that Oath,* They shall *be made uncapable of Sitting and Voting in this* House, *as it is a thing unprecedented in former Times, so is it, in Our humble Opinion, the highest Invasion of the Liberties and Priviledges of the* Peerage, *that possibly may be, and most destructive of the Freedom, which they ought to enjoy as Members of* Parliament, *because the priviledges of Sitting and Voting in* Parliament *is an Honor they have by Birth, and a Right so inherant in them, and inseparable from them, as that nothing can take it away, but what by the Law of the Land, must withal, take away their Lives, and corrupt* their Blood; *upon which ground we do here enter our Dissent from that Vote, and our Protestation against it*

Buckingham	*Aylisbury*	*Howard* E. of Berks	*Shaftsbury*
Bridgwater	*Bristol*	*Mohun*	*Clarendon*
Winchester	*Denbigh*	*Stamford*	*Gray Roll.*
Salisbury	*Pagitt*	*Hallifax*	*Say & Seal*
Bedford	*Holles*	*Delamer*	*Wharton*
Dorset	*Peter*	*Eure*	

The *next Protestation* was against the Vote of committing the Bill in the words following;

The Question being put whether the Bill Entituled An Act to prevent the Dangers, which may arise from Persons disaffected to the Govern-

ment, should be commited, It being carried in the Affirmative, and We after several days' debate, being in no measure Satisfied, but still apprehending that this Bill doth not only subvert the Priviledges, and birthright of the Peers, by imposing an Oath upon them with the penalty of losing their Places in Parliament; but also, as We humbly conceive, stick at the very root of Government; it being necessary to all Government to have freedom of Votes and Debates in those, who have power to alter, and make Laws, and besides, the express words of this Bill, obliging every Man to abjure all Endeavors to alter the Government in the Church; without regard to anything that rules of Prudence in the Government, or Christian compassion to Protestant Dissenters, or the necessity of Affairs at any time, shall or may require. Upon these Considerations, We humbly conceive it to be of dangerous consequence to have any Bill of this Nature, so much as Committed, and do enter our Dissents from that Vote and Protestation against it,

Buckingham	*Bristol*	*Shaftsbury*
Winton	*Howard of Berks*	*Wharton*
Salisbury	*Clarendon*	*Mohun*
Denbigh	*Stamford*	*De la mer*

Which Protestation was no sooner entered and subscribed the next day, but the great Officers and Bishops raised a *storm* against the Lords that had Subscribed it; endeavouring not only some severe proceedings against their *persons,* if they had found the House would have born it, but also to have taken away *the very liberty of Entering Protestations with Reasons;* but that was defended with so great Ability, Learning, and Reason by the Lord *Holles,* that they quitted the Attempt, and the Debate run for some hours either wholly to raze the Protestation out of the Books, or at least some part of it, the Expression of *Christian compassion to Protestant Dissenters* being that, which gave them most offence; but both these ways were so disagreeable to the honor and priviledg of the House, and the Latter to common Sense and Right, that they despaired of carrying it, and contented themselves with having voted *That the Reasons given in the said Protestation, did reflect upon the Honor of the House, and were of dangerous consequence.* And I cannot here forbear to mention the *Worth, and Honor, of that Noble Lord Holles,* suitable to all his former life, that whilst the Debate was at the height, and the Protesting Lords in danger of the *Tower;* he begged the House to give him leave to put his Name to that *Protest,* and take his Fortune with those Lords, because his sickness had forced him out of the House the day before, so that not being at the Question, he could not by the rules of the House Sign it. This Vote against those twelve Lords begat the next day this following *Protestation* signed by 21.

Whereas it is the undoubted priviledg of each Peer in Parliament *when a Question is past contrary to his Vote and judgment, to enter his Protestation against it, and that in pursuance thereof, the* Bill *entituled An Act to prevent the dangers which may arise from persons disaffected to the Government, being conceived by some Lords to be of so dangerous a Nature, as that it was not fit to receive the countenance of a Committment, those Lords did protest against the Commitment of the said* Bill, *and the House having taken exceptions at some expressions in their Protestation; those Lords who were present at the Debate, did all of them severally and voluntarily declare, That they had not intention to reflect upon any Member, much less upon the whole House, which, as is humbly conceived, was more than in strictness did consist with that absolute freedom of Protesting, which is inseparable from every Member of this House, and was done by them meerly out of their great Respect to the House, and their earnest desire to give all satisfaction concerning themselves, and the clearness of their intentions. Yet the House not satisfied with this their Declaration but proceeding to a Vote, that the reasons given in the said Protestation do reflect upon the honor of the House, and are of dangerous consequence;*

which is in our humble Opinion, a great discountenancing of the very liberty of Protesting. We whose Names are under Written, conceive ourselves, and the whole House of Peers, *extreamly concerned that this great Wound should be given (as we humbly apprehend) to so essential a priviledg of the whole peerage of this Realm, as their liberty of Protesting, do now (according to our unquestionable Right) make use of the same liberty to enter this our Dissent from, and Protestation against the said Vote,*

Bucks	*Denbigh*	*Hallifax*	*Holles*
Winton	*Berks*	*Audley*	*Delamer*
Bedford	*Clarendon*	*Fitzwater*	*Grey Roll*
Dorset	*Aylisbury*	*Eure*	
Salisbury	*Shaftsbury*	*Wharton*	
Bridgwater	*Say & Seal*	*Mohun*	

After this Bill being committed to a Committee of the whole House, the first thing insisted upon by the Lords against the Bill; was, that there ought to be passed some *previous Votes* to secure the Rights of *Peerage,* and Priviledg of *Parliament* before they entered upon the debate, or Amendments of such a Bill as this; and at last two previous *Votes* were obtained, which I need not here set down, because the next Protestation hath them both in *terminis.*

Whereas upon the debate on the Bill *entituled An Act to prevent the Dangers which may arise from Persons disaffected to the Government,* It was ordered by the house of Peers the 30th of *Aprill* last, *that no Oath should be imposed by any* Bill, *or otherwise, upon the Peers with a penalty in case of Refusal, to lose their Places, or Votes in* Parliament, *or liberty to debate therein; and whereas also, upon debate of the same, the* Bill *was ordered the Third of this instant* May, *that there shall be nothing in this* Bill, *which shall extend to deprive either of the Houses of* Parliament, *or any of their Members, of their just ancient Freedom, and priviledg of debating any Matter or business which shall be propounded, or debated in either of the said Houses, or at any Conference or Committee, of both, or either of the said Houses of* Parliament, *or touching the Repeal, or Alteration of any Old, or preparing any new Laws, or the redressing any publick Grievance; but that the said Members of either of the said Houses, and the assistance of the* House of Peers, *and every of them, shall have the same freedom of Speech, and all other Priviledges whatsoever, as they had before the making of this Act.*

Both which Orders were passed as Previous directions unto the Committee of the whole House, to whom the said Bill was committed, to the end that nothing should remain in the said Bill, which might any ways tend towards the depriving of either of the Houses of *Parliament*, or any of their Members, of their ancient freedom of Debates, or Votes, or other their priviledges whatsoever. Yet the House being pleased, upon the report from the Committee, to pass a Vote, That all Persons who have, or shall have Right to sit and Vote in either House of *Parliament*, should be added to the first enacted Clause in the said Bill, whereby an Oath is to be imposed upon them as Members of either House, which Vote *We whose Names are under Written being Peers of this Realm, do humbly conceive, is not agreeable to the said two Previous Orders*, and it having been humbly offered, and insisted upon by divers of us, that the *Proviso* in the late Act *Entituled An Act for preventing Dangers, that may happen from* Popish *Recusants;* might be added to the Bill depending, *Whereby the Peerage of every Peer of this Realm, and all their Priviledges, might be preserved in this Bill, as fully as in the said late Act.* Yet the House not pleasing to admit of the said Proviso, but proceeding to the passing of the said Vote, *We do humbly upon the Grounds aforesaid, and according unto our undoubted Right, enter this our Dissent from, and Protestation against the same.*

Bucks	*Berks*	*Denbigh*	*Eure*
Bedford	*Bridgwater*	*Dorset*	*De la mer*
Winton	*Stamford*	*Shaftsbury*	*Pagitt*
Salisbury	*Clarendon*	*Wharton*	*Mohun*

This was their last Protestation; for after this they altered their Method, and reported not the Votes of the Committee, and parts of the Bill to the House, as they past them, but took the same Order as is observed in other Bills, not to report unto the House, untill they had gone through with the Bill, and so report all the Amendments together. This they thought a way of more Dispach and which did prevent all Protestations, untill it came to the House; for the Votes of a Committee, though of the whole House, are not thought of that weight, as that there should be allowed the entering a Dissent of them, or Protestation against them.

The Bill being read over at the Committee, the Lord Keeper objected against the form of it, and desired that he might put it in another Method, which was easily allowed him, that being not the Dispute. But it was observeable the Hand of *God* was upon them in this whole Affair; their Chariot-wheels were taken off, they drew heavily. A Bill so long designed, prepared, and of that Moment to all their Affairs, had hardly a sensible Composure.

The first part of the Bill that was fallen upon; was, whether there should be an Oath at all in the Bill, and this was the only part the Court-Party defended with Reason: for the whole Bill being to enjoin an Oath, the House might reject it, but the Committee was not to destroy it. Yet the *Lord Hallifax* did with that quickness, Learning, and Elegance, which are inseparable from all his Discourses, make appear, that as *there really was no Security to any State by Oaths*, so also, no private Person, much less Statesman, would ever order his Affairs as relying on it, no Man would ever sleep with open Doors, or unlockt up Treasure, or Plate, should all the Town be sworn not to Rob; So that the use of multiplying Oaths had been most commonly to Exclude, or disturb some honest Consciencious Men, who would never have prejudiced the Government. It was also insisted on by that Lord and others, that the Oath imposed by the Bill, contained Three Clauses, the two former Assertory, and the last Promissory, and that it was worthy the Consideration of the Bishops, Whether *Assertory Oaths*, which were properly appointed to give testimony of a matter of Fact, whereof a Man is capable to be fully assured by the evidence of his Senses, be lawfully to be made use of to Confirm, or Invalidate Doctrinal Propositions, and whether that Legislative power, which imposes such an Oath, doth not necessarily assume to itself and Infallibility? And, as for *Promissory Oaths*, It was desired that those Learned Prelates would consider the Opinion of *Grotius de jure Belli & pacis, lib. 2. cap. XIII.* who seems to make it plain that those kind of Oaths are forbidden by our *Saviour Christ, Mat. 5.34,37.* and whether it would not become the Fathers of the Church, when they have well weighed that and other places of the *New Testament;* to be more tender in multiplying Oaths, than hitherto the great Men of the Church have been? But the Bishops carried the Point, and an Oath was ordered by the major Vote.

The next thing in Consideration, was about the *Persons* that should be enjoined to take this Oath; and those were to be, *all such as enjoyed any beneficial Office or Employment, Ecclesiastical, Civill, or Military;* and no farther went the Debate for some hours, untill at last the Lord Keeper rises up, and with an eloquent Oration, desires to add *Privy Counsellors, Justices of the Peace*, and *Members of both Houses;* The two former particularly mentioned only to usher in the latter; which was so directly against the two Previous Votes, the first of which was enrolled amongst the standing Orders of the House, that it wanted a Man of no less assurance in his Eloquence to propose it, and he was driven hard, when he was forced to tell the House, that they were *Masters of their own Orders,* and Interpretation of them.

The next consideration at the Committee was *the Oath itself,* and it was desired by the Countrey Lords, that it might be clearly known, whether it were meant all for an Oath, or some of it a Declaration, and some an Oath? If the latter, then it was desired it might be distinctly parted, and that the Declaratory part should be subscribed by itself, and not sworn. There was no small pains taken by the Lord Keeper and the Bishops, to prove that it was brought in; the two first parts were only a *Declaration,* and not an *Oath,* and though it was replied that to declare upon one's Oath, or to abhorr upon one's Oath, is the same thing with *I do Swear;* yet there was some difficulty to obtain the dividing of them, and that the Declaratory part should be only Subscribed, and the rest Sworn to.

The Persons being determined, and this division agreed to, the next thing was the parts of the *Declaration,* wherein the first was; I A. B. *do declare that it is not lawful upon any pretence whatsoever, to take up Armes against the King.* This was liable to great Objections; for it was said it might introduce a great change of the Government, to oblige all the Men in great Trust in *England,* to declare that exact Boundary, and Extent, of the Oath of *Allegiance,* and inforce some things to be Stated, that are much better involved in Generals, and peradventure are not capable of another way of expression, without great wrong on the one side, or the other. There is a Law of *25 Edward 3.* that Armes shall not be taken up against the *King,* and that it is Treason to do so, and it is a very just and reasonable Law; but it is an idle question at best, to ask whether Armes in any case can be taken up against a lawful Prince, because it necessarily brings in the debate in every Man's mind, how there can be a distinction then left between Absolute, and Bounded Monarchies, if *Monarchs* have only the fear of *God,* and no fear of human Resistance to restrain them.

And it was farther urged; that if the chance of human Affairs in future Ages, should give the *French King* a just Title and Investiture in the Crown of *England,* and he should avowedly own a design by force, to change the Religion, and make his Government here as Absolute as in *France,* by the extirpation of the Nobility, Gentry, and principal Citizens of the *Protestant* Party, whether in such, or like Cases, this *Declaration* will be a Service to the Government, as it is now establisht. Nay, and it was farther said, that they overthrow the Government that suppose to place any part of it above the fear of Man: For in our *English* Government, and all bounded Monarchies, where the Prince is not absolute, there every individual Subject is under the fear of the King, and His People, either for breaking the Peace, or disturbing the common Interest that every Man hath in it, or if he invades the Person or Right of his Prince, he invades his whole People, who have bound up in him, and derive from Him, all their Liberty, Property, and Safety. As also the Prince himself, is under the fear of breaking that Golden Chain and Connexture between Him and his People, by making his interest contrary to that they justly and rightly claim. And therefore neither our Ancestors, nor any other Country free like ours, whilst they preserved their Liberties, did ever suffer any *mercenary, or standing Guards to their Prince,* but took care that his Safety should be in Them, as theirs was in Him. Though these were the Objections to this Head, yet they were but lightly touched, and not fully insisted upon, until the debate of the second Head, where the Scope of the Design was opened clearer, and more distinct to every Man's capacity.

The second was, *And that I do abhorr that Traiterous Position of taking Armes by His Authority against His person.* To this was objected, That if this be meant an Explanation of the Oath of Allegiance to leave men without pretense to oppose where the individual person of the King is, then it was to be considered, that the proposition as it is here set down is universal, and yet in most cases the position is not to be abhorred by honest or wise men: For there is but one case, and that never like to happen again, where this position is in danger to be Traiterous, which was the Case of the *Long Parliament*, made perpetual by the King's own Act, by which the Government was perfectly altered, and made inconsistent with itself; but it is to be supposed the Crown hath sufficient warning, and full power to prevent the falling again into that danger. But the other cases are many, and such as may every day occurr, wherein this position is so far from Traiterous, that it would prove both necessary and our duty. The *Famous instance of Henry 6* who being a soft and weak Prince, when taken Prisoner by his Cousin *Edward 4.* that pretended to the Crown, and the great Earl of *Warwick*, was carried in their Armies, gave what orders and Commissions they pleased, and yet all those that were Loyal to him adhered to his Wife and Son, fought in a pitcht battel against him in person, and retook him. This was directly taking up Armes by His Authority against his person, and against those that were Commissioned by Him, and yet to this day no Man hath ever blamed them, or thought but that, if they had done other, they had betrayed their Prince. The great Case of *Charles 6. of France*, who being of a weak and crazie Brain, yet governed by himself, or rather by his Wife, a Woman of passionate, and heady humour, that hated her Son the *Dolphin*, a vigorous and brave Prince, and passionately loved her Daughter; so that She easily (being pressed by the Victory of *Henry 5. of England*) complied to settle the Crown of *France* upon Him, to marry her Daughter to Him, and own his Right, contrary to the Salique Law. This was directly opposed with Armes and Force by the *Dolphin*, and all good *French Men*, even in his Father's lifetime. A third instance is that of *King James* of blessed Memory, who when he was a Child, was seized, and taken Prisoner by those, who were justly thought no friends to His Crown, or Safety, and if the case should be put, that a future *King* of *England* of the same temper with *Henry 6.* or *Charles 6 of France*, should be taken

Prisoner by *Spaniard, Dutch,* or *French,* whose overgrowing power should give them thoughts of vast Empire, and should, with the person and Commission of the King, invade *England* for a Conquest, were it not suitable to our Loyalty to join with the Son of that King, for the defence of his Father's Crown and Dignity, even against his Person and Commission? In all these and the like cases it was not justified, but that the strict Letter of the Law might be otherwise construed, and when wisely considered, fit it should be so, yet that it was not safe either for the Kingdom, or person of the King and his Crown, that it should be in express words sworn against, for if we shall forswear all Distinctions, which ill Men have made ill use of, either in *Rebellion* or *Heresy,* we must extend the Oath to all particulars of Divinity, and Politiques. To this the aged Bishop of *Winchester* replied, That *to take up Armes in such cases, is not against, but for the person of the King.* But his Lordship was told that he might then as well, nay much better, have left it upon the Old Oath of *Allegiance,* than made such a wide gapp in his new *Declaration.*

The third and last part of the Declaration was *or against those that are Commissioned by him.* Here the mask was plainly pluckt off, and *Arbitrary Government* appeared bare-faced, and a *standing Army* to be established by Act of Parliament, for it was said by several of the Lords, That *if whatever is by the King's Commission, be not opposed by the King's Authority, then a standing Army is Law whenever the King pleases;* and yet the King's Commission was never thought sufficient to Protect, or justify any man, where it is against his Authority, which is the Law; this allowed alters the whole Law of *England,* in the most essential and Fundamental parts of it, and makes the whole Law of *property* to become *Arbitrary,* and without effect, whenever the King pleases.

For instance, if in a Suit with a great Favourite, a man recovers House and Lands, and by course of Law be put into Possession by the Sheriff, and afterwards a Warrant is obtained by the interest of the person, to command some Souldiers of the standing Army to take the possession and deliver it back, in such a case, the man in possession may justify to defend himself, and killing those who shall violently endeavour to enter his house, the party, whose house is invaded, takes up Armes by the King's Authority against those, who are Commissioned by him. And it is the same case, if the Souldiers had been Commissioned to defend the House against the Sheriff, when he first endeavored to take the possession according to Law; neither could any Order, or Commission of the King's, put a stop to the Sheriff, if he had done his duty in raising the whole force of that County to put the Law in execution; neither can the Court, from whom that Order proceeds, (if they observe their oaths, and duty) put any stop to the execution of the Law in such a case, by any commance or commission from the King whatsoever; Nay, all the Guards, and standing forces in *England,* cannot be secured by any Commission from being a direct Riot, and unlawful Assembly, unless in time of open War and Rebellion. And it is not out of the way to suppose, that if any King hereafter, shall contrary to *the petition of Right,* demand, and levie Money by Privy-Seal, or otherwise, and cause Souldiers to enter, and distrain for such like illegall Taxes, that in such a case any Man may by Law defend his house against them; and yet this is of the same nature with the former, and against the words of the Declaration. These instances may seem somewhat rough, and not with the usual *reverence* towards the Crown, but they alleadged, they were to be excused, when all was concerned, And without speaking thus plain, it is refused to be understood; and, however happy we are now, either in the present Prince, or those we have in prospect, yet the suppositions are not extravagant, when we consider, Kings are but Men, and compassed with more temptations than others; And, as the Earl of *Salisbury,* who stood like a Rock of Nobility, and *English* Principles, excellently replied to the Lord Keeper, who was pleased to term them *remote Instances,* that they would not hereafter prove so, when the Declaration had made the practise of them Justifiable.

These Arguments enforced the Lords for the Bill to a change of this part of the *Declaration,* so that they agreed the second, and third parts of it, should run thus; *And I do abhorr that Traiterous position of taking Armes by His Authority, against his person, or against those, that are commissioned by Him according to Law, in time of Rebellion, or War, acting in pursuance of such Commission.* Which mends the matter very little; for if they mean the King's Authority, and his lawful Commission, to be two things, and such as are capable of Opposition, then it is as dangerous to the Liberties of the Nation, as when it run in the former words, and we only cheated by new Phrasing of it. But if they understand them to be one and the same thing, as really and truly they are, then we are only to abhorr the Treason of the position of taking Armes by the King's Authority against the King's Authority, because it is Non-sense, and not practicable; and so they had done little but confest, that all the Clergy and many other Persons, have been forced by former Acts of this present *Parliament,* to make this Declaration in other words, that now are found so far from being Justifiable, that they are directly contrary to *Magna Charta* our Properties, and the Established Law and Government of the Nation.

The next thing in course was, the Oath itself, against which the Objection lay so plain, and so strong at the first entrance, *Viz.* That *there was no care taken of the Doctrine, but only the Discipline of the Church.* The Papists need not scruple the taking this Oath; for Episcopacy remains in its greatest Lustre, though the Popish Religion was introduced, but the King's Supremacy is justled aside by this Oath, and makes better room for an *Ecclesiastical One,* in so much that with this, and much more, they were inforced to change their Oath, and the next day bring it in as followeth. *I do swear that I will not endeavour to alter the Protestant Religion or the Government either of Church or State.* By this they thought they had salved all, and now began to call their Oath *A Security for the Protestant Religion, and the only good design to prevent Popery,* if we should have a Popish Prince. But the Countrey Lords wondered at their confidence in this, since they had never thought of it before, and had been but the last preceeding day of the Debate by *pure Shame* compelled to this Addition; for it was not unknown to them, that some of the *Bishops* themselves had told some of the *Roman Catholick Lords* of the House, that *care had been taken that it might be such an Oath, as might not bear upon them.* But let it be whatever they would have it, yet the Countrey Lords thought the addition was unreasonable, and of as dangerous consequence as the rest of the Oath. And it was not to be wondered at, if the addition of the best things, wanting the Authority of an express divine Institution, should make an Oath *not to endeavor to alter,* just so much worse by the addition. For as the Earl of *Shaftsbury* very well urged, that it is a far different thing to believe, or to be fully persuaded of the truth of the Doctrine of Our Church; and to swear *never to endeavor to alter;* which last, must be utterly unlawful, unless you place an *Infallibility* either in the Church, or Your Self, you being otherwise obliged to alter, whenever a clearer, or better light comes to you; and he desired leave to ask, where are the Boundaries, or where shall we find, how much is meant by the *Protestant Religion.* The Lord Keeper thinking he had now got an advantage, with his usual Eloquence, desires it might not be told in *Gath,* nor published in the Streets of *Askalon,* that a Lord of so great Parts, and Eminence and professing himself for the Church of *England,* should not know what is meant by the *Protestant* Religion. This was seconded with great pleasantness by Divers of the Lords the Bishops; but the Bishop of *Winchester,* and some others of them were pleased to condescend to instruct that Lord, that the *Protestant* Religion was comprehended in 39 *Articles,* the *Liturgie,* the *Catechisme,* the *Homilies,* and the *Canons.* To this the Earl of *Shaftsbury* replied, that he begged so much Charity of them to believe, that he knew the *Protestant* Religion so well, and was so confirmed in it, that he hoped he should *burn* for the witness of it, if Providence should call him to it: But he might perhaps think some things *not necessary*, that they accounted *Essential*, nay he might think some things *not true*, or agreeable to the Scripture, that they might call *Doctrines of the Church*. Besides when he was to swear *never to endeavor to alter*, it was certainly necessary to know *how far the just extent of this Oath was;* but since they had told him that the Protestant Religion was in those 5 *tracts*, he had still to ask, whether they meant those whole Tracts were the *Protestant* Religion, or only that the Protestant Religion was contained in all those, but that every part of these was not the Protestant Religion. If they meant the former of these then he was extreamly in the dark to find the Doctrine of *Predestination* in the *18. and 17. Article* to be owned by so few great Doctors of the Church, and to find the *19. Article* to define *the Church* directly as the *Independents* do. Besides the *20. Article* stating the Authority of the Church is very dark, and either contradicts itself, or says nothing, or what is contrary to the known Laws of the Land; besides several other things in the *39 Articles*, have been Preached, and Writ against by Men of great Favor, Power, and Preferment in the Church. He humbly conceived the *Liturgie* was not so sacred, being made by Men the other day, and thought to be more differing from the dissenting *Protestants*, and less easy to be complied with, upon the advantage of a pretense well known unto us all of making *alterations* as might the better *unite* us; instead whereof, there is scarce one alteration, but *widens* the breach, and no *ordination* allowed by it here, (as it now stands last reformed in the *Act of Uniformity*) but what is *Episcopall;* in so much that a *Popish Priest* is capable, when converted, of any Church preferment without *Reordination;* but no *Protestant Minister* not Episcopally ordained, but is required to be reordained, as much as in us lies *unchurching* all the *forreign Protestants*, that have not Bishops, though the contrary was both allowed, and practised from the beginning of the Reformation till the time of that Act, and several Bishops made of such, as were never ordained Priests by Bishops. Moreover the *Uncharitableness* of it was so much against the Interest of the *Crown, and Church of England* (casting off the dependency of the whole Protestant party abroad) that it would have been *bought* by the *Pope* and *French King* at a vast summ of Money; and it is difficult to conceive so great an advantage fell to them meerly by chance, and without their help; so that he thought to endeavor to alter, and restore the Liturgy to what it was in *Queen Elizabeth's* days might consist with his being a very good Protestant.

As to the *Catachisme*, he really thought it might be mended, and durst declare to them, it was not well that there was not a better made.

For the *Homilies* he thought there might be a better Book made, and the *3. Homily* of *Repairing* and *keeping clean of Churches*, might be omitted.

What is yet stranger than all this, The *Canons* of our Church are directly the *old Popish Canons*, which are still in force, and no other; which will appear, if you turn to the *Stat. 25. Henry 8. cap. 19* confirmed and received by *I. Elizabeth* where all those Canons are established, untill an alteration should be made by the King in pursuance of that Act; which thing was attempted by *Edward the 6th.* but not perfected, and let alone ever since, for what reasons the Lords the Bishops could best tell; and it was very hard to be obliged by Oath *not to endeavour to alter* either the English Common-Prayer book, or the Canon of the Mass. But if they meant the latter, *That the Protestant Religion is conteined in all those, but that every part of those is not the Protestant Religion,* then he apprehended it might be in the Bishops' Power to declare *ex post facto* what is the Protestant Religion or not, or else they must leave it to every man to judge for himself, what parts of those books are or are not, and then their Oath had been much better let alone. Much of this nature was said by that Lord, and

Others, and the great Officers, and Bishops were so hard put to it, that they seemed willing, and convinced to admit of *an Expedient*. The *Lord Wharton* an Old and Expert Parliament Man of eminent Piety and Abilities, beside a great Friend to the Protestant Religion, and Interest of *England*, offered as a cure to the whole Oath, and what might make it pass in all the 3 parts of it, without any farther debate, the addition of these words at the latter end of the Oath, *Viz. as the same is or shall be established by Act of Parliament*, but this was not endured at all, when the Lord *Grey of Rollston*, a worthy and true *English* Lord, offered another Expedient, which was the addition of words, *by force or fraud*, to the beginning of the Oath, and then it would run thus, *I do swear not to endeavor by force or fraud to alter;* this was also a *cure* that would have passed the whole Oath, and seemed as if it would have carried the whole House. The Duke of *York* and Bishop of *Rochester* both seconding it; but the Lord Treasurer, who had privately before consented to it, speaking against it, gave the word and sign to that party, and it being put to the question, the major Vote answered all arguments, and the Lord *Grey's* Proposition was laid aside.

Having thus carried the question, relying upon their strength of Votes, taking advantage that those expedients that had been offered, extended to the whole Oath, though but one of the 3 Clauses in the Oath had been debated, the other two not mentioned at all, they attempted strongly at nine of the Clock at night to have the whole Oath put to the question, and though it was resolutely opposed by the Lord *Mohun*, a Lord of great *courage*, and *resolution* in the Publick Interest, and one whose own personal merits, as well as his Father's, gave him a just title to the best favors of the Court; yet they were not diverted but by as great a disorder as ever was seen in that House proceeding from the rage those unreasonable proceedings had caused in the Country Lords, they standing up in a clump together, and crying out with so loud a continued Voice *Adjourn*, that when silence was obtained, Fear did what Reason could not do, cause the question to be put only upon the first Clause concerning *Protestant Religion*, to which the Bishops desired might be added, *as it is now established*, and one of the eminentest of those were for the Bill added the words *by Law*; so that, as it was passed, it ran, *I A. B. do swear that I will not endeavor to alter the Protestant Religion now by Law established in the Church of England.* And here observe the words *by Law* do directly take in the *Canons* though the Bishops had never mentioned them. And now comes the consideration of the latter part of the Oath which comprehends these 2 Clauses, viz. *nor the Government either in Church or State*, wherein the Church came first to be considered. And it was objected by the Lords against the Bill that it was *not agreeable to the King's Crown and Dignity, to have his Subjects sworn to the Government of the Church equally as to Himself;* That for the Kings of *England* to swear to maintain the Church, was a different thing from enjoining all His Officers, and both His Houses of Parliament to swear to them. It would be well understood, before the Bill passed, what the *Government of the Church* (we are to swear to) is, and what the *Boundaries* of it, whether it derives no Power, nor Authority, nor the exercise of any Power, Authority, or Function, but from the *King as head of the Church*, and from *God* as through him, as all his other Officers do?

For no Church or Religion can justify itself to the Government, but the *State Religion*, that ownes an entire dependency on, and is but a branch of it; or the *independent Congregations;* whilest they claim no other power, but the exclusion of their own members from their particular Communion, and endeavor not to set up a Kingdom of Christ to their own use in this World, whilest our Saviour hath told us, that His Kingdom is not of it, for otherwise there would be *Imperium in imperio,*[15] and two distinct Supream Powers inconsis-

---

15. A kingdom within a kingdom.

tent with each other, in the same place, and over the same persons. The Bishops alleadged that *Priesthood* and the *Power* thereof, and the *Authorities* belonging thereunto were derived immediately from *Christ*, but that the *license of exercising that Authority* and Power in any Country is derived from the *civil Magistrate:* To which was replied, that it was *a dangerous thing to secure by Oath, and Act of parliament those in the excercise of an Authority, and power in the King's Country, and over His Subjects, which being received from Christ himself, cannot be altered, or limitted by the King's Laws;* and that this was directly to set the *Mitre above the Crown.* And it was farther offered, that *this Oath was the greatest attempt that had been made against the King's Supremacy since the Reformation;* for the King in Parliament may alter, diminish, enlarge, or take away any Bishoprick; He may take any part of a Diocess, or a whole Diocess, and put them under Deans, or other Persons; for if this be not lawful, but that Episcopacy should be *jure divino,* the maintaining the Government: as it is now, is unlawful; since the Deans of *Hereford,* and *Salisbury,* have very large tracts under their jurisdiction, and several Parsons of Parishes have Episcopal jurisdiction; so that at best that Government wants alteration, that is so imperfectly settled. The Bishop of *Winchester* affirmed in this debate several times, that there was no Christian Church before *Calvin* that had not Bishops; to which he was answered that the *Albigenses* a very numerous People, and the only visible known Church of true believers, of some Ages, had no Bishops. It is very true, what the Bishop of *Winchester* replied, that they had some amongst them, who alone had power to ordain, but that was only to commit that power to the Wisest, and Gravest Men amongst Them, and to secure ill, and unfit Men from being admitted into the Ministery; but they exercised no jurisdiction over the others. And it was said by divers of the Lords, that they thought Episcopal Government best for the Church, and most suitable for the Monarchy, but they must say with the Lord of *Southampton* upon the occasion of this Oath in the Parliament of *Oxford*, *I will not be sworn not to take away Episcopacie*, there being nothing, that is not of Divine Precept, but such circumstances may come in human affairs, as may render it not Eligible by the best of Men. And it was also said, that *if Episcopacy be to be received as by Divine Precept, the King's Supremacy is overthrown,* and so is also the opinion of the Parliaments both in *Edward 6.* and *Queen Elizabeth's* time; and the constitution of our Church ought to be altered, as hath been shewed. But the Church of *Rome* itself hath contradicted that Opinion, when She hath made such vast tracts of ground, and great numbers of Men exempt from Episcopal jurisdiction. The Lord *Wharton* upon the Bishop's claim to a Divine Right, asked a very hard question, *viz. whether they then did not claim withall, a power of Excommunicating their Prince,* which they Evading to answer, and being pressed by some other Lords, said they never had done it. Upon which the Lord *Hallifax* told them that that might well be; for since the Reformation they had hitherto had too great a dependance on the Crown to venture on that, or any other Offence to it, and so the debate passed on to the third Clause, which had the same exceptions against it with the two former, of being unbounded How far any Man might meddle, and how far not, and is of that extent, that it *overthrew all Parliaments,* and left them capable of nothing but giving Money. For what is the business of Parliaments but the alteration, either by adding, or taking away some part of the Government, either in Church or State? And every new Act of Parliament is an alteration; and what kind of Government in Church and State must that be, which I must swear upon no alteration of Time, emergencie of Affairs, nor variation of human Things, never to endeavor to alter? Would it not be requisite that such a Government should be given by God himself, and that withall the Ceremonie of Thunder, and Lightening, and visible appearance to the whole People, which God vouchsafed to the Children of *Israel* at Mount *Sinai?* and yet you shall nowhere read that they were sworn to it by any oath like this: nay on the Contrary, the Princes and the Rulers, even those recorded for the best of them, did make several variations. The Lord *Stafford*, a Noble Man of great Honor and Candour, but who had been all along for the Bill, yet was so far convinced with the debate, that he freely declared, there ought to be an addition to the Oath, for preserving the freedom of debates in Parliament. This was strongly urged by the never to be forgotten, Earl of *Bridgwater*, who gave reputation, and strength to this *Cause of England;* as did also those worthy Earls *Denbigh, Clarendon,* and *Aylisbury,* Men of great Worth and Honor. To Salve all that was said by these, and the Other Lords, The Lord Keeper and the Bishops urged, that there was a Proviso, which fully preserved the Priviledges of Parliament, and upon farther enquiry there appearing no such, but only a Previous vote, as is before mentioned, they allowed that that Previous vote should be drawn into a *Proviso,* and added to the Bill, and then in their opinion the Exception to the Oath for this cause was perfectly removed; but on the other side it was offered, that a positive absolute Oath being taken, a Proviso in the Act could not dispence with it without some reference in the body of the Oath, unto that Proviso; but this also was utterly denied, untill the next day, the debate going on upon other matters, the Lord Treasurer, whose authority easily obtained with the major Vote, reassumed what was mentioned in the Debates of the proceeding days, and allowed a reference to the Proviso, so that it then past in these words, *I A. B. do swear that I will not endeavor to alter the Protestant Religion now by Law Establisht in the Church of England, nor the Government of this Kingdom in Church, or State, as it is now by Law established, and I do take this Oath according to the meaning of this Act and the Proviso contained in the same, so help me God.*

There was a passage of the very greatest observation in the whole debate, and which with most clearness shewed what the great Men and Bishops aimed at, and should in order have come in before, but that it deserved so particular a consideration, that I thought best to place it here by itself, which was, that upon passing of the Proviso for preserving the Rights, and Priviledges of Parliaments made out of the Previous Votes, It was excellently observed by the Earl of *Bullingbrook,* a Man of great Abilitie, and Learning in the Laws of the Land, and perfectly stedfast in all good *English* Principles, that *though that Proviso did preserve the freedom of Debates and Votes in Parliament, yet the Oath remained notwithstanding that Proviso* upon all Men, that shall take as a prohibition either by Speech, or Writing, or Address, to endeavor any alteration in Religion, Church, or State; nay also upon the *Members* of *both Houses* otherwise than as they speak, and vote in open Parliaments or Committees: for this Oath takes away all *private Converse* upon any such affairs even one with another. This was seconded by the Lord *De la mer,* whose Name is well known, as also his Worth, Piety, and Learning; I should mention his great Merits too, but I know not whether that be lawful, they lying yet unrewarded. The Lord *Shaftsbury* presently drew up some words for preserving the same Rights, Priviledges, and Freedoms, which Men now enjoy by the Laws established, that so by a side Wind we might not be deprived of the great Liberty we enjoy as *English Men,* and desired those words might be inserted in that Proviso before it past. This was seconded by many of the formentioned Lords, and prest upon those terms, that they desired not to countenance, or make in the least degree anything lawful, that was not already so, but that they might not be deprived by this dark way of proceeding of that Liberty was necessary to them as Men, and without which Parliaments would be rendered useless. Upon this all the great Officers showed themselves, nay the Duke of *Lauderdale* himself, though under the Lord of two Addresses, opened his mouth, and together with the Lord Keeper, and the Lord Treasurer, told the Committee in plain terms, that they intended, and designed to prevent Caballing, and conspiracies against the Government that they knew no reason why any of the King's Officers should consult with Parliament Men about Parliament business, and particularly mentioned those of the Armie, Treasury, and Navy; and when it was Objected to them, that the greatest part of the most knowing Gentry were either Justices of the Peace, or of the Militia, and that this took away all converse, or discourse of any alteration, which was in truth of any business in Parliament, and that the Officers of the Navy, and Treasury, might be best able to advise what should be fit in many cases; and that withall none of their Lordships did offer anything to salve the inconvenience of Parliament Men being deprived of discoursing one with another, upon the matters that were before them. Besides it must be again remembered, that nothing was herein desired to be countenanced, or made lawful, but to preserve that that is already Law, and avowedly justified by it; For without this addition to the Proviso, the Oath rendered Parliaments but a *Snare* not a *Security* to the People. Yet to all this was answered sometimes with passion, and high words, sometimes with Jests, and Raillery (the best they had) and at the last the major Vote answered all objections, and laid aside the addition tendered.

There was another thing before the finishing of the Oath, which I shall here also mention, which was an *additional Oath* tendered by the Marquess of *Winchester,* who ought to have been mentioned in the first, and chiefest place for his conduct, and support in the whole debate, being an expert Parliament Man, and one whose Quallity, Parts, and Fortune, and owning of good Principles, concurr to give him one of the greatest places in the esteem of good men. The additional Oath tendered, was as followeth, *I do swear that I will never by Threats, Injunctions, Promises, Advantages, or Invitation, by or from any person whatsoever, nor from the hopes, or prospect of any Gift, Place, Office, or Benefit whatsoever, give my Vote other than according to my Opinion and Conscience, as I shall be truly, and really persuaded upon the debate of any business in Parliament; so help me God.*

This Oath was offered upon the occasion of swearing Members of Parliament, and upon this score only, that if any new Oath was thought fit (which that Noble Lord declared his own Judgment perfectly against) this certainly was (all considerations, and circumstances taken in) most necessary to be a part, and the nature of it was not so strange if they considered the *Judge's* Oath,[16] which was not much different from this. To this the Lord Keeper seemed very averse, and declared in a very fine Speech, that it was an *Useless Oath;* for all Gifts, Places, and Offices, were likeliest to come from the King, and no Member of Parliament in either House, could do too much for the King, or be too much of His side, and that Men might lawfully, and worthily, have in their Prospect, such Offices, or Benefits from Him. With this the Lords against the Bill, were in no tearms satisfied, but plainly spoke out *that Men had been, might, and were likely to be, in either House, too much for the King, as they called it,* and that whoever did endeavour to give more power to the King, than the Law and constitution of the Government had given, especially if it tended to the Introducing an *Absolute* and *Arbitrary* Government might justly be said to do too much for the King, and to be corrupted in his judgment by the prospect of advantages, and rewards; Though, when it is considered that every deviation of the Crown towards Absolute power, lessens the King in the love, and the affection of his People, making Him become less their Interest, A wise Prince will not think it a Service done Him.

And now remains only the last part of the Bill, which is the penalty different according to the quallifications of the Persons *All that are, or shall be Privy Counsellors, Justices of the Peace, or possessors of any beneficial Office, Ecclesiastical, Civill, or Military, are to take the Oath when summoned, upon pain of £.500 and being made uncapable of bearing Office, the Members of both Houses are not made uncapable but liable to*

---

16. Judges had to take an oath to do common right to all the king's people, notwithstanding any command of the king to the contrary.

the penalty of £.500 if they take it not. Upon all which the considerations of the Debate were, That those Officers, and Members of both Houses are of all the Nation the most dangerous to be sworn into a mistake, or change of the Government, and that, as to the Members of both Houses, the penalty of £.500 was directly against the latter of the 2. Previous Votes, and although they had not applied the penalty of Incapacity unto the Members of both Houses, because of the first Previous Vote in the Case of the Lords, neither durst they admit of a Proposition made by some of themselves, *that those that did not come up, and Sit as Members, should be liable to the taking the Oath, or penalty, untill they did so.* Yet their Ends were not to be compassed without invading the latter Previous Vote, and contrary to the Rights and Priviledges of *Parliament* enforce them to swear, or pay £.500 every Parliament, and this they carried through with so strong a Resolution, that having experienced their misfortunes in replies for several hours, not one of the party could be provoked to speak one word. Though, besides the former arguments, it was strongly urged, that this Oath ought to be put upon Officers with a heavier penalty than the *Test* was in the Act of the immediate preceding Session against the *Papists,* by which any Man might sit down with the loss of his Office, without being in the danger of the penalty of £.500 and also that this Act had a direct retrospect (which ought never to be in Penall Laws) for this Act punishes Men for having an Office without taking this Oath, which office, before this Law pass, they may now lawfully enjoy without it. Yet notwithstanding it provides not a power, in many cases, for them to part with it, before this Oath overtake them; For the clause *whoever is in Office the 1. September* will not relieve a Justice of the Peace, who, being once Sworn; is not in his own power to be left out of commission; and so might be instanced in several other cases; as also the members of the House of Commons were not in their own power to be unchosen; and as to the Lords, they were subjected by it to the meanest condition of Mankind, if they could not enjoy their Birthright, without playing Tricks suitable to the Humour of every Age, and be enforced to swear to every fancy of the present times. Three years ago it was *All Liberty and Indulgence*,[17] and now it is *Strict and Rigid Conformity* and what it may be, in some short time hereafter, without the Spirit of Prophesying might be shrewdly guessed by a considering Man. This being answered with silence, the Duke of *Buckingham*, whose Quality, admirable Wit, and unusual pains, that he took all along in the debate against this Bill, makes me mention Him in this last place, as General of the party, and coming last out of the Field, made a Speech late at night of Eloquent, and well-placed Nonsense, showing how excellently well he could do both ways, and hoping that might do, when Sense (which he often before used with the highest advantage of Wit, and Reason) would not; but the Earl of *Winchilsea* readily apprehending the Dialect, in a short reply, put an end to the Debate, and the major Vote *ultima ratio Senatuum, & Conciliorum*,[18] carried the Question as the Court, and Bishops would have it.

This was the *last Act* of this *Tragi-Comedy*, which had taken up sixteen or seventeen whole days' debate, the House sitting many times till eight or nine of the Clock at night, and sometimes till Midnight; but the business of *priviledg* between the two Houses gave such an interruption, that this Bill was never reported from the Committee to the House.

I have mentioned to You divers Lords, that were Speakers, as it fell in the Debate, but I have not distributed the Arguments of the debate to every particular Lord. Now you know the Speakers, your curiosity may be satisfied, and the Lords I am sure will not quarrel about the division. I must not forget to mention those great Lords, *Bedford, Devonshire,* and *Burlington,* for the Countenance and sup-

---

17. The reference is to Charles II's Declaration of Indulgence of 1672.
18. The ultimate purpose of senates and of councils.

port they gave to the *English* Interest. The Earl of *Bedford* was so brave in it, that he joined in three of the Protests; So also did the Earl of *Dorsit,* and the Earl of *Stamford,* a Young Noble Man of great hopes, The Lord *Eure,* the Lord *Viscount Say and Seal,* and the Lord *Pagitt* in two; the Lord *Audley* and the Lord *Fitzwater* in the 3d. and the Lord *Peter,* a Noble Man of great Estate, and always true to the maintenance of Liberty, and Property in the first. And I should not have omitted the Earl of *Dorset,* Lord *Audley,* and the Lord *Peter* amongst the Speakers: for I will assure you they did their parts excellently well. The Lord *Viscount Hereford* was a steady Man among the Countrey Lords; so also was the Lord *Townsend,* a Man justly of great Esteem, and power in his own countrey, and amongst all those that well know him. The Earl of *Carnarvon* ought not to be mentioned in the last place, for he came out of the Countrey on purpose to oppose the Bill, stuck very fast to the Countrey party, and spoke many excellent things against it. I dare not mention the *Roman Catholick* Lords, and some others, for fear I hurt them; but thus much I shall say of the *Roman Catholick* Peers, that if they were safe in their Estates, and yet kept out of Office, their Votes in that House would not be the most unsafe to *England* of any sort of Men in it. As for the absent Lords, the Earl of *Ruttland,* Lord *Sandys,* Lord *Herbert of Cherbury,* Lord *North,* and Lord *Crew,* ought to be mentioned with Honor, having taken care their Votes should maintain their own interest, and opinions; but the Earls of *Exceter,* and *Chesterfield,* that gave no proxies this Sessions, the Lord *Montague of Boughton,* that gave his to the Treasurer, and Lord *Roberts* his to the Earl of *Northampton,* are not easily to be understood. If you ask after the Earl of *Carlisle,* the Lord *Viscount Falconbridge,* and the Lord *Berkeley of Berkeley* Castle, because you find them not mentioned amongst their old Friends, all I have to say, is That the Earl of *Carlisle* stept aside to receive his Pension, the Lord *Berkeley* to dine with the Lord Treasurer, but the Lord *Viscount Falconberg,* like the Noble Man in the

Gospel, went away sorrowfull, for he had a Great Office at Court; but I despair not of giving you a better account of them next Sessions, for it is not possible when they consider that *Cromwell's* Major General, Son in law, and Friend,[19] should think to find their Accounts amongst Men that set up on such a bottom.

Thus Sir, You see the Standard of the *new Partie* is not yet set up, but must be the work of another Session, though it be admirable to me, how the *King* can be enduced to venture His Affairs upon such *weak Counsels,* and *of so fatal consequences;* for I believe it is the first time in the World, that ever it was thought adviseable, after fifteen years of the highest Peace, Quiet, and Obedience, that ever was in any Countrey, that there should be a *pretense* taken up, and a reviving of former miscarriages, especially after so many Promises, and Declarations, as well as Acts of Oblivion, and so much merit of the Offending party, in being the Instruments of the King's Happy Return, besides the putting so vast a number of the King's Subjects in utter despair of having their crimes ever forgotten; and it must be a great Mistake in Counsels, or worse, that there should be so much pains taken by the Court to debase, and bring low the House of Peers, if a *Military Government* be not intended by some. For the Power of *Peerage,* and a *standing Army* are like two Buckets, the proportion that one goes down, the other exactly goes up; and I refer you to the consideration of all the Histories of ours, or any of our neighbor Northern Monarchies, whether standing forces Military, and Arbitrary government, came not plainly in by the same steps, that the Nobility were lessened; and whether whenever they were in Power, and Greatness, they permitted the least shadow of any of them. Our own Countrey is a clear instance of it; For though the *White Rose* and the *Red* changed fortunes often to the ruine, slaughter and beheading of the great Men of the other side; yet nothing could enforce

---

19. The reference is to Henry Ireton.

them to secure themselves by a standing force. But I cannot believe that the King Himself will ever design any such thing; for He is not of a temper Robust, and Laborious enough, to deale with such a sort of Men, or reap the advantages, if they be any, of such a Government, and I think, He can hardly have forgot the treatment his *Father* received from the Officers of his Army, both at *Oxford*, and *Newark*; T'was an hard, but almost an even choice to be the Parliament's *Prisoner*, or their *Slave*; but I am sure the greatest prosperity of his Armes could have brought him to no happier condition, than our King his Son hath before him whenever he please. However, This may be said for the honor of this Session, that there is no Prince in Christendom hath at a greater expence of Money, maintained for two Months' space, a Nobler, or more useful dispute of the Politiques, Mystery, and secrets of Government, both in Church and State, than this has been; Of which noble design no part is owing to any of the Countrey Lords, for they several of them begged, at the first entrance into the Debate, that they might not be engaged in such disputes, as would unavoidably produce divers things to be said, which they were willing to let alone. But I must bear them witness, and so will you, having read this, that they did their parts in it, when it came to it, and spoke plain like *old English* Lords.

I shall conclude with that, upon the whole matter, is most worthy your consideration, That the *design is to declare us first into another Government more Absolute, and Arbitrary, than the Oath of Allegiance, or old Law knew,* and then make us *swear unto it,* as it is so established: And less than this the Bishops could not offer in requital to the Crown for parting with its Supremacy, and suffering them to be sworn to equal with itself. Archbishop *Laud* was the first Founder of this Device; in his Canons of 1640.[20] you shall find an Oath very like

---

20. Archbishop William Laud's Canons of 1640, "Constitutions and canons ecclesiastical, treated upon by the … convocations … of Canterbury and York … ," imposed an oath upon all archbishops, bishops, priests, and deacons "for the preventing of all innovations in doctrine

this, and a Declaratory Canon preceding *that Monarchy is of divine Right,* which was also affirmed in this debate by our Reverend Prelates, and is owned in Print by no less Men than Arch Bishop *Usher,* and B. *Sanderson;* and I am afraid it is the avowed opinion of much the greater part of our dignified Clergie. If so, I am sure they are the most dangerous sort of Men alive to our *English* Government, and it is the first thing ought to be lookt into, and strictly examined by our Parliaments; 'tis the *leaven* that corrupts the whole lump; for if that be true, I am sure Monarchy is not to be bounded by human Laws, and the *8. chap. of I. Samuel,*[21] will prove (as many of our Divines would have it) the Great Charter of the Royal Prerogative, and our *Magna Charta* that says *Our Kings may not take our Fields, our Vineyards, our Corn, and our Sheep* is not in force, but *void* and *null,* because against divine Institution; and you have the *Riddle* out, why the Clergy are so ready to take themselves, & impose upon others such kind of Oaths as these, they have placed themselves, and their possessions upon a better, and a surer bottom (as they think) than *Magna Charta,* and so have no more need of, or concern for it. Nay what is worse, they have truckt away the Rights and Liberties of the People in this, and all other countries wherever they have had opportunity, that they might be owned by the Prince to be *Jure Divino,* and maintained in that Pretention by that absolute power and force, they have contributed so much to put into his hands; and that *Priest,* and *Prince* may, like *Castor* and *Pollux,* be worshipt together as Divine in the same temple by Us poor Lay-subjects; and that *sense*

---

and government." In addition to swearing that the doctrine, discipline, and church government as established in the Church of England contained all things necessary to salvation, they had to swear not to "ever give my consent to alter the government of this Church ... as it stands now established."

21. In this chapter of the Bible the people of Israel ask Samuel, their elderly judge, to allow them to have a king like other peoples. Samuel resists but at God's urging warns them of the ill consequences of monarchy. When they still persist God instructs Samuel to "make them a king."

and *reason, Law, Properties, Rights,* and *Liberties,* shall be understood as the Oracles of those Deities shall interpret, or give signification to them, and never be made use of in the world to oppose the Absolute, and Freewill of either of them.

Sir, I have no more to say, but begg your Pardon for this tedious Trouble, and that you will be very careful to whom you communicate any of this.

FINIS.

Anonymous

Vox Populi:
OR THE
Peoples Claim
TO THEIR
PARLIAMENTS
SITTING,

To Redress Grievances, and Provide for
the COMMON SAFETY;
BY
The known Laws and Constitutions of the Nation:

Humbly Recommended to the KING and *Parliament*
at their Meeting at *OXFORD*, the 21th of *March*.

---

*Rex merito debet Retribuere Legi, quia Lex tribuit ei, facit enim Lex quod ipse
sit Rex.* Bracton, lib. 3.c.9 fol. 107.

The King ought deservedly to give the Law his due, because the Law gave
it him; for the Law makes him a King.

Prov. 22.28. *Remove not the Ancient Land-mark* (or Bound) *which thy Fathers have set.*

LONDON,
Printed for *Francis Smith* at the *Elephant* and *Castle* near the
Royal Exchange in *Cornhill*, 1681.

*T*his anonymous pamphlet was part of the new Whig party's campaign to pressure Charles II to agree to a bill that would exclude his Catholic brother, James, from the throne. Charles had countered these efforts by abruptly proroguing or dismissing parliaments, which had the effect of terminating any pending exclusion bill and aborted the influence of the Whig-dominated House of Commons. When the Parliament of March 1679 returned from its summer recess the following October, Charles immediately prorogued it for a full year. Members resumed business in October 1680 only to find the Parliament dissolved barely four months later. It was a newly elected parliament summoned to convene at Oxford in March 1681 to which this tract is addressed. The repeated disruptions of parliaments justified complaints that little useful business had been accomplished.

"Vox Populi," however, rises above its immediate political moment by assembling timely legal maxims amplifying the importance of law and Parliament and emphasizing the limitations of the monarch. It then provides a brief history of the antiquity and significance of parliaments. All this harked back to the views of the men of the 1640s and the "good old cause," a similarity that enabled the Crown and the Tories to raise the spectre of Whigs intent upon another civil war.

"Vox Populi" may have energized Whigs but was ignored by Charles, who peremptorily dismissed the new parliament on 28 March 1681 merely a week after it convened. A secret stipend from Louis XIV ensured that this was the last parliament Charles would ever need to call.

Vox Populi:
Or, the Peoples Claim to Their Parliaments Sitting, to Redress Grievances and to Provide for the Common Safety, by the Known Laws and Constitutions of the Nation.

Recommended to the King and Parliament at their meeting at *Oxford*, &c.

Since the Wonderful Discovery and undeniable Confirmation of that horrid Popish Plot which designed so much ruine and mischief to these Nations, in all things both Civil and Sacred, and the unanimous Sence and Censure of so many Parliaments upon it, together with so many publick Acts of Justice upon so many of the Traitors; it was comfortably hoped before thirty Months should have past over after the Detection thereof, some effectual Remedies might have been applied to prevent the further attempts of the Papists upon us, and better to have secured the Protestants in their Religion, Lives and Properties. But by sad experience we have found, that notwithstanding the Vigorous Endeavours of three of our Parliaments to provide proper and wholsome Laws to Answer both ends: Yet so prevalent has this Interest been, under so potent a head the *D.* of *Y.*[1] as to stifle in the Birth all those hopeful Parliament-Endeavours; by those many Surprizing and Astonishing Prorogations and Dissolutions which they have procured, whereby our fears and Dangers have Manifestly increased, and their Spirits heightened and incouraged to renew and Multiply fresh Plottings and Designs upon us.

But that our approaching Parliament may be more successful for our Relief before it be too late, by being permitted to sit to Redress our Grievances, and to perfect those Good Bills which have been prepared by the former Parliaments to this purpose; these following

1. Charles II's brother James, Duke of York.

Common Law Maxims respecting King and Parliament, and the Common and Statute Laws themselves (to prevent such unnatural Disappointments and Mischiefs) providing for the sitting of Parliaments till Grievances be redressed, and publick Safety secured and provided for, are tendered to consideration.

Some known Maxims taken out of the Law-Books.

1. Respecting the King.

That the Kings of England *can do nothing as Kings but what of right they ought to do.*

That the King can do no *wrong,* nor can he die.

That the King's Prerogative and the Subject's Liberty are determined by Law.

That the King hath no Power but what the Law gives him.

That the King is so called from Ruling well, Rex a bene Regendo [viz. *according to Law*] *Because he is a King whilst he Rules well, but a Tyrant when he Oppresses.*

That Kings of England *never appear more in their glory, splendor and Majestick Soveraignty, than in Parliaments.*

That the Prerogative of the King cannot do wrong, nor be a Warrant to do wrong to any. Plowd. Comment. *fol.* 246.

2. Respecting the Parliament.

That Parliaments constitute and are laid in the Essence of the Government.

That a Parliament is that to the Common-Wealth which the Soul is to the Body, which is only able to apprehend and understand the symptoms of all Diseases which threaten the Body politick.

That a Parliament is the Bulwark of our Liberty, the boundary which

keeps us from the Innundation of Tyrannical Power, Arbitrary and un-
bounded Will-Government.

That Parliaments do make new and abrogate Old Laws, Reform
Grievances in the Common-Wealth, settle the Succession, grant subsidies;
And in summe, may be called the great Physician of the Kingdom.

From whence it appears and is self evident if Parliaments are so
absolutely necessary in this our constitution, That they must then
have their certain stationary times of Session, and continuance, for
providing Laws, essentially necessary for the being, as well as the well
being of the People; and Redressing all publick Grievances, either by
the want of Laws, or of the undue Execution of them in being, or
otherwise. And suitable hereunto are those Provisions made by the
Wisdom of our Ancestors as recorded by them both in the Common
and Statute-Law:

First, What we find hereof in the *Common Law.*

The Common Law, (saith my Lord *Coke*), is that which is
founded in the immutable Law and light of Nature, agreeable to the
Law of God, requiring Order, Government, Subjection and Protec-
tion, &c. Containing ancient usages, Warrented by Holy Scripture,
and because it is generally given to all, it is therefore called Common.

And further saith, *That in the Book called* The Mirror of Justice *appeareth the whole frame of the ancient common Laws of this*
Realm from the time of K. Arthur, 516. *till near the Conquest;*
which Treats also of the Officers as well as the diversity and Dis-
tinction of the Courts of Justice (which are Officinae Legis*) and*
particularly of the High Court of Parliament by the name of Coun-
cil General or Parliament; so called from Parler-la-ment, *speaking*
judicially his mind: And amongst others gives us the following Law
of King Alfred *who Reigned about* 880.

Le Roy Alfred *Ondeigna pur usage perpetual que a deux foits per*
l'an ou plus sovene pur mistier in temps de peace se Assembler a

Londres, *pur Parliamenter surle guidement del people de dieu co-ment gents soy garderent de pechers, viverent in quiet, receiverent droit per certain usages et saints' Judgments.*

King *Alfred* Ordaineth for a usage perpetual, that twice a year or oftner if need be, in time of peace, they shall Assemble themselves at *London,* to Treat in Parliament of the Government of the People of God, how they should keep themselves from Offences, should live in quiet, and should receive right by certain Laws and holy Judgments.

And thus (saith my Lord *Coke*) you have a Statute of K. *Alfred* as well concerning the holding of this Court of Parliament twice every year at the City of *London,* as to manifest the threefold end of this great and Honourable Assembly of Estates; As,

First, That the Subject might be kept from offending; that is, that Offences might be prevented both by good and provident Laws, and by the due Execution thereof.

Secondly, That men might live safely and in quiet.

Thirdly, That all men might receive Justice by certain Laws and holy Judgments; that is, to the end that Justice might be the better administered, that Questions and Defects in Laws might be by the High Court of Parliament planed, reduced to certainty and adjudged. And further tells us that this Court being the most Supream Court of this Realm, is a part of the frame of the Common Laws, and in some cases doth proceed Legally, according to the ordinary course of the Common Law, as it appeereth, 39 E. 3. f. *Coke Inst. ch. 29. fol. 5.* To be short, of this Court it is truly said, *Si vetestatem spectes est antiquissima, si dignitatem est honoratissima, si jurisdictionem est capacissima.* If you regard Antiquity, it is the most Ancient, if Dignity the most Honourable, if Jurisdiction the most Soveraign.

And where question hath been made whether this Court continued during the Heptarchy, let the Records themselves make answer, of which he gives divers Instances in the times of King *Ine, Offa, Ethelbert*. After the Heptarchy, K. *Edward* Son of *Alfred*, K. *Ethelston, Edgar, Ethelred, Edmond, Canutus*. All which (he saith) and many more are extant and publickly known; proving by divers arguments, that there were Parliaments, unto which the Knights and Burgesses were summoned both before, in, and after the Reign of the Conqueror, till *Hen.* 3. time; and for your further satisfaction herein, see 4. E. 3. 25. 49 *Ed.* 3. 22, 23. 11 H. 4. 2. *Litl. lib.* 2. c. 10.

Whereby we may understand,

1. That Parliaments are part of the frame of the Common Law, [which is laid in the Law and Light of Nature, right Reason and Scripture].

2. That according to this Moral Law of Equity and Righteousness, Parliaments ought frequently to meet for the common peace, safety and benefit of the People, and support of the Government.

3. That Parliaments have been all along esteemed an essential part of the Government, as being the most ancient, honourable and Soveraign Court in the Nation, who are frequently and perpetually to sit, for the making and abolishing Laws, Redressing of Grievances, and see to the due administration of Justice.

4. That as to the place of Meeting, it was to be at *London* the Capital City, the Eye and Heart of the Nation, as being not only the Regal Seat, but the principal place of Judicature, and residence of the chief Officers, and Courts of Justice, where also the Records are kept, as well as the principal place of Commerce and Concourse in the Nation, and to which the People may have the best recourse, and where they may find the best accomodation.

5. The Antiquity of Parliaments in this Nation, which have been so ancient that no Record can give any account of their Beginning, my Lord *Coke* thus tracing from the *Brittans*, through the *Saxons, Danes* and *Normans* to our days.

So that not to suffer Parliaments to sit to answer the great ends for which they were Instituted, is expressely contrary to the Common Law, and so consequently of the Law of God as well as the Law of Nature, and thereby Violence is offered to the Government itself, and Infringement of the People's fundamental Rights and Liberties.

Secondly, What we find hereof in the Statute-Law.

The Statute Laws are Acts of Parliament which are (or ought to be) only Declaratory of the Common Law, which as you have heard is founded upon right Reason and Scripture; for we are told, that if anything is enacted contrary thereto, it is void and null: As *Coke Inst.* 1. 2. c. 29. f. 15. *Finch* p. 3. 28 H. 8. c. 27. *Doct. and Stud.*

The first of these Statutes which require the frequent Meeting and Sitting of Parliaments, agreeable to the Common Law, we find to be in the time of *Ed.* 3. viz. *4 Ed.* 3. & *ch.* 14. In these words:

Item it is accorded that a Parliament shall be holden every Year once, or more often if need be.

The next is in the 36 of the same K. *Ed.* 3. c. 10. *viz.*

Item, For the maintenance of the said Articles *and* Statutes, *and Redressing of divers* Mischiefs *and* Grievances *which daily happen, A* Parliament *shall be holden* every year, *as at another time was ordained by a Statute,* viz. the aforementioned, in his 4th year. And agreeable hereto, are those Statutes upon the Rolls, *viz. 5 Ed.* 2.-1 R. 2. No. 95.

By which Statutes it appeareth, that Parliaments ought Annually to meet, to support the Government, and to redress the Grievances which may happen in the Interval of Parliaments; That being the great End proposed in their said Meetings. *Now,* For Parliaments to meet Annually, and not suffered to sit to Answer the Ends, but to be Prorogued or Dissolved before they have finished their Work, would be nothing but a deluding the Law, and a striking at the foundation of the Government itself, and rendering Parliaments altogether Useless; for it would be all one to have No Parliaments at all, as to have them turned off by the Prince before they have done that they were called and intrusted to do. For by the same Rule whereby they may be so turned off One Session, they may be three Sessions, and so to threescore, to the breaking of the Government, and introducing Arbitrary Power. To Prevent such intollerable Mischiefs and Inconveniencies, are such good Laws as these made in this King's time, and which were so Sacredly observed in after times, That it was a Custom, especially in the Reigns of Henry 4. Henry 5. Henry 6. to have a Proclamation made in *Westminster-Hall* before the end of every Session, *That all those who had any matter to present to the Parliament, should bring it in before such a day, for otherwise the Parliament at that Day should Determine.* Whereby it appears the People were not to be eluded nor disappointed by surprizing Prorogations and Dissolutions, to frustrate and make void the great ends of Parliaments.

And to this purpose saith a late Learned Author, That if there was no Statute, or anything upon *record extant, concerning the Parliament's* sitting *to redress grievances, yet that I must believe, that it is so by the fundamental Law of the Government, which must be Lame and imperfect without it; [For, otherwise the Prince and his Ministers may do what they please, and their Wills may be their Laws].*

Therefore it is provided for in the very Essence and Constitution of the Government itself; and this (saith our Author) *we may call the Common Law, which is of as much value (if not more) than any Statute, and of which all our good Acts of Parliament and* Magna Charta, *itself is but Declaratory; so that though the King is intrusted with the formal part of summoning and* pronouncing the dissolution of Parliaments, which is *done by Writ; yet the Laws which Oblige him (as well as us) have determined how, and when he shall do it; which is enough to shew, that the King's share in the Soveraignty, that is in the Parliament, is cut out to him by Law,* and not left at his disposal.

The Next Statute we shall mention, to inforce this fundamental Right and Priviledge, is the 25th *Ed.* 3. *ch.* 23. called the *Statute of Provisors,* which was made to prevent and Cut off the Incroachments of the Bishops of *Rome,* whose *Usurpations* in disposing of Benefices occasioned intollerable Grievances, wherein, in the Preamble of the said Statute, it is expressed as followeth.

> *Whereupon the Commons have prayed our said Soveraign Lord the King, that sith the Right of the Crown of* England, *and the Law of the said Realm is such, that upon the* Mischiefs *and Damage which happeneth to his Realm, he* ought *and is* bounden *of the* accord *of his said People in his Parliament, thereof to make Remedy and Law, in avoiding the Mischiefs and Damage which thereof cometh; That it may please him thereupon to provide Remedy. Our Soveraign Lord the King seeing the Mischiefs and Damage before named, and having regard to the said Statute made in the time of his said Grandfather, and to the Causes contained in the same, which Statute holdeth always his force, and was never defeated or annulled in any point, and by so much is bound by his Oath to do the same, to be kept as the Law of this Realm, though that by Sufferance and Negligence it hath since been attempted to the contrary. And also having regard to the grievous Complaints made to him by his People in divers Parliaments holden heretofore, Willing to ordain Remedy for the great Damages and Mischiefs which have happened and daily do happen by the said Cause,* &c. *By the assent of all the great Men and Commonality of his said Realm, hath Ordained and Established,* &c.

In which preamble of the Statute we may observe, (1.) The intollerable grievance and burden, which was occassioned by the illegal Incroachments of the See of *Rome.* (2.) The many Complaints the People had made, who in those dark times, under Popery were sensible of, groaning under those Burdens. (3.) The Endeavours used in vain by former Parliaments to Redress the same, And to bring their

Laws in being, to have their Force and Effect. (4.) The acknowledgment of the King and Parliament, that the Obligation hereto was
upon the King.

(1.) From the Right of the Crown, which obliged every King to
pass good Laws. (2.) The Statute in force. (3.) The King's *Oath* to
keep the Old and pass new Laws for his People's safeguard, which
they should tender to him. (4.) From the sence of the People, expressed in their Complaints; and, (5.) From the Mischief and Damage which would otherwise ensue.

And therefore by the desire and accord of his People, He passes
this famous Law. The Preamble whereof, is here recited.

Another *Statute* to the same purpose you find 2. R. 2. No. 28

*Also the Commons in Parliament, pray, that for as much as Peti-
tions and Bills presented in Parliament by divers of the Commons,
could not heretofore have their Respective Answers; That therefore
both their Petitions and Bills in this present Parliament, as also others which shall be presented in any future Parliament, may have a
good and Gracious Answer and Remedy ordained thereupon before
the departing of every Parliament: And that to this purpose, a due
Statute be ensealed* [or Enacted] *at this present Parliament, to be
and remain in Force for all times to come.*

To which the King Replied:

The King's Answer.

THE *King is pleased that all such Petitions delivered in Parliament, of
things* (or matters) *which cannot otherwise be determined; A good and
Reasonable Answer shall be made and given before the Departure of Parliament.*

In which excellent Law we may observe, (1.) A Complaint of former remisness, their Bills having aforetime been passed by, their

Grievances Unredressed, by unseasonably Dissolving of Parliaments before their Laws could pass. (2.) That a Law might pass in that very Parliament to rectifie that Abuse for the future. And, (3.) That it should not pass for a temporary Law, but for perpetuity being of such absolute Necessity, that before the Parliaments be dismissed, Bills of common Right might pass.

And the King agreed hereto.

Suitable hereto, we have my Lord Chief Justice *Coke,* that great Oracle of the Law, in his *Instit.* 4. B. p. 11. Asserting, *Petitions being truly preferred* (though very many) *have been Answered by the Law and Custom of Parliament, before the end of Parliament.*

This appears saith he, by the ancient Treatise *De Mode tenendi Parliamentum,* in these Words faithfully Translated. *The Parliament ought not to be ended while any Petition dependeth undiscussed, or at the least to which a determinate Answer is not made.* Rot. Par. 17. E. 3. No. 60. 25 E. 3. No. 60. 50 E. 3. No. 212. 2 R. 2. 134. 2. R. 2. No. 38. 1 H. 4. 132. 2 H. 4. 325. 113.

And that one of the principal ends of calling Parliaments, is for redressing of Grievances that daily happen, 36 E. 3. c. 10. 18 E. 3. c. 14. 50 E. 3. No. 17. *Lyons Case, Rot. Par.* 1. H. 5. No. 17. 13 H. 4. No. 9.

And that as concerning the departing of Parliaments, *It ought to be in such a manner: saith* Modus Tenendi. *viz. To be demanded, yea and publickly Proclaimed in the Parliament, and within the Palace of the Parliament, whether there be any that hath delivered a Petition to the Parliament, and hath not received Answer thereto; if there be none such, it is to be supposed, that every one is Satisfied, or else Answered unto at the least, so far forth as by the Law he may be. And which custom was observed in after Ages, as you have heard before.*

Concerning the Antiquity and Authority of this Ancient Treatise, called *Modus tenendi Parliamentum* (saith my Lord *Coke)* whereof we make often use in our Institutes: Certain it is, *that this* Modus *was*

*Rehearsed and Declared before the Conqueror at the time of his Conquest,
and by him approved for* England, *and accordingly he according to*
Modus *held a Parliament for* England, *as appears* 21 E. 3. fo. 60.

Whereby you clearly perceive, that these wholsome Laws are not
only in full agreement with the Common Law and declarative
thereof, but in full accord with the Oath and Office of the Prince,
who has that great trust by the Law lodged with him for the good
and benefit, not hurt and mischief of the People, *viz.*

First, these Laws are very suitable to the Office and Duty of a
Ruler, and the end for which he was instituted by God himself, who
commands him to do Judgment, and Justice to all; especially, to the
Oppressed, and not to deny them any request for their relief, protec-
tion or welfare, 2. *Sam.* 22.3. 1 *Chron.* 13.1, to 5. 2 *Chron.* 9.8.19.5. &c.
Est. 1. 13. Our Law Books enjoining the same, as *Bracton* Lib. 1. c.2.
Lib. 3. c.9. *fol.* 107. *&c. Fortiscue,* ch. 9. *so.* 15.c.7. *fol.* 5. 11. *Coke* 7. Book
Reports, *Calvin's* Case *f.* 11.

Secondly, they are also in full Harmony with the King's Coronation Oath Solemnly made to all his Subjects, viz. *To grant, fullfil, and
defend all rightful Laws which the Commons of the Realm shall choose,
and to strengthen and maintain them after his Power.*

Thirdly, These Laws are also in full agreement, and oneness with
Magna Charta itself, that Antient Fundamental Law which hath
been Confirmed by at least Forty Parliaments, *viz. We shall deny, We
shall defer to no Man Justice and Right,* much less to the whole Parliament and Kingdom, in denying or deferring to pass such necessary
Bills which the People's needs call for.

Object. But to all this which hath been said, it may be objected,
That several of our Princes have otherwise practised by Dissolving or
[as laterly used, by] Proroguing Parliaments at their pleasures, before Grievances were Redressed, and Publick Bills of Common
Safety Passed, and that as a Priviledge, belonging to the Royal Prerogative.

Answ. *To which it is Answered, That granting they have so done: First, it is most manifest that doth not therefore create a right to them so to do; according to that known maxime,* a facto ad jus non valet Consequentia, *especially, when such Actions are against so many express and positive Laws, such Principles of Common Right and Justice, and so many particular Ties and Obligations upon themselves to the contrary.*

Secondly, But if it had been so, yet neither can Prerogative be pleaded to Justify such Practices, because the King has no Prerogative, but what the Law gives him; and it can give none to destroy itself, and those it protects, but the contrary. *Bracton* in his Comments, *pag.* 487. tells us, *That although the Common Law doth allow many Prerogatives to the King, yet it doth not allow any, that He shall wrong, or hurt any by his Prerogative.* Therefore 'tis well said, by a late Worthy Author upon this point, *That what Power or Prerogative the Kings have in Them, ought to be used according to the true and genuine intent of the Government; that is for the Preservation and Interest of the People. And not for the disappointing the Councils of a Parliament, towards reforming Grievances, and making provision for the future Execution of the Laws; and whenever it is applied to frustrate those ends, it is a Violation of Right, and Infringment of the King's Coronation Oath, who is obliged to Pass or Confirm those Laws His People shall chuse.* And tho He had such a Prerogative by Law, yet it should not be used, especially in time of Eminent danger and distress. The late King in his Advice to his Majesty that now is, in his Eikon Basilike 239. *Tells him that his Prerogative is best shewed, and exercised, in Remitting, rather than exacting the Rigor of the Laws, there being nothing worse than Legal Tyranny.*

Nor would he have him entertain any Aversion or Dislike of Parliaments, which in their right Constitution, with freedom and honour, will never Injure or Diminish His Greatness, but will rather be as interchangings of Love, Loyalty and Confidence, between a Prince and his People.

It is true, some Flatterers and Traitors have presumed, in defiance to their Countries' Rights, to assert that such a boundless *Prerogative* belongs to Kings. As did Chief Justice *Trisilian*, &c. in Richard 2's time; *Advising him that he might Dissolve Parliaments at pleasure;* and, *that no Member should be called to Parliament, nor any Act past in either House, without His Approbation in the first place;* and, *that whoever advised otherwise were Traitors.* But this Advice you read was no less Fatal to himself, than Pernicious to his Prince. *Baker's Chron.* p. 147, 148, and 159.

King James *in his Speech to the Parliament* 1609. *Gives them assurance, That he never meant to Govern by any Law, but the Law of the Land; tho it be disputed among them, as if he had an intention to alter the Law; and Govern by the absolute power of a King; but to put them out of doubt in that matter, tells them, That all Kings who are not Tyrants, or Perjured, will bound themselves within the limits of their Laws. And they that persuade the contrary, are Vipers and Pests, both against them and the Common-wealth.* Wilson. K. J. p. 46.

The Conclusion.

1. If this be so, That by so great Authority (*viz.* so many *Statutes* in force, The fundamentals of the Common Law, the Essentials of the Government itself, *Magna Charta*, The King's Coronation Oath, so many Laws of God and Man); the Parliament ought to sit to Redress Grievances and provide for Common Safety, especially in times of Common Danger. (And that this is eminently so, who can doubt, that will believe the King; so many Parliaments, The Cloud of Witnesses, the Publick Judicatures, their own sense and experience of the manifold Mischiefs which have been acted, and the apparent Ruine and Confusion that impends the Nation, by the restless Attempts of a bloody Interest, if speedy Remedy is not applied.)

Then let it be Queried, Whether the People having thus the Knife at the Throat, Cities and Habitations Fired, and therein their Persons fried, Invasions and Insurrections threatened to Destroy the King and Subjects, Church and State; and as so lately told us, (upon Mr. *Fitz Harris's* commitment),[2] the present Design on Foot was to Depose and Kill the King; and their only remedy hoped for under God to give them Relief thus from time to time, Cut off, *viz.* Their Parliaments, who with so much care, cost and pains are Elected, sent up, and Intrusted for their help, turned off *re infecta,*[3] and rendered so insignificant by those frequent Prorogations and Dissolutions.

Are they not therefore justified in their important Cries, in their many Humble Petitions to their King, Fervent Addresses to their Members, earnest Claims for this their Birthright here Pleaded, which the Laws of the Kingdom, consonant to the Laws of God and Nature, has given them?

2. If so, what then shall be said to those who advise to this high Violation of their Countrie's Rights, to the infringing so many just Laws, and exposing the Publick to those desperate hazards, if not a total Ruine?

If King *Alfred* (as *Andrew Horne* in his *Mirror of Justice* tells us) hanged *Darking, Segnor, Cedwine, Cole,* and Forty Judges more, for Judging contrary to Law; and yet all those false Judgments were but in particular and private Cases; What Death do those Men deserve, who offer this violence to the Law itself, and all the Sacred Rights of their Country? If the Lord Chief Justice *Thorp* in *Edward 3's* time, for receiving the Bribery of One hundred pounds was adjudged to be Hanged as one that had made the King break his Oath to the Peo-

2. Edward Fitzharris was an Irish Catholic informer employed by the Court against the Whigs. The House of Commons attempted to impeach him, presumably in hopes of implicating Danby and the Duke of York in the Popish Plot. When the Lords refused to cooperate the Commons passed a resolution of the House of Commons that no inferior court could proceed against Fitzharris. Nevertheless he was brought to trial in King's Bench in 1681 charged with a seditious libel and an intent to bring in the French to overthrow the king. He was found guilty and executed.

3. An incomplete thing.

ple; How much more guilty are they of making the King break his Coronation Oath that perswade him to Act against all the Laws for holding Parliaments, and passing Laws therein, which he is so solemnly sworn to do? And if the Lord Chief Justice *Tresilian* was Hanged, Drawn, and Quartered for Advising the King to Act contrary to some Statutes only; what do those deserve that advise the King to Act not only against some, but against all these Ancient Laws and Statutes of the Realm?

And if *Blake* the King's *Council* but for Assisting in the Matter and drawing up Indictments by the King's Command contrary to Law, though it is likely he might Plead the King's Order for it, yet if he was Hanged, Drawn and Quartered for that, what Justice is due to them that assist in the Total Destruction of all the Laws of the Nation, and as much as in them lies, their King and Country too? And if *Usk* the under Sherif (whose Office it is to Execute the Laws) for but endeavouring to aid *Tresilian, Blake* and their *Accomplices* against some of the Laws, was also with Five more Hanged, Drawn and Quartered; What punishment may they deserve that Aid and endeavour the Subvertion of all the Laws of the Kingdom? And if *Empson* and *Dudley* in *Henry* the Eight's time, though two of the King's privy Councel, were Hanged for Procuring and Executing an Act of Parliament contrary to the Fundamental Laws of the Kingdom, and to the great vexation of the People; so that though they had an Act of Parliament of their side, yet that Act being against the known Laws of the Land, were Hanged as Traitors for putting that Statute in Execution: then what shall become of those who have no such Act to shelter themselves under, and who shall Act not only contrary to, but to the Destruction of the Fundamental Laws of the Kingdom, and how Harmonious such Justice will be, the Text tells us, *Deut.* 27.17. *Cursed be he that removeth his Neighbour's Landmark: and all the People shall say,* Amen.

That this present Session may have a happy Issue, to answer the great ends of Parliaments, and therein our present Exigencies and Necessities, is the incessant Cry and longing Expectation of all the Protestants in the Land.

FINIS.

Parliament
and the
Succession

[Elkanah Settle, 1648–1724]

THE
CHARACTER
OF A
Popish Successour,
AND WHAT
ENGLAND
MAY EXPECT
From Such a One.
Humbly offered to the Consideration of
BOTH HOUSES
OF
PARLIAMENT,
Appointed to meet at
OXFORD,
On the One and twentieth of *March*, 1680/1.

LONDON,
Printed for *T. Davies*. MDCLXXXI.

*T*his anonymous tract, with its arguments that no Catholic could inherit the English throne, was part of the Whig party's vigorous campaign to exclude James, Duke of York, from succeeding his brother. It has been attributed to the temperamental and vacillating Restoration poet and playwright Elkanah Settle.

Settle left Oxford in 1666 without taking a degree, but found quick success in London when he was just eighteen with his play, "Cambyses, King of Persia; a Tragedy." Other plays followed, and for a time he was a favorite of the Court. He became a competitor and later enemy of Dryden, with whom he traded barbs in a series of pamphlets. When the Court wearied of Settle, he approached the Whigs. His strong Protestantism was evident in his next play, "The Female Prelate, being the History of the Life and Death of Pope Joan," produced in 1680 and dedicated to the Earl of Shaftesbury. The following year, allegedly at Shaftesbury's behest, he wrote the political tract reprinted here, "The Character of a Popish Successour."

This timely and provocative tract aroused great excitement, provoked a flurry of replies, and went into two editions. Settle followed it with a revised, and yet more adamant, version later the same year. By 1683 with the king's crackdown on Whigs in full swing, Settle turned against them in a tract that exposed the popish plot of 1678 as a fraud and heaped abuse on Shaftesbury and his party. His new-found hostility to the Whigs was so intense that Settle even published hostile tracts on the dying speeches of William Lord Russell and Algernon Sidney. By the time of James II's accession Settle was a staunch Tory, publishing a poem in honor of the new king's coronation and even enlisting as a soldier in James's army. After the Glorious Revolution he continued to publish but was understandably shunned by both political parties. He did manage to obtain the post of city poet for London, however, and settled down to produce pageants and plays.

"The Character of a Popish Successour," however flighty the politics of its author, is of constitutional value as it musters the full Whig political and constitutional arsenal upon which the exclusion movement rested.

The Character of a Popish Successour, and What *England* May Expect from Such a One.

It has been my Fortune to be a *Subject* and a *Native* of that part of the *World*, where almost three years last past I have scarce heard anything, but the continual Noise of *Popery* and *Plots*, with all the clamourous Fears of a jealous *Kingdom*, about my Ears. And truly, I must plainly confess, I am not so ill a *Commonwealthsman*, but that I am glad to see my Country-men disturbed in a Cause, where *Religion*, *Liberty*, and *Property* are at stake. If their Jealousies are just, and their Fears prophetick, in God's Name let them talk. Every good Man ought to be so far from silencing any Reasonable Murmurs, that 'tis rather his Duty to bear a Part in a Choir so Universal. And if we see the Great and Wise Men of our Nation, like true *English* Patriots, strugling and toiling to prevent our threatening Calamities, let us take delight to behold them restless and uneasie, rolling about our troubled Sea, like *Porpoises* against a Tempest, to forewarn us of an approaching Destruction.

But amidst our evident Danger, we see another sort of People daily flattering and deluding us into a false and fatal Security. And sure none are so little our Friends, or indeed so void even of Humanity itself, as those who would lull us asleep when Ruine is in view. But since Zeal and Hypocrisy, naked Truth and artificial Falshood, have oftentimes alike Faces, I cannot but think it the Duty both of a *Christian* and an *English* man, to unravel the Treachery of those false Arguments which they raise to destroy us.

As first, they say, *Why should we stand in fear of Popery, when in the present Temper of* England *'tis impossible for any Successour whatever to introduce it?*

And next, amidst our groundless Fears (say they) *Let us consider what the Prince is that appears so dreadful a* Gorgon *to England. A Prince that on all accounts has so signally ventured his Life for*

his King and Country: A Heroe of that faithful and matchless
Courage and Loyalty: A Prince of that unshaken Honour and Res-
olution, that his Word has ever been known to be his Oracle, and his
Friendship a Bulwark wherever he vouchsafes to place it; with such
an infinite Mass of all the Bravery and Gallantry that can adorn a
Prince. Why, must the change of his Religion destroy his Human-
ity, or the advance to a Crown render his Word or Honour less Sa-
cred, or make him a Tyrant to that very People whom he has so often
and so chearfully defended? Why, may there not be a Popish King
with all these Accomplishments, that whatever his own private De-
votions shall be, yet shall publickly maintain the Protestant Wor-
ship, with all the present Constitution of Government, unaltered?

Yes, now I say something! If this *Rara avis in terris*[1] can be found,
then *England* were in a happy condition. But, alas! What signifie all
the great past Actions of a Prince's Life, when *Popery* at last has got
the Ascendant? All Vertues must truckle to Religion; and how little
an Impression will all his recorded Glories leave behind them, when
Rome has once stampt him her Proselyte?

But since unlikely things may come to pass, let us seriously examine how far the Notion of such a *Popish Successour* consists with Reason, or indeed has the least shadow of possibility.

If to maintain and defend our *Religion* be any more than a Name,
it is impossible for any Man to act the true Defensive Part, without
the Offensive too: And he that would effectually uphold the *Protes-*
tant Worship, Peace, and Interest, is bound to suppress all those potent and dangerous Enemies that would destroy them; for all other
Defence is but Disguise and Counterfeit.

If then the Wisdom of several Successive Monarchs, with a whole
Nation's unanimous Prudence, and indefatigable Care for the Protestant Preservation, has determined, That those Popish Priests who

---

1. A rare bird on earth.

have sworn Fealty to the See of *Rome*, and taken Orders in Foreign
Seminaries, are the greatest Seducers of the King's Liege People, and
the most notorious Incendiaries and Subverters of the Protestant
Christianity and Loyalty; and for that cause their several Laws declare them Traitors; by consequence these are the potent and dangerous Enemies which, in defence of the Protestant Case, this Popish
King is obliged to suppress and punish, and these the very Laws he is
bound to execute.

And though, perhaps, till the Discovery of the late Plot, for several
Ages we have not seen that Severity inflicted on Popish Priests, as
the Laws against them require; and why? Because the flourishing
Tranquillity of the *English* Church under this King and His Father's
Reign, rendered them so inconsiderable an Adversary, that the natural tenderness of the Protestant People of *England* not delighting
in Blood, did not think it worth their while either to detect or prosecute them, and therefore has not made them the common Mark of
Justice.

But under the Reign of an *English* Papist, when the Fraternity of
their Religion shall encourage the Pope to make his working Emissaries ten times more numerous; when, if not the hope of Publick
Patronage, yet at least their confidence of Private Indulgence, Con-
nivance, and Mercy, emboldens the Missive Obedience of his Jesuitical Instruments, whilst the very Name of a Popish Monarch has the
Influence of the Sun in *Egypt*, and daily warms our Mud into Monsters, till they are become our most threatening and most formidable
Enemies. And if ever the Protestant Religion wanted a Defender, 'tis
then. If the Word, Honour, or Coronation-Oath of a King be more
than a Name, 'tis then or never he is obliged to uphold the Protestant Interest, and actually suppress its most apparent and most notorious Enemies.

Well then, for Argument's sake, by the vertue of a strong Faith, (a
Faith so strong as may remove Mountains) let us suppose we may

have such a *Roman Catholick* King, as shall discountenance Pope and Popery, cherish Protestantism, and effectually deter and punish all those that shall endeavour to undermine and supplant it: and then let us examine what this King, thus qualified, must do.

First then, in continuing the Ecclesiastick Jurisdiction, Honours, and Preferments in the Hands of the Protestant Clergy, he must confer his Favours and Smiles on those very Men, whom (by the Fundamentals of his own uncharitable Persuasion, which dooms all that die out of the Bosom of the *Romish* Church to a certain state of Damnation) he cordially believes do preach and teach, and lead his Subjects in the direct way to Hell: And next, at the same time he must not only punish and persecute, but perhaps imprison and hang those very only Righteous Men, whom from the bottom of his Soul he believes can only open them the Gates of Paradise: whilst in so doing he cannot but accuse himself of copying the old *Jewish* Cruelty. Nay, in one respect he out goes their Crime; for he acts that knowingly, which they comitted ignorantly. For, by the Dictates of his Religion he must be convinced, that in effect he does little less than save a *Barabbas*, and crucify a *Jesus*.

A very pretty *Chimaera!* Which is as much as to make this Popish King the greatest Barbarian in the Creation; a Barbarian that shall cherish and maintain the Dissenters from Truth, and punish and condemn the Pillars of Christianity, and Proselytes of Heaven: Which is no other than to speak him the basest of Men, and little less than a Monster. Besides, at the same time that we suppose that King that dares not uphold nor encourage his own Religion, we render him the most deplorable of Cowards; a Coward so abject, that he dares not be a Champion even for his God. And how consistent this is with the Glory of a Crowned Head, and what hope *England* has of such a Successour, I leave all Men of Sense to judge.

Besides, What mismatched incongruous Ingredients must go to make up this Composition of a King! His Hand and Heart must be of no Kin to one another. He must be so inhuman to those very darling *Jesuits* that like *Mahomet's* Pidgeon infused and whispered all his Heavenly Dreams into his Ears, that he must not only clip their Wings, but fairly Cage them too, even for the charming Oracles they breathed him. And at the same minute he must leave the wide and open Air to those very Ravens that daily croak Abhorrence and Confusion to them, and all their holy Dreams, and their false Oracles. Thus whilst he acts quite contrary to all his Inclinations, against the whole bent of his Soul, what does he but publickly put in force those Laws for the Protestant Service, till in fine, for his Nation's Peace, he ruines his own, and is a whole Scene of War within himself? Whilst his Conscience accusing his Sloth on one side, the *Pope* on the other, *Rome's* continual Bulls bellowing against him, as an undutiful unactive Son of Holy Mother Church, a Scandal to her Glory, a Traitor to her Interest, and a Deserter of her Cause; one day accusing the Lukewarmness of his Religion, another the Pusilanimity of his Nature; all *Roman Catholick Princes* deriding the feebleness of his Spirit, and the tameness of his Arm: till at long run, to spare a Faggot in *Smithfield*,[2] he does little less than walk on hot Irons himself. Thus all the Pleasure he relishes on a Throne, is but a kind of *Good-Friday* Entertainment. Instead of a Royal Festival, his riotting in all the Luxury of his Heart, to see *Rome's Dagon* worshipped, *Rome's* Altars smoak, *Rome's* Standard set up, *Rome's* Enemies defeated, and his victorious Mother Church triumphant; his abject and poor-spirited Submission denies himself the only thing he thirsts for. And whilst the Principles he sucks from *Rome* do in effect in the Prophet's words bid him, *Rise, slay and eat*, his Fear, his unkingly, nay unmanly Fear, makes him fast and starve.

However, if there be such a King in Nature, as will not defend his

2. Smithfield became notorious during the reign of Mary Tudor as the place where many Protestants were burned to death as heretics.

own Religion, because he dares not; but sneaks upon a Throne, and in obedience to his Fear shrinks from the Dictates of his Conscience, and the Service of his God: If, like *Jupiter's* Log, such a King can be, and Fate has ordained us for a Popish Prince, pray Heaven shrowd the Imperial Lion in this innocent Lambsskin. But I am afraid we shall scarce be so happy; and I shrewdly suspect, that all those cunning *Catholick* Trumpetters who in all Companies sound the Innocence of a *Popish Successour,* and flatter us with such a hopeful, harmless, peaceful Prince in a *Papist,* have a little of the *Romish* Mental Reservation in the Promises they make us, and no small *Jesuitical* Equivocation in the Airy Castles they build us.

But I have heard some say, *Why, may there not be a zealous Prince of any Religion, who still out of the meer Principles of Morality, shall have that tenderness and sense of his People's Peace, as to trouble himself about Religion no farther than concerns his own Salvation; and therefore continue the Administration of Laws and Devotion in the same Channel he found them?*

And all this his meer Morality shall do! Alas! alas! If he's a Bigot in Religion, all his Morals are Slaves to his Zeal. Nay, grant him to be the most absolute Master of all the *Cardinal Vertues,* there's not one of them that shall not be a particular Instrument for our Destruction. As for Example, allow him *Fortitude,* suppose him a Prince of matchless Courage. So much the worse; what does that but make him the more daring, and more adventurous, in pushing on the Cause of *Rome,* and with a more undaunted and manly patience bear all the Oppositions he meets in the way. If he be a Man of *Justice,* that still makes for *Rome:* for whilst he believes the *Pope* to be *Christ's* Lawful Vicar, and that that Office includes the Ecclesiastical Supremacy, no doubt but he'll think it as much the Duty of his *Christianity* to give the Pope his Right, as to take his own. And in *Christ's* own Words, that *give unto* Caesar *the things that are* Caesar's, *and unto God those things that are God's,* he'll certainly judge the *Pope's*

Restoration as great a piece of Justice, as his own Coronation. Then
if he be a Master of *Temperance,* in the properest sense of this Moral
Vertue, *viz.* a Man that can govern his Passions, that's still as bad:
For he that has the most bridled Passions, has always the firmest and
steadiest Resolutions. Who so renowned for Constancy, so fixt in his
Resolves, and so unalterable in his determined Purposes, as that
Philip of *Spain,* who was never heard to rage, or scarce seen to frown?
Nay, History gives this Character of him, That after the discovery of
his Queen's Adultery with his own Son, at the same minute that he
ordered her a Bowl of Poison, he did not so much as change his Look
or Voice, either to his treacherous Son, or his incestuous Wife. And
what so fit a Pillar for *Popery,* as such Constancy in a King?

But if we take *Temperance* in its larger signification, *viz.* the self-
denial of a Man's Worldly Appetites; still worse and worse: For a Riotous Luxurious Monarch bounds his Ambition wholly in the
Pleasures of a Crown, resigns his Reins to his Charioteers, and leaves
the Toil of Power to his Subordinate Magistrates, like the Work of
Fate to Second Causes; whilst his Intemperance so slackens his Zeal,
that it unbends those very Nerves, which otherwise might be more
strenuously wound up for our Destruction.

And lastly, If he has *Prudence,* that's worst of all. That's his only
winning Card; the only leading Vertue that manages his Policies and
Conduct with that Care and Art, till he effects the Business of *Rome,*
and ripens that mighty Work to a perfection, which otherwise an
overforward fool-hardy Zeal, by ill management, might destroy.

Thus his very *Cardinal Vertues* are the absolute Hinges that open
the Gates to *Rome.* Alas! Where Superstition rules the day, all Moral
Vertues are but those lesser Lights that take their Illumination from
that greater Orb above them. And thus, what boots it in a Popish
Heir, to say he's the truest Friend, the greatest of *Heroes,* the best of
Masters, the justest Judge, or the honestest of Men? All meer treach-

erous Quicksands for a People to repose the least glimpse of Safety in, or build the least Hopes upon.

But I have heard a great many say, *It cannot enter into their thoughts, that a Popish Successour will ever take such an inhuman and so unnatural a Course to establish Popery, it being so absolutely against the* English *Constitution, that it can never be introduced with less than a Deluge of Blood. Surely his very Glory should withhold him from so much Cruelty, considering how much more it would be for his Immortal Honour, to have the universal Prayers than the Curses of a Nation. And one would think a King would so much more endeavour to win the Hearts, than the Hatred of his People, that certainly in all probability this excentrick Motion, this disjointing the whole Harmony of a World, should be so ungrateful to him, that no Religion whatever should put such a thought into his Head.*

And all this his Glory shall do? His Glory! The Glory of a *Papist!* A pretty Airy Notion. How shall we ever expect that Glory shall steer the Actions of a *Popish Successour,* when there is not that thing so abject that he shall refuse to do, or that Shape or Hypocrisie so scandalous he shall not assume, when *Rome* or *Rome's* Interest shall command; nay, when his own petulant Stubbornness shall but sway him? As for example; For one fit he shall come to the *Protestant* Church, and be a Member of their Communion, notwithstanding at the same time his Face belies his Heart, and in his Soul he is a *Romanist.* Nay, he shall vary his Disguises as often as an *Algerian* his Colours, and change his Flag to conceal the Pirate. As for instance; Another fit, for whole Years together, he shall come neither to one Church nor the other, and participate of neither Communion, till ignobly he plays the unprincely, nay the unmanly Hypocrite, so long, that he shelters himself under the Face of an *Atheist,* to shroud a *Papist.* A Vizor more fit for a *Banditto,* than a Prince. And this methinks is so wretched and so despicable a Disguise, that it looks like being ashamed of his God.

Besides, If Glory could have any Ascendant over a *Popish Successour*, one would think the Word of a King, and the Solemn Protestations of Majesty, ought to be Sacred and Inviolable. But how many Precedents have we in *Popish* Princes to convince us, their strongest Engagements and Promises are lighter than the very Breath that utters them. As for Example's sake; How did their Saint *Mary* of *England*[3] promise the *Norfolk* and *Suffolk* Inhabitants the unmolested continuation of the *Protestant* Worship, calling her God (that God that saw the falseness of her Heart) to witness, *That though her own Persuasion was of the Romish Faith, yet she would content herself with the private Exercise of her own Devotion, and preserve the then Protestant Government, with all her Subjects' Rights and Privileges, uninjured.* Upon which those poor, credulous, honest, deluded Believers, on the security of such prevalent Conjurations, led by the mistaken Reverence they paid to a protesting Majesty, laid their Lives at her Feet, and were the very Men that in that Contest of the Succession placed her on a Throne. But immediately, when her Sovereign Power was securely established, and his pious Holiness had bid her safely pull the Vizor off, no sooner did *Smithfield* glow with Piles of blazing Hereticks, but Chronicles more particularly observe, that no People in her whole Kingdom felt so signal Marks of her Vengeance, as those very Men that raised her to a Throne. Her Princely Gratitude for their Crowning her with a Diadem, Crowned them with their Martyrdoms.

But since we have mentioned her Princely Gratitude, 'twill not be amiss to recollect one Instance more of so exemplary a Vertue. In the Dispute betwixt hers, and the Lady *Jane Grey's* Title to the Crown, it

3. Mary Tudor.

was remarkable, that all the Judges of *England* gave their unanimous Opinions for the Lady *Jane's* Succession, except one of them only, that asserted the Right of *Mary:*[4] But it so fell out, that this Man proving a *Protestant,* (notwithstanding of all the whole Scarlet Robe he had been her only Champion) was so barbarously persecuted by her, that being first degraded, then imprisoned and tortured for his Religion, the cruelty of his Tormentors was so savage, that with his own hand he made himself away to escape them. And well might the violence of his Despair sufficiently testify his Sufferings were intolerable, when he fled to so sad a Refuge as Self-murder for a Deliverance.

But here says another Objection, *Suppose that the Conservation of a Nation's Peace, the Dictates of a Prince's Glory, and all the Bonds of Morality, cannot have any influence over a Popish Successour; yet why may there not be that Prince, who in veneration of his Coronation-Oath, shall defend the Protestant Religion, notwithstanding all his private regret; and inclinations to the contrary? When rather than incur the infamous brand of Perjury, he shall tie himself to the performance of that, which not the force of Religion itself shall violate? And then, how can there be that Infidel of a Subject, after so solemn an Oath, that shall not believe him?*

Why, truly I am afraid there are a great many of those Infidels, and some that will give smart Reasons for their Infidelity: For, if he keeps his Oath, we must allow, that the only Motive that prompts him to keep it, is some Obligation that he believes is in an Oath. But considering he is of a Religion that can absolve Subjects from their Allegiance to an Heretical Excommunicated Prince, nay depose him, and take his very Crown away; why may it not much more release a

---

4. Sir Richard Morgan, chief justice of common pleas who died in 1556, is probably the judge referred to here. *Foxe's Book of Martyrs* claims that Morgan, who had pronounced sentence against Lady Jane Grey, was so troubled by her execution that he went mad.

King from his Faith to an Excommunicated Heretical People, by so much as the Ties of Vassals to Monarchs, are greater than those of Monarchs to Vassals?

But 'twill not be amiss, for strengthening this Argument, to give the World an Instance of the power of an Oath with a *Roman Catholick* King.

There is a famous Gentleman on the other side the Water,[5] whom we all very well know, (pray Heaven we live not to be better acquainted with him than we desire) that once took the strongest of Oaths, the Sacrament, *That he would never invade nor make war upon Flanders.* But whether or no his *Confessour* found some *Jesuitical* Loophole from that Sacrament, or that the Body and Blood of *Christ* could not hold him, we see that *Flanders* of late years has not lived so merrily, nor so peaceably, as so Royal a Voucher (one would have thought) might have assured them they should.

And now let us a little balance the difference between the Breach of his Oath, and that of a *Popish* Princess in *England.* All the Motives that could provoke him to the breach of his Oath, was only his Ambition, a Lust of being Great. And at the same time that he is an Invader of his Neighbouring Princes, his Conscience must tell him his Conquests are at best but so many glorious Robberies, and all his Trophies but shining Rapines. Was it not the sense of this that made *Charles* the Fifth, who may be also called *Great,* after all his Victories, retire from a Throne into a Cloister, out of meer remorse for all the Streams of Blood he had shed, to make the last part of his Life an Attonement for the Faults of the first?

And then if a *Roman Catholick* can break an Oath only for the pleasure of Conquering, which he knows is doing ill; shall not a *Popish* Prince in *England* have ten times more inclination to break an Oath for the propagation of his own Faith, which his Conscience

5. Louis XIV.

tells him is Meritorious? For, besides the specious flattery, *That Kings can do no ill;* and *That all Crimes are cancelled in a Crown,* he has Religion to drive the Royal *Jehu* on; Religion, that from the beginning of the World, through all Ages, has set all Nations in a Flame, yet never confesses itself in the wrong. Besides, how can a *Popish* Prince, in attempting to establish his own Religion, believe he does his Subjects an Injustice in that very thing in which he does God Justice; or think he injures them, when he does their Souls right? Alas! no: When *Rome* by her insinuating Witchcrafts has lifted the full Bowl of her Inchantments to his Lips, what will his holy enthusiastick Rage do less than the hot-brained drunken *Alexander?* All his best Friends, and every honest *Clytus* that dares but thwart his Frenzy, is presently his Frenzy's Sacrifice: only with this difference; the frantick *Alexander,* after his drunken Fit was over, in his milder and more sensible Intervals, with all the compunctions of penitence, could mourn and groan for what his blinder Rage had murdered. But Religious Frenzy leaves that eternal Intoxication behind it, that where it commits all the Cruelties in the World, 'tis never sober after to be sorry for it. Thus whilst a *Popish* King sets his whole Kingdom in a combustion, how little does he think he plays a second *Nero?* Good consciencious Man, not he. Alas! he does not tune his Joys to the Tyrannick *Nero's Harp,* but to *David's* milder and more sacred *Lyre;* whilst in the height of his pious Ecstasy he sings *Te Deum* at the Conflagration. Thus with an arbitrary unbounded Power, what does his licencious holy thirst of Blood do less, than make his Kingdom a larger Slaughter-house, and his *Smithfield* an Original Shambles? Thus the old *Moloch* once again revives, to feast and riot on his dear Human Sacrifice. And whilst his fiery Iron Hands crush the poor burning Victim dead, the propagation of Religion, and the Glory of God, as he calls it, are the very Trumpets that deafen all the feeble Cries of Blood, and drown the dying Groans of what he murders.

Thus whilst the Bonds of Faith, Vows, Oaths, and Sacraments

can't hold a *Popish Successour,* what is that in an Imperial Head, but what in a private Man we punish with a Gaol and Pillory; whilst the perjured Wretch stands the universal Mark of Infamy, and then is driven from all Conversation, and like a Monster hooted from Light and Day. But the *Pope* and a Royal Hand may do anything; there's a Crown in the case to gild the Deeds his Royal Engins act.

———————*Et quod*
Turpe est Cerdoni, Volesos Brutosque, decebit.[6]

They are still that adorable Sovereign Greatness we must kneel to, and obey. What if a little perjured Villain has sworn a poor Neighbour out of a Cow or a Cottage! Hang him, inconsiderable Rogue, his Ears deserve a Pillory. But to Vow and Covenant, and forswear three Kingdoms out of their Liberties and Lives, that's Illustrious and Heroick. There's Glory in great Atchievements, and Vertue in Success. Alas! a vast Imperial *Nimrod* hunts for Nobler Spoils, flies at a whole Nation's Property and Inheritance. A Game worthy a Son of *Rome,* and Heir of Paradise. And to lay the mighty Scene of Ruine secure, he makes his Coronation Oath, and all his Royal Protestations, (those splendid Baits of premeditated Perjury) the Cover and Skreen to the hidden fatal Toil laid to insnare a Nation.

But now to their main Objection: *Some People will tell us, That 'tis wholly impossible for any Popish Successor, by all his Arts or Endeavours whatever, to introduce Popery into* England.

To this I answer, If he's a Papist that says so, he knows he belies his Conscience; for our late Hellish Plot[7] is a plain Demonstration, that their whole Party believed it possible. For did not the late Secretary St. *Coleman's* Records[8] tell us, *That the pestilent Northern*

6. And that which is a disgrace for Cerdonus will be decent or fitting for the Volesuses and Brutuses.

7. The supposed Popish Plot of 1678.

8. Edward Coleman, a convert to Catholicism, became a victim of the Popish Plot scare. He served as secretary to the Duke and later the Duchess of York. His correspondence with Catholics abroad about the restoration of Catholicism in England appeared to investigators to involve a plot to kill Charles II. He was executed in December 1678.

Heresy was to be rooted out, and *that now they had as much hopes of accomplishing that Sacred Work of* Rome, *as they had in Queen* Mary's *days?* Could anything be plainer, than that the subtle *Jesuits* had formed a Design to effect it? For it is contrary to Reason, and even Nature itself, (as bloody as their Principles are) to think they aimed at the Life of their King, and would play the Regicides only to commit the blackest of Murders, for meerly Murder's sake. No: They had the assurance under a presumptive Popish Heir, of making a National Conversion; and how little privy soever he might possibly be to their principal and hellish Blow, yet they had that perfect insight into the very Soul of a *Papist,* that they were satisfied that under that Notion it was impossible for him to be otherwise than a Man of *Rome's* right stamp, and their Heart's own liking. And if under such a Successour, their hopes of a Nation's Conversion were equal to those in Queen *Mary's* time, no doubt the converting Means must have been as Bloody or Bloodier than hers. For if after the short Infancy of seven years' Reformation, under the Protestant *Edward* the Sixth's Reign, there wanted Fire and Faggot to restore the *Pope;* how much more will he want them for his Restoration, after an Exclusion of almost Sevenscore years together, with all the necessary Difficulties of regaining his Empire, where his Throne has been so long demolished? Nay, in *Edward's* Days the only detestation of the Fopperies, Idolatries, and Superstitions of *Rome,* was all that went to make a *Protestant Reformation.* Alas! the Beast was then but young: But his Horns are since grown stronger, and his Teeth and Tallons sharper: For, since that, we have had the notorious *Paris* and *Irish* Massacres,[9] when at one riotous Festival above 100,000 bleeding Protestant Hearts were all gorged by the devouring Monster in a Night. Add to these, the successive Villanies of Gunpowder-Treasons, Fired Cities, with Plots against Kings and Kingdoms, which serve to heighten the Protestant Abhorrency. And if after all this we must still be con-

9. The Paris massacre was the St. Bartholomew's Day massacre of August 1572; the massacre of Protestants in Ireland occurred in October 1641.

verted, most certainly his Holiness must follow *Nebuchadnezzar's* Example, and heat his Fiery Furnace seven times hotter than formerly.

Thus far we are convinced that the *Jesuits* believed it possible; and they are too cunning and politick a sort of People, to be deceived with Shadows, or make Mountains of Mole-hills. And that it may not be objected, *That their Zeal has blinded their Reason,* let us but rightly consider, how far the first Foundations of *Popery,* (*viz. Arbitrary Power*) may be laid in *England.* First, then, if a *Papist* Reign, we very well understand that the Judges, Sheriffs, Justices of the Peace, and all the Judiciary Officers, are of the King's Creation: And as such, how far may the Influence of Preferment on baser Constitutions, culled out for his purpose, prevail even to deprave the very Throne of Justice herself, and make our Judges use even our *Protestant Laws* themselves to open the first Gate to Slavery. Alas! the Laws, in corrupted Judges' hands, have been too often used as barbarously as the Guests of *Procrustes,* who had a Bed for all Travellers; but then he either cut them shorter, or stretched them longer, to fit them to it. Well, but if the Publick Ministers of Justice betray the Liberty of the Subject, the Subject may petition for a Parliament to punish them for it. But what if he will neither hear one, nor call the other? Who shall compel him? The intailed Revenues of the Crown are much larger than his *Popish* Predecessors ever enjoyed, notwithstanding all the Branches of it that terminate with the Life of this present King. Besides, if this will not do, there's no doubt but he'll find sufficient Assistance from the *Pope, English Papists,* and Foreign Princes. And then having but a prudent Eye, and a tenacious Hand, to manage his Exchequer, we shall find he'll never call that People he shall never have need of. And then where are our Parliaments, and a Redress for all the Grievances and Oppressions in the World? But all this while the *Pope* is not Absolute, there wants a Standing Army to crown the Work. And he shall have it; for who shall hinder him? Nay, all his Commanders shall be qualified, even by our present Protestant Test, for the Employment. He shall have enough Men of the Blade out of one half of the Gaming-houses in Town, to Officer twice as many Forces as he shall want. 'Tis true, they shall be Men of no Estates nor Principles; but they shall fight as well as those that have both: For People are ever as valiant that have their Fortunes to raise, as those that have them to defend: nay, of the two they shall be more faithful to him; for they have no Property to be concerned for, and will more zealously serve him, by reason their whole Interest and Estates lie in him? And that this Army may be more quietly raised, how many Honourable Pretences may be found? Perhaps the greatest and most importunate Preservation of his Kingdom shall call for it; and then, upon second thoughts, instead of defeating some Foreign Enemy, they are opportunely ready to cut our Throats at home, if we do not submit, and give all that this King shall ask. And then I hope none will deny, but his Revenue may be as great as he and his Popish Counsellors shall think fit to make it.

Thus far we have given the Pourtracture of a *Popish King*. And now let us take a Draught of his Features in his Minority; that is, whilst he is only a *Popish Heir Apparent*.

Imagine then a long and prosperous Reign of a *Protestant* Prince, a Prince so excellently qualified, that true Original of Clemency, Goodness, Honour, all the most dazling Beams of Majesty: That with all his Sacred Princely Endowments he renders himself so true a Viceregent of Heaven in his Three Kingdoms, so near an Image of God in the moderation of his Temper, and the dispensation of his Laws, that even the nearness of his affinity to Heaven should entitle him to the dearest Care of it. And to prove him the dearest Care of Heaven, imagine likewise that Heaven has given him a People of those loyal and grateful Principles, looking up with that thankful Allegiance, and kneeling with that humble Veneration to the best of Kings, the Authour of their Prosperity, and the Founder of his Kingdom's Glory, that they have made it the greatest study of their Obedience to deserve so good a King. Witness in all Exigences their cordial tendering their Lives to serve him, and so far endeavouring to strengthen his Scepter and his Sword, till perhaps they have added those Gems to his Crown, that all his Princely Ancestors could never boast of: Being so truly strenuous in rendering their Purses and Fortunes his absolute Votaries, till they have made his Revenue more than trebbly exceed all his Royal Predecessors: And not stopping here, but upon all occassions continuing their generous and unwearied Bounty. Nay, that too, not always where his People's safety, and his Kingdom's Glory, but where his private Satisfaction called for it; as if they were resolved to yield their Hands and Hearts so entire a Sacrifice to Majesty, that they would gratify even his softest Wishes, studying to sweeten his Fatigue of Empire with all the Pleasures of a Throne.

Now let us suppose, after a long Tranquillity of this matchless Monarch's Reign, That the immediate Heir to his Crown and a part of his Blood, by the Sorceries of *Rome* is cankered into a *Papist*. And to pursue this Landscape, we see this once happy flourishing Kingdom so far (as in all Duty and Reason bound) concerned for themselves, their Heirs, and their whole Country's safety, till with an honest, cautious, prudent Fear they begin to inspect a Kingdom's universal Health; till weighing all the Symptoms of its State, they plainly descry those Pestilential Vapours fermenting, that may one day infect their Air, and sicken their World; and see that rising Eastern Storm engendering, that will once bring in those more than *Egyptian* Locusts, that will not only fill their Houses and their Temples, but devour their Labours, their Harvests, and their Vintages. Thus they so long survey their threatened Country's Danger, till with a more than Prophetick horrour, they manifestly discover all the inseparable Concomitants of a *Popish Successour;* and, like true Patriots, anticipate their Woes, with a present sense of the future Miseries they foresee.

With these just Resentments of their dangerous State, 'tis easie to conclude what follows. What is this *Popish Heir* in the Eye of *England*, but perhaps the greatest and only Grievance of the Nation, the universal Object of their Hate and Fear, and the Subject of their Clamours and Curses? At whose Door lie their Discontents and Murmurs; But 'tis Murmurs so violent, that they thrust in amongst their very Prayers, and become almost a part of their Devotions: Murmurs so bold, that they dare approach the very Palace, nay Throne and Ear of Majesty. And whenever the People of *England* reflect on this Heir as their King in Reversion, they have reason to look upon him as no better than *Jupiter's* Stork amongst the Frogs. Yes, notwithstanding all his former Glories and Conquests, his whole Stock of Fame is so lost and buried in his Apostacy from the Religion, and consequently the Interest of these Protestant Kingdoms, that all his Services are cancelled, and his whole Mass of Glory corrupted.

Suppose likewise this *Popish* Heir for many years so blest in the Tenderness and Friendship of the best of Kings, that there is not that Favour or Honour within the reach or wish of Majesty, that he has not made it the Study of his whole Reign to confer upon him; whilst his Greatness and Lustre have been so much his dearest darling Care, as if the promoting his Interest had been the Support of his own; till in short he has had so large a share in the Bosom of this Royal *Pylades*, this kindest and most gracious of Princes, as if one Soul had animated them both.

On this Foundation, as great Affections are not easily removed, and Sympathy is that Bond which Human Power can never dissolve, suppose moreover, that this inseparable Tie continues so long, notwithstanding all the Changes of Principles and Religion, a Biass so heavy that it almost overturns a Kingdom. Yet still the force of Nature and Friendship surmounts them all, and stands that zealous unshaken Bulwark, for the protection and safety of this dearest part of himself; till at length he does little less than act so over-fond a *Pelican*, that he exhausts even his own Vitals to cherish him.

Thus whilst the long and lawful Fears of a drooping Nation have fully and justly satisfied them, that the kindest and most favourable Aspect of a Majesty that smiles on *England*, through the defence and Interest of a *Popish Heir*, shines but like the Sun through a Burning-glass, whose gentlest morning Vernal Beams, through that fatal *Medium*, do but burn and consume what otherwise they would warm and cherish; what can the Consequence of this unhappy Friendship be, but that the very Souls and Loyalties of almost a whole Kingdom are staggered at this fatal Conjunction; till I am afraid there are too many, who in detestation of that one gangrened Branch of Royalty, can scarce forbear (how undutifully soever) to murmur and revile even at that Imperial Root that cherishes it? Insomuch that those very Knees that but now would have bowed into their very Graves to serve him, grown daily and hourly so far from bending (as they ought) to a Crowned Head, till they are almost as stubborn as their Petitions and Prayers have been ineffectual.

Thus whilst a *Popish Heir's* extravagant Zeal for *Rome* makes him shake the very Throne that upholds him, by working and incroaching on the Affections of Majesty for that Protection and Indulgence that gives Birth and Life to the Heart-burnings of a Nation; what does he otherwise, than in a manner stab his King, his Patron, and his Friend, in his tenderest part, his Loyal Subjects' Hearts? Which certainly is little less than to play the more lingering sort of Parricide; a part so strangely unnatural, that even Savages would blush at; yet this Religion, incorrigible remorseless Religion, never shrinks at.

Thus whilst the Universal Nerves of a whole strugling Nation bend their united force against the Invasion of Pope and Popery, in studying to prevent Tyranny, they grow jealous of Monarchy. And fearing lest their Loyal Aid to the Father of their Countrey should unhappily contribute to the strengthening of the Subverters of their peace and liberty, instead of that Tributary-gold which once they so cheerfully showered at their Dread Soveraign's feet, now on the contrary the protection of a Popish Successor makes them so far from supplying the real and most pressing Necessities of Majesty, that they are rather well pleased and triumph in his greatest wants, and that perhaps when his Glory, nay possibly when his nearest Safety calls for their Assistance.

Thus what does this Popish Heir in tying up the hands of a whole Nation from their just devotion to their King, but only this, In return for the accumulated honours heaped upon him, he most inhumanly starves the very hand that fed him. An Ingratitude that even an Infidel would be ashamed of. But this Religion, incorrigible remorseless Religion, never blushes at.

Besides, if there can be a Son of that Royal Martyr *Charles* the First, a Prince so truly pious, that his very Enemies dare not asperse his Memory or Life with the least blemish of Irreligion; a Prince that sealed the *Protestant Faith* with his blood; who in his deplorable Fate and ignominious Death, bore so near a resemblance to that of the Saviours of the World, that his Sufferings can do no less than seat him at the right hand of Heaven. If, I say, there can be a Son of that Royal Protestant, of that uncharitable *Popish* Faith, who by the very Tenets of his Religion dooms all that die without the bosome of their Church, irreparably damned; then consequently he must barbarously tear up his Father's sacred Monument, brand his blessed memory with the name of Heretick; and to compleat the horrid *Anathema*, he most impiously execrates the very Majesty that gave him being.

Then in fine, provided and granted that we have an Heir to the Imperial Crown of *England* perverted to the *Romish* Faith, and consequently of that depraved constitution and principles, that he has neither charity for the Stock from whence he sprang, concern or care for the safety, peace, glory or prosperity of the best of Patrons, Friends and Kings; nor lastly, any remorse for all the groans of an afflicted Kingdom. What promises can we give ourselves of his future Reign, when we have all these fatal prognosticks before hand? *Ex pede Hercules.*[10] Or is it likely, he will have greater care and tenderness for a Nation's peace, when he shall be seated on a Throne, and have more power to take it from them?

But says a Critick to all this, *Suppose this Popish Heir undoubtedly believes (as a Papist must do) that there's no way to Heaven but his own; should he so far comply with the glory or interest of his King, though a Father or a Brother, on the one side, and the quiet and safety of a Nation on the other, as to renounce his principles of Christianity, and conform to theirs? What were that, but to purchase their peace with his own damnation; and to sacrifice his own Soul, for their worldly interests? And certainly neither Duty, nor Allegiance, nor any tie whatever, ought to extort that from him. And then, if all the grievances of a Kingdom lie at his door, alas, the worst can be said of him is, that if he be any occasion of it, 'tis his unhappiness, and not his fault. More especially, provided he is only passive, and that we plainly see that during his being this Popish Heir, he acts nothing that may encourage or favour Popery in the least.*

Pray, by the way, How must it follow that if we do not plainly see him act, that therefore he must not act? Does no man act, but he that publickly treads the Stage? Does no man sit at the Helm, but he that visibly holds the Rudder? Does no wind stir the troubled Sea into a Tempest, but what the poor Mariners both hear and feel? No Storm, but that which lightens in their Eyes, and thunders in their Ears, to warn them 'tis coming? Alas, alas, the greatest Hurricanes are only made by subterranean Winds. A secret, silent, underground working Mine of ruine, which never bursts out till it destroys, and which no man hears or sees till he is lost.

10. From the foot of Hercules.

But to return to the objection, *The grievance of a Nation may be his unhappiness, and not his fault,* &c. That is, in short, he cannot help it. Very right. And so when this *Popish* Heir comes to the Crown, and promotes the *Romish* Interest with all the Severity, Injustice, and Tyranny, that Religious Cruelty can invent, his answer will be, he cannot help it, or at least cannot withstand those irresistible motives that prompt him to their execution, which is the same thing. The injunctions of his conscience make him as active now in the ruining a Kingdom's peace, as he was passive in it before. For who can be so void of common sense, as not to know that the same impulse of conscience that makes a man a *Roman Catholick,* will make him act like one when opportunity serves? And what greater opportunity to establish *Popery,* than for a *Papist* to wear a Crown? And though perhaps the stubborn *English Genius* will not easily bend to the Superstition of *Rome,* yet since his Almighty Friend the *Pope,* the undisputed Keeper of the Keys of *Paradice,* will no doubt assign him no common Diadem in Heaven for so glorious a Task as a Nation's conversion, who then will not make that sacred Work the study of years, which cannot be accomplisht in a day, for such a Reward? Especially when he has these two infallible arguments to spur him on in so godly a Cause: First then, he is of a Religion that makes human Merit the path to salvation. *Merit,* the *Roman Catholick* Exchequer, *Rome's* bottomless Golden Mine. *Merit,* that makes the frighted dying sinner starve his own blood, and pawn his Estate to redeem his soul. *Merit,* that drains the Wealth of Nations into the priestly Coffers, and makes the Luxury of a World the pampered riotous Church-man's Inheritance. *Merit,* that can make a *Loretto* Chappel vie with a *Venetian Arsenal;* and *Rome's* Altars, Cloisters, and Convents, rise so high, so rich, so numerous, and so magnificent, though the impoverisht Widow's groans, and the naked Orphan's cries do little less towards the building than a second *Amphion.* Nay *Merit,*

that can consecrate Daggers, and kill Kings. Thus whilst he has the
Wonder-working *Merit* for his Tutor, what greater and more Meritorious act to canonize him a Saint of the first magnitude, than the
converting of an Apostatized Heretical Kingdom?

And then next, he is of Religion that does not go altogether in the
old fashion Apostolical way of preaching and praying & teaching all
Nations, &c. but scourging, and wracking, and broiling them into
the fear of God. A Religion that for its own propagation will at any
time authorize its Champions to divest themselves of their humanity, and act worse than Devils, to be Saints. And thus whilst neither
the cries of blood can deter him on the one side, and so no Tyranny
comes amiss to him; and next, that he has the undeniable assurance
of the greatest blessings of Eternity to encourage him on the other;
With these advantages, who would not be as active as a second *Rom-
ulus,* and with all his utmost vigour and pride, build up his *Rome's*
new Walls, though he made his nearest, nay the Nation's dearest
blood their Cement.

And thus what is a *Popish* Heir, but the most terrible and the most
dangerous of *England's* Enemies, and of all our Foes has the most inflexible invincible Enmity. Nay, the very outrages of Thefts, Murders, Adulteries, and Rebellions, are nothing to the pious Barbarities
of a *Popish* King. The Murderer and Adulterer may in time be re-
claimed by the precepts of Morality, and the terrors of conscience.
The thief by the dread of a Gallows may become honest. Nay, the
greatest Traitor, either by the fear of death, or the apprehensions of
Hell, may at last repent. But a *Papist* on a Throne has an unconfut-
able vindication for all his proceedings, challenges a Commission
even from Heaven for all his Cruelty dares act. And when the Inchantments of *Rome* have toucht his tongue with a cole from her Altars, what do his Enthusiasms make him believe, but that the most
savage and most hellish Dooms his blinded zeal can pronounce, are

the immediate Oracles of God? and all the apology a poor Nation can expect from him, is, *He cannot help it.*

I, *but,* (says the wisest Criticks we have met with yet) *if these be the dangers of a Popish King, why have we not such strong, such potent Laws made before this popish Heir come to the crown, that it shall be impossible for him ever to set up* Popery, *though he should never so much endeavour it?*

To this I answer; To endeavour to set up Popery by Law, even with the Laws that we have already against it, is impossible, and therefore the very supposition of the projection that way is nonsense. And on the other side, to conclude he'll endeavour to do it against Law, and so to make new Laws on purpose for him to break them with their fellows, is worse nonsense than the other. Besides, Who shall call this King to question for breaking these Laws, if he has the power and will to do it? I fancy that the only nearest illustration I can make upon this point in creating new Laws against Popery in case of a Popish Successor, is as politick a piece of work in the kind, as building the Hedge to fence in the Cuckow. 'Tis true, I will not deny, but a Popish King may be totally restrained from all power of introducing Popery, by the force of such Laws that may be made to tie up his hands; but then they must be such as must ruine his Prerogative, and put the executive power of the Laws into the hands of the people. If a King of *England* were no more than a *Stadt-holder* in *Holland,* or a *Duke* of *Venice,* no doubt Popery would have little hopes of creeping into *England;* which is in short, he that is no King, can be no Tyrant. But what Monarch will be so unnatural to his own blood, so ill a Defender, and so weak a Champion for the Royal Dignity he wears, as to sign and ratify such Laws as shall entail that effemenacy and that servility on a Crown, as shall render the Imperial Majesty of *England* but a Pageant, a meer Puppet upon a Wire? If then no King will assent to make Laws to do it this way, and no Laws can do it the other, all laws against Popery, in case of a Popish Successour, are as I told you before, but building the Hedge, &c. For indeed, how can the force of Laws made by a Protestant Predecessour, and a Protestant Parliament, in any sort bind a Popish Successour, when the very first advance of the Pope's Supremacy introduces that higher power, those Canonick Ecclesiastick Laws, which no Secular, or any Temporal Court can or may controul? Laws that shall declare, not only all the Statutes and Acts of Parliament made against the Dignity of Mother Church, void and null, but the very Lawmakers themselves as Hereticks, wholly uncapable of ever having any right of making such Laws. No doubt then, but that fire that burns those Heretick Lawmakers, shall give their Laws the same Martyrdom.

With this certain prospect, both of the Ruin of their Estates, Lives, and Liberties, where lies the sin in the Commons of *England* to stand upon their guard against a *Popish* Successor? Ay, a God's name let them stand upon their guards, and use all expedients to keep out *Popery* and *Tyranny,* provided still that we preserve the sacred Succession in its right line; for that we are told both King and people are obliged in conscience to defend and uphold.

I think I need not insist further in multiplying arguments to prove how far 'tis impossible to do one without the other; but on the other side let us examine how the defending and establishing a *Popish* Successor, is an obligation on our Duties or Consciences.

First then, let us fancy we see this *Popish* Heir on his Throne, and by all the most illegal and arbitrary means, contrary to the whole frame and hinges of the *English* government, introducing *Popery* with that zeal and vigour, till his infatuated conscience has perverted the King into a Tyrant. And not to stop here, If the Constitution of the *English* Majesty makes a King supreme Moderator and Governour both Ecclesiastick and Civil; What does this *Popish* King by admitting the *Pope's* Church-supremacy, but divest himself of half his Royalty, whilst like the junior King of *Brainford* in the play, he resigns and alienates the right and power of Majesty to an Invader and Usurper? And whilst we are thus enslaved by a Medley-Government betwixt Tyranny and Usurpation, by establishing a *Papist* on a Throne, we are so far from preserving the Crown, that is, the Imperial Dignity, in a right line of Succession, that we do not preserve it at all, but on the contrary extirpate and destroy it, whilst by enthroning a *Papist* we totally subvert and depose the very Monarchy itself. And can it be the duty of either *English* men or Christians, to have that zeal for a corrupted leprous Branch of Royalty, that we must ruine both Religion, Government, and Majesty itself, to support him? How much more consistent would it be with the honest, prudent, and lawful means of a Nation's preservation, to take out one link out of the whole Chain of Succession, than by preserving that, to break the whole to pieces? Next let us see, who 'tis the Commons of *England* would render uncapable of inheriting the Imperial Crown; a Prince of the Royal Blood, nurst and bred up in the Protestant Allegiance and Faith, and afterwards seduced and perverted to the *Romish* principles and Superstition. And what's that, but a Prince whom the unanimous Voice both of King and People (for such are the Laws of *England*) have declared guilty of High-Treason, as we find it in the first Statute in the 23d of *Elizabeth*.

Statute.

Be it declared and enacted by the Authority of this present parliament, That all persons whatever, which have, or shall have, or pretend to have power, or shall by any way or means put in practice to absolve, perswade, or withdraw any the Queen's Majestie's Subjects, or any within her Highness's Realms and Dominions, from their natural Obedience to her Majesty; or withdraw them for that intent from the Religion now by her Highness's Authority establisht within her Highness's Dominions, to the

Romish *Religion, or to make them, or any of them, to promise any Obedience to any pretended Authority of the See of* Rome, *or any other
Prince, State, or Potentate, to be had or used within her Dominions; or
shall do any Overt Act to that intent or purpose; and every of them, shall
be to all intents adjudged to be Traitors; and being thereof Lawfully convicted, shall have Judgment to suffer and forfeit as in case of High-
Treason.*

*And if any person, shall after the end of this Sessions of Parliament, by
any means be willingly Absolved, or withdrawn as aforesaid, or willingly
reconciled, or shall promise any such obedience to any such pretended Authority, Prince, State, or Potentate, as is aforesaid; then every such person,
their Procureres and Councellors thereunto, being thereof lawfully Convicted, shall be tried and judged, and shall suffer and forfeit as in cases of
High-Treason.*

Nor was this Act any more than a Confirmation and Explanation of
an Act made before in the 13th year of her Reign; *Where 'tis likewise
declared, That if any person, or persons, shall willingly receive or take any
Absolutions, or Reconciliations from the See of* Rome, *that they and their
Seducers shall be equally guilty of High Treason.* Nay, we have an Act
even in *Henry* the 8th's Reign, in which is declared, *That any man
that shall refuse the Oath of* Henry's *Supremacy in renunciation of the
Pope, shall be guilty of High Treason.*

If then we have a Popish Heir presumptive of the same brand that
these Laws have markt him out, I would ask what crime 'tis in the
people of *England* to endeavour to disable a Traitor from wearing a
Crown? Besides, they consider they are under a regulated and
bounded Government, a Government where no man stands or falls
but by his own act and decree; whilst the whole dispensation of
Meum and *Tuum* are made by every man's self, or his Representatives. Since then the people of *England* as the Lawmakers are an essential part of the Government, and are fully assured in the Reign of

a Papist, that Right will be destroyed, why should not they be as active and vigorous for their own Royal Inheritance, and Sacred Succession of Power, as a King for his? Nay they ought to be the more vigorous of the two. For the King in defending a *Popish* Heir, protects but that Successor, whose Tyranny he shall never live to see (since it commences but from his Grave), but the people of *England* in Asserting their Rights and Liberties, and defending themselves and their Heirs, do oppose that Tyranny which they both live to see and feel. And that they may assure themselves they shall feel it, if ever a Papist mounts this Throne, then all their Murmurs, their Petitions, Protestings and Association Votes will be remembered to the purpose. He that has gone a long and tiresome Journey, through Brakes and Briars to a splendid Palace, when once in possession, will send out to Root up all those Thorns, and weed those Thistles that gored him in the way. Alas! too sure he'll make good that old promise of God to the seed of the woman, *He'll crush their Heads, that bruised his heels.* And would it not be hard, that the folly and fall of one man, should renew our old *Adam's* misfortune, and entail a Curse on our whole English Generation? If the policy of *Rome*, like the old Serpent's subtilty, has puft him up into an ambition and lust of being equal to God's; may he have *Adam's* success too, whilest the Protestant hearts and hands of *England,* stand like the Angel's Flaming Sword to expel him from that once hereditary Paradice, which now his Apostacy has justly forfeited and lost.

Besides, that the disinheriting of an Heir to the Crown of *England* may not appear a thing so illegal, or indeed so monstrous as some people would make it, I would only refer those vehement assertors of the inviolable right of succession, to our own Chronicles for their confutation. For they'll find not only the succession was scarce ever kept for Three Kings' Reigns together, in a direct line of descent, since the Conquest; but that the Crown and Succession were frequently disposed and setled by Acts of Parliament. I shall need in-

stance but in some few particulars; In the 25. of *Henry* the *8th.* we
find the Parliament ordering the Succession, and enacting, *That the
Imperial Crown of this Realm shall be to King* Henry *the* 8th, *and to the
Heirs of his body lawfully begotten on Queen* Ann, *and the Heirs of the
bodies of such several sons respectively, according to the course of inheritance; and for default of such Issue, then to the sons of his body in like manner; and upon failure of such issue, then to the Lady* Elizabeth, *&c.* By
the same Statute is every subject at full age obliged by an Oath to defend the contents of this, and the refusal made misprision of Treason. In the 28th year of his Reign, was that Act repealed, and the
Parliament entailed the Crown on the Heirs of his Body by Queen
Jane, the Lady *Mary* and the Lady *Elizabeth* being both declared illegitimate, the first as the Daughter of *Katherine,* formerly his
Brother's Wife, and divorced; and the last as the Daughter of *Anne
Boleign,* attainted of High Treason. *And in case he died without issue,
then the Parliament empowered him by the same Act to dispose of the Succession by his own Letters patents, or his last Will. In the 35th* year of his
Reign the *Parliament granted the Succession to* Edward, *and for want
of heirs of his body, to the Lady* Mary, *and the heirs of her body; and for
want of such heirs, to the Lady* Elizabeth; *but both subject to such conditions as the King should limit by his Letters patents, or by his last Will
signed by his hand; and if the King left no such conditions by his Will, or
under his Letters patents, then either of them should enjoy the Imperial
Crown with the limitations only made in that Act.* By these Acts we
may plainly see that the succession of the *English* Crown was wholly
subjected to the disposal, determinations, and limitations of Parliament. And that we may be well assured that that right lay in them,
Henry the *8th* was a Prince of that wisdom and prudence, and so far
from submitting to Parliaments, that we may be very well assured,
that he would never have complimented them with a power that was
not their due. If he had thought in the least that he could have disposed of the Succession himself, no doubt but he would have chal-

lenged the prerogative, had he had it to challenge. And as in every one of these three Acts they declared that their zeal for setling the Succession was for prevention of those mischiefs, and that bloodshed that might possibly be occasioned by future disputes; Here 'tis observed, that whilst they thus bandied the Succession so many various ways, by three several Acts in one King's Reign, they did not so much respect the preservation of the Right Heir, as the Kingdom's safety. For had they been so passionately tender for the next of blood in that age, as some would have us be in this, they would never have excluded the Lady *Mary* and *Elizabeth* from the Crown in one Act, or never have readmitted them again in another. Besides one thing is remarkable in these Acts of Parliament, *viz.* the last Act of Parliament gives the Succession to those very Ladies whom the King and Parliament had before declared and recorded illegitimate. Nay, they had proceeded so far, as to make it Treason for any man by writing or printing to say or declare that either the Lady *Mary* or the Lady *Elizabeth* were legitimate; and yet afterwards these were no impediments to debar them from a Throne. And *England* was never more blest, than under the long and glorious Reign of that excellent Princess *Elizabeth*, how illegitimate soever she had been rendered. I shall only cite one Act more, and that is the 13. of *Elizabeth*, where 'tis made Treason to *affirm the Right of succession of the Crown to be in any other than the Queen; or to affirm that the Laws and Statutes made in Parliament, do not bind the Right of the Crown, and the descent, limitation, inheritance, and governance thereof.* If after so plain and evident proofs of the undeniable power of Parliaments, we meet so many snarlers against the proceedings of the last, I know no excuse they can make for themselves, but by owning their ignorance to be as great as their impudence.

If then (which no man in his right wits can deny) our Religion, Lives, and Liberties are only held by a Protestant Tenure, and the Majesty of *England* not only by the force of his Coronation Oath, but by all the ties whatever ought to be the pillar and bulwark of the Protestant Faith, and at the same time granting that we have a Popish Prince to inherit the Imperial Crown of *England*, he ought certainly in all Justice as little to ascend this Throne, as *Nebuchadnezzar* ought to have kept his when the immediate blast of Heaven had made him so uncapable of ruling as a King, that he was only a companion fit for brutes and savages. And if he had no injustice done him when he was thrust out into his proper Element, to feed and herd with the Beasts of the field; a Papist Heir of *England* with that persuasion and principles so destructive to the *British* State, has as little wrong done him in being debared from the Succession, as a fitter Guest for a Cloister than a Throne. I remember story tells us, That the Mother of *Paris*, the Son of King *Priam*, dreaming before his birth she had brought forth a firebrand that should one day set their *Troy* in flames, immediately upon this the afflicted King as a true Father of his Countrey, notwithstanding all the compunctions of Nature, and ties of blood, was so far from cherishing even his own Race, and a Branch of himself, that he ordered the Infant to be bred up amongst Swains, as the Son of a Shepherd, where divested of all his Princely Fortunes, and ignorant of his own high blood, he should end his days in ignoble obscurity. And all this out of the prophetick horror but of a dream, that seemed to threaten the peace and safety of his Kingdom. And how much more reason has the present Power of *England*, for effectually opposing Popery by disinheriting a Popish Successor, when under a Popish Monarch, our *Troynovant* has the undeniable assurance of being put into a flame; when *Priam's* fear was but a Dream? How fabulous soever this Story may appear, yet I am certain we have too much reason to esteem the moral of it Oraculous. And surely our present greatest Sticklers for an unbroken Succession of the Crown, must of all mankind set but a very little price upon their Countrey, and conclude our *England* the most inconsiderable part of Christendom, when the interest of one man shall outweigh that of Three Kingdoms, with the whole safety of Religion it-self, and the Glory of God to fill up the Ballance. But indeed they are resolved to be positive: and be the next of Blood a Papist or a Mahumetan, yet if he be born to it, let him Govern us; And truly I cannot forbear to repeat one of their commonest Arguments, and as they think strongest; which is, If the Son of a private Gentleman, though a Papist, shall inherit and quietly possess his hereditary Es-tate; is it not hard, nay barbarous injustice, That the Son of a King, and the Heir of a Crown, should lose his Patrimony of Three King-doms for being a Papist?

Though this Argument, as *Argumentum a Fortiori*, has mighty sound in it, yet how feeble will it appear, when the Analogy shall be examined!

That Papist Gentleman that's born to an Estate, may peaceably inherit it, yes, and with some reason for it: For he's a Subject of a Protestant Kingdom, and as such has Protestant Laws to rule him. He can neither force his Neighbour or his Tenant to Mass, or im-prison or burn them for Hereticks, nor seize their Estates as forfeited to *Rome,* whilst he is a Papist. His Religion is only to himself, and if he takes any violent or unlawful course to propagate his own persua-sion, he's not so big but he may be brought into *Westminster-Hall* to answer for it. Nay, possibly the Papist Subject under a Protestant Government, may sometimes behave himself as a more harmless and quiet Commonwealth's-man, than a Protestant himself, if for no other than his own preservation, as not daring to awaken that Jus-tice that may inflict the penal statutes against him for his Recusancy.

But how directly contrary to all this is the influence of a Romish Heir, when there is not one of all these destructive qualities (of which a private man can ne're be guilty) that he on the other side shall not vigorously and undoubtedly put in execution, when once the acqui-sition of a Crown has Enabled him for it, as we have at large dis-coursed before? And if the Princely Popish Heir be disinherited, when a private Gentleman escapes, 'tis not for his Religion, for that may be alike in both; but for his uncontroulable power of establishing that Religion, which a Royal station will inevitably give him.

Alas, the Protestant strength is above the fear of any little Popish Beasts of prey: It only behoves their safety, to hunt the Imperial Lion down.

If then the English Blood boils so high, and the access of a Papist to a Throne must necessarily meet a passage so difficult, with all these solid Bars between; if his Religion were as Honourable as 'tis invincible, what deathless Fame, and what eternal Trophies might a Popish Heir atchieve, if the welfare of a King and Kingdoms could so far influence him, as freely of himself to make the union of King and people a work of his own creation, by slacking the fatal strength of a too generous Brother's over-violent Friendship; and so rendering our universal peace his inclination, and not necessity?

I remember in the old Roman History, when a long Plague had reigned in *Rome*, and an Earthquake had opened a prodigious Gulph in the middle of the *Forum*, their *Consulteo Oracle* told them, that neither the Plague should be stopt, nor the breach closed, till the most noble Victime in *Rome* had appeased their angry Deity. When *Curtius*, a Noble Youth of *Rome*, of the best and highest *Roman* quality, most Princely adorned, and most gallantly mounted on Horseback, with a look so gay and so cheerful, more like that of a Bridegroom than a Sacrifice, amidst a Thousand wondering tender eyes around him; rode headlong into the yawning Pit. Thus falling, unterrified at so dreadful a precipice for his Country's deliverance, he extorted the promise of the Oracle; for the Pestilence ceased, and the closing Earth sealed up his Grave.

The voluntary resignation of a Popish Heir, would be no less signal National service in the present exigance of *England*, than that of *Curtius* in *Rome*; only 'tis attended with milder circumstances. Our State, as dangerous as it is, does not require any sanguinary sacrifice.

The Cure he might make to all our plagues, would be only the easier oblation of quitting the doubtful prospect of a remote and Craggy Throne; and that too, to refix a shaking Crown, to regain the hearts of a whole Nation, and build himself that Pyramid of Honour, which would outshine the wearing a Diadem.

Besides, let Plotting but once end, and the Pendant Sword, which like that of *Damocles* hangs but by a Hair over our Sovereign's Head, be safely sheathed, and give Nature fair play, the little disparity of their years considered, the resigning of a Crown in all human probability, would not appear at so much distance, and such uncertainty, altogether so extravagant an offering, especially when 'tis made for a King and Brother's safety and glory, a Kingdom's peace and prosperity, nay indeed the whole repose of Christendom, when the concordance of the King and Parliament is the greatest means for strengthening those foreign Alliances, that may give check to the fatal growth of *France*.

Nay, above all this, what immortal glory would it bring even to the Romish Religion itself, when a Prince so immediately allied to a Crown, shall voluntary lay aside the hopes and pretensions to a temporal Diadem, for an immortal one? And how many more, at least more hearty Converts would so transcendent an example of piety make, beyond the utmost severer influence of a Throne? Nay, I may even without flattery say, the deed would make him so adorable, that for losing a Crown, he would almost raise himself an Altar.

But *Rome* (Heaven knows) has other work in hand, she'll have no proselites of that kind of creation; her mode of conversion, I assure you, lies quite another way. Besides, her Champions are not made of so pure and so refined an *Ore*, their *Minerals* are more coarse, and more alloyed. Her Saints, in spight of all their heavenly contemplations, have still so much of Earth about them, that like the feet of *Daniel's* Image, they are a mixture between Iron and Clay.

But to sum up all; If no reason must or shall prevail, and that right or wrong a Papist must succeed, when all the inseparable cruelties of Pope and Popery shall surround us; suppose the worst that may be, that the dreadful approach of certain slavery, so opposite to the freeborn genius of *England*, has exasperated them into a spirit of Rebellion; What is it but the pestilential Air of reigning Popery, that bloats and swells them into that Contagion? And if the Popish King summons all his Thunder to punish them for it, What can the greatest favourer of *Rome* make more on it, than that he warps them crooked, and then breaks them to pieces because they are not straight? And what's the whole sum of a revolting Nation under a Popish Tyrant, but using a violent cure, to expel an universal poison?

But here will some pretended pious objectors say, *How shall we dare to revolt? Remember we are Christians, and we must obey, or at least yield a passive obedience to our King; be his Religion, Principles, or Government never so Tyrannick, he is still the Lord's Anointed, and our native Soveraign.*

I would ask what this Lord's Anointed is? And who 'tis our Native Soveraign, when instead of being free Subjects, Pope and Tyranny shall rule over us, and we are made Slaves and Papists? We are bound indeed by our Oaths of Allegiance, to a constant Loyalty to the King and his Lawful Successours. Very right; by that Oath we are bound to be his lawful Successour's Loyal Subjects; but why his Loyal Slaves? Or how is an arbitrary absolute Popish Tyrant, any longer a Lawful Successour to a Protestant establisht and bounded Government, when lawfully succeeding to this limitted Monarchy, he afterwards violently, unlawfully, and tyrannically over-runs the due bounds of power, dissolves the whole Royal constitution of the Three Free States of *England*, and the Subjects' Petition of Right? Whilst wholly abandoning those Reins of Government which were his lawful birthright, and making new ones of his own illegal creation, he makes us neither those freeborn Subjects we were when we took that Oath, nor himself that King we swore to be Loyal to. But alas! that Bugbear *passive obedience* is a notion crept into the world, and most zealously, and perhaps as ignorantly defended. There never wanted the authority even of Holy Writ itself on all occasions to vindicate everything; and there's scarce a precedent in the oldest Historick part of the Bible, that shall not by an extorted Application, be appropriated even to the duty and necessity of all ages, places and constitutions of the world. For example, *They'll tell you that the Prophet* Samuel *makes this answer to the* Jews *that desired a King, That he would make their Sons and Daughters Slaves, and give their Fields, their Vineyards, and their Olive-yards, &c. to his Servants, and all this and much more they must expect from a King, &c. And ye shall cry out in that day, because of your King that you have chosen, and the Lord will not hear you in that day. Which was as much, as if the Prophet had said, If a King shall, as he may do this, you have no redress but to your Prayers for his conversion, and they perhaps too shall not be heard.* He does not tell them they might revolt or rebel to redress themselves; no, Heaven forbid he should. For what was the King they desired, but like those of the Nations about them? And what were those Kings but Absolute? In their own breath lay the voice of the Laws, and *Sic volo sic Jubeo*[11] was a Decree or Statute; and if they voluntarily submitted, and vowed allegiance to a King so absolute, and so arbitrary, as such they ought to obey him. And as they freely would run all risks of whatever might follow, it was their own choice, and *Volenti non fit Injuria.*[12] Here indeed a passive obedience was due; But what's this to a King of *England?* 'Tis not here, *Sic volo sic Jubeo,* here 'tis first *sic vult populus,* and then comes *sic jubet Rex.*[13] Here all our Laws and Decrees by which we are governed, are of the people's choice; first made by the Subject, and then confirmed by the King. Here a King cannot take our Sons and Daughters, or our Fields and Vineyards away, unless we please to give him them.

If the Three States of *England,* which we suppose the whole Body

---

11. Thus I will, and thus I command.
12. There is no injury (injustice) to one who is willing.
13. Thus wills the people; thus does the king command.

of *England* lawfully convened in Parliament, shall submit to such an arbitrary Majesty, to have their *Magna Charta* abolisht, their Religion and Liberties destroyed, and to have Popery and Arbitrary power set up, and yield to have the Right of Lords and Commons extirpated, and all devolve into the King, so that like the old Kings of *Israel,* he may set up Idols and molten Calves, and make us bow down and worship them; if they will do all this, then indeed we are his lawful Slaves, and as such, 'tis our duty to pay him an entire, undisputed obedience.

I would only beg the world seriously to consider how Monarchy itself is acquired and founded, and then the duty of Subjects will be more easily discerned.

Monarchy can be acquired but Two ways.

First, by the choice of the people, who frequently in the beginning of the world, out of the natural desire of safety, for the securing a peaceful Community and Conversation, chose a single person to be their Head, as a proper supream Moderator in all differences that might arise to disquiet that Community. Thus were Kings made for the people, and not the people for the King.

The other acquisition of Monarchy, was by Conquest. The glory and pleasure of Reigning grew so tempting, that (especially in later Ages) they spured on ambitious minds to obtain that by force, which in the infancy of Time, and the first original of Nations, appears to be generally the people's choice, and not compulsion.

However, whether choice or compulsion, yet after possesion, and the people's submission, the Right of Kings is sacred.

Now Conquest is twofold.

The first sort is, where the Conqueror wholly over-runs a Nation, or People, and like those that take Towns by storm, destroys and depopulates, kills or enslaves; and then establishes Religion, Rights and Laws, solely at the will of the Conqueror.

The other kind is, when the vanquisht come to capitulate before they yield, and only surrender upon terms.

Such was our last *Norman* Conquest, when the Inhabitants of *Kent*, and the Bishops of *London* upon a parley, prevailed with him (as our Records attest) to confirm their Customs and Rights establisht and granted them by *Edward* the Confessour, whilst the Lenity of the Conquerour, contenting himself with no larger a Prerogative than their last *Saxon* King had possest before him; submitted to make their own native common Laws of *England*, the Standard of his Justice, and the continuation of their Ancient Priviledges the cement of their new Allegiance.

In this mild Channel ran the English Monarchy, till in the Reign of *Henry* the *3d*, the *Magna Charta* was confirmed; which indeed was but a monumental Register of the Liberties and Immunities of English men, enjoyed before (though not so fixt) in their pious *Edward's* Reign. In this state has the Majesty of *England*, the Dignity of Parliaments, and the Liberty of the people (bating their former servility to *Rome*) continued ever since. And if now at last, Popery must and shall come in (as by Law it cannot) and consequently must be restored by Arbitrary power: If a new Monarchy, then a new Conquest; and if a Conquest, Heaven forbid we should be subdued like less than English men; or be debared the Common Right of all Nations, which is, to resist and repel an Invader if we can.

But to sum up all this, I must say, the most vehement Disputants against the people's Right of defending themselves, must at least acknowledg thus much, that whenever a Popish King shall by Tyranny establish the Pope's Jurisdiction in *England*, undoubtedly in the Eye of God he is guilty of a greater sin, than that people can be, that with open Arms oppose that Tyranny. For by introducing Popery by Tyranny, by one unjust power he establishes another as unjust; and by one ill, defends a worse: whereas the people of *England*, in taking

Arms against that Tyranny, defend a just Right, *viz.* their Religion, Lives and Liberties.

Thus when a Popish *Monarch* shall subvert all Right, and violate all Laws, till oppressing a wretched Nation, more like a *Lupus Agri*[14] than *Pater Patriae,* he so wholly perverts the Duty of his great Office, and defaces in himself the nearest Image of a Deity, by so falsly representing his Viceregent; Imagine on the other side, a persecuted deplorable People, even abandoned by God, and so exasperated by injustice till they struggle against the Yoke, and the Horrour of this *Gorgon* in spight of all their Native Duty, has hardened them into disobedience, and then what can a poor Nation expect but vengeance and destruction? If this be our Rod of Iron, this the King ordained to rule over us, What signifies all our long pudder about a Plot, give the Papists that point, and allow them all they dare ask, that there neither is nor has been any Popish Plot: That the Evidence are perjured, and that *Coleman's* Letters, *Godfrey's* Murder, and *Bedlow's* dying Attestations, *&c.* are nothing to the purpose. Grant this and twice as much more: yet allowing at the same time, that Providence has decreed us a Papist and a Bigot for a King; no matter then for Plotters, Jesuits, or Ruffians; The very essence of a Popish successor is the greatest Plot upon *England* since the Creation. A Plot of God himself to scourge a Nation, and make Three Kingdoms misarable. As for the other Plot, what was it but a secret Confederacy between a handful of feeble Villains, the Limbs of the Roman *Hydra*? But, alas! with all their designs they were but men, and as such we have seen them both detected and defeated. But if we are predestined for a Romish Government, that's a Plot indeed, a design formed by the irresistable decrees of Heaven either for our sins, or what cause to itself best known, to lay a groaning Country in ruine. Nay the ruin is so universal, we must give it no bounds. For upon the supposition of a Popish Heir,

14. Wolf of the field.

we must not conclude that 'tis only the poor distressed Protestants that shall feel the smart, and stand the mark of slavery and Martyrdom. A Popish King has that pestilential influence, that he blasts even the very party he smiles upon, and entails a Curse upon his dearest darling Favourites. As for instance, if after this King's Reign, steps up a Protestant Prince (for surely the whole Royal Blood must not all follow his Apostacy, and degenerate *in secula seculorum*) then what becomes of the Popish Interest in the next Generation, and all that flourishing party, whom either the Witchcrafts of *Rome*, or the Contagion of *Regis ad exemplum*[15] has nurst up for ruine? 'Tis the greatest toil of the next King's Reign, to make those severer Statutes for future Ages, to suppress the insolencies and follies of the past; whilest those very Idols that were Saints but yesterday, are now crusht and dasht to pieces.

Thus a Popish King undoes at once, the Heretick party in his own Reign, and the *Roman Catholick* in the next. And then who is it, that he either does or can make happy? Why nothing but an Atheist, he that believes there is no God, and so makes the name of the most fashionable Religion, the Bawd to his pleasures and preferments; or at best that Latitudinarian Believer, that can kneel to a Crucifix today, and burn it tomorrow. This and this only Principle, can be safe under a Papist; and these are the only men that in their right wits ought to be unconcerned at the danger of a Popish Successour.

FINIS.

---

15. At the example of the king.

[William Cavendish, Duke of Devonshire, 1640–1707]

REASONS

FOR

His Majesties Passing

THE

BILL

OF

EXCLUSION.

IN A

LETTER

To a FRIEND.

LONDON:

Printed for *J. W.* and sold by *Langly Curtis,* 1681.

*W*illiam Cavendish, dashing nobleman, ardent Whig, and leading member of Parliament, is considered the author of this exclusionist tract.

In the limelight from the start of the Restoration, Cavendish was one of four young noblemen chosen to bear Charles II's train at his coronation in April 1661. He was elected to Parliament for Derby that same year and was a leading member of Parliament for the next twenty years. His service was characterized by his anxiety to protect both the Protestant faith and the role and dignity of Parliament. These aims eventually brought him into league with the Whig opposition. When Parliament met in 1676 after a prorogation of fifteen months, it was Cavendish who moved that the overlong recess meant Parliament was, in fact, dissolved. He was later an urgent inquirer into the details of the supposed popish plot of 1678.

Cavendish's concern for the Protestant faith made him fear the accession of Charles's brother, the Catholic Duke of York, to the throne. In 1679 he was among the battery of Whigs Charles brought into the Privy Council in hopes of forming a coalition. With the others Cavendish supported suggestions to protect their religion without disturbing the succession. Unfortunately this government coalition broke down the following year, and he resigned from the Council. By 1681, when the short pamphlet reprinted below was written, he had come to the conclusion that there could be no compromise: James must be excluded. The tract assesses the position of the king within the government and the role of religion within a state, then calls upon Charles to deny his brother the throne for the public good. Cavendish had been influenced by the philosophy of Thomas Hobbes but, as this tract demonstrates, rejected it arguing that the king should bow to the will of the people. This work makes a compelling, and reasoned, plea. Only a single edition was published.

With the collapse of the exclusion campaign Cavendish prudently avoided discussions and subsequent plots against the Duke of York. Nevertheless he remained loyal to his more impulsive friends. He appeared as a witness for William Lord Russell at the latter's trial, even, apparently, offering to change clothes with him in prison so Russell might escape.

On James's accession Cavendish kept his distance from the rebellion of Charles's Protestant son, the illegitimate James Duke of Monmouth. After Monmouth's defeat, however, Cavendish retired from Court and devoted himself primarily to the building of Chatsworth. At home he abandoned at last the caution that had kept him safe and joined in attempts to bring William of Orange to England. When William finally landed Cavendish worked hard for his triumph. The duke sat in the Convention Parliament where he argued for the deposition of James and the elevation of a new king rather than a regent. He was later sworn to William's Privy Council. At the coronation of William and Mary he was given the signal honor of bearing the crown. A faithful friend, he also worked to reverse the attainders of Lord Russell, Algernon Sidney, and other Whigs.

Reasons for His Majesties Passing the Bill of Exclusion.

I Am not ignorant that you have lately heard Reports to my disadvantage, concerning some matters relating to the Publick: and though I flatter myself (much more I confess from your Partiality to me, than any Merit I can pretend to) that you do not think the worse of me for them; yet because one cannot be too sure of what one values so highly, as I do your Esteem, I take the liberty to give you some account of my Thoughts of the present posture of Affairs, that if I am not so happy as to continue still in the good opinion you have formerly had of my firmness to the Publick Interest, I may learn at least in what particular you conceive I have varied from it. Which last, though perhaps less welcome than the first, will yet be owned as a very great mark of your Friendship, since I assure myself, you have too much Charity for me to impute my Errours in this kinde to any worse cause than want of Understanding.

I must confess, I have had no great Veneration of late for some Men, who though extreme zealous in appearance for things of Publick Concern, and particularly for the Bill for Excluding the Duke of *York* from the Succession to the Crown, have yet taken such Methods for the obtaining that Bill, as (with respect to their Popularity) looked to me, as if they had rather wished it should be denied, than granted.

I mean a sort of men that pass with the Vulgar for very publick Spirits, yet are no otherwise for the Publick Good, than as they think it may conduce to their own private Designs. If matters be not disposed for them to leap into a great Place, or to be restored to some Office they have formerly enjoyed, and in which they have discovered Principles far different from what they now profess: if every one they have a prejudice to be not immediately removed, or perhaps if they fancy themselves the most likely to head the Rabble, should things fall into confusion; they will be sure with great appearance of Zeal to press things of less moment, and which they think will be denied, lest anything that really tends to Settlement should be granted. And they are for the most part gainers by this, for their Vehemence, which proceeds from dark and hidden causes, seldom fails of being mistaken by the Vulgar for a true and hearty Love of their Country. I believe His Majesty will finde these men harder, I am sure less necessary to be satisfied, than the Nation. And therefore I hope you will not wonder if I, who care not much for a great Office if the Bill of Exclusion do pass, or to be popular with the Rabble if it do not, cannot heartily concur with all that seems to be aimed at by that sort of people.

I suppose you have heard which way I have declared my Opinion concerning that Bill, when I thought it to any purpose. But give me leave (with as little reflection upon the Causes of the breach of the last Parliament, as the subject will permit) to tell you, what in my poor judgment may most conduce to the passing it in the Parliament which is to meet at *Oxford.* I cannot imagine how popular Speeches in either House, or angry Votes that are not always backt with the strongest Reason, much less the Pamphlets that fly about in the Intervals of Parliament, can signifie much to the obtaining this Bill; for to what purpose are Arguments to the People to prove the necessity of that, which they are so fully convinced of already?

I should rather think it worthy the Wisdom of the next Parliament, to consider what Arguments are most likely to prevail with the King himself in this matter; and instead of such Addresses as carry the least shew of Menace in them, which cannot but be offensive, since to suppose a King capable of Fear, is the worst Complement can be made him; instead of angry Votes which may alienate the Hearts of the people yet farther from His Majesty, and make him more averse from granting their reasonable Desires, and consequently from consenting to this Bill, to lay before him such Reasons for it, as may convince him that it is his own particular Interest to pass it.

I do not mention the House of Lords, being too well assured of the Loyalty of that Noble Assembly, to doubt of their passing anything for which His Majesty shews the least Inclination. Taking it then for granted that this Bill only sticks with His Majesty, no Arguments are of moment to obtain it, but such as ought to be of weight with Him; and those I conceive to be of this Nature.

One Objection must first be removed: for since Kings, of all Men living, ought to have the greatest regard to Justice, we must not suppose that His Majesty can ever consent to this Bill, till he be satisfied of the Justice of it. I shall therefore endeavour to prove, not only that it is just, but agreeable to the very intention and design of Government.

It seems to me to be an undeniable Position, that Government is intended for the safety and protection of those that are Governed; and that where the Supreme power is lodged in a single Person, he is Invested with that power, not for his own greatness or pleasure, but for the good of the People. The Tyrannies in *Aristotle's* time, and those that continue to this day in the Eastern parts, must certainly have degenerated from a better kind of Government by some accident or other; since what people can be supposed to have been so void of sense, and so servilely inclined, as to give up their Lives and Liberties to the unbounded disposal of one man, without imposing the least condition upon him? For admit, according to Mr. *Hobbes,* that Monarchical Government is formed by an Agreement of a Society of Men, to devolve all their power and interest upon one Man, and to make him Judge of all Differences that shall arise among them; 'tis plain, that this can be for no other end, than the Security and protection of those that enter into such a Contract; otherwise, you must suppose them Mad-men, voluntarily to strip themselves of all means of Defence, against the fury and violence of one of their number, rather than continue in a state of War, where at the worst, they are as free to Rob, as they are subject to be Robbed. 'Tis hard therefore to conceive, that Absolute Monarchy could ever have been constituted by consent of any Society of Men, (besides that we see those that live under them, would be glad to shake off their Yoke if they could) but 'tis probable they may have been raised by the Ambition and Valour of some Prince, or Succession of Princes, or by the people's supineness in suffering themselves to be enslaved by degrees, and so being at last forced to submit, when 'twas too late to oppose.

I have insisted the longer upon this Argument, because another depends upon it, which comes nearer the present Question; for if no Reason of Government can be assigned, but the Safety and Protection of the People, it follows naturally, that the Succession of Princes in Hereditary Monarchies, cannot be binding, nor ought to be admitted, where it proves manifestly inconsistent with those ends. I need not instance in all the cases that incapacitate a Prince to perform the Office of a Chief Governour; but I can think of no disability so strong or so undeniable, as his being of a different Religion from that which is generally owned by the People.

Religion, considered only in a Politick Sense, is one of the chief Supports of Civil Government; for the fear of corporal Punishments, nay of Death itself, would often prove insufficient to deter men from refusing Obedience to their Superiours, or from breaking their Laws, without those stronger ties of Hope of Reward, and Fear of Punishment in another Life. The *Romans*, of a fierce and rude people, were made tractable by *Numa*, and submitted to such Laws and Customs as he thought fit to introduce, not so much by their being convinced of the reasonableness of those Laws, as by the finding a way to perswade them, that all his new Constitutions were the Dictates of a Divinity, with whom he pretended daily to converse. This sense of Religion raised that People afterwards to that incredible exactness of Order and Discipline; and the belief they had the Gods on their side, made them run so intrepidly upon Dangers, that *Cicero* observes, that though some Nations excelled them in Learning and Arts, others equalled if not exceeded them in Valour and Strength, 'twas to Religion, and their respect to Divine Mysteries, that they owed their Conquest of the World. But this very Religion, that is the Bond of Union between a Prince and his People, when both profess the same, must of necessity produce the contrary Effects, and be the seed of the most fatal Disorders, nay of the Dissolution of Governments, where they differ. The same Conscience that ties the People's Affections fastest to the Prince in the first case, dissolves all manner of Trust, all bonds of Obedience, in the second.

It is impossible that a Prince should signifie anything towards the support of the People's Religion, being himself of another; nor would it ever be believed, if he could. And how can that Government subsist, where the People are unanimously possest with a belief that the Prince is incapable of protecting them in that which for the most part the value above all other considerations? I know no instance can be given in this *Northern* part of the World, even in those Kingdoms that have varied from their Original Constitution and are become Absolute, that a Prince of a different Religion from the People, was ever admitted to the Crown. Queen *Mary* here in *England* met with some opposition; yet she could not be said to be of a different Religion from the People: for *Popery* was so far from being extirpated in her days, that she found a Parliament that joined with her in the restoring of that Religion. But in *France,* when the King of *Navarre,* a Protestant,[1] was presumptive Heir to the Crown, the States assembled at *Blois* (as all Historians of that Time agree) had certainly Excluded him, and the rest of that Branch that were *Protestants* from the Succession, if they had not parted abruptly, upon the Death of the Duke of *Guise* and his Brother. Nay some affirm, that the King himself, though of the Established Religion, was not out of danger of

---

1. Henry of Navarre, a Protestant, became Henry IV in 1589 after the long French Wars of Religion but was not fully accepted by the French Catholic party until he converted to Catholicism in 1593.

being Deposed, upon a Suspicion of his favouring too much the *Protestant* Faction, in opposition to the League. After the King's Death the Hereditary Right was without Dispute in the King of *Navarre;* but he found none to assist him in the making good his Title, but the *Protestant* Party, of whom he was the Head, and some Creatures of his Predecessour, that took his part more out of Hatred to the League, than Affection to him. This Prince was at last indeed admitted to the Crown, upon his Conversion to the Church of *Rome.* But that would not have sufficed, nor would the Generality of the People, who were extremely zealous for their Religion, ever have trusted one that had been of another, had he not happened to be a Prince of incomparable Courage and Conduct, who through Seas of Blood, and after many Victories, forcing his Entrance into the Capital City, made his way to the Throne by Conquest, rather than by a voluntary Admission of the People. It is observable by the way, that the Bishops and Clergy of *France* were so far from setting up a Divine Right of Succession above the Religion established, that most of them opposed him even after his Conversion, all of them before; and the Pulpits rung with such bitter Invectives against him, (only upon the account of Religion) as perhaps no Age can parallel. This I should think might serve for Instruction to some Bishops, that I could name, who by maintaining that nothing ought to overrule the Hereditary Right of Succession, must either confess, that their Religion deserves not so much to be defended as the *Romish* doth, or that they themselves are not so zealous in the defence of it as they ought to be. Let these Assertors of Divine Right tell me, if in *France*, at this day the most Absolute Monarchy in *Europe*, and where the Succession is held most Sacred, a *Protestant* Prince would be admitted to the Crown.

And here in *England*, besides the consideration of Religion, that of Property is not to be neglected, since what security can be given that Abbey-Lands, in which most Landed men in the Kingdom have a share, would not be restored to the Church under the Reign of a Popish Prince? The Objection that a Prince may be of the Church of *Rome,* and yet not change the Establisht Religion, is frivolous. For though there may be a possibility of his not attempting it, deterred perhaps by the people's universal detestation of Popery, or discouraged by the ill success of former Attempts; this amounts to no more, than that he will not bring Popery in, because he cannot. But is this all that a King of *England* is obliged to do, by the Oath which he takes at his Coronation? An Oath not only a Crime for him to take, (if he be a Papist) but impossible for him to keep. For can a Papist defend that Religion to the utmost of his power, which cannot be fully secured but by the suppression of his own? Can he be a fit Head of the Protestant Interest abroad, who (while he continues of the Church of *Rome*) must wish there were never a Protestant left in the world? If he be incapable of doing this, that is, if the ends of Government cannot be obtained in the ordinary course of Succession, the State must of necessity fall into Confusion, if there be not an extraordinary power lodged somewhere, to provide for its preservation.

That Power here in *England,* is in a Parliament, and has often been made use of; but I conceive, for the Reasons above mentioned, never more justly than upon this occasion.

And though the Justice of this Bill be very clear, I think the next thing yet easier to prove, which is, That it is His Majesty's real Interest to pass it. For if this Government be so constituted, that the King having the Hearts of his People, is one of the most considerable Princes in *Europe,* but without them signifies but little, either at home or abroad, as I doubt that is the case; and if nothing can contribute more to the alienating the people's Affections from him, than his denying this Bill, one would think there needed no other Motives to induce His Majesty to pass it. But besides, I should not think this unworthy of His Majesty's Consideration, if there are some persons to whom he may have a just prejudice; and who if they cannot bring to pass what-ever they propose to themselves, will still be endeavouring to make the Breach wider; whether the denial of this Bill may not furnish them with too plausible Arguments with the People, to refuse such necessary demands as His Majesty may make for the Safety of the Kingdom, or the support of his Alliances; and whether on the contrary, the passing it may not very much disappoint those Counterfeit Patriots, by taking from them the best pretence they have of stirring up the People to Sedition.

Nay, who knows but the refusal of this Bill may exasperate the Nation to that degree, that a Title may be set up on pretence of a former Marriage,[2] by the help of false Witnesses, which though as ridiculous in itself, as injurious to His Majesty's Reputation, may yet put the whole Kingdom into a flame?

The Expedient of taking away all Regal Power from a Popish Successor, and leaving him only the Name of a King, can be no satisfactory security to the Nation, unless such a Form of Government were setled during the Life of his Predecessor. For otherwise the Successor, (having a right to the Crown, which without an Act to exclude him he will have) may not only pretend that the Predecessor cannot give away his Prerogative, but probably may succeed in opposing it, by the difficulty that is always found in the introducing of New Constitutions. Now whether this Expedient (being put in practice during the Life of the present King) be not as good for the people, as the Bill, I shall not now dispute; but as to the King himself, I think 'tis clear, that nothing can be less for his Honour or Interest, than to admit of such an Expedient.

The Objection that this Bill may Disunite *Scotland* from *England*, seems not very weighty. For first, we know not but a Free Parliament there, may pass a Bill to the same effect; but if they do not, the Disunion cannot happen, unless the Duke outlive the King; and in that

2. The reference here is to James Scott, Duke of Monmouth, Charles II's illegitimate son.

case, will continue but during his Survivance, for the next Successor will unite the Kingdoms again. This inconvenience therefore, if it be at all, will be of so short continuance, as cannot be of weight to ballance with those present and visible Mischiefs that may fall upon the Nation for want of this Bill.

Some have fancied, and I hope 'tis but a fancy, that the King has made a Solemn promise to his Brother, never to pass it. I will suppose the worst. If His Majesty have made such a promise, I conceive, with submission, it is void in itself. For if he have taken an Oath at his Coronation to maintain the Establisht Religion, and in order to that, it be necessary to pass this Bill, I doubt no subsequent promise can absolve him from the performance of that Oath. In the next place, all promises are understood to be for the advantage of him that makes them, or of him they are made to, or both. But the performing this would not only be ruinous to His Majesty, but of no advantage to his Royal Highness: for how great soever his Merit and Vertues are acknowledged to be, he lies under a circumstance that makes it impossible for him to come to the Crown (though this Bill never pass) but by Conquest; and that way he may have it, notwithstanding all the Acts that can be made to oppose him.

I shall add no more to the trouble I have given you upon this Subject, but that I am for this Bill, because I think it just and necessary, not because it is contended for by a Party: for I hold myself as free to differ with that Party, when I think them in the wrong, as to agree with them when they have reason of their side. This may be an Errour, at least may be subject to mis-construction, in a time that most things are so; but I hope you that have known me long, will judge more charitably of

SIR,
Your most Humble Servant.
FINIS.

B. T. [Sir Benjamin Thorogood, d. 1694]

Captain Thorogood

His Opinion of the Point of

SUCCESSION,

To a Brother of the Blade in

SCOTLAND.

*T*his intriguing tract was one of nearly two hundred titles that appeared during the campaign to exclude James, Duke of York, from the throne. Its Tory author vigorously mustered his party's objections to any alteration in the succession, taking care to refute every Whig argument. What is especially remarkable about the piece is Thorogood's readiness to rebut Whig elevation of Parliament by vehemently attacking that institution's claim to represent the English people.

Both Whig and Tory agreed that European Protestantism was in peril. But while the Whigs saw this as a reason why the Catholic James must not become king, Thorogood finds it the reason he must. James has martial skills, and tampering with the succession would so weaken England that it could not rescue Europe from Louis XIV's ambitions for a universal monarchy. Where the Whigs claim to preserve monarchy by removing a disastrous heir, Thorogood claims a change in the succession would fundamentally alter the government and make monarchy elective. And whereas Whigs defend Parliament's right to make such a change, Thorogood denies that power.

Only God or man can change the constitution. God shows no sign of wanting it changed and as for man, Parliament cannot speak for the people because it does not represent most of them. Thorogood then produces a stunning assault on anomalies in the English electoral system.

The tract, which ends abruptly in midsentence, was written in the form of a letter to a friend and appeared in a single edition. It is signed with the initials B. T., presumably B. Thorogood. The most likely author is Sir Benjamin Thorogood, a London Tory. If Thorogood did indeed write it, he was among those Anglican Tories to feel the sting of winning the battle but losing the war. The man who advanced James's claims to the throne, even questioning the basic authority of the king in Parliament, was one of six London aldermen dismissed by then King James in October 1687 for their unwillingness to support his religious policy. A year later, when the fear of an invasion by William of Orange provoked James to reverse his policies, he restored the old London charter and reinstated Thorogood and some other ousted aldermen. Many other aldermen refused to resume their posts. Sir Benjamin lived to see the Glorious Revolution.

Dear Jack,

AS I covet nothing so much as to see the Exorbitant Power of *France* reduced to its ancient bounds; so I am sensible no Nation upon Earth can stop the rapid Course of their Victories but Ours, whose Valour still fills their hearts with no less fear than their late Successes have done with ambition. But I confess the consideration of Our present unhappy differences makes me dread losing the opportunity of rescuing enslaved *Christendom* from their Tyranny, and Our own Glory from the stains of Infamy, contracted by the over-long repose of our Arms. This fear I look upon to be well-grounded, since no less a thing is said to be in agitation than a change in the very Fundamentals of our Government, which like a distemper that seizes the noble Parts, must (after the long struglings and conflicts of the contending parties), extremely weaken, if not absolutely destroy it, as is evident by the no less impious than doleful examples of all Ages; And if that should once happen, (which God in his Mercy prevent), who would be able to resist the mighty Force of *France?* Or what could *England* (which alone, if, united, is capable to prevent it), expect but with the rest of *Europe,* (and upon harder conditions than any other Nation) be swallowed up in the Universal Monarchy?[1] To prevent which, since nothing can more effectually contribute than a firm and lasting Union among Ourselves, which is morally impossible to be attained, if once the ancient and fundamental form of Government, under which this Nation has (to its Immortal Renown, and its Enemies' Terror), flourished so many Generations, be now abolished. I thought fit in a Soldierly manner, and *en Cavalier,* to shew you that the just exclusion of His Royal Highness[2] from the Imperial Crown

---

1. There were fears in the late seventeenth century that Louis XIV meant to conquer Europe and make himself a universal monarch.

2. This reference is to James Stuart, Duke of York, brother of Charles II. The author frequently refers to him in this tract as "R. H."

of this Realm, (in case the King should die without Issue) is absolutely impossible; and this I do on no other account, but because I believe it may do my Country good, whose Interest, as well as Glory, it will be, to have a Prince of Martial Spirit Reign over Us, by whose Valour Our almost withered *Lawrels* may once more be planted in *French-ground*, moistened and made fat with the Bloud of our implacable Enemies, and nourished and reared up to that Strength and Vigour they formerly enjoyed by the Courage and Conduct of our Ancestors.

You know it is the common Theme of the Town-Scriblers, that *Monarchy* is a meer Human institution, alterable in *Part;* or in the *Whole,* as often as the *Governour* and *Governed* shall think it necessary for their common Safety. That the *King* for the time being[3] is the Supreme *Governour,* and the whole Aggregate of People the *Governed.* That these being not otherwise easily to be assembled, are some personally, and the rest by their Representatives in Parliament. That whatever Law or Sanction, the King, with the advice and consent of his People so convened does Enact, binds the whole Nation; and that consequently it is in their Power to exclude His R. H. the Succession, or, which is the same thing, to turn the *Hereditary Monarchy* into an *Elective.*

This Position, (how injurious soever to a Successor), is more dangerous to a Prince Regnant, who if weak, easy, or inconsiderate, may, through hope, or fear, be prevailed upon to yield to his own dethroning, and exchange his actual Royalty for an Annuity or yearly Pension; whereas, the other loses only a possibility of a Crown, with this further advantage, That *most Men will think him worthy of wearing it, because not the want of Courage and Magnanimity, but of Interest and Power creates his Misfortune.* Whatever then shall be said to shew the impracticableness of this Position here in *England,* is as much intended to secure the Possession of His most Sacred Majesty, or any

3. This refers to the distinction made between the king de facto and the king de jure, that is a king in fact and a king by right.

other that shall lawfully fill the Throne, as the possibility which His *R. H.* now has, or any other Heir Apparent may have in after Ages. It is indeed a Royal Cause, and as such to be maintained by the Swords and Pens of all good Subjects, of which number I profess myself to be one, and in evidence of my Loyalty say,

1. That since *England* is *de facto* a Hereditary Kingdom, and every King for the time being, with the help of his *Parliaments* entrusted with the Government of it as such; it follows, that as he cannot alien or subject it to another Crown or Person, because the alienation of a Kingdom is so far from being comprehended in the Government of it, by him (to whom first committed) and his Heirs, that it is directly repugnant and inconsistent with it, so he cannot alter the course and order of Succession, which is a kind of alienation, because it transfers the Title to one who (without such an Act) would have none; and consequently any Monarch attempting the Destruction of the very Form and Essence of such a Government, may be thought rather to frustrate in some measure part of the Trust reposed in him, and stray from his Duty, than vitiate his Successor's Title to the Kingdom.

2. If both Houses of Parliament should be allowed to have a share in the Government in a coordinate manner with the King, then the King and they (having the Supreme Power of Governing a Hereditary Monarchy committed to their Charge, and nothing else), have no authority to alter or destroy it; because a Power to support and maintain a Government, and change and dissolve it, is absolutely inconsistent with itself.

3. This great trust was reposed in them either by *God* or *Man;* if by *God*, then 'tis certain it cannot warrantably be altered without his positive command infallibly known as such; If by *Man*, we are under the disability until his express Will and Pleasure be made known to us, in a plain, evident and indisputable way.

God has not yet revealed us his Will or Desire to change our Government, nor are we to look for such extraordinary Injunctions at this time, when the light of the Gospel has sufficiently cleared all the Errors and Doubts that might hinder our Duty; And it is an act of equal Folly and Impiety to attempt an Innovation upon the supposition of being able to know certainly and unquestionably the Will of *Man*, since that knowledge will (to any that seriously considers the Constitution of this Kingdom) appear absolutely impossible. For if by *Man* we understand (as we must) the whole Complex of the People, or the *Governed*, we cannot possibly be satisfied of their being after a full and mature deliberation, desirous of a Change, because we have, or at least will use no other way of knowing their minds, but by their *Representatives* in Parliament; and these whom we commonly call *Representatives* are either not so at all; or if they be, do not derive their Power from a third part of the Nation, and consequently cannot impart a knowledge to us, which they themselves never had, or execute an Authority which was never given them, according to the old Maxim, *nemo dat quod non habet;*[4] The reason why they may be thought to be no Representatives at all, is, because if the ultimate and last result of Power, such as is doubtless the disposing of the Crown, be in the King and Parliament only, it cannot rationally be said, That the Parliament is the People which is always to be the party Governed; it being as impossible that they should at one and the same time, and in the same respect, be both *Governours* and *Governed*, as it is for me to be *Master* and *Servant*, in regard to myself singly and alone. But to waive this, which may possibly be looked upon as a subtilty or strained Notion; I say that the Parliament as now usually Elected, is not at all the Representative of the People; I mean so as to have such an actual or virtual Deputation or Commission from every individual person, as may enable them to exercise all the Acts relating to Government, as arbitrarily, and without controll; as if all the People were personally present, and consenting to such Acts. For none

---

4. No one can give away what he does not have.

have Votes in Elections, but *Free-holders* of at least forty Shillings a Year, and *Citizens* and *Burgesses,* and consequently all *Lessees* for Years, *Grantees* of *Annuities* for Years: *Men* that live upon the Interest, and Product of their Money: The greatest part of the *Clergy,* all *Soldiers,* and *Seamen* in general, most of the young *Nobility* and *Gentry,* who besides their possibilities of Remainders, seldom have anything for their maintenance but their Parents' allowances; And in fine, the whole number of *Labourers, Servants, Artificers,* and *Tradesmen,* not residing in, or at least free of Cities and Boroughs, are totally excluded, and consequently no more represented by the Parliament, than the Attorney you authorized to appear for you this Term in a Suit at *Westminster,* is warranted by the Authority you gave him, to appear likewise for me without my knowledge or privity; And what can be more unequal, not to say unjust, than that a numerous and upon due computation the far greatest part of the nation, that are Passengers in the great Ship of the Commonwealth, as well as the rest, should be debarred their right of choosing a *Master* or *Pilot,* to whose Skill and Care they commit their common safety? Have they not their *Liberty,* their *Property,* their *Religion;* and in a word, the present enjoyments of this, and in some measure the hopes of a future *Life* to be secured or hazarded by the good or ill Conduct of their *Governour?* And must this, all this be left to the Arbitrary Power and Discretion of such, as by chance, perhaps more than merit, have acquired the Possession of some Land, or are free of Boroughs and Cities? If a Freehold of forty Shillings *per annum,* entitles one to as great a share of the Legislative Power, as that of five thousand Pounds does another, what shew of Reason can there be, why one whose Goods and Chattels amount to ten times the value of such a Freehold, and has peradventure a Stock of Reputation, Honesty and Wisdom as many degrees beyond him, should not be equally concerned in the Government?

But allowing *Free-holders, Citizens* and *Burgesses,* some Mysterious and Sacred *Right*, exclusively of all others, of delegating the Representatives, and irrevocable Attorneys of the whole Kingdom; yet surely there should be such a proportion and equality between them, as would render this mighty Power vested in them, agreeable to Right Reason, and the very nature of Government. But we see no such thing for the meanest Borough; For *Example, Old Sarum* deputes as many men to serve in Parliament, as the greatest County in *England*, with equal Authority, not only of consulting and debating, but likewise of giving their determinative and decisive Voices in all matters and things whatsoever.

Cornwall which is the two and fiftieth part of the Kingdom, makes above an eleventh part of the *House of Commons;* and yet *London, Southwark,* and *Westminster,* which in the Power of Men and Riches, is judged to be a sixth of the whole Nation, is in the Representative but the sixty-fourth part. And this Solecism alone in the very constitution of the Government will make it forever impossible to have the People Represented in any just and rational manner; unless perhaps such course might be taken, as is practiced in *Holland,* where each Province sends as many Deputies as it pleases, with power of proposing and debating, but not of resolving by the Votes of the Persons, but of the Provinces.

It may be here objected that our present Constitution has appointed no other way for choosing Representatives; and that therefore we ought to acquiesce. To this I Answer, that it may very well fall out, that nothing may be a clearer and greater hinderance to our having a true and evident knowledge of the People's Desires and Inclinations by their Representatives, than our very Laws; For *example,* at present the *Oaths of Allegiance, Supremacy,* and the *Test,* are to be taken by all the Members of both Houses of Parliament. But if in this, or any after-age, almost the whole, or the far greater part of the Nation, should become true *Presbyterians,* who abhor our *Royal* as much as the *Papal Supremacy,* or *Quakers* that indeed scruple all

Oaths, or *Papists* that cannot well be supposed willing to renounce the whole substance of their Religion; could the few, (who by taking such *Oaths,* would then be rendered capable of sitting in Parliament), be properly accounted the *Representatives* of a Nation, that could not otherwise look upon them, than as men wicked, irreligious, and perjured, and consequently move forward to heighten than heal their Miseries; To which end no man can be rationally supposed to depute another? No sure, and therefore when Laws which are made for the People, (and not the People for the Laws) do cross and thwart the Right and Interest of the major part of the Society, they then not being able to effect what they were designed for, become useless, and die.

A further Objection will be, that the constant opinion of all Ages has put it beyond doubt, that the Parliament is the Representative of the People; and that all the Acts they pass, do virtually include the consent and agreement of every individual person in the Kingdom. To this I would very readily agree provided it would be allowed me on the other hand, (as appears by all our Law Books), that *Monarchy* is *Jure natura,* and unalterable without apparent Violence by any Human Power whatsoever; But if the arrogance or malice of some will carry them so far as to trample upon all the Positive and Fundamental Laws of the Land, and publish daily in Print, to the manifest hazard of the State, that all Forms or kinds of Government, are changable at the Will and Pleasure of the People, into that *Species* which shall by them be thought the most agreeable, to their Natures and Inclinations; I hope it will not be looked upon as a Crime in me, if following the way they chalked out for me, and waiving the common received opinion, I likewise speculatively pry, into the very Constitution and Frame of parliaments, thereby to shew the impossibility of altering the *Succession.* But to clear all Objections as far as possible, I say, That the supposition, of the Parliament's representing the People, is a fiction of Law, well devised by the Wisdom of our Ancestors, for quieting and appeasing the minds of all particular men, who could not have a stronger Motive of Submission, or of not believing themselves injured than their being accounted parties and privy to all Acts of Parliament; But this fiction of Law cannot reach the Actual Legislators, as such, since they cannot be supposed to wrong themselves, though they might those by whom commissioned. The Parliament, then when it alters or repeals Laws, lops off the exuberancies and excrescencies, which by the design or heedlesness of the Managers, grow up in the Government, curbs the Pride, Avarice and encroachments of great Persons bounds and limits reciprocally the Prince's Prerogative and Subject's Liberty; and in fine lends its healing hand towards the removing anything that is dangerous or noxious to the Body Politick as first constituted, then, I say, it may well enough for its greater Strength and Authority, be allowed the Representative of the whole Body of the People. But if instead of applying fit remedies for its preservation and continuance, they should go about to annihilate or dissolve it, which must inevitably be attended with violent concussions and universal calamities, it cannot, as I said before, be accounted their Representative; because the consequence of such an Act must immediately influence every individual Member of the Society; and 'tis but reason that the common concernment of the ruine or happiness of all; should be left, not by fiction of Law, but in reality, to be weighed by their own Judgment. For if (as some would have it) the Power of Dominion was originally in the People, and by them transferred on *one, few* or *many* of themselves, 'tis evident that as every one was actually aiding by his choice and agreement in erecting such a Dominion, so it's necessary he should by the same means concur to its change and destruction.

If it should be said that our Government was first established not by the Votes of Individuals, but by Representatives in the Nature of Parliaments, as now constituted; I Answer, that it could not be, because of the inequality of the choice, which is certain was not in the beginning; (for until the 8th. year of *Henry* the *6th*. as is plain by the Statute then made, the Electors of Knights of the Shire were not under a necessity of having forty Shillings *per annum* to expend) or if it was, let our Adversaries prove when and where it first began; if they cannot, but confidently and positively affirm it was so, and we as confidently and positively deny it, then 'tis evident, we being in possession, that the advantage will be on our side, for *in aquali jure melior est conditio possidentis.*[5]

4. Having thus far endeavoured to prove that the Parliament is not the Representative of the People. I further say, That allowing them to be so, yet 'tis certain they assemble not of themselves, but by the King's Writ, which sets forth the occasion of their being called *viz.* To advise and consult, &c. *De arduis & urgentibus negotiis Regni,* of the great and pressing Affairs of the Kingdom. Now the Kingdom being Hereditary at the time of issuing forth the Writ, and they summoned to appear and give their advice concerning the good Estate and Defence of it as such, 'tis plain they cannot change, alter or destroy it, no more than a Physician sent for, to remove the Pains and Oppressions of Sickness, can lawfully stab or poison his Patient, who through rage or folly may yield his assent to his own destruction. 'Tis ridiculous and foolish to think that even the very Country would not with high Indignation resent such an attempt, since they know full well that the Election of Members to constitute the Body Politick of a Parliament, was never intended to destroy the Head and most essential part of it, I mean the Hereditary Kingship, which abstractedly from this or that man, who may give an ill Precedent, and therefore is not intrusted with an absolute disposal of it, is the very Life and Soul of the Government, and without which it must infallibly crumble into pieces.

5. We all know that a Body Politick, which is the Work and Crea-

---

5. In Aquilian law the condition of the possessor is the better.

ture of Man, has many resemblances with the Body Natural, which is the Creature of God; for as this aims always at its ease, happiness and long preceptions of the pleasures of this Life, and consequently dreads and abhors Death or Dissolution which puts an end to all, so the other is constant and unwearied in the pursuit of the like ends to that degree, that by its very constitution and essential form we attribute to it a kind of Immortality, whence comes the known Maxim received into our Laws, *That the King never dies,* that is, that Kingship, not the Persons to whom it is inherent or annexed for this, or that time, is beyond the reach of Fate and Time that puts an end to all things. This then being so, we cannot rationally conclude that our present Sovereign has Will or Power to destroy himself, that is, Hereditary Kingship, which made him what he is, and is as essential to the Politick Capacity he is in, as Supreme Governour, as the rational Soul is to his natural Capacity, as man. To say or judge otherwise, would be no less, than to put him to break all the sacred ties of Love which bind him so strongly to himself, and suppose him capable to be in some measure his own Executioner, and a *Felo de se* of Monarchy, than which there can be no greater Indignity offered to the Majesty of a Prince whom we all know to be Just, Merciful and Generous to others; and who therefore must so much the more signally practice those Vertues towards himself, by how much self-respect exceeds that due to another.

6. And lastly, 'Tis evident by several Statutes, that all Knights of the Shires, and their Electors are to be Inhabitants and Residents in the respective Counties the day of the Writ, and that likewise the Citizens and Burgesses are to be men resident, dwelling and free in the Cities and Boroughs for which they are to be chosen; And right reason teaches us that none ought by sinister and unjust means to step into Authority, if therefore anyone be previously disabled and uncapable to exercise Power by a positive Law, or openly by deceits, calumnies or corruption thrust himself into the Seat of Justice, 'tis

certain all his Proceedings and Sanctions do carry a nullity and in-
sufficiency in themselves, and affect none, besides the Maker, who
by endeavouring to exercise a Legislative Power against Law and
Reason, makes his violation of them so much the more manifest.
This often happens in choosing of Parliament-men in our days,
when those that live in the *North* are chosen for the *South,* and men
that never saw the Cities or Boroughs before the time of Election
made their Representatives, with this further addition of disability,
that they gain Votes by Bribes, Threats, and many unlawful Artifices,
as by loading their Competitors with the most odious calumny of
being Courtiers, Pensioners, Papists, Atheists, and what not, though
they know them to have more love for their Country and their Religion than themselves. I know nothing that can more effectually
frustrate the Decrees and Resolves of Law-makers than this, and
therefore leave it to impartial and indifferent men to judge whether
such a practice, if it should intervene, would not exclude any Society
of Men from excluding another from his Right.

Upon the whole matter then the present Monarchy is so founded,
that neither the King nor the Parliament can possibly alter the true
and essential form of it; and consequently his *R. H.* cannot be barred
his Right of Reigning over us, if he survive his Brother, whose Life he
values beyond the Crowns and Kingdoms he can leave him, whom
God long preserve in Peace and Plenty, and the unfeigned affection
of his People.

As for the Examples which are alledged to evince the contrary, and
urged so confidently by the Gentleman that is the Author of the *Word
without Doors*[6] they do not at all scare me, for the Question is not
whether *de facto,* but whether without violation of Justice and the
Principles of right Reason, our Monarchy may be changed? For no
man ever doubted but Power, Rebellion and Faction with the con-

6. J. D., "Word without Doors concerning the bill for succession" [London, 1679], Wing
D48. Two further editions were published in 1680.

currence of timorous and easy Princes did often turn things into Tragical Confusions, and unhinge the whole frame of *Governments*, but far be it from us to ground the lawfulness of our Actions upon so weak a Topick as that of *Example,* since we know that no Crime can be perpetrated, no Usurpation introduced, no Violation offered even to Heaven itself, but will be all warrantable, if their being subsequent to a like practice of former Ages frees them from Guilt. Rebellion is as ancient as the Creation, it first divided the Court of Heaven, and deprived *Lucifer* and his Accomplices of their Glory, and then threw Man out of the Garden of *Eden,* and the state of Innocence into a rough tract of the Earth, and yet rougher anguishes and perplexities of Sin. An obedience to God's Command to *encrease and multiply* was not long paid, when of the few Inhabitants of the World, one, and he the most harmless too, fell a Sacrifice to his Brother's envy and maker's affection. Idolatry (the *Jews* only excepted) was the common Worship of Mankind, and whatever Species of Christianity was first planted in this Island, 'tis certain that Popery not many Years since was the legal and known Religion universally embraced by the People; yet God forbid we should now pretend Rebellion, Murder, Idolatry and Popery to be all lawful because we find ancient times memorable for such impieties. 'Tis no plea in Divinity to alledge the prescription which sin has gained upon us, as an excuse.

The alterations successively made in the *Jewish* Commonwealth are nothing pertinent to the matter for whose proof they were brought, for they were either by a previous command or subsequent approbation of God manifested to his Prophets introduced and continued for their respective portions of time, and when we have such visible dispensations of the divine Will imparted to us, we will then be as active in our Obedience and Submission to God as the Authors of such Pamphlets are in their Malice and Disloyalty to their King; but till then we hope no man will expect that, because God who is the Sovereign Author of all Governments, and knows the ways and methods that are most suitable to their happiness, has often changed the form he prescribed to the *Jews;* Therefore we Men that are possessed with Interest, Passion, and Ambition may do the like upon Motives no ways certain or evident.

His Example of *Don Sancho,* who by the approbation of the three Estates took the Crown which was the right of his Nephews, is no less impertinent to his purpose, for he himself allows in the *4th.* page of his Pamphlet, that in *Spain* the next Heir cannot succeed but by the approbation of the Nobility, Bishops and States of the Realm. If so, is not that Kingdom in a manner Elective? And what parity is there between it and ours, where the next Heir is actual King without the Ceremonies of Coronation or the consent, choice or agreement of any? He is yet more unfortunate in the Case of *Hugo Capetus,* who by the choice (as he says) of the States of *France* invaded the Throne, to the prejudice of *Charles* Duke of *Lorrain* the next Heir; For whereas his Position was in the beginning, That any Government was alterable or ammendable by the mutual consent of the *Governours* and *Governed,* he now very learnedly proves this, by saying that the States alone did exclude *Charles* of *Lorrain;* which surely are not the absolute Governours, at least without the lawful King at the head of them, in any Hereditary Government in the World. If they be, an actual Prince may be deposed with as much Justice as an Heir can be excluded the Succession, and so (for ought we know) his *R. H.* being once removed out of their way, the next attempt will be against His Majesty.

His Story of *William Rufus* and his Brother *Henrie's* successively enjoying the Crown is to as little purpose as his Foreign Examples; for as it is certain that neither of them had any right whilst *Robert* Duke of *Normandy* was living, so their being admitted Kings by the consent of the Realm (that is, I suppose, of a Parliament) gave them no Title at all, by this Gentleman's supposition, who says that in such Cases the Will of the Governours and Governed must concur. The same Answer serves to defeat the pretended Legality of all his other examples, and therefore I leave him to bemoan his Ignorance, or plead Drunkenness (for his Discourse was delivered in a Tavern) as an excuse of his impertinencies. And I hope none of us will be so Unchristian or Impolitick as to think, that because by the Treasons and Conspiracies of ambitious, disloyal and designing Persons, the Crown was now and then transferred from one Family to another we now must do the like, when the occasions of such innovations are perfectly taken away, not only by the conjunction of the White and Red Roses, but likewise by the meeting of the Bloud Royal of the three Kingdoms in the Person of our present Monarch. To attempt this, were to bring all the evils upon the People to which the unsteddy course of Human Affairs can possibly subject them, For where a gap is once opened to Ambition and snatchings one from another, the most bloudy Commotions imaginable succeed, in which necessity obliging the parties to the practice of promiscuous Violences, Depredations and Slaughters, the People at last wearied with the Cruelties and Calamities of War, and to purchase quiet at any rate, often give up their Liberty to the Conquerour, and make the publick Desolations of their Country its Grave; so terrible an Example of which we had in the late Troubles,[7] that surely none, but such as are Betrayers of the *English* Liberty, or destined for Slavery, will venture the like Transgression the second time.

It will be said, that his *R. H.* has embraced the Papal Religion, which will be as destructive to the Temporal and Eternal Well-fare of the whole Kingdom, in case he should come to the Crown, as it is to his own Soul, and therefore, to prevent so universal a mischief, it is necessary his particular Interest should be sacrificed to the publick. To this I Answer,

1. No man ever yet gave any particular convincing instance of his

7. The reference is to the English civil wars.

being a Papist, besides his not conforming to the Religion now established by Law, or not taking such Oaths as would make him capable of enjoying all the great Offices of the Kingdom, to which his Birth and Merit without them might justly entitle him; But this Nonconformity is agreeable not only to all the Classes and Subdivisions of Protestantism, but to all the other Forms and Modes of Worship in the World, and his unwillingness to swear, proceeds, for ought we know, rather from a belief that all Oaths are unlawful, as not only many of old Christians, our present Quakers, but the most refined and ingeniously learned of all Modern Sects the Socinians, maintain, than that he thinks the matter of those the Law now requires to be Damnable or Heretical, and therefore we may as well say that he is a *Presbyterian, Independent,* or *Quaker,* or *Socinian;* or, which is yet worse, a *Turk* or *Jew,* as that he is a *Papist:* and to speak Truth our too much curiosity, and strict scrutiny into this matter, is far less warrantable than his concealing his opinion; for *Who art thou that judgest another Man's Servant? To his own Master he standeth or falleth; yea he shall be holden up, for God is able to make him stand.*

Therefore judge nothing before the time, until the Lord come, who both will bring to light the hidden things of Darkness, and will make manifest the Counsels of the hearts.

2. If he be a *papist* now, who can tell but the powerful operations of the Holy Spirit may by changing his Sentiments concerning Sacred things remove those jealousies and fears with which we are now so strongly possest, and add to his future happiness the temporal blessings we so much dread to lose? Faith is the Gift of God, and he being most just and merciful, will we hope bestow it where it may have the kindest reception, and bring forth its Fruits in greatest Plenty, that is on a Prince whose natural Endowments and moral Vertues are so eminent as, (if enlivened by true Faith as we hope they are) to enable him when a King to conquer the Atheism, Irreligion, Debauchery and other swarms of Evils, with which the Age abounds,

by his Example, as well as the Enemies of the Crown by his Valour. 'Tis our Duty then to wait the leisure of Providence, and not by a rash, not to say a wicked attempt, endeavour to deprive him of his right, and ourselves of the happiness his enjoying the Religion, as well as the Kingdom, of his Ancestors, may possibly secure unto us; nor do I see any satisfactory reason, why he should be so severely used, allowing no hopes of his Conversion or Return to the Church of *England*, for our Religion is sufficiently guarded by several Acts of Parliament, which he can never repeal. And besides, His present Majesty is (thank God) Strong, Active, and Vigorous, and likely enough either to outlive his *R. H.* or leave him so old and crazy as to want briskness answerable to his zeal, to attempt any notable change or innovation in the Government.

3. *Popery* in the single Person of the Prince, whatever is said to the contrary, is consistent enough with the Welfare of the Subjects, though of another Perswasion, as appears in *Germany*, where in many Places the Body of the People are of the Reformed, and the Prince of the *Romish* Religion, without diffidence or fear, or the narrow Spirit of Persecution of either side.

4. By the Principles of the Church of *England*, no Prince can be deposed, or forfeit his Right to the Sovereignty, purely upon the score of Religion; and as long as that Church is in being, and the rule and managment, next after the King, of all things as well Spiritual as Temporal, is by the Laws of the Land in its hands, and the hands of such as are Members of it, and obedient Children to the Practice and Discipline of so pious and charitable a Mother, 'tis evident that none else can be proper Judges, or have cognizance of the point now in debate, but they; and therefore his *R. H.* appeals to them, and is not at all concerned at what others can do, who doubtless have as great a desire to dethrone the King as to bar the Succession, could it be done with as much security and safety; For as he who intentionally and deliberately would destroy an Infant in the Mother's Womb, by causing

an abortion, would never scruple the bringing of him to an untimely
end after his coming into the World, did not the Law appoint Death
for the Punishment of this, though not of the other. So he, that on
the account of Religion, would exclude another from the possibility
he has to a Crown, would make no conscience of discharging an actual Prince, from his Royal Function, upon the same or other motives, were not his possession fenced and guarded by the Law, which
makes all such attempts High-Treason, and so exposes him to all the
evils attending so great a Crime.

But after all, why so much rancor, hatred and aversion against his
R. H.: who of all men living is the most passionate Lover of his
Country, and under whom, if ever it should be his lot to wear the Imperial Crown, it would undoubtedly be as happy as under any that
swayed the *English* Scepter since the Conquest; having so many
Princely Qualities, though now clouded and kept concealed from the
eyes of the Nation, by the artifice of his Adversaries, as would fill the
hearts of all true *English-men* with Love and Respect, and those of
his Enemies, whether Domestick or Foreign, with Fear and Confusion; For he is a Prince of a Noble Presence and affable Behaviour,
with a mixture of pleasantness in his Words and Actions, that wins
powerfully the affections of all that approach him. His discourses are
always pertinent and solid, free from Flourishes and a vain and
empty Ostentation of Wit, which sorts better with the levity of mim-
ical Heroes, upon a Theatre, than the true Grandeur of real Princes
in a Court.

He is of a most high Spirit, and invincible Courage, of mature
Wisdom, and singular Industry and Application to business, wary in
Council and quick in Execution; He hates above all things a perpet-
ual fluctuation and unsteddiness in the Measures and Politicks of
Government, because it makes it a Riddle to itself as well as to all
other Nations, and forces it to wander and stray from the proposed
Ends, having no clue of reason to guide it through so many

Labyrinths of Confusions, and therefore is constant and inflexible in his Resolutions, whilst suitable to the true Interest of the Nation, which often created him great and dangerous Enemies, every one hoping in the uncertainty and variety of Councils to be able to get the Ministry into his own hands, and therefore looking upon him with an Eye of Envy, as the hinderance and main obstacle of their ambitious purposes.

He is true and firm to his Friends and Servants, whom not chance or fortune, but parts and merit, with a long and unstained reputation of Honesty, places in his Favour; and as his love is not to the Persons, but their Vertues, so his hatred extends only to their Vices, and ends as soon as they begin to give any visible signs of their Repentance; and whatever is said to the contrary by some of his Enemies, who would scare the rest, and harden them in their wickedness, by putting them into a despair of forgiveness, he is not of a vindictive Spirit, for none ever yet fell otherwise than gently by his means, or smarted any longer under his indignation, than they continued obstinate and willful in the pursuit of his and the Country's disquiet, as might be proved by a thousand instances too tedious to be here recounted. In short, he is of a Martial and Souldierly Temper, patient of cold, heart, hunger, thirst and all the toils and fatigues naturally incident to War either by Sea or Land; his Valour is sprightly, but not rash; his Conduct wary and secure, and the events of his Battels and Engagements[8] still Fortunate and Succesful, all which would certainly make the *English* Nation (for whose Genius Providence has fitted him) readier to shed their Bloud to acquire him new Crowns, than deprive him of those Nature has already entitled him to, after the Death of his Brother, had not the inveterate malice of some rest-

---

8. James had experience in both the army and the navy. During the 1650s he served in the French army under the Vicomte de Turenne, the greatest general in Europe at the time, and later in the Spanish army. During his brother's reign he commanded the English fleet against the Dutch winning the battle at Lowestoft. He remained involved in naval affairs, although fears for his safety kept him from continuing to command in person.

less and Factious Spirits possessed them with an opinion of his having designed for so many years to involve them in Bloud and Slaughter; the falshood of which will easily appear, to any that consider his
actions all along since his and the King's Return from their Exile, to
which such Practices as are now afoot drove them.

I.

As it is doubtful whether he renounced the Religion, wherein he was
Educated, and embraced *Popery* more than *Socinianism*, or any other
form of Christianity distinct from the National Worship; so it is certain, that he always adhered to the True Interest of *England:* I mean
the Glory and Preservation of the *Monarchy*, which His Royal Father
consigned to his Posterity, Sealed with his Blood, shed by Men out-
doing in Practice (though not in Principles) the *Modern Reformers.*

II.

He hath made it his Business to free his Majesty's Subjects from their
Fatal Longings after a *Commonwealth,* to which the Contagion of
the late Times had Enslaved them; And by his Addresses, Sollicita-
tions, and Preferments, with which he was able (when in Power) to
Reward such brave Souls as signalized their Loyalty to his Father or
Brother in the Disorder of their Affairs; He hath brought that Virtue
in fashion again, and made more Converts to the Royal Authority,
than all the Orthodox Clergy with their Preachings and Arguments,
(how Learnedly and Industriously soever handled), were able to do.
  Quis enim Virtutem amplectitur ipsam, Praemia si tollas?[9]—The
Truth of this will appear easily to any, that will take the trouble to
consider, how notably the Reverence due to Majesty is impaired, and

---

9. For who will welcome virtue itself, if you take away all its rewards?

how Universally the *Anti-monarchical Principles* are spread within these Seven or Eight Years, since upon the misconceived Jealousies of the People, He declined the Influence He had upon the State, by his Great Imployments.

III.

Through the Power, which his Fidelity and Ability gave him over the King, He hath procured the chiefest Places of Strength in the Nation; And most of the great Trusts, as well Civil and Religious, as Military, to be confered upon known Royalists, and sworn Enemies to such, as under the specious pretence of securing our Liberties, would again involve Us in the same Calamities, from which, Providence hath so lately Delivered Us.

IV.

He hath been by his Advice and Influence over the great Ministers the Principal Opposer of all the *French Agents*, who in subservience to Their Interest, were often tampering for promoting of an *Arbitrary Government*, and of making the King's Interest both distinct from, and opposite to that of his People. And this He hath done in Obedience to the *Fundamental Laws*, for which he always testified a great Veneration, and to prevent the ill Effects constantly attending such Pernicious Councels: For He well knew from the History of some of his Progenitors, that an Attempt to remove the *Antient Boundaries and Land-marks of Government, never misses opening a way of Discord and Confusion; Of which, Ambitious Men taking Advantage, by their wheedling Practices, often perswade the* People *that are Heady, Valiant, and Jealous of their Liberty, to run into Rebellion; which as it generally terminates in the Ruine of the* Prince, *or* Subject, *so it often Enslaves both to the Power of a* Foreign Enemy; *For which Rea-*

son He always held the Constitution of the Kingdom as Sacred and Inviolable, in reference to the People, as He now does in regard of his own Right.

V.

It was This *Active and Vigilant Prince,* that (possessed with Flames of Love towards the City of *LONDON,* as violent as those that reduced it to Ashes),[10] exposed his person to a Thousand Dangers, to Rescue it from Destruction. He busied those Hands (destined for *Managing of Scepters*) in Breaking open Pipes and Conduits for Water, reached Buckets as nimbly as any of the Common People; cleared the Streets from the Throngs and Crouds, that hindered the carrying away of their Goods, Appointed his *Servants* and *Guards* to Conduct them to secure places: And in fine, for several Nights and Days, (without Sleep, or rest from Labour), was seen in all parts, giving the necessary Orders for preventing the further spreading of the Conflagration, as if Love (which usually works Miracles), had Multiplied him, or rather given him a kind of Ubiquity. And this He did, partly to shew his Gratitude to his Beloved *Londoners,* whose Minion He was, but chiefly to save the *Magazine* of the Strength and Treasure of the Kingdom from Desolation and Ruine.

VI.

Whatever is said of his Inclination to *Popery,* or the Humour of the *French Nation,* 'tis Evident, He understands, and pursues the Interest of *England* so well, that to check the Torrent of their Victories, by creating them work at home, he forwarded (as much as possibly he could) an Alliance, which *Monsieur Rohux,* a *French* Gentleman pro-

---

10. The great fire of London had occurred in 1665. James played an active role in trying to save the population and limit the damage.

posed to His Majesty for the Securing of *Foreign Protestants;* And it had in all probability come to a very happy Issue, had not *Monsieur Rovigny Leiger,* Embassador from *France* at this Court, prevented it, by corrupting one *Monsieur de Verax,* That after the Insurrection in the *Vivarets,* fled hither, and rid some time in the Guards; who (through Necessity, or Frailty), made Sale of the whole Secret, (and with It, of the Safety of his Friend, and the *Protestant Religion* in *France*), for Two Hundred *Pistols.* Upon notice of which Treachery, *Monsieur Rohux* retired into *Switzerland,* where being Seized by a Party of *French Horse,* he was conveyed to the *Bastile;* and after some time's Imprisonment, broken upon the Wheel at the place of Execution.

VII.

It was against his Will that the first and last *Dutch* Wars were commenced, yet the resolution being taken, by those, whose Will is a Law, in sheathing, or unsheathing the Sword of the Subjects, he valiantly, and for the Glory of the *English* Nation, in the *First,* with many Thousands of their Souldiers and Seamen, sunk a great part of their Fleet, blew up their Admiral, and with him the very Reputation of their Naval Power, thought before Invincible,[11] and by Sacking of *Scheveling* made proud *Amsterdam* tremble, for which great Services, as *England* shall ever be indebted, so the Parliament, then sitting, was pleased to vote him £.100,000 as a small acknowledgment of his Merit, and their Affections; and *London,* and all other Places, entertained him with Acclamations of Joy. Thus you see the vicissitude of Human Affairs, and how Fortune, which then opened the Hearts and Cities of the Kingdom, for his Reception, now shuts them, and all the Avenues to the Crown against him, which may

11. This is a reference to the naval battle at Lowestoft.

serve as an Example to *Perkin Warbeck*,[12] who never did anything to recommend him, besides the effect of Chance, his being a Protestant, how little reason he has to rely upon the Affections of a Multitude, that so easily forgets the real worth of their Darling Prince.
———Nor did he less deserve the hatred of his Enemy, and love of his Country in the last War, in which, though with the many notable Disadvantages of the Wind and Tide, being at Anchor when set upon, and the succeeding Mist, he yet behaved himself with that Gallantry, as made *De Ruiter* own us to be Invincible, and more than men, and particularly, that His R. H. exceeded all the Admirals in *Christendom*, as much by his Bravery, as he did by his Birth having, in the heat of the Engagement, (when Refitting, would lose the Benefit of his Orders, and Action), changed Ships oftener than Great Generals at Land, have done their Horses.

VIII.

It was this Zealous Prince, for the Honour and Safety of *England*, that advised the forming of the *Triple League*, which was the wisest Conjunction, and most for the Glory of the King's Reign, and the Preservation of His Dominions, that ever he entered into. And this he did, not only to curb *France*, whose Power he saw was already overgrown, but to save all the weaker Parts of *Christendom* from the Attempts of the stronger; For he knew that while that *League* continued firm, the King of *Sweden*, and the *States* of *Holland*, would have construed all Designs upon us in *England* as done against those of the same Interest with themselves, and in favour of whose Security, they had entered into that *Alliance*.

---

12. Warbeck was an infamous pretender of the late fifteenth century who claimed to be Richard, Duke of York, one of the two young princes who disappeared from the Tower during the reign of their uncle, Richard III. Warbeck rallied enemies of the Tudors on his behalf and was banished by Henry VII. He returned in an effort to capture the throne by force. After his defeat he confessed his imposture, was imprisoned, and subsequently was hanged.

IX.

He was so great a *Stranger* to the breaking of the *Triple League,* and seizing the *Dutch Smyrna* Fleet, that Sir *Edward Sprag,*[13] who was known to be his Creature, was not thought fit to be entrusted with the Secret, which occasioned the *Miscarriage* of the Design, and the Eternal Glory of his Highness.

X.

He hath not only maintained Correspondence with Foreign Princes, by His Majesty's *approbation,* for securing the well-fare of the Nation, but likewise endeavoured to draw them into an *Alliance* with us, to oppose the *French* particularly, or any other Foreign Enemy, that by Counsel, or Action, would endeavour the overthrow of our *Legal Government.* And besides many evidences of this, which are needless to mention at present, the secret Counsel, which, by His Majesty's Consent, he gave to our several *Ambassadors* abroad, and are yet to be seen, together with the many Letters he wrote to the same purpose, do uncontrollably demonstrate it.

XI.

It was He, that when the late Expedition into *Flanders,* was thought really Designed against the *French,* put all his Equipage into a readiness, and vowed to retrieve the Reputation of *England,* by Death or Conquest. But a *Great Man,* then at the Helm,[14] (now for his many

13. Sir Edward Spragge, admiral of the English fleet in 1667 during the Second Dutch War, was blamed for his part in the humiliation that occurred when the Dutch fleet sailed up the Thames to Chatham where the greater part of the English fleet lay at anchor, most ships without their crews. There, with little opposition, the Dutch burned the English ships and left only when they had used up their fireships. As they retreated they added insult to injury by towing the English flagship, the *Royal Charles,* away with them.

14. The "Great Man, then at the Helm" was Edward Hyde, Earl of Clarendon, that old royalist, champion of Charles I, chancellor of Charles II, and father-in-law of James, Duke of York. Clarendon had become unpopular for his power and wealth and his prudish manners so

Villanies confined to the Hold), thought fit by his *Advice* to make a *Mock-General*, for a *Mock-Army*, not daring to put such a great Indignity upon any, that had Sense to understand, or Courage to revenge it, which occasioned that Imposition of Peace, under which all the *States* of *Christendom* do, more or less, feel the heavy pressures of the *French* Insolence, whereas, had not that Mercenary Lord put a stop to the Parliament's Proceedings, and the Duke's Resolutions, *Europe* had in a few years been restored to its Tranquility.

XII.

He was so far from consenting to, or cooperating in any part of the *Popish Plot*, that *Oats* and *Bedlow*,[15] (the two Poles on which the whole Frame of it has its motion and circumgyration) did solemnly clear him, as appears by their several *Depositions*, and the *Journals* of both Houses of *Parliament*.

XIII.

It was the *Duke*, who, when Father *Bedingfield*[16] brought him the *Treasonable Letters* concerning the *PLOT,* immediately shewed them to the King, that so the *Conspirators* and their *Papers* might be seized, and the Truth sifted to the Bottom.

---

at odds with a decadent Court. He was even charged with a desire to keep parliaments in check and to have the king govern without them and with a standing army. Clarendon became the scapegoat for the Dutch disaster. He was threatened with impeachment, fled into exile, and was formally banished by the House of Lords.

15. Titus Oates and William Bedloe were both instrumental in spinning the web of allegations about a Catholic plot to overthrow the Protestant monarchy that triggered the Popish Plot panic of 1678/79.

16. Father Bedingfield was James, Duke of York's, Jesuit confessor. He received a packet of letters supposedly containing information about a Catholic plot and turned them over to the king.

XIV.

It is he, who this Summer, at *Windsor*, facilitated the *Treaty* of *Alliance*, made between This and The Crown of *Spain*, for the Common Security of both Nations, against all Enemies whatsoever, and to the unspeakable Advantage of our Merchants in that Country, and all other parts of the *Spanish* Dominions.

XV.

The incredible Expences of the Crown having drained His Majesty's *Exchequer*, to that degree, that he wanted Money for defraying the *Vast Charges*, of *Maintaining* and *Defending Tangier*, his *R. H.* rather than so Important a Place, for the Trade of the *Streights*, should fall into the hands of the *Moors*, and, perhaps, by them be delivered up to worse Enemies, generously disbursed a very considerable Sum of Money, for its Preservation; and by that Action shewed how sollicitous he is about the Well-fare of *England*, even at the very time, when it contrives his Destruction, which is an infallible Evidence of his being in his Nature and Principles very averse from Animosity and Revenge. To which his Enemies have reported him so addicted, that in the opinion of many, he is accounted irreconcilable; whereas he is so much of a contrary temper, that as he equals *Caesar* in his Greatness of Mind, and firmness of Resolution; so he out-does him in the particular Character of *Remembering all things but Injuries*. Christianity has made him so unalterable in this Point; that as Thousands of Examples do manifest his Sincerity in it, so his common and constant saying, *viz.* that *as he never forgets good turns, so he can easily forgive bad ones*, is an invincible proof of his Inclination. He needs no *Cicero* to plead the Cause of the Guilty, or heap upon him extravagant Praises for his Mercy to his Enemies in Distress; His own *Genius* leads him to the practice of that Gallantry, without the Intercession or Flattery of others. *Marcus Marcellus* was not with more readiness and affection received into *Caesar's* Favours, than all Adversaries may be into his, upon quitting those Crimes, for which he is now Vogued inexorable; And, were it his Fortune to have the full knowledge of this particular Virtue spread as far as the Effects have reached, I am confident it would be impossible for the Malice of a few, to impose upon others, so, as to make them continue their violent Actions against him, and think that their Security, (which is really their Hazard) instead of Repenting, to go on to greater Ills upon so groundless and malicious a supposition.

Lastly, as he believes that none deserves to have Obedience paid to him, when a King, that is Unruly and Refractory to his Prince's Command when a Subject, so he is submissive to his Majesty's Pleasure, even beyond the Prescript of Law, having now the third time, with the manifest hazard of his Person, besides the difficulties and inconveniencies of travelling, quitted his Native County, upon the first notice of his Commands.

Thus you see what a Prince *England* is weary of, and that as a weak and diseased Stomack, nauseates even the best Restorative, so our Nation in the Confusions and Distractions the fear of losing its Liberty has put it into, dreads none so much as him, who of all men living, if a King, would be the most able and willing to Defend them. But I hope *Scotland* understands his Merit, and its own Interest better,[17] and will secure him that Ancient Throne, whose Splendor is much abated, since that Kingdom is, by the Absence of their Kings, in a manner become a Province; if he fills it once with an exclusion from ours, it will soon regain its first Lustre, and your name will be as glorious, as ours will be detestable to Posterity. But however, as I would not have the happy Union of the two Kingdoms dissolved, so I hope that either our Repentance will recall him, or that, *Alexander*

17. In November 1679, a few months after the introduction of the first bill to exclude James from the throne, James was sent to Edinburgh as commissioner to the Scots Estates.

like, his own victorious Sword, will in time cut this Gordian Knot of the Succession, and Establish him in his Right. To which, as I doubt not but you will be assisting, so you need not question the help of all Loyal men here, and particularly of

Jan. 3. 1679.   Your humble
                                                 Servant
                                                      B. T.

Algernon Sidney, 1622–1683

The Very COPY of a

PAPER

Delivered to the

SHERIFFS,

Upon the Scaffold on *Tower-hill*, on *Friday Decemb. 7.* 1683.

By Algernoon Sidney, Esq;

Before his Execution there.

*T*his final testament of the renowned republican philosopher and politician Sir Algernon Sidney provides a vivid reminder of the persistence of that "good old cause" for which Vane had suffered more than twenty years before.

Sidney had an active military and political career, beginning in 1642, when he joined his father, the lord deputy of Ireland, in suppressing the Irish rebellion. Back in England he had enlisted as an officer in the Earl of Manchester's army, determined, he later wrote, to uphold the common rights of mankind, the laws of the land, and the true Protestant religion. When wounds he received at Marston Moor made soldiering impossible, he sat in the Long Parliament for Cardiff. Sidney played no part in the trial of Charles I and later opposed the engagement oath. Nevertheless, in 1652 he served on the Council of State. He was present when Cromwell entered the chamber and forcibly evicted the Rump. He later opposed the Protectorate. In 1659 when the Long Parliament was restored Sidney was among those who returned to the Commons where he was again elected to the Council of State. He was one of four commissioners appointed to mediate between the kings of Sweden and Denmark and was therefore out of England when Charles II was recalled and the Restoration took place.

Unlike Vane, Sidney was not among those individuals specifically exempted from pardon. Nevertheless he chose to remain abroad, unwilling to live under suspicion or to plead repentance. After some seventeen years of self-imposed exile he returned to England to settle his private affairs. Once home he got immersed in the exclusion debate and decided to remain. Sidney made four unsuccessful attempts to win election to Parliament. His involvement in Whig intrigues with the French damaged his reputation. Although he apparently never plotted armed resistance, he was arrested in 1683 after the so-called Rye House Plot on three charges of treason: for consultations to levy war against the king; for sending a man to Scotland to conspire with the Scots; and for the sentiments expressed in Discourses Concerning Government, *his unpublished manuscript written to refute Sir Robert Filmer's* Patriarcha, or the Natural Power of Kings Asserted. *Indeed, Sidney's manuscript would be used by the judge as the crucial second witness against him.*

Sidney defended himself vigorously despite the usual liabilities suffered by those charged with treason and the additional burden of facing the notorious Judge Jeffreys on the bench. His witnesses discredited the only direct witness against him, Lord Howard of Escrick. Nevertheless he was found guilty, sentenced on 26 November 1683, and beheaded on 7 December. Instead of a scaffold speech he handed the sheriffs the essay reprinted here and passed another copy to a friend.

When the two-page "Last Paper" was published, it caused a sensation and quickly went into three editions. It was reprinted with government approval on the premise that it would demonstrate that Sidney was a traitor. Contrary to tradition these last words were not repentant but defiant. He denounced the injustice of his trial and embraced the theories of his Discourses Concerning Government *and of the "good old cause." Indeed Sidney ended with thanks to God for permitting him to die for that cause in which he was engaged from his youth.*

Men, Brethren, and Fathers; Friends, Countrymen, and Strangers;

IT May be expected that I should now say some Great matters unto you, but the Rigour of the Season, and the Infirmities of my Age, encreased by a close Imprisonment of above Five months, doth not permit me.

Moreover, we live in an Age that maketh Truth pass for Treason: I dare not say anything contrary unto it, and the Ears of those that are about me will probably be found too tender to hear it. My Trial and Condemnation doth sufficiently evidence this.

West, Rumsey, and *Keyling,*[1] who were brought to prove the Plot, said no more of me, than that they knew me not; and some others equally unknown unto me, had used my Name, and that of some others, to give a little Reputation unto their Designs. The Lord *Howard*[2] is too famous by his Life, and the many Perjuries not to be denied, or rather sworn by himself, to deserve mention; and being a single Witness would be of no value, though he had been of unblemished Credit, or had not seen and confessed that the Crimes committed by him would be pardoned only for committing more; and even the Pardon promised could not be obtained till the Drudgery of Swearing was over.

This being laid aside, the whole matter is reduced to the Papers

1. It was on the basis of information from these three men that charges were brought against Whigs for plotting to murder Charles II and launch a general insurrection. Sidney, among others, was arrested, charged, and convicted. Josiah Keeling, an oil merchant, first to inform the Privy Council of the Rye House Plot, was followed by Colonel John Rumsey and Robert West, who reported their knowledge of two plots, the Rye House Plot and a more general insurrection. Keeling was rewarded and given a post but was dismissed for Jacobitism after the Glorious Revolution and died in prison. Both his story and West's wild and inconsistent account have earned them comparison with Titus Oates.

2. William Lord Howard was indeed famous as an informer. He played that role during the Popish Plot and made himself useful to the Restoration government as an informer against his former associates among the sectaries. At the trial of Lord Stafford he gave evidence against his own kinsman in addition to evidence against Sidney, Russell, and John Hampden's grandson, John.

said to be found in my Closet by the King's Officers, without any other Proof of their being written by me, than what is taken from suppositions upon the similitude of an Hand that is easily counterfeited, and which hath been lately declared in the Lady *Car's* Case[3] to be no Lawful Evidence in Criminal Causes.

But if I had been seen to write them, the matter would not be much altered. They plainly appear to relate unto a large Treatise written long since in answer to *Filmer's* Book,[4] which by all Intelligent Men is thought to be grounded upon wicked Principles, equally pernicious unto Magistrates and People.

If he might publish unto the World his Opinion, That all Men are born under a necessity derived from the Laws of God and Nature, to submit unto an Absolute Kingly Government, which could be restrained by no Law, or Oath; and that he that hath the Power, whether he came unto it by Creation, Election, Inheritance, Usurpation, or any other way had the Right, and none must Oppose his Will but the Persons and Estates of his Subjects must be indespensably subject unto it; I know not why I might not have published my Opinion to the contrary, without the breach of any Law I have yet known.

I might as freely as he, publickly have declared my Thoughts, and the Reasons upon which they were grounded, and I persuaded to believe, That God had left Nations unto the Liberty of setting up such Governments as best pleased themselves.

That Magistrates were set up for the good of Nations, not Nations for the honour or glory of Magistrates.

3. This reference is probably to the petition of Lady Mary Carr on behalf of herself and her husband, Robert Carr, the younger, to settle the estate of Sir Robert Carr. This petition before the House of Lords in 1664 caused considerable debate before it was eventually amended and approved by the Parliament.

4. This large treatise was Sidney's *Discourses Concerning Government*, which was apparently written between 1681 and 1683 but not published until fifteen years after Sidney's death. Sir Robert Filmer's book, *Patriarcha: A Defence of the Natural Power of Kings Against the Unnatural Liberty of the People*, which provoked Sidney to write his *Discourses*, was first published in 1680, after Filmer's death, but had been circulated in manuscript form prior to publication.

That the Right and Power of Magistrates in every Country, was that which the Laws of that Country made it to be.

That those Laws were to be observed, and the Oaths taken by them, having the force of a Contract between Magistrate and People, could not be Violated without danger of dissolving the whole Fabrick.

That Usurpation could give no Right, and the most dangerous of all Enemies unto Kings were they, who raising their Power to an Exorbitant Height, allowed unto Usurpers all the Rights belonging unto it.

That such Usurpations being seldom Compassed without the Slaughter of the Reigning Person, or Family, the worst of all Villanies was thereby rewarded with the most Glorious Privileges.

That if such Doctrines were received, they would stir up men to the Destruction of Princes with more Violence than all the Passions that have hitherto raged in the Hearts of the most Unruly.

That none could be Safe, if such a Reward were proposed unto any that could destroy them.

That few would be so gentle as to spare even the Best, if by their destruction a Wild Usurper could become God's Anointed; and by the most execrable Wickedness invest himself with that Divine Character.

This is the Scope of the whole Treatise; the Writer gives such Reasons as at present did occur unto him, to prove it. This seems to agree with the Doctrines of the most Reverenced Authors of all Times, Nations and Religions. The best and wisest of Kings have ever acknowleged it. The present King of *France*[5] hath declared that Kings have that happy want of Power, that they can do nothing contrary unto the Laws of their Country, and grounds his Quarrel with the

5. Louis XIV was then king of France.

King of *Spain, Anno.* 1667. upon that Principle. King *James* in his Speech to the Parliament *Anno.* 1603.[6] doth in the highest degree assert it. The Scripture seems to declare it. If nevertheless the Writer was mistaken, he might have been refuted by Law, Reason and Scripture; and no Man for such matters was ever otherwise punished, than by being made to see his Errour; and it hath not (as I think) been ever known that they had been referred to the Judgment of a Jury, composed of Men utterly unable to comprehend them.

But there was little of this in my Case; the extravagance of my Prosecutors goes higher: the above-mentioned Treatise was never finished, nor could be in many years, and most probably would never have been. So much as is of it was Written long since,[7] never reviewed nor shewn unto any Man; and the fiftieth part of it was produced, and not the tenth of that offered to be read. That which was never known unto those who are said to have Conspired with me, was said to be intended to stir up the People in Prosecution of the Designs of those Conspirators.

When nothing of particular Application unto Time, Place, or Person could be found in it, (as hath ever been done by those who endeavoured to raise Insurrections) all was supplied by *Innuendoes.*

Whatsoever is said of the Expulsion of *Tarquin;* the Insurrection against *Nero;* The Slaughter of *Caligula,* or *Domitian;* The Translation of the Crown of *France* from *Meroveus* his Race unto *Pepin;* and from his Descendants unto *Hugh Capet,* and the like, applied by *Innuendo* unto the King.

They have not considered, that if such Acts of State be not good, there is not a King in the World that has any Title to the Crown he bears; nor can have any, unless he could deduce his Pedigree from the

6. For James I's speech to his first Parliament, 22 March 1603/4, see *CJ* I, 142–46.

7. Thomas West, editor of *Discourses Concerning Government* (Indianapolis, 1990), xviii, reckons it was written between 1681 and 1683, more recently than Sidney claims here.

Eldest Son of *Noah,* and shew that the Succession had still continued in the Eldest of the Eldest Line, and been so deduced to him.[8]

Everyone may see what advantage this would be to all the Kings of the World; and whether that failing, it were not better for them to acknowledge they had received their Crowns by the Consent of Willing Nations; or to have no better Title unto them than Usurpation and Violence, which by the same ways may be taken from them.

But I was long since told that I must Die, or the Plot must Die.

Least the means of destroying the best Protestants in *England* should fail, the Bench must be filled with such as had been Blemishes to the Bar.

None but such as these would have Advised with the King's Council, of the means of bringing a Man to death; Suffered a Jury to be packed by the King's Solicitors, and the Under-Sheriff; Admit of Jury-men who are not Freeholders; Receive such Evidence as is above mentioned; Refuse a Copy of an Indictment, or to Suffer the Statute of 46 *Ed.* 3.[9] to be read, that doth expresly Enact, It should in no Case be denied unto any Man upon any occasion whatsoever; Overrule the most important Points of Law without hearing. And whereas the Stat. 25 *Ed.* 3.[10] upon which they said I should be Tried, doth Reserve unto the Parliament all Constructions to be made in Points of Treason, They could assume unto themselves not only a Power to make Constructions, but such Constructions as neither agree with Law, Reason, or Common Sence.

By these means I am brought to this Place. The Lord forgive these Practices, and avert the Evils that threaten the Nation from them. The Lord Sanctify these my Sufferings unto me; and though I fall as

---

8. This patriarchal theory that kings derive their right to govern in a line of descent from Noah is the theory upon which Filmer bases his notion of divine right in *Patriarcha.*

9. There were no acts passed in 46 Edward III. Sidney probably means to cit 45 Edw. III, cap. 1, A Confirmation of the Great Charter and the Charter of the Forest in all Points.

10. 25 Edw. III, stat. 5, cap. 2 (1350), A Declaration which Offences shall be adjudged Treason.

a Sacrifice unto Idols, suffer not Idolatry to be Established in this Land. Bless thy People, and Save them. Defend thy own Cause, and Defend those that Defend it. Stir up such as are Faint; Direct those that are Willing; Confirm those that Waver; Give Wisdom and Integrity unto All. Order all things so as may most redound unto thine own Glory. Grant that I may Die glorifying Thee for all Thy Mercies; and that at the last Thou hast permitted me to be Singled out as a Witness of thy Truth; and even by the Confession of my Opposers, for that OLD CAUSE in which I was from my Youth engaged, and for which Thou has Often and Wonderfully declared thy Self.

We do appoint *Robert Horn, John Baker,* and *John Redmayne,* to Print this Paper, and that none other do Presume to Print the same.

Peter Daniel.
Sam. Dashwood.

London.
Printed for *R. H. J. B.* and *J. R.* and are to be
sold by *Walter David* in *Amen Corner,* MDCLXXXIII.

The King's
Inalienable
Prerogative

[John Brydall, b. 1635?]

THE
ABSURDITY

Of that New devised

State-Principle,

(*VIZ.*)

That in a Monarchy, *The Legislative Power is Communicable to the Subject, and is not radically in Soveraignty in one, but in More.*

In a Letter to a Friend.

Ουκ ἀγαθὸν πολυκοιρανίη, εἰς κοίρανος ἔστω
Haud Multos regnare bonum est, Rex unius esto.

LONDON,
Printed for *T. D.* and are to be sold by
Randal Taylor, near *Stationers Hall*, 1681

*T*his essay in the form of a letter has been attributed to John Brydall, the author of some thirty-six published treatises, most of which dealt with the law.

Little is known about Brydall's personal life. He was a native of Somerset. He was educated at Jesus College, Cambridge, and Queen's College, Oxford, then went on to Lincoln's Inn. While there he served as captain of a foot regiment raised for the king by the Inns of Court. He seems to have been noted for his pike exercises. Brydall later became secretary to Sir Harbottle Grimston, who served as master of the rolls from 1660 until his death in 1685. Between 1673 and 1700 Brydall published numerous treatises, for some reason all anonymously. At his death he left another thirty treatises still in manuscript.

Brydall was a champion of prerogative and absolute royal power. The emergence of the Whigs and the challenge of the exclusion crisis provoked him to write on political, as opposed to legal, theory. In the tract reprinted here he stoutly defends the absolutist concepts of Jean Bodin and the views of Sir Robert Filmer, whose Patriarcha *had been published the previous year. As Sidney and the Whigs harked back to the principles of the "good old cause," Brydall was among those who harked back to the principles of the absolutist defenders of monarchy. Both Sidney and Brydall demonstrate the longevity of the old quarrel as it resurfaced in the new political situation of an impending Catholic succession. "The Absurdity of That New Devised State-Principle" appeared in only a single edition.*

SIR,

YOU cannot but remember, that at our last Meeting, there happened betwixt us, a hot dispute touching Co-ordination, occasioned by your reading the day before a Tract, not long since exposed to publick view, and Intituled, by the Author thereof, *An Account of the Growth of Knavery,* &c. In a Letter to a Friend,[1] (In Answer to Two Pamphlets, the one styled, *An Account of the Growth of Popery and Arbitrary Government in* England;[2] The other, *A seasonable Argument to perswade all the Grand Juries in* England *to Petition for a New Parliament*);[3] In which said Tract there are some Passages that seem very distastful to your Palat, but more especially that Sentence (pag. 44 & 45.) concerning the Legislative Power thus expressed by our Author.

"The Making of Laws," sayes he, "is a peculiar and incommunicable Priviledge of the Supream Power; And the Office of the Two Houses in this Case, is only Consultive or Preparative, but the Character of the Power, rests in the Final Sanction, which is in the King; and effectually the passing of a Bill is but the Granting of a Request; The Two Houses make the Bill 'tis true, but the King makes the Law, and 'tis the Stamp, and not the Matter that makes it Currant."

This piece of Doctrine [say you] is very strong and Heterodox; for it contradicts, not only your own darling Sentiments, but also the opinion of many other Persons in this Nation, who hold, That the Legislature resides not in the King only, but in him, and in the Two Houses of Parliament; so that you, and those other Persons fancy a Mixture, or Co-ordinacy in the Supremacy itself, making the *English* Monarchy a Compound of Three Co-ordinate Estates.

This same opinion, say you, is founded upon the Authority of the

1. Roger L'Estrange, "An Account of the Growth of Knavery" (London, 1678), Wing L1193.
2. Andrew Marvell, "Account of the Growth of Popery" (Amsterdam, 1677), Wing M860.
3. Andrew Marvell, "A Seasonable Argument to Perswade All the Grand Juries" (Amsterdam, 1677), Wing M885.

Law Books, which tell us, That every Statute must be made by the King, Lords and Commons; And if it appear by the Act that is made by Two of them only, it is no Statute, as appears by 4 H. 7.18.b. *Co. Lit.* 139.b. *Co. 4. Inst. f. 25. Co. 2. Inst.* 157. 158. 334. *Bulstrod's* Reports, *Dominus Rex & Allen, v. Tooley.*

These same Authorities I allow as well as you, but then it must be with this distinction, that the Two Houses of Parliament, are in a sort Co-ordinate with His Majesty *Ad aliquid* to some Act, or Exercising the Supream Power that is to say, there is an equal Right in the King and the Two Houses of a Negative Voice in respect of new Laws to be Enacted, or old to be repealed. But if you intend by Co-ordination (as indeed you do) a Fellowship with the King, in the very Supremacy itself, you are much beside the Cushion, and truly in the wrong side of the Hedge too. Because it is repugnant to the nature thereof, and a clear Contradiction, If it be true as it is, that the King is our only Soveraign, there can be no such thing, as a Co-ordinate or Co-equal Power; If they be Co-partners in the Soveraignty, in what a fine Condition are we, that must be obliged to Impossibilities. For we must obey three Masters, Commanding contrary things. The Two Houses may as well injoin us to do them Homage, which is, and ought to be performed only to the King, as to challenge a Corrival Power with the Soveraignty of Royalty. 'Tis true, no Law can be imposed on us, without the consent of the Two Houses, yet this doth not make them Co-ordinate with their Prince in the very Supremacy of Power itself, but still leaves the Power of Ordaining Supreamly in him as in the Fountain, though the Efflux or Exercise of that Power be not solely in his Will, but expects the Consent of his People; And therefore 'tis very curiously expressed by the Learned Mr. *Hooker*,[4] *That Laws do not take their Constraining Force from the Quality of such as devise them, but from the Power that doth give them the strength of Laws: Le Roy le*

4. Richard Hooker, *Of the Laws of the Ecclesiastical Polity*, book I, chap. 10, 8.

veult, the King will have it so, is the Interpretative Phrase pronounced at the King's passing of every Act of Parliament: "And it
was," sayes Sir *Henry Filmer* in that most excellent discourse called
Patriarcha, "the Antient Custom for a long time, till the dayes of
Henry 5. that the Kings, when any Bill was brought unto them, that
had passed Both Houses, to take and pick out what they liked not,
and so much as they chose was Enacted for a Law: but the Custom of
the later Kings hath been so Gracious, as to allow alwayes of the entire Bill (and sometimes with a Tacking too) as it hath passed both
Houses."[5]

So much (Sir) in general, touching your fancied Corrivality of
Power, I come now to a more close and minute Application, and I
argue thus:

If the Two Houses have a Joint and Co-equal Authority with their
King in making Laws and the like, it must be one of these two wayes,
either it must be *Primitively* Seated in them, or it belongs to them
by *derivative participation*.

First, the Two Houses of Parliament cannot have this Co-ordinate
Power vested in them Primitively or Radically; For are not Both
Houses Summoned by the King's Writ? Do they not sit in Parliament by Virtue only of the Authority Royal? Can either the Lords
or Commons or both together Lawfully convene themselves, appoint
the time and place of their own Meeting? Our Books of Law can tell
you (Sir) that the Power of Convocating and keeping of Assemblies
of Subjects; the Power of Calling, Holding and Proroguing of Parliaments is an Essential Part, and Inseparable Privilege of the *English*
Regality.

All able Jurists and Politicans very well know, that the King is
Caput Principium & Finis Parliamenti,[6] solely made and Created by

---

5. The passage cited is from *Patriarcha*, chap. 31, by Robert, not Henry Filmer.
6. The head, beginning, and end of Parliament.

him, and unto him only can be ultimately resolved. And therefore surely it must be the most unreasonable thing that ever was in the World, that Subjects Assembled by their Soveraign's Writ, should have a Co-equality of Power with their Prince, without whose call they could not meet together, and at whose will and pleasure they are Dissolved in Law, and bound to betake themselves to their own Habitations: And return to the *Status quo* of Private Persons and Subjects, whereas Supremacy is a Publick and indelible Character of Lawful Authority.

But farther, can the Two Houses of Parliament pretend to be before our First King in time, can they outvy him in Seniority? Surely, no. As for the Lords, *Bracton* affirms, that the Earls and Barons were Created by the King, and assumed to him only for Counsel and Advice; which infers undoubtedly, that the Power they are invested withall, is not by a Contrivement or Reservation (as some Fanaticks fancy) at the supposed Making of the First King, but proceeds, *ex Indulto Regum* from the gratuit Concessions of our Princes.

But it was Objected by you in our Disceptation as it hath been by others heretofore, that the very Style of *Comites*[7] and Peers, implies a Co-ordinative Association with the King in the Government; they are in Parliament his *Comites*, his Peers.

I Answer, that Mr. *Bracton* tells us, *Rex parem non habet in Regno suo,* the King has no Peer, and offereth us another Reason of the Style of *Comites, Quia sunt in Comitatu,*[8] without any Relation to Parliament, because they are either in the Train of the King, or because placed in each County, *ad Regendum Populum,*[9] and so assumed to the King to the like end that *Moses* did his under-Officers, in Governing his People. They were not only to be Companions as to his Person, but in respect of his Cares; *Pares Curis, solo diademate dis-*

---

7. Companions, or court.
8. Because they are in the court or retinue.
9. For ruling or governing the people.

pares.[10] They are the Highest, and in the nature of Privy-Counsellors, but Created by the Soveraign Prince (the Fountain of Honour) and so not equal unto him, though exalted above Fellow-Subjects. To be short, if this word [*Comites*] should imply a Co-ordinative Society, it must needs follow that the Commons must be the King's Peers too, for they are as much Co-ordinate with His Majesty as the other; And so let's set up Three Thrones, One for the King, another for the Lords, and a Third for the House of Commons.

I would advise you (Sir) to make a Voyage, next long Vacation, into *France,* and argue there at the *French* Court, from the Denomination of *Pares Franciae,* and see what Thanks you shall have for your Logick. Thus much for the Lords, I must have a touch at the Commons too.

As for the Commons, they surely will not pretend to exceed the Lords in Antiquity: If what Sir *Robert Cotton* (that Famous Antiquary) relates, in some part of his *Posthuma* Works, be truth; And he hath been pleased in this very manner to express himself.[11]

As this great Court or Council, consisting of the King and Barons, ruled the great Affaires of State, and Controlled all Inferiour Courts; so were there certain Officers, whose transcendent Power seemed to be set to bound in the Execution of Princes' Wills, as the Steward, Constable and Marshal fixed upon Families for many Ages. They as Tribunes of the People, or *Ephori* amongst the *Athenians,* grown by an unmannerly Carriage, fearful to Monarchy, fell at the Feet and Mercy of the King, where the daring Earl of *Leicester* was slain at *Evesham.* This Chance and the Dear Experience *Henry* the Third himself had made at the Parliament at *Oxford* in the Fortieth year of

10. Equals in cares (responsibilities), unequal by the crown alone.
11. From "A Brief Discourse concerning the Power of the Peers, and Commons of Parliament, In point of Judicature," *Cottoni Postuma: Divers Choice Pieces of that Renowned Antiquary, Sir Robert Cotton,* J. H. [James Howell] Esq., ed. (London, 1679), 348–49.

his Reign, and the Memory of the many streights his Father[12] was driven unto, especially at *Runney Meade* near *Stanes*, brought this King wisely to begin, what his Successor fortunately finished in lessening the Strength and Power of His great Lords. And this wrought by searching into the Regality, they had Usurped over their peculiar Soveraigns (whereby they were (as the Book of Saint *Alban's* termeth them) *Quot Domini, Tot Tyranni*),[13] and by weakening that Hand of Power which they carried in the Parliaments, by Commanding the Service of many Knights, Citizens and Burgesses to that General Council. Now began the frequent sending of Writs, to the Commons their Assents, not only used in Money, Charge and Making Laws (for before all Ordinances passed by the King and Peers) but their Consent in Judgments of all natures, whether Civil or Criminal.

By what I have here offered out of Sir *Robert Cotton*, and elsewhere before in this Discourse; It is as clear as the Sun at Noon day, That the Two Houses of Parliament are not *Co-aetaneous* with the First King, much less before him, and consequently the Legislature cannot be said to be Originally and Radically seated in the Lords and Commons.

Secondly, As I have made it appear that the Architectonick Power Paramount of making Laws in Parliament was never Natively, and formally seated in the Two Houses, so I come now to prove that the Supream Legislative Authority was never vested in them, by way of Emanation, or derivation from the Imperial Crown of this Nation.

Now if they have derivatively such a power, it must be one of these two wayes, either by way of Donation or Usurpation: Again, if they have it *via Donationis*, by way of Grant, they must have it either by

---

12. King John.
13. As many as there are lords, so many are there tyrants.

way of Division or by way of Communication: But they cannot challenge it by either of these same wayes.

1. The Houses of Parliament may not challenge a Co-ordination in the Supremacy by way of Division or Partition; For *Suprema potestas,* is an Entity or being Indivisible; as it is subordinate to none but God Almighty; so it admitteth no *Co-ordinate, Collateral, Co-equal* or *Corrival Power.* To make *Majestatem in Majestate, Regnum in Regno,* more than one Soveraign in a Kingdom, is inconsistent with *Supremity;* for Supream admits neither of Equal nor Superiour, and to affirm it, is *Contradictio in Adjecto.*[14] And therefore you may read, that *Henry de Beauchamp* Earl of *Warwick* for the singular favour that King *Henry* the Sixth bare to him, Crowned him King of *Wight:* But we could never find (sayes *Cook*) any Letters Patents of this Creation, because (as some hold) the King could not by Law, Create him a King within his own Kingdom, because there cannot be Two Kings in one Kingdom, or if such there be, they are but *Reguli* or *Proreges,* Kings to their Subjects, and Subjects to the Supream King.

So *Oedipus* King of the *Thebans* having Issue Two Sons, *Polynices* and *Eteocles,* ordained that after his Decease, his Two Sons should alternative by Course, Reign in his Kingdom. But what was the event? *Fratres de Regni Haereditate dissidentes singulari certamine Congressi mutuis vulneribus ceciderunt.*[15]

Let any Man look upon the Estate of the *Roman* Empire, when it was divided by *Constantine* the Great amongst his Three Sons, *Constantinus, Constantius* and *Constans;* Or upon the Estate of the Western Empire, after the Division made by *Lotharius, Lewis* and *Charles,* Sons of *Ledovicus Pius;* And he will find most sad and horrible Confusions ensued on such Partitions. But letting pass Forreign Countries, we must not pretermit the miserable Estate within this

14. A contradiction in terms.
15. The brothers disagreeing about the inheritance of the kingdom met in single combat and killed each other.

Kingdom, under the Heptarchy until all was Re-united under one Soveraign; And this is the Reason that in *England, Scotland* and *Ireland,* the Royal Dignity is descendible to the Eldest Daughter or Sister, *Co. 4 Inst. f. 243 & on Lit. fol.* 165. a. For *Regnum non est divisible:*[16] And so was the Descent of *Troy.*

> *Praeter te sceptrum Ilione quod gesserat olim*
> *Maxima Natarum Priami.*[17]

2. As the Two Houses cannot have a Co-ordinate Power with the King, by way of Division; so neither can they challenge to themselves a Co-ordination in the Supremacy itself by way of Communication; for the Prerogative of Legislation (as many others) is so naturally intrinsically inherent in the Supremacy (for where Majesty is, there must be the Power Legislative), that it cannot be transferred or separated from the Crown, or so Communicated to Both Houses, as to denude or disrobe the King of that Sacred Supream Right which God has given to him, as his Vice-regent on Earth.

Ea quae Jurisdictionis sunt & pacis (sayes our *Bracton*) *ad nullum pertinent nisi ad Coronam, & dignitatem Regiam, nec à Coronâ separari poterunt, cum faciant ipsam Coronam,* Lib. 2.c.24.[18]

The old Statute of *Praerogativa Regis* tells us, That our King can grant no Prerogative to the prejudice of the Crown. And thereupon whatsoever a King of this Land Grants to his Subjects, or to any other that is essentially in the Crown of this Kingdom, that is to say, really annexed to the Person of a Man, as he is King of *England,* as that the parting with it, makes him to be no King, or a less King than he ought to be in Dignity or Royal Power the Grant is void, the Grant how large soever, It must be understood with this Limitation, *Salvo Jure*

---

16. For the kingdom is not divisible.

17. Before you [is] the scepter which Ilione, the eldest of the daughters of Priam, formerly wielded.

18. Those things having to do with jurisdiction and peace pertain to no one else but the Crown, and the royal dignity, nor could they be separated from the Crown, even though they support the Crown.

Coronae. And how tender our Former Kings and their Subjects have been of the Rights and Prerogatives of the Crown, Pray (Sir) at your good leasure consult the Statutes of 28.E.1.c.2 & 20. 34.E.3.c.15 & 17. 5.R.2.c.13. 11.R.2.c.9. 9.H.5.c.1. 28.H.6.c.2 & 27.E.1.c.5.

With our Municipal Laws do concurr Two Famous Jurists, I mean, *Gothofrede* and *Suarez.*

The former returns an Answer to this *Quaere, Potestne Princeps Regalia alteri Cedere?*

Potest (sayes he) *His temperamentis adjectis, ut ne Regalia Jura sua cedat sine summâ necessitate, ac ut ea cedat ex causâ necessariâ, ut ne ea tota cedat: Deinde ut quaecunque cedit suopte motu, ac sua sponte sciens, prudensque cedat,* Principatûs Jure Excepto: *quod etsi nominatim non fuerit exceptum, tacitè tamen exceptum intelligitur (cum adversus omnes Regalia possidentes, in suo Regno, Jus instituendae Actionis habeat) adeo ut Jus id nullo tempore possit praescribi.*

The latter *viz. Suarez* sayes thus, *Regnum est veluti quoddam Officium quod incumbit propriae Personae, cui confertur, & non tam est propter ipsam, quam propter eos, qui regendi sunt, & ideo non potest Rex, vel Regina tale onus à se separare, etiam quoad usum, vel administrationem, ita ut non maneat apud ipsum suprema potestas, & Obligatio Regendi; non ergo transferri potest illo modo Administratio Regni in Regem, Ratione Matrimonii.*[19]

19. [From Gottfried or Godfrey] Query: Can the Prince cede the royalty to another? He can, given a special set of proportionate circumstances, lest he cede his royal rights without supreme necessity; and that he cede them from a necessary cause, so that he not cede all of them. Then that whatever he cedes by his own motion, and that he may cede it spontaneously knowing and prudently, With The Exception Of The Rights Of Princely Rule: because even if what is made an exception were not named explicitly, it is still tacitly understood to be excepted (although he may have a right of initiating action against all those possessing royal rights in his kingdom) and besides the right that at no time it be able to be set forth in writing.

The latter, namely, Suarez, says thus. Rule is similar to a certain office that is properly incumbent upon a certain person on whom it is conferred, and not so that it is on account of that very person, instead of those who are to be ruled, and therefore a king or a queen cannot separate such a burden from themselves, even as regards use, or administration, so that the supreme power does not remain with him or her; and the obligation to govern therefore can-

The sum of all that I have said as to the point of Communication is this; That however the prime essential Constitutives of Monarchy, in the exercise of them, may be intrusted by the King to the Subject by way of Delegation to ease his Burden and to facilitate his Royal Charge, yet in so doing, he does not, he cannot divest himself of the Soveraign Power, nor of any of those Sacred Rights and Prerogatives that are naturally and intrinsecally inherent in his Imperial Crown.

In the last place, as the Two Houses cannot challenge to themselves by way of Grant (that is to say neither by Division, nor by Communication) a Co-ordination in the very Supremacy of Power itself (and consequently there cannot be any such thing as a Co-equality of Power in the Legislature); so neither can they make forth a good and Lawful Title to themselves, for a Fellowship in the Legislative Power, *via usucapionis,* by virtue of any Custom or Prescription; For no immemorial Custom can hold good, when there be Authentical Records to the Contrary; And whether there be not such, I will appeal unto your own good self.

Antiently the Law Enacted began thus, *Rex Statuit,* the King Ordains, and before the Laws and Statutes in each King's Reign from the time of *Edward* the First to this day, I find the Title or Introduction thus expressed as follows.

7.Edward 1. the Statute of Mortmain, *We therefore by Advice of our Prelates, Earles, Barons and other Subjects, have provided, made and Ordained.*

9.Edward 2. The Statute of Sheriffs——*Our Lord the King, by the Assent of the Prelates, Earles, Barons and other great Estates, hath Ordained and Established.*

5.Edward 3. Statute de Natis ultra Mare, *Our Lord the King by the Assent of the Prelates, Earles, Barons and other Great Men, and all the*

---

not be transferred in that manner in which the administration of the kingdom is transferred to the king by reason of matrimony.

Commons of the Realm, hath Ordained and Established these things under Written.

3.Richard 2.c.3.————*Our Lord the King, by the Advice, and Common Consent, &c. hath Ordained and Established.*

4.Edward 4.c.1.————*Our Lord the King, by the Advice, Assent Request and Authority aforesaid, hath Ordained and Established.*

1.Richard 3.c.2.————*Therefore the King will, it be Ordained by the Advice and Assent of the Lords Spiritual and Temporal, and the Commons of this Present Parliament.*

1.Henry 7.c.7.————*The King our Soveraign Lord, by the Advice and Assent of the Lords Spiritual and Temporal, at the Supplication of the Commons ordaineth.*

1.Henry 8.c.7.————*The King our Soveraign, by the Assent of the Lords Spiritual and Temporal, and the Commons ordaineth.*

1.Edward 6.c.4.————*Wherefore the King our Soveraign Lord, at the humble Petition and Suit of the Lords and Commons, doth Ordain, Declare and Enact, by the Assent of the Lords Spiritual and Temporal, and of the Commons in Parliament Assembled.*

1. Mary c.1.————*Be it therefore Enacted by the Queen our Soveraign Lady, with the Assent of the Lords Spiritual and Temporal, and of the Commons in this present Parliament Assembled.*

5. Elizabeth c.5.————*Be it Enacted by the Queen's Most Excellent Majesty, with the Assent of the Lords Spiritual and Temporal, and the Commons in this present Parliament Assembled.*

1. James c.2. *Be it therefore Enacted by the King's Most Excellent Majesty, by and with the Assent and Consent of the Lords Spiritual and Temporal, and the Commons in this present Parliament Assembled.*

16. Charles 1.c.1. *Be it Enacted by the King's Most Excellent Majesty, with the Consent of the Lords Spiritual and Temporal, and the Commons in this present Parliament.*

12. Charles 2. *nunc Regis* c. 11. *Be it Enacted by the King's Most Excellent Majesty, with the Advice and Consent of the Lords and the Commons in this present Parliament.*

Thus (Sir) by the Title or Introduction of our Statutes in each King's Reign (from King *Edward* the First, to this very day) it is clearly proved, that the Two Houses cannot challenge a Co-ordinate Power with the King in making Laws in Parliament by Usage, or Prescription, the Legislative Authority being only in the King, though the use of it be restrained to the Consent of the Lords and Commons in Parliament; *Le Roy fait les Liex avec le Consent des Seigniors, & Communs, & non pas les Seigniors & Communs avec le Consent du Roy;* The King makes the Laws with the Consent of the Lords and Commons, and not the Lords and Commons with the Consent of the King. In a word, the Soveraign is the sole Legislator, it is His Stamp and Royal Will, and that alone which gives Life, and Being, and Title of Laws to that which was before, but Counsel and Advice; All marks of Supremacy being still in him, nor is it an Argument of Communicating his Power, that he restrains himself from exercising some particular Acts without Consent of Parliament, for it is by virtue of his own Grant, that such after-Acts shall not be valid. He hath not divided his Legislative faculty, but tied himself from using it, except by the Advice and Consent of the Peers, and at the Request of the Commons, their Rogation must precede his Ratification. Wherefore upon what has been said, I may very well pronounce our Author's words.

That the Making of Laws is a peculiar and incommunicable priviledge of the Supream Power; And the Office of the Two Houses in this Case is only Consultive or Preparative, but the Character of the Power, rests in the final Sanction which is in the King; And effectually the passing of a Bill is but the granting of a Request; the Two Houses make the Bill 'tis true, but the King makes the Law, and 'tis the Stamp, and not the Matter, that makes it Currant.

FINIS.

Anonymous

THE

ARRAIGNMENT

OF

Co-Ordinate-Power;

WHEREIN ALL

Arbitrary Proceedings

Are laid open to all H o n e s t

ABHORRERS

AND

ADDRESSERS:

With a Touch at the

London-Petition

AND

CHARTER.

Plebs aut humiliter servit, aut superbe dominatur, Tacit.

Albeit by the sufferance of the King of *England,* Controversies between the King
and His People are sometimes determined by the High-Court of Parliament,
and sometimes by the *Lord Chief Justice:* Yet all the Estates remain in full
Subjection to the King, who is not bound to follow their Advice, neither to consent to their Requests, *Bodin de Rep. l.1.c.2.*

---

*Irridenda est eorum socordia, qui praesenti potentia credunt se extingui posse
sequentis aevi memoriam,* Tacit. l.4.

Printed for *T. Hunt,* Anno Dom. MDCLXXXIII.

*T*he author of this tract hid his identity so well that it remains a mystery. He is likely to have been a barrister however, as he claims expertise in the law and familiarity with the views of barristers. The publication of this tract in 1683, the year of the Rye House Plot, coincided with, and appears to be a part of, fierce government repression of Whigs and dissenters and a propaganda campaign against their ideology. Charles and his party demanded unity, obedience, and control.

"The Arraignment of Co-Ordinate-Power" disparages the institution of Parliament at a time when Charles II had no intention of summoning another. Indeed the King had secretly promised Louis XIV he would not do so. For two decades there had been a parliament in session all but two years. In 1683 none was held or anticipated. The first five chapters of "The Arraignment of Co-Ordinate-Power" reprinted below consider the antiquity and role of Parliament in relation to that of the King and the judicial powers of the two houses. Because the remainder of the tract treats more narrow questions of law, it has been omitted.

The author begins by directing attention to two documents of 1681 that claim for Parliament great power, especially judicial power: the debates of the House of Commons in October 1680, published in 1681; and the petition of the mayor and aldermen of London in January 1681. The author's quarrel with the former is its claim that barristers believe "the proceedings of the House of Commons are Things above them, and which they have neither Power or Ability to make determination of the same." This he proposes to answer. The second document, the London petition, complained about the interruption of public justice during the prorogation of Parliament. The petition figured prominently in the indictment the Crown brought against London in 1683 to force that Whig stronghold to surrender its charter.

The tract is a clear exposition of the Tory viewpoint in the 1680s. Its title page sports a quotation from Bodin that prepares readers for what is to come: "Albeit by the sufferance of the King of England, Controversies between the King and His People are sometimes determined by the High-Court of Parliament, and sometimes by the Lord Chief Justice: Yet all the Estates remain in full Subjection to the King, who is not bound to follow their Advice, neither to consent to their Requests." The dedication to Lord Noble complains that "It is against the Liberty of the Subject, that Loyal and Obedient Subjects should be either Terrify'd or Dismay'd by their own Representatives, whose Electors . . . cannot give away all their own Rights, Power and Freedoms unto them, without His Majesties Consent, or the Promulgation of a known Law, and leave nothing to themselves for a Self-preservation." Only a single edition of the tract seems to have been published.

The Power of the Parliament of this Kingdom.

I *Cannot presume that He or They that writ the* Pamphlet *printed for* Richard Baldwin *on the* 28 of June 1681.[1] *was so well acquainted with* Benchers, Ancients, *and most of the* Barresters *of the several* Inns of Court, *as he pretends to be; for assuredly then in that Paper there had not been so much of the Language of* Billingsgate,[2] *and so little of that of* Westminster-Hall *therein to be found. Now for that it is therein said,* That the Inns of Court-men have declared, that the proceedings of the House of Commons are Things above them, and which they have neither Power or Ability to make determination of the same. *By these words this Writer being so great an intelligent* Athleta, *let us consider the Power of the Parliament,* &c.

THE Power of the *Parliament* of this Kingdom being agreed by most Men, if not by all, to have no other Limits, save only such as are set by the Law of Nature preceptive, and the dispersed Divine Laws, written and declared in the Sacred Volumes of the Old and New Testaments, whose Acts by conjecture bear a relation thereunto, yet are always subject to the mistakes of Human Frailties. The Doubts that at this time seem necessary to require a Dispute, are, to whom and to what this Name *The Parliament* is due, and what things cannot be done but by the Concurrence of all the Three Estates, *Lords Spiritual* and *Temporal*, and *Commons;* what Power the King hath over both or either Houses of *Parliament:* which not being rightly understood by the greater part of the People, much hath passed for current, to the endangering a Relapse to the whole Kingdom, that otherwise would have plainly appeared counterfeit, and base Alloy:

1. "An Exact Collection of the most considerable Debates In the Honourable House of Commons, at the Parliament Held at Westminster the One and twentieth of October, 1680" (London, 1681).
2. A prison.

For the clearing of which, I shall, with some brevity and demonstration, state and argue these Ten Questions following.

I. What the Parliament is?

II. Whether the name Parliament hath been, or can properly be given to any part or parts of this Body?

III. What Power the Lords in Parliament have as a Judicial Court of Record, touching particular Suits between the King and Subject, or between Subject and Subject?

IV. Whether the House of Commons *be any Judicial Court of Record, touching particular Suits between the* King *and* Subject, *or between* Subject *and* Subject?

V. Whether the House of Commons *alone can make any Ordinance to bind any of the* Commonalty, *but their own Members; or where some Contempt is committed, by breaking the present Priviledges belonging to the Members of that House?*

VI. Whether the House of Commons *alone have any Power to imprison any of the Commonalty, for Breach of their* Votes *or* Ordinances, *unless a Member of the House, or where there is a Contempt committed by Breach of the* Priviledges *belonging to the* Members, *being such as before is mentioned?*

VII. Whether the Lords *alone, or the* Lords *and* Commons *together, (without the* King) *can make Ordinances to imprison, bind the Persons and Estates of the Subject, where there is no Suit before them between the* King *and a* Subject, *or between* Subject *and* Subject; *or where it doth not concern the regulating their own Members, or where there is no Contempt committed against their Proceedings given them by the Law of* England?

VIII. Whether there be not greater reason to be given, that taking men into Custody by a Vote *of the* House of Commons, *where their Priviledges are not concerned, should be within the Statute of 27.E.3.1. and the 16R.2. then for the High Court of* Chancery *to hold Cognizance of a Cause after Judgment given in a Court at Law?*

IX. Whether the Priviledges of Parliament *as now pretended to be used, be not an Oppression to the People?*

X. Whether the House of Commons *can prohibit a Councellor at Law to speak in behalf of his Client?*[3]

CHAP. I.

Q.1. *What the Parliament is?*

The *Parliament* is the *Common Councel,* or great Court of the Kingdom: A Body Politick, consisting of the Three Estates aforesaid, whereof the *King* is the Head, the *Lords,* the *Noble Members* in person, and the *Commons* the inferiour Members. By their Representatives the two latter called by the *King's Writ,* in which Councel or Court alone old Laws may be annulled, abrogated, restrained, enlarged, or so declared, as shall bind other *Courts* or New Laws made by the *King,* done with the advice and consent of the *Lords* and *Commons,* and not otherwise.

Every part of this being indeed a description of the *Parliament,* is made good by the Writ of *Waste* and other Writs upon Statutes and in Authors of great Reputation in this Kingdom. The *Parliament* is called *Commune Concilium Angliae,* the Common Councel of *England;* and *Magna Curia,* the Great Court. And there is great reason it may be so called, there being, in effect, the common advice and judgment of the whole; amongst others, I instance these in the Margent.

From this name *Parliament,* some persons before the Statute *13 Car. 2.*[4] were of Opinion, That both or either *Houses of Parliament,*

---

3. The sections dealing with questions 1 through 5 are included below.
4. 13 Car. II, c.1 (1661), An Act for Safety and Preservation of His Majesty's Person and Government Against Treasonable and Seditious Practices and Attempts, condemns the opinion that both houses of Parliament, or either of them, has a legislative power without the king.

had a Legislative Power without the *King;* since which time the like Principle hath been revived, that both or either Houses of *Parliament* hath a co-ordinate power and share in the Government with the *King,* and that this is the ancient Constitution of the Government of this Kingdom, as the *London-Petition*[5] gravely asserts it. As if it would stand with any colour of reason, that the *King,* who by His *Prerogative* hath the sole Sanction of Laws, which is the only reason of our Obedience; that the *King,* to whom the protection and preservation of the Laws of the People, their Lives, Liberties, and their Estates, with the whole Kingdom, are especially committed; That the *King,* who is exempt from Human Laws, and may command the Laws themselves for the Publick Good; and by whom only *Parliaments* can be called, and at His Pleasure dissolved; and who indeed is *Anima Republicae,* God's Lieutenant, *Salus Populi,* and an Emperour in His own Dominions, should have Associates and Collegues joined with His Royal Person, and yet these persons be only called *Counsellors* and *Advisers.* As if it were not necessary that in every Commonwealth, that some one Authority should be established, that is superiour and above all Laws.

First, To supply the defect of Laws.

Secondly, To correct the severity of Laws: Because the event of future matters cannot be foreseen, and so every Act that is the exercise of Supreme Power, doth suppose that the Agent hath a proportionable power to itself.

The Chronologers and Historians that do keep within the compass of their own bounds, do prudently and safely say, That the name *Parliament* is a name of no great Antiquity; that it is a *French* word,

---

5. In January 1681 the mayor and council of London petitioned the king to summon a parliament, complaining about the interruption of public justice during its prorogation. This petition figured in the indictment against the city in King's Bench in 1683 as the Crown moved to force London to surrender its charter. See Ogg, *England in the Reign of Charles II,* 636–39.

derived from *Parler-le-ment*, that is, to speak one's mind, and to discourse freely; that before the time of King Henry I to signifie the *King's great Court, or Councel*. On the contrary, some persons that affect Popularity, and make it their studies to enlarge the Jurisdictions of the Commons, are not contented with that old name, *The King's great Court, or Councel;* where the Rights and Liberties of the Subject are as well, if not better secured and maintained, than they are in the same Court called by the new name, *The Parliament*.

These kind of men have such Fancies, and imperfect, and partial Animadversions for this name, *The Parliament*, that instead of making this name serviceable to the *King*, and His Subjects, they endeavour by misrepresentation, and otherwise, to ease His Majesty of great Trouble, and give the *Commons* dominion, and make the *Laws* subservient unto them. And so King *Charles I.* complained, That the Oaths of Allegiance and Supremacy to defend the Crown, and assist and defend all Jurisdictions, Priviledges and Authorities belonging to Us, obliges them not, they are to be associated in these Regal Powers; the Sword and Scepter may be in Pictures and Statues, but not in the King's hand alone.

So I find in *Vox Populi*, a Pamphlet printed 1681.[6] that when they came to mention King *Alfred's* appointing the meeting of an Assembly, Pur Parlementer de grandment de People, the which signifies to discourse freely concerning the great Affairs of the People; They, on purpose to delude the Vulgar, falsly translate these words, to mean, *That they shall assemble themselves at* London, *to treat in* Parliament *of the Government of the People*.

2. They say the Court of *Parliament* is the most ancient Court. Let this Court be called by what Name you please, be it either *Wittena Gemot. Geredner Micellemod*, as Mr. *Campden* hath it, or the *Sen-*

---

6. See "Vox Populi," 656–57 above.

ate of the King's great Court, the *Parliament* Treaty or Assembly, as the Statute of 7 E.i. and the 13 *Car.* 2.15. calls it; Yet by the Laws of *England,* never any of these Courts had a share in the Government, as government of the People, as hereafter will appear.

This Court, by the name of the *King's great Court,* may well be called the most *Ancient Court;* for there were Kings before there were Laws, witness that Story of King *Lucius* and *Eleutherius,* and that *Kings* had *Councels* before *Courts.*

This Kingdom flourished as much, if not more, before the Name of *Parliament* was known. The Parliament of *Paris,* which is the ancientest, was established and constituted in the time of King *Philip le Bel,* in the year 1294. That of *Toulouse* during the Reign of *Charles VII.* in the year 1444. That of *Bordeaux* in the time of the said *King,* in the year 1451. That of *Dauphin* in the time also of the said King: But by the Authority of King *Lewis XI.* His Son, at *Dolphin,* then inhabiting in *Dolphin* in the year 1459. The Parliament of *Dion* and of *Province* in that time of the said King *Lewis;* That of *Rouen* in the time of King *Lewis XII.* in the year 1553, and so it would be absurd to say, That *Parliamenta est Curia Antiquissima,* that we took the Name *Parliament* from the *French,* whose first Court of *Parliament* was held at *Paris,* in the year 1294, as aforesaid.

Such like ancient *Parliaments,* were those of *Magna Carta,* held in the 9th year of Henry 3 afterwards, wherein some time the assent of the *Lords* and *Commons* were not at all mentioned; such like most ancient Courts was that held at *Clarendon* in *Normandy,* in the time of King *Henry II.* wherein those excellent Laws were made against *Thomas A Becket,* yet no *House of Commons* were ever there: The which shews, That good Laws have been made for the People to their own contents by His Majesty, without any consent of the *Commons, Pes Regis sepes legis sospes Civis.*

Polidore Virgil says, That before the time of King *Henry I. Reges*

non consuevisse populi conventum consultandum causa raro facere. That
it was very rare or seldom, that the Kings of *England,* before the time
of King *Henry I.* called an Assembly of the People, to know their advice and counsel; For, saith he, the Vulgar that came to consult in
such Assemblies were unlearned, *Cuivis proprium est nihil sapere;* they
had so little knowledge, they did but hinder, instead of giving a dis-
patch to the King's Council. Some persons appeared in respect of
their Tenures, the which might cause some opposition to be made on
their behalf, But at this time of day it is not material to search into
Antiquity, concerning the time when, and place where the *Commons*
first met and sat, either together with the Lords, or by themselves,
but chiefly concerning their Power: However, thus far I will concur
with the *Petitioners* and *Presenters,* that the Name *Parliament* is the
most famous Idol that ever was, to be thus bowed down to, and worshipped in respect of time, before it ever was born or heard of in the
world. Concerning this mixture of Power, let us first look into the
danger of it.

First, The Poets are against this mixture:

> *Nulla fides Regni sociis omnisque potestas*
> *Impatiens consortis erit.*[7]

So concerning *Ruffinus,* the treacherous Tutor of *Arcadius,* that
endeavoured to supplant him by the help of King *Alericus:*

> *Iam non ad calumnia rerum*
> *Injustos crevisse quaeror tolluntur in altum*
> *Ut lapsu graviore ruant.*
> *Apprehensa veste morantem*
> *Increpat Archadium scandat sublime tribunal*
> *Participem Sceptri socium declaret honoris.*[8]

---

7. The allies of the realm have no faith, and all power is averse to a partner.
8. I no longer complain that the unjust have grown to the heights. They are raised aloft so
that they may fall the more heavily. Seizing a garment, he rebukes the Arcadian who is delay-
ing. He mounts the lofty tribunal. He declares that a sharer of royal power is an ally.

The truth whereof we find in the Emperour *Constans*, that when he suffered his two Brothers *Tiberius* and *Heraclius*, to be his Fellow Consorts in the Government, he cut off both their Noses, lest afterwards they should enjoy the dignity of being *Emperours.*

And so it is observed of *Constantine* and *Maxentius, Nullam Regni societatem diu esse patientem consortis.* For the like cause Henry 2. put out his Brother *Robert's* eyes. And when Henry 2. out of his great care to his Son, caused him to be crowned King; and at the Solemnity of the Feast made on that occasion, carried up the first Dish to his Son's Table, to honour his Son the new King, and waited likewise upon him. But before the Feast was ended, King Henry 2. said, *Eius penitet! Penitet me extulisse hominem.* It repented him he had made his Son a Consort in the Government; so in a short time he did see, (when it was too late) that a *Crown* is no Estate to be made over in Trust; and what trouble would ensue thereupon both to himself and the whole Kingdom.

So the Adoption of *Pisoky Galba*, was the cause of *Pisor's* Ruine, *Cornelius Tacitus Hist. I.*

In the *36 Fable* of *Aesop*, concerning the *Husbandman*, and the *Wood;* the Husbandman petitions *Jupiter* but for so much Wood as would only make him a Hatchet Helve, the which Petition being granted, the *Husbandman* cut down the whole Wood; upon the Moral of which Fable, Mr. *Ogilby* pleasantly saith:

> *Who Weapons put into a Mad-man's hands,*
> *May be the first the Error understands;*
> *But Kings that Subjects with their Swords do trust,*
> *If They do suffer, seems not much unjust.*

So concerning *Julius Caesar*, and his Collegue *Bibulus Augustus, Lepidus* and *Antonius.*

> *Noxia res, plures Domini,*
> *Multos imperare malum,*   } *Rex unicus esto.*
> *Non bene, turba regit populum,*

It is not good that many Rule, let one
Whom *Jupiter* approves be *King* alone.

His Majesty is the *Exis*, the Soul of Human Things; the Bond of Society, which cannot otherwise subsist; the vital Spirit, whereby so many millions of Men do breath, and the whole nature of things; His Majesty hath peculiar Rights to himself, called *Sanctimonia summae potestatis*, the which are sacred and individual.

In the presence of His *Majesty*, both, or either *Houses of Parliament*, have no Power to command: And, as *Rivers* lose their Name and Power, at the Mouth or Entrance into the Sea; and the Stars their light, in the presence of the Sun: So the Power of both or either *Houses of Parliament*, is but upon sufference, in the presence of their Sovereign His Majesty.

It is said concerning *Arbates, Rex Medorum Tanta erat Regia illa veneratio honorem deferens ei insidere Sellae quam vocabunt Thronon Basilicôn capitale esset, Praescribi à subditis nequit immunitus ab obedientia principis vel ipsius correctione, vel ut eum non possit appellari quia potestas praecipiendi judicandi & castigandi omnino intrincise est potestate Principis respectu subditorum.*

Multum falluntur qui existimant cum Regis acta quaedam sua nolunt rata esse nisi a Senatu aut alio coetu aliquo probentur partitionem fieri potestatis nam quae acta eo in modo rescinduntur intelligi debent rescindi Regis ipsius Imperio quo eo modo sibi cavere volunt ne quid fallaciter impetratum pro vera ipsius voluntate haberetur.[9] Dr. *Taylor* is of the same

---

9. Arbates, the King of the Medes: so great was the royal veneration deferring honor to him that it was a death sentence for him to occupy the seat called the throne of Kings. Unable to be subjected to limits by his subjects, he was immune to princely obedience or to his own emendation or to being hailed to court because owing to the regard of his subjects the power of instructing, judging, and chastising is by nature inherent in a prince's power.

Those are deceived who think that when they do not want certain acts of the King to be ratified unless first approved by the senate or some other assembly, a division of power can come about. For acts that are rescinded by the power of the King himself: Which power they will want to beware of lest in some way that which has been obtained deceitfully be considered as in accordance with his will.

opinion, who saith, That the consent of the People gives no Authority to the *Law;* therefore it is no way necessary to the Sanction and Constitution, saving only to prevent Violence, Rebellion, and Disobedience; as for Example:

Asivius Gallus cum Tiberius simulate partem sibi Reipublicae petisset, interrogato inquit Caesar, quam partem Reipublicae tibi mandari velis, mox cum vultu offensionem confectasset. Non se ideo interrogasse ait ut divideret quae seperari nequirent, sed ut sua confessione argueretur unum esse Reipublicae corpus atque unius animo regendum.

Decius Imperator cum decimum filium suum imperiali diademate proponeret insignari renuit filius dicens, vereor ne si fiam Imperator, dediscam esse filius, malo non esse Imperator quam filius indevotus imperet, pater meus meum imperium scit parere humiliter imparanti nam parentum affectum exuit qui male suprapositum filium extinguit prius enim claudi & nutriendi sunt pueri & cum processerant quis procedere debent invite ascendunt.[10]

That is, *Decius* the Son refused to receive the Crown, and participate in the Government with his Father *Decius;* for in respect of the difficulty that did attend *Supreme Power,* he said he had rather be no *Emperour,* than after the acceptance thereof, prove to be a disobedient Son.

Erat ipsi pelvis aurea in qua tam ipse Amasis *quam convive omnes semper pedes lavabunt contusa ergo pelvi statuam Dei ex illa fecit. Et in*

---

10. Asivius Gallus, when Tiberius by a pretense had sought a part of the commonwealth for himself, questions him, "Caesar," he says, "what part of the commonwealth do you want mandated to you?" (Soon he mitigates the offense with a look.) He says that he does not ask the question in order to divide what cannot be separated but so that it might be made clear that by his own admissions the commonwealth is a single unit and should be ruled by the will of single man.

When the emperor Decius nominated his own son for the honor of an imperial crown, the son refused saying: I fear that if I become emperor, I would forget how to be a son. I prefer not to be emperor rather than rule as an undevout son. My father knows that I am unprepared to wear my royal authority lightly. Indeed, I who kills a son who has been himself placed in authority strips the parents of natural feelings. For in earlier times the lame and halt had to be cared for, and when they had advanced as far as they should, they ascended unwillingly.

ea urbis parta collocavit ubi erat commodissimum Aegyptii irantes ad statuam studiose eam coluerunt quo Amasis cognito accersitis Aegyptiis exposuit statuam ex pelvi factam esse ex qua prius levarit pedes modo autem religiose ab illis coliunt igitur eadem est mea quae pelvis ratio uti enim prius fuerint plebeius nunc tamen Rex vester sum honorare igitur me & venerari voce jubeo hac quidem ratione Aegyptios sibi reconciliavit & equum judicarent ipsi servare.[11]

But yet to come nearer to the purpose: Admit that the Two Houses have a share in making *Acts* by their advice and consent only, yet they have no power in the *Government* itself, either before or after the *Statutes* made; for that the sole *Empire* is in the *King,* the *King* is the only *Supreme Governour of this Realm;* in all the world there is no other Sovereignty touching the Regality of the Crown of *England, 4 Inst. 89.* The Lord Bishop of *Lincoln,* p. 4. printed 1679.

The King hath sufficient power to do *Justice* in all Cases within His Dominions.

Curia Domini Regis nos debet deficere conquerentibus in justicia exhibenda.

Eum à quo aliquis constituitur esse superiorem constituto, id est cujus affectus perpetuo pendet a voluntate constituentis.

All external Actions are under the Command of the Civil Power, in order to the Publick Government; and if they were not, the Civil Power sufficiently provided for the acquiring the ends of its institution, so all that God made were not good.

That the Information against Sir *John Elliot* is good Law, notwith-

---

11. He had a golden bowl in which both Amasis and his dinner guests always washed their feet. But he broke up the bowl and cast it into a statue of a god, and he placed it in that part of the city where it was most convenient for Egyptians to approach and devoutly worship it. When Amasis learned of this, he summoned the Egyptians and exposed the statue as being made from a bowl in which he had earlier bathed his feet. But now it was worshipped by them with religious awe. Therefore the rationale underlying my present situation is the same as that of my bowls. For I used to be a plebeian but I am your King. So I order you to honor me and venerate me with words. On this basis he in fact reconciled the Egyptians to him and they thought it just to serve him.

standing the *Vote* of the Commons for making him reparation for damages;[12] for the *Statute* saith, For that to the King it belongeth at all times and seasons to defend, force of Armour, and all other force against the Peace at all times, and to punish them that shall do the contrary; and hereunto the Subjects are bound to aid our Sovereign Lord the King at all seasons when need shall be. And so the Civil Rights of the Subject are under a general Protection, otherwise Sovereign Power cannot subsist. And as these *Statutes* extend to punish Force within the Lords House, so the Book of *3 E.3. 19 Bro. Corone 161.* extends to punish a Peer for departing the Parliament without the King's Licence; much more for a Commoner, that pretends that whatsoever is acted and done in their House, is acted and done in a Superior Court, and cannot be called in question in any of His Majesty's Courts in *Westminster-Hall,* and the reason is, for that the King hath no Peer in his own Land.

That it is the Rights of the Crown, to declare all *Acts of Parliament* to be void unto which the King doth not freely consent at the time of the making thereof.

So it was when the *Prelates* and *Citizens* had obtained an Act of Parliament, That if anything was done by any of what estate or condition he be contrary to their *Franchises,* that it should be redressed in the next *Parliament;* and so from *Parliament* to *Parliament,* and they shall be made quit of the Exchequer.

---

12. Sir John Eliot and two other members of the House of Commons were arrested and imprisoned on 3 March 1628/9 after forcibly detaining the Speaker the previous day to prevent an adjournment of Parliament. Charles I was determined to make an example of Eliot for his outspoken opposition to royal policies. When the three members—Eliot, Denzil Holles, and Benjamin Valentine—were finally indicted, it was for seditious words spoken during the actual session as well as for violence to the speaker. This flew in the face of the Commons' insistence upon freedom of speech during its debates. The judges found in favor of the Crown. The three men were fined but refused to pay. Holles escaped, Eliot died in prison in 1632 (possibly for want of food), and Valentine was finally released in February 1640 just as the Short Parliament was to be elected. In July 1641 the Long Parliament resolved that the proceedings against the three men had been a gross breach of privilege. In 1668 on the motion of Holles himself the judgment of 1630 was at last reversed on a writ of error.

So great was the King's Prerogative before the Statute *8 H.5. cap. 1.*
for the care and safety of the Subject, that if a *Parliament* was summoned by Writ under the *Teste* of the King's Lieutenant, during the
time that the *King* was in Foreign Parts beyond the Sea, at the King's
Return, such Parliament was dissolved.

Thus having shewed what the *Parliament* is, what Power the *King*
hath over both or either House of *Parliament*, and what kind of share
both or either House of *Parliament* can pretend to in the Government, what danger there is in a Colegislative Power, I descend to the
second Question.

CHAP. II.

Q. 2. *Whether the Name of* Parliament *can properly be given to any Part or
Parts of this Body, not being the Whole?*

In all Bodies, whether Natural or Politick, there is one Name which
is proper only to the whole taken together, and divers Names proper
to the Members respectively, as the whole reasonable Creature is
called Man, and the parts by several other Names, and the chief the
Head, the rest the Arms, &c. And so the whole irrational Creature is
called a Horse, a Dog, or such like, according to their difference; but
of the parts one is called the Head, &c. A Man shall scarcely in an
Age hear any person never so ignorant call the Head of a Man, a
Man; or of a Horse, a Horse. In Bodies Politick, the Whole is called
the Empire, the Kingdom, the State, the City, the Colledge, but the
Members by particular Names: As the *Emperour*, the *King*, the *Head*,
the *Nobles*, and the *Commons;* the *President*, the *Mayor*, the *Master*,
&c. Doth ever anyone call the Mayor of *London*, or the Aldermen,
(though many) the City? No, the reason is plain, because in truth that
is the name of the Whole, which consists of the Mayor, Aldermen
and Commonalty, whereof the Mayor and Aldermen are but Parts,

though but chief ones; so the Name the *Parliament*, is the Name due to the Whole, and not to any Part or Parts not being the Whole, nor can properly be given to them. The Commandment which God gave unto *Adam*, was to impose Names to all, significant to every Creature, but to give to every particular Part, or to some Part, not being the Whole, the same Name, would not only be repugnant to the definition of a Name, but also destroy the end for which Names were given, which is, that one thing may be distinguished from another; which cannot be, if the same Name be given to a Part, which belongeth to the Whole. And there would follow Confusion, besides Absurdity. *Uno Absurdo dato, mille sequuntur;* one Absurdity being admitted, infinite do follow. It is likewise a Rule, *Nemo praesumendus est velle absurdi.* And shall we have so base an opinion of our wise Ancestors, as to think they gave the Name *Parliament* to a part of that *Parliament*, which is so absurd as hath been said.

May it not come to pass, that if the King, and the Lords in the Upper House, and the Commons in the Lower House, differ in opinion; the one by the Name of *Parliament*, ordain for one thing, and the other against it, and what remedy will there be, but such as may prove worse than the Distemper, *Unde summam confusionem sequi necesse est cognitionem de re eadem pro jure potestatis;* when the dispute arises concerning the Right of Power, of necessity it is, great confusion must follow.

There is more reason, that if the Name proper to the whole Parliament may be given to a part, that it should be given to the King the Head, than to any other part; for that the Head is the supreme and most noble, in respect of its regent part of all natural Bodies. The head of a Man by *Plautus* is called *divinissimum*, and so it is, and must be in the Head Politique.

Hence it is, that great mistakes have come from this word *Parliament*, and great confusion hath arisen from these words of Sir *Edward Cooke*, in respect of the Priviledge of the Commons; *That the*

Justices should not in any wise determine the Priviledges of this High Court of Parliament, for it is so high and mighty in its nature, that it may make new Laws; and that which is Law, they may make no Law; and the determination and knowledge of the Priviledges belongeth to the Lords of Parliament, and not to the Justices.

In which words it is very plain, that the word *Parliament* is *Nomen collectivum,* and means the King, Lords and Commons; for it is they jointly that can make Laws. And that which is Law, is by them to be made no Laws; and so the House of Commons alone are but a Society, and a distinct Court, the determination of whose Priviledges belong to the Lords, and cannot be called the Parliament: Nor can this Name be given to the King alone, or to the King and Lords, or to the Lords and Commons, or to the King and Commons; for then we should have several Parliaments, which cannot be allowed by the Laws of *England.*

CHAP. III

Q. 3. What Power the Lords in Parliament have as a Judicial Court of Record, touching particular Suits between the King and a Subject, or between Subject and Subject?

Their Power is to hear and determine matters duly brought before them, either by Presentment, or Impeachment from the *House of Commons* Information on behalf of His Majesty, or complaint of any particular person grieved by Error, or corrupt Judgment, Decree, Sentence, or other unjust pressure; but with these Limitations:

I. *That the Suits before that, which by the known Laws or course of Equity of the Realm the Party ought to have had, to avoid that Judgment, Decree or Sentence, which is against the same Laws or course of Equity.*

II. *That the Defendant be called and admitted to make his defence as in other Courts of the King, as in all Justice he ought.*

III. *That if the Defendant deny the matter alledged, it must be proved either by Record, or Witnesses upon Oath.*

IV. *That the Judgement, Sentence, Decree or Ordinance of the Lords in such Cases, be only such as by the known Laws or course of Equity of the Kingdom it ought to have been given in Chancery, King's Bench, Common Pleas, or other Courts of the King.*

For the office of the *Lords* in these Cases, is *jus dicere*, to say what the Law saith, and not *jus dare*, to give Law as they please. If the *Lords* in the Cases aforesaid were not limited, then in effect they might do as much as the whole *Parliament*, for the *Judgments*, *Decrees*, and *Ordinances*, would make *Laws* if there were none to warrant them, it being in truth nothing less, if they have liberty to proceed as they will, and give what *Judgments*, *Decrees* and *Ordinances* they please, and those to be held good.

And for what do the *Judges* attend in the *Upper House*, and not in the *Lower*, unless it be to inform the *Lords* what the Law is, as in the 7 H.7.20.[13] It is, *That the Lords with their advice proceed to correct erroneous Judgments*. In the Case of the 21 E.3.46. which I cited before, the Lords in *Parliament* gave Judgment for repealing a Patent, being against *Law*. But because they had not (as the *Common Law* required) first awarded a Writ of *Scire Facias*, to summon the Patentee to shew cause if he could, to maintain the Patent, the Judgment was by the Lords in Parliament held erroneous, and therefore reversed. And if the Lords were so clear of that opinion, having better consulted what the Law was, which we must intend they did, as to condemn their own former Judgment; methinks it should satisfie any reasonable person, who labours not to be troublesome herein.

13. 7 Hen. VII, cap. 20 (1491), the reversal of the attainder of Thomas last Lord Roos and restitution of his son Edmund.

Besides, it were against reason, destructive to *Property, Liberty,* and all manner of Repose, to make the common Law uncertain, which is a great misery to a People. It is well said, *Misera est servitus, ubi jus est vagum;* where Law is wanting, there is miserable servitude. That Judgments, Decrees, and Ordinances, not warrantable by Law, or course of Equity of the Kingdom, or the Parties' consent should bind unquestionably, for that man could not call anything his own, or enjoy any security, which are the ends of all Society: *Omnis Societas eo intendit ut suum cuique fit salvum communi opere & conspiratione.* All Society tends to this, that every one may by the common aid and design, as it were, enjoy what is his own in safety.

That the Lords do not sit or act anything as they are a peculiar, Judicial Court, by so much as the Election of the People, for the King is the only Fountain of Honour; nor have they consent to do what they please with the People, or their Estates, I suppose all men unconcerned that know anything of the Policy, Law or Government of the Kingdom, will confess.

The chief Reason why an Act of Parliament binds all, (if it were so intended it should) is in effect every one, both King and People, by himself, or his Representative, is consenting thereunto; in which regard the Lawyers hold, and truly too, That an Act of Parliament (they mean a Free Parliament, for such only are according to the Frame and excellent fundamental Policy of this State) cannot be said to do any wrong, relying upon a Maxim in Law, *Volenti non fit injuria,* a thing is not a wrong to him that willeth it, as it is with the People and their Representatives, so in this it is with the King and his Representatives.

Moreover, unless the Lords have the consent of the Commons, who do represent all the Commons *England,* and have power from them, as joining with the King in doing of such things as cannot be done but by the concurrence of all the Estates of the Kingdom, they take upon themselves and exercise as great an arbitrary Power as may be; and how vast and pernicious a Crime that hath been esteemed in all Ages, see *Wingate's* Abridgment,[14] Title, *Accusation,* and *Stat. 17 Car. I cap. 10.*[15] *&c.* If the Lords had any such Power, it would have appeared by the Records of the Lords House; but it doth not appear, therefore it follows, that they have no such Power or Authority.

To conclude, The Lords in Parliament never claimed such unlimited and arbitrary Power, the which certainly they would have done, if it had belonged unto them. The Lords at this time are contented with the Legal Power and Jurisdiction that always hath been allowed them, if they be not incroached upon therein by others.

Let us now see if the House of Commons are contented with that Jurisdiction which the Law allows them likewise.

CHAP. IV.

Q. 4. *Whether the* House of Commons *be any Judicial Court of Record, touching particular Suits between the* King *and a* Subject, *or between* Subject *and* Subject?

Although I do acknowledge, and that most willingly, That they are an Honourable Assembly, and have privity in the promulgation of Laws, and are a kind of Court of Record as touching the Members of their own House, if they be remiss, or offend, *quasi Parliament-men,* that is, if they offend in anything which is contrary to the course of Proceedings of the House; and also for preserving their necessary Priviledges of that House, given and allowed them by the Law, without which it may be probable, they may be hindered in attending the

14. Edmund Wingate, *An Exact Abridgment of All Statutes in Force and Use. From the Begining of Magna Charta, untill 1641. With a Continuation, under Their Proper Titles of All Acts in Force and Use, untill the Year, 1670* (London, 1670). This collection was continued down to the year 1681 and reprinted in that year.

15. An Act for regulating the Privy Council and for taking away the court commonly called the Star Chamber, 1642.

Service of the *Common-weal*, for which they are elected and set up; yet I hold they are no *Judicial Court of Record*, to determine Suits between the *King* and a *Subject*, or between *Subject* and *Subject*, upon these Reasons.

1. Because they have not the means whereby to know the truth, as by Law and in Reason is required; for they cannot administer an Oath to a Witness to make any kind of Evidence, either before themselves, or any other Court whatsoever. And that is clear, not only by the opinion of all persons that know the *Laws*, but by this, that it doth not appear that ever any Oath was administered by them *quasi Parliament-men, Knights, Citizens*, and *Burgesses*, otherwise why should Sir *William Scroggs*, late Chief Justice, be sent for by one of their Members to desire his assistance and advice in the House? And when he was there, then to make use of him to have an Oath or Oaths administered by him before them, to make out such Evidence as might prove acceptable unto them.

2. Yea, when any Committee, or the House itself, hath been desirous to be satisfied by *Affidavits*, the direction hath been, and the like is practised at this very day, That an *Affidavit* is to be made before the *Lords*, or else in the *Chancery*, the which is a most strong evidence, that they cannot administer an Oath themselves. And can it stand with any colour of reason, that if the *Law* had made them such a Court, it would have denied the means; for, *qui negat medium, negat finem;* he that denies the means, destroys the end; whereas the meanest Court that is, without scruple exerciseth that power.

3. They cannot take a *Recognizance*, and the Defendant ought in many Cases to be bailed, if he tender Bail; and if he so doth, he ought not to be imprisoned, but delivered; and there is no *Court of Record*, but may take a *Recognizance*, which is but an obligation upon *Record*.

4. There is not any Record of any Suit to be found between the *King* and *Subject*, or between *Subject* and *Subject*, adjudged, and determined by the Commons alone.

5. The Commons are so far from being a Court of Record, that their Journal Book did but begin in the time of King *Edward 6:* and some say *1 Henry 7.* concerning his Marriage. It must be intended, that if the Commons had any such Power, they would have exercised the same as well as the *Lords,* especially considering, that in most, if not in all Parliaments, there hath been in the House of Commons some men greatly learned in the Laws, as conscientious to perform that Trust and Duty, which if Judges, they ought to have performed; and the People by nearness of degree, or other causes, more likely to apply themselves unto them for redress, rather than to the Lords. And as to criminal Causes, it is a great Argument they are no Court of Record.

CHAP. V.

Q. 5. Whether the House of Commons *alone can make any Order or Ordinance to bind any of the* Commonalty, *but their own Members; or where some Contempt is committed, by breaking the present Priviledges belonging to the Members of that House?*

The House of Commons have a twofold Power, touching those persons that sent them, the Commonalty from whom they derive part of it; and that is limited by the Writ, and by the Indenture: The other for regulating their Members, and maintaining their Priviledges, as before is expressed; but I hold they cannot by any Ordinance of theirs, and the common People, or their Estates, by reason of any Suit between Subject and Subject, because, they have no *Judicial Court of Record,* as before is proved; and that they cannot where there is no Suit.

　The Writs whereupon the Members of the Commons House are chosen, without which they could not be directly so, the Election and Authority given by the Commons, is to do and consent to such things as are to be treated and concluded by the Common-Council of the Kingdom, which consists of the Three Estates. And that appears plainly by the Writ and Indenture of Election, admitting the common people had any such power; yet not having given it, they cannot by an Authority derived, for the people work otherwise, for Authority must exactly be pursued: As for instance, If a Letter of Attorney be made to two to do a thing, one of them cannot do it without the other. So if a Commission be granted by the King to twenty men, nineteen of them cannot do anything without the other, unless there be a special Clause in the Commission that enables part of them so to do. If two men refer their differences to the award of three, two of these three can do nothing; yea, in Authority, every circumstance of time, place and manner, must be observed. And it is great reason so to be, for to whom the Authority is given by his or their acceptance, he or they agree to the qualifications.

It would be of mischievous consequence for the Lower House, if they might make one Law touching the Goods, Contracts and Inheritance of the common People, and the Lords the quite contrary, concerning the Goods, Contracts, and Inheritance of Noble-men, and a third touching the Grants, Goods, and Inheritance of the Crown.

As it is in the Natural Body, so it is in the Body Politick of this *Common-weal,* the Goods of each of the Three Estates hath dependency in the good of the other two, and one cannot be prejudiced, but the other will suffer.

Altera poscit opem res ut conservat amice.[16]

As for instance, If the Revenues of the Crown be wasted, will not the other two Estates be grieved at it? I fear much the former times have found it so, and therefore Princes by reason of their extremities that they have often been put unto, have consented to Acts of Re-

16. One thing demands aid in one way, another in another that each may be preserved on good terms.

sumption of the Lands of the Crown alienated away. This mischief hath taken deep root in the Fortunes and Affections of the Subjects, when Princes, to repay the Breaches of their own Revenues, have often resumed the possessions of their people, as *Edward* the 2d the 5*th* and 8*th* year of Reign, *Omnes donationes per Regem factas ad dampnum & diminutionem Regis & Coronae suae*. King *Richard* the 2d in the 10*th* year of his Reign, did the like of all Grants made to unworthy men by his Grandfather, and recalled all Patents dated since the 40*th* year of the Reign of King *Edward* the 3d. Thus did Henry 5. in the 20*th* year of his Reign, and Henry 6. in the 23d year of his Reign, and Edward 4. in the 3d and 12th year of his Reign, Henry the 7th in the third year of his Reign, with all Offices of his Crown, granted either by the Usurper, or his Brother. Neither is this in itself unjust, since the reason of State as Rules of best Government, the Revenues and Profits, *Quae ad sacrum Patrimonium Principis*, should remain firm and unbroken. And certainly *Theodosius* was in the right, who said, *Periculosis simum animal est pauper Rex*, a poor King is a dangerous Creature. And so the Citizens of *Constantinople* found it, when *Constantinus Peleologus*, in whose time the famous City of *Constantinople* was took by *Mahomet the Great*, in the year 1452, the miserable Emperour who had in vain gone from door to door, to beg or borrow money to pay his Soldiers, which the *Turks* found in great abundance when he took the City.

So Sir *Richard Baker* tells us a Story of a *Jew* in King *John's* Reign, would not pay his Taxation, till the King caused every day one of his great Teeth to be pulled out by the space of seven days; and then he was content to give the King a £.1000 of Silks, that no more might be pulled out, for he had but one left.

Again, If the common People decay, will not the King suffer many ways in the Customs and Aids he may expect from them, to defend the Kingdom against Foreign Invasions, and other ways?

The Common-weal hath a Supreme Property in the Estates and

Persons of every one, and may only by the joint consent of the Three Estates, *scilicet,* by Act of Parliament, dispose the same as shall be thought fit. Now if the House of Commons alone by their Ordinance bind the common People, their Persons and Estates as they please, then may they deprive the other two Estates, and that whether the King or Lords will or no, the which is against Reason.

Admit the Commons should make an Ordinance, That every third Person of the Common-weal should go to *Pensylvania* in *America,* and place themselves there, would not this prejudice the King, and the Lords too; It is most apparent it would.

In the ninth year of King *Henry* the *4th* an Act of Parliament was made, that all the *Irish People* should depart the Realm, and go into *Ireland* before the *25th* of *December* following, the which Act was a terrour to the People, and utterly against the Law; Besides, *Solomon* saith, *That the Honour of a King, is in the multitude of his People.*

Perchance it will be objected, That the House of Commons doth not claim any power to make any Ordinance of a new Law, but declaratory of the old, and that to bind only during Parliament.

Truly if their Ordinance have such power, that whatsoever they declare therein to be Law, and must bind all the Commons of *England* during that Parliament, may they not when they please, in effect, make a new Law, by declaring that there is such an old one; and by that means during Parliament, take and dispose all the Money, Plate, and personal Estate of the Commons of *England,* and imprison and banish any of them; and when the Parliament is done and ended, and all gone, what relief will it yield the people that the Ordinance hath now no farther duration? They will have but a lame remedy; but this they need not to fear falling lower, for

Quin jacet in terram non habet unde cadet.[17]

17. He who lives in the earth has no place from which to fall.

The Authority given them by the people, is no more to make Ordinances continue during Parliament, than forever; nor is there anything in the Indenture, in the Writ, or in the King's Warrant to the Chancellor, wherein there is Authority given that hath any shadow of such a thing. *Nemo potest in alium transferre quod ipse non habet:* The Commonalty cannot assign that to their Representatives, which they never had themselves. The Law cannot be altered for a certain time, but by the assent of the Three Estates, for then why not for 100 years, or for 1000, as well as 100, and then what need of Statutes? You know we have many Statutes made but for a little time.

Anonymous

THE

KING'S Dispensing Power
Explicated & Asserted.

*T*his tract appeared without a title page, leaving uncertainty not only as to its author but also to the place and date of publication. Because it directly concerns the nature of the king's power to dispense with laws, however, it was almost certainly published in defense of James II's Declaration of Indulgence issued on 4 April 1687.

In an attempt to remove the legal liabilities against Roman Catholics, James had issued a declaration granting religious toleration to them as well as to Protestant dissenters. Charles II had failed to make good a similar declaration in 1672, and James was clearly cautious in his approach. He had already purged some of its most likely opponents—the most rigid Anglican magistrates—from their posts across the realm. His declaration relied upon his prerogative powers to *suspend penal laws outright, although in the case of the Test Act of 1673 he merely ordered that the oaths and declaration it required not be administered. He anticipated his actions would be endorsed by the next Parliament. A year later, with the meeting of Parliament postponed, he reissued his Declaration, again on the strength of his prerogative powers of dispensing with and suspending laws.*

    James's action elicited a storm of protest and a flurry of pamphlets on the extent of the royal power to dispense with or suspend a law, or in this instance a batch of laws. "The King's Dispensing Power" defends James's action and provides a detailed explanation of the royal power to dispense with laws as then understood by supporters of the Crown. The tract appeared in only a single edition.

The Introduction.

There being a sort of Men in this Kingdom, who think themselves no longer Happy, than they are in a Capacity to Destroy all those that dare not commit the Conduct of their Souls unto them, do all they can to Asperse the Government *and call the most Odious Reflections imaginable on* Majesty *itself. And, that their Design may be the more successfully accomplished, they boldly affirm, That His Majesty intends nothing less than an Introducing* Popery *in an Arbitrary way; an Insinuation equally Malicious and Unjust, and directly contrary to the Stream of the King's Proceedings, which are for the Establishing* Liberty of Conscience *on such Just and Equal Foundations, as may make it* Unalterable, *and secure to all the free Exercise of their Religion* forever. *However, the Cry is, That nothing but Popery, in Dominion; That nothing but a Getting the Legislative Power into the hands of Roman Catholicks, is the Design; and the chief Argument urged to perswade the People to believe so much, is taken from His Majesty's* Dispensing *with some Laws, and putting some Papists into Places of Trust and Profit. But such as impartially weigh all Circumstances, cannot but conclude, That seeing all men, of what Perswasion soever, in Matters Religious, put most* Confidence *in those that are of their own Religion (if men of Principle) it's Unreasonable to expect His Majesty should not do so too. And seeing there are a multitude of Laws that Deprive the King of their Service, if the Dispensing Power be really a Part of* His *Just Prerogative, it must be acknowledged to be highly Rational, that His Majesty, to the end He may have the Service of those He can mostly Trust, should make use of it. And so long as His Majesty keeps within those limits, our Learned Lawyers universally Recognize to be the Boundaries of the Prerogative, there is no Wrong done Us. The King doth but exercise a Just Power for His own greater Safety; and what is further to be Regarded, this Prerogative is not only exercised for the sake of the King and the Papist, but moreover for the Relief of the Protestant Dissenter, who hath been a long time laid aside, as an useless Member of our Body Politick.*

In a word, His Majesty is Resolved to do His uttermost, that the Persecuting Power, *which hath proved most fatal to these Kingdoms, be destroyed, which can never be, so long as the Government is Lodged with those, who are for Persecution. It is Liberty of Conscience, to the want of which most of our Late Miseries must be imputed, that the King desires to Establish, which can never be effected, if those in Places of greatest Trust and Profit be against it. And daily Experience assures us, That although there are many brave Gentlemen of the Church of* England *Communion, who will most heartily concur with His Majesty, that this most Glorious Design be obtained, yet there are not enough of that* Church, *so nobly disposed to do it: for which reason should none but those, who can qualify themselves as by Law required, be Imployed in the Government, we must count on our being once more a Miserable People. The Laws made in the Late King's Reign*[1] *having deprived His present Majesty of the Service of a Great Part of His Subjects, it's become Impossible for the King, so long as these Laws are strictly observed, to do what is necessary towards the Settlement of the Nation's Peace, or the Advance of His People's Happiness. If then it be in the Power of the King to* Dispense *with those Laws, the Arguments for the doing it will be found after the strictest Scrutiny to be Impregnable. Thus much is so very plain and manifest, that I doubt not but every Good man will be of the same Opinion with me,* viz. If the *Dispensing* Power be a Jewel Inherent in the Imperial Crown of *England,* it is become absolutely necessary, that the King, in the present Juncture, make use of it.

Our Enquiry therefore must be, Whether it be in the Power of the King to Dispense with those Laws, that Deprive Him of the Service of His Subjects, and with such other Laws as are a manifest Grievance to the Subject?

And that what I do in this *may be for the Greater Satisfaction of those who are thoughtful about it, I will shew what is meant by a* Dispensation, *and in what Cases His Majesty may Dispense with our Laws: In*

---

1. The Test Acts passed in 1673 and 1678.

doing which, I shall have a fair Occasion to evince, That although the Dispensing Power is at this time necessarily exercised in order to the Establishing our Liberty, yet it can never be used to Destroy it.

SECT. I.

The Dispensing Power *Explicated; That It Is a Jewel Inherent in the Imperial CROWN Fully Proved.*

A *Dispensation* imports more than *Interpretation,* but less than *Abrogation,* and is a Voluntary Act of the Prince's Grace and Favour, exempting particular Persons, or a Community from the Obligation of a Law, that still continues in its Being, to Oblige those who have not a Dispensation given them.

It is more than *Interpretation,* because Interpretation doth not Release to any the Obligation of a Law, it only declares that it doth not oblige in this or the other Case.

It is less than *Abrogation,* for by an Abrogation the Law is absolutely Revoked. When a Law is *Abrogated,* there remaineth no Obligation on any at any time; But though the Law be *Dispensed* with, yet the Obligation abides on those, who have not a Dispensation; or, if it be General to a Community, it must be only for a *time.* Some Limitation, either as to *Persons* or *Time,* there must be in a Dispensation, to distinguish it from Abrogation. The Obligatory Power is taken off, which must be either from *Some* Persons only, or from *All;* If from All, it must be for *Some* Time only, or *forever.* If the Obligation be removed from *Some* only, or from *All* for *some time* only, it is a *Dispensation,* and the Law continues in Being: But if the Obligation be taken away from *All* forever, it is an *Abrogation,* and the Law ceases to be a Law. For which reason, the Learned, when they write of Dispensations, do thus express themselves: *Dispensatio importat amotionem Obligationis Praecepti in casu, & quoad aliquid, vel aliquos, vel quoad omnes ad aliquod tempus;* adding, *Si enim Dis-*

pensatio esset Universalis ad omnis, & insuper perpetua, procul dubio re ipsa esset Revocatio.[2]

This Dispensation, which falls short of Abrogation, belongs not to Legislation, but to Jurisdiction, which is entirely in the Person of the King, and according to our Constitution, the King may Dispense with whatever is but *Malum Prohibitum,* and with all those Laws that Deprive Him of the Service of His Subjects.

To clear this, it must be Observed, That amongst our Laws, some are Declarative of what is Evil in itself, and they cannot be Dispensed with. What is *Malum in se,* is *Malum omni respectu,* it is Evil in every circumstance, even to every Person, and at all times. And those Laws that fall under this Line, are so far from coming within the Circle of the Dispensing Power, that they cannot be abrogated by those that are Intrusted with the Legislation. On which occasion some esteeming Liberty of Conscience to be Established by the Law of Nature, affirm, That to Restrain it, is *malum in se,* and that therefore all Poenal Laws for Religion were *ab initio,* void and null. But be the Legislative power as Immense and Boundless, as our Lawyers generally averr, yet the *Dispensing* Power is confined within a narrower Compass, and is not strong enough to vacate what is *malum in se.* However, what is but *malum Prohibitum* may be Dispensed with; that is, those things that are Unlawful, only because made so by some particular Act or Statute, may be Dispensed with. Though there were weighty Reasons moving those, with whom the Legislative Power is Intrusted, to make such Laws, yet the things were not Unlawful to be done, antecedent to the making the Law, and are therefore called *Mala Prohibita,* in contradistinction to *Mala per se.* And notwithstanding, the making these Laws are for the *General* Good, yet they may prove Inconvenient to some *particular persons,* as soon as made,

---

2. Dispensation means the removal of the obligation of a rule in a case and refers to a certain thing, or certain people, or even to all people at a certain time; adding, for if dispensation were universal in regard to everyone, and moreover perpetual, without any doubt it would really be a revocation.

and to *many* more in Process of time; and therefore it is requisite, that with the King a Dispensing Power be Lodged, whereby the Parties grieved may find Relief. So our Lawyers, *Dispensatio mali Prohibiti est de jure Domino Regi concessa propter impossibilitatem praevidendi de omnibus particularibus, & est mali prohibiti provida Relaxatio, utilitate seu necessitate pensata.*[3] *Vaughan* hath it more fully *thus.* An Act of Parliament which generally Prohibits a thing upon Poenalty, which is Popular, or only given to the King, may be inconvenient to divers Particular Persons, in respect of Person, Place, Time, &c. For this cause the Law hath given Power to the King, to Dispense with Particular Persons. But that Case touches not upon any Inconvenience from the Largeness of the King's Dispensation, in respect of Persons, Place or Time, which the Law leaves Indefinite to the Person of the King, as the Remedy of Inconveniences to Persons and Places, by the Poenal Laws, some of which may be very inconvenient to many Particular Persons, and to many Trading Towns, others but to few Persons and Places, and the Remedy by Dispensation, accordingly must sometimes be to great numbers of persons and places, and sometimes to fewer.

The distinction between *malum per se,* and *malum prohibitum,* is grounded on that old Rule, taken from the Case of *II Hen. 7.* where it is with great strength of Reason affirmed, *That with* malum prohibitum, *by Statute the King may Dispense, but not with* malum per se. What is said by our Lawyers in the Explications they give of this Distinction, we need not trouble ourselves with, it being sufficient to our purpose, that it is warranted by our Law-Books, That *where a Statute prohibiteth anything upon a Poenalty, and giveth the Poenalty to the King, or to the King and Informer, there the King may Dispense.*

But as for the *Dispensing Power,* touching those Laws, which De-

---

3. Dispensation of a prohibited evil is in principle conceded to the dominion of the king on account of the impossibility of foreseeing all the particularities, and the relaxation of the prohibited evil is provided by a considered utility or necessity.

prive the King of His Subjects' Service, it is grounded on a *Prerogative inseparably incident to the Person of the King*, of which our Laws are as Tender as of the People's Rights. And that I may the more clearly state this Case, I will do it as near as I can in the words of Sir *Edward Coke*, the Great Oracle of our Laws, who is well known to be rather more concerned for the Liberty and Property of the Subject, than for the Prince's Prerogative.

This great Lawyer assures us, that no Act of Parliament can bind the King from any Prerogative, which is Sole and Inseparable to His Person, but that he may by a *Non Obstante*[4] Dispense with it. And He instanceth in a Case of the same Nature, with what is at this time under debate, declaring, That a Soveraign Power to Command any of his Subjects to Serve Him, for the Publick Weal, is Solely and Inseparably annexed unto his Person, and that therefore this Royal Power cannot be Restrained by Act of Parliament, neither in *Thesi*, nor in *Hypothesi*,[5] but that a King, by his Royal Prerogative, may Dispense with it, for upon Commandment of the King and Obedience of the Subject, doth His Government consist. So far Sir *Edward*.

Besides, our Lawyers universally hold the Service of the Subject to be due to the King before any Judicial or Municipal Laws had their Being, and therefore due *Jure Naturali*. The Reasons they give for this, are Cogent, as, 1. That Government and Subjection were long before any Municipal or Judicial Laws. 2. For that it would have been in vain to have prescribed Laws to any but to such as owed Obedience before, in respect whereof they were bound to Observe them. *Frustra feruntur Leges nisi subditis, & Obedientibus;*[6] and for this cause it is, that the Prince is termed our *Natural* Lord, and *we* His *Natural Subjects*, and our Allegiance *Natural*, it being due to him by the Law

---

4. With nothing impeding or standing in the way.
5. Neither in the thesis nor in the hypothesis.
6. Laws are proposed in vain unless proposed to those who are subject to them and who obey them.

of Nature, which is *Immutable*, for *Jura Naturalia nullo Jure Civili dirimi possint;*[7] So that if we should strictly pursue this Argument, we must conclude, that those Acts of Parliament which deprive the King of His Subjects' Service, are rather *ab initio*, void and null, than Indispensable. Thus an Act of Parliament in the time of *Henry 3. De Tallagio non Comedendo*, (Title Purveyance *Rasta*) which barrs the King wholly of Purveyance is void, as it appears in *Co. lib. fol. 69*.

However, I insist not on this, it being my design at this time to urge what about the Dispensing Power, hath been long ago universally taken for Good Law, which I shall most effectually perform, by giving not only the Opinion of our Learned Lawyers, but by adding some of the many Cases Judicially determined by our Judges.

By the *4 Hen. 4. c. 32.* it is ordained, That no *Welshman* be made Justice, Chamberlain, Chancellor, Treasurer, Sheriff, Steward, Constable of a Castle, Receiver, Escheator, Coroner, nor chief Forrester, nor other Officer, nor Keeper of the Records, nor Lieutenant in any of the said Offices, in no parts of *Wales*, nor of the Counsel of any *English* Lord, notwithstanding any Patent made to the contrary with this Clause *(non Obstante quod sit Wallicus natus)* and yet (saith Sir *Edward Coke*) without Question, the King may Grant with a *Non Obstante*.

By the *8 Rich. 2.c.2.* it is Ordained and Assented, That no man of the Law shall be from henceforth Justice of the Assizes, or of the Common Deliverance of Jails, in his own Country, and yet the King (said *Coke*) with Special *Non Obstante*, may Dispense with this. And the Reason is, because this belongs to the Inseparable Prerogative of the King, *viz*. His Power of Commandment to Serve.

Furthermore, whenever a particular Statute interferes with the Prerogative, that is Incident inseparably to the Person of the King, the King's Dispensation, with a *Non Obstante*, is Good, although the Statute be most Express to the contrary. Thus the Royal Power, to

7. Natural laws can be set aside by no civil law.

pardon Treasons, Murders, Rapes, &c. is a Prerogative Incident Solely and Inseparably to the Person of the King. And although there is an Act of Parliament to make the Pardon of the King void, and to restrain the King to Dispense by *Non Obstante,* and to disable Him, to whom the pardon is made, to Take or Plead it, yet it shall not bind the King, but that He may Dispense with it. And this is well proved (saith my Lord Ch. J. *Coke*) by the Act 13 *Rich. 2. parl. 2. c. 1.* For by this it was Enacted, That no Charter of Pardon from henceforth be allowed, by whatsoever Justices, for Murders, Treason, Rape of a Woman, nor be specified in the said Charter, and if it be otherwise, be the Charter Disallowed. It must be observed, that this was the surest way that the Parliament could take to Restrain the King to pardon Murder, unless that He pardon it by Express Terms, which they thought the King would not, for they knew, that the King could not be Restrained by any Act to make a Pardon; For *Mercy* and a Power to Pardon, is a Prerogative incident Solely and Inseparably to the Person of the King: And it hath been *oft-times adjudged,* that the King can pardon Murder by General Words, without any express mention with *Non Obstante* the said Act.

To come more close to the Case before us; by the Statute of *23 Hen. 6. c. 8.* it is provided, that all Patents made, or to be made, of any Office of a Sheriff, for term of years, for Life in Fee-simple, or in Taile, are void, and of no Effect; any Clause or *Parole de Non Obstante* put, or to be put into such Patents to be made, notwithstanding.

This Statute of *Hen. 6.* was made (as appears by the Purview of the Act) to Redress the many Grievances and Oppressions the King's Leige People were exposed unto by those Sheriffs that Held their Offices for Terms of Years, &c. and it did Revive those Statutes that were long before made to the same effect, *viz. 14 Ed. 3 & 42 Ed. 3.* And it was further Ordained, That whosoever shall take upon him, or them, to Accept or Occupy such Office of Sheriff by Vertue of such Grants or Patents, shall stand perpetually Disabled to be or bare the Office of Sheriff, within any County of *England,* by the same Authority. And notwithstanding that, by this Act, I. The *Patent is made void*; 2. The *King is restrained to Grant* Non Obstante; 3. The *Granter* Disabled *to take the Office*; Yet the King (to use Sir *Edward's* own Words) by His Royal Soveraign Power of Commanding, may Command by His Patent (for such Causes as He in His Wisdom doth think meet and profitable for Himself and the Common-Wealth, of which He himself is solely Judge) to serve Him and the Weal-Publick as Sheriff of such a County, for Years or for Life, &c. And so was it Resolved by All the Justices of *England*, in the *Exchequer Chamber*. *2 Hen. 7. 66.*

SECT. II.

The Safety of taking a Dispensation Evinced.

This is more than enough to evince, That the Dispensing Power is no New Thing, for, above Two hundred years ago it hath been Judicially Resolved by all the Judges of *England*, That the King, by a *Non Obstante*, may Dispense with those Laws that Deprive Him of the Service of His Subjects, and by comparing the Statutes made in the Late King's Reign with those of *14 Ed. 3. 42 Ed. 3. & 23 Hen. 6.* 'twill appear, That the Reason of the Old Statutes was more weighty, and the Caution taken to prevent a *Non Obstante* Greater than what is in the New; and yet then the King might Dispense, and therefore much rather may His Present Majesty do it. And seeing the Dispensation exempts from the Obligation of the Law, they who are Dispensed with, though not Qualified, are secure enough, from the Poenalty; for, where there is no Transgression, there no Poenalty is Incurred; and where no Obligation, there no Transgression. Thus much must be inculcated, A Dispensation, I say, is more than a Security from the Punishment, for it releaseth unto those that have it, the Obligation of the Law, and therefore they cannot be fully esteemed either Violaters of the Law, or liable to the Punishment, especially considering that this Case hath been very Lately determined Judicially by His Majesty's Judges, who are a Skreen between the Severity of the Law, and those Gentlemen that act according to the Judges' Resolutions, on which account, whoever in Obedience to His Majesty's Command, do Serve the King, and Unqualified, enter on Places of Trust with a Dispensation, in which is a *Non Obstante* to the Act of Parliament, they are most safe.

Not only a particular Dispensation will be good Security, but a Dispensation under the Broad Seal, to all that cannot conform to the Church of *England*, will be sufficient, such a Dispensation especially, if but for a time, is vastly different from Abrogation, for it doth *only* exempt *Dissenters* from the Obligation of that Law, that continues to bind all those who do Conform, even when by Abrogation as has been already noted, the Law is absolutely vacated, and obliges none.

That where the King can Dispense with particular Persons, He is not confined to *Number*, or *Place*, but may Licence as many, and in such places as He thinks fit, is abundantly proved by those Arguments, that evince it to be in the Power of the King to grant Dispensations to a Body Corporate, or Aggregate, as well as to Private persons.

Whoever desires further satisfaction touching this matter, will *see* enough in our Law-Books, particularly in *Vaughan's Reports*, where there are gathered together a Multitude of Precedents of Licences to Corporations.

SECT. III.

The King's Exercise of His Dispensing Power Cannot Hurt Liberty of Conscience.

THE King's *Dispensing Power*, in those Instances, wherein His Majesty Exercises it, and the *Safety* of those, who, though they cannot take the Imposed Tests, do yet, under the Protection of a Dispensation, enter on Places of Trust and Profit, being Cleared, I will go on to shew, that the nature of a Dispensation is such, as makes it manifest, that a Law establishing Liberty of Conscience, cannot be prejudiced by the Dispensing Power.

In the Description given of a Dispensation, it is express, that it is *Mali prohibiti provida relaxatio,* it being an Act of the Prince's Grace and Favour, designed for the *Relief* of the Oppressed, for which reason, that Law, which gives Ease to All and Oppresses none, falls not within the Compass of a Dispensation. It would be scarce Sence to say, That a Law, by which the Peace and Quiet of the Subject is Established, may be Dispensed with; for, to turn it into plain English, it must be thus, The Obligation of that Law, by which the Peace and Quiet of the Subject is Secured, must be Released to this or the other man, that thereby they may Enjoy the greater Peace; that is, Their Ease shall be secured by taking away their Security. In like manner, the Talk of a Dispensing with a Law, to the end the Subject may be Oppressed, is much to the same purpose, for it is to say, that by giving Relief to a man you Oppress him. A Dispensation is an Instrument of Ease; To give a Dispensation then, to the end you may Oppress, is to give Ease, that thereby you may grieve and afflict those who are Oppressed.

If we look into this Matter a little more closely, 'twill with much Evidence appear to be Impossible for the Dispensing Power to Hurt Liberty of Conscience, for whenever a Law for Liberty is enacted, all Poenal Laws for Religion must be Repealed, so that no man can be exposed to Suffer for his Conscience, until a new Poenal Law be made, which cannot be done by the *Dispensing Power.* Though the Dispensing Power exempts from the Obligation of a Law in Being, yet it gives not Being to a Vacated Law. If then all Poenal Laws for Religion be Abolished, Liberty of Conscience can meet with no Molestation. For, unless there be some Poenal Law in force against this or the other Religion, no man can be exposed to any Poenalty for his

Conscience. There must be a New Law enacted, or our Liberty remain firm; and seeing the Dispensing Power cannot Repeal nor make a Law, we are in no Danger from the Prerogative in this Respect.

And whereas it is maliciously suggested, That if the King may Dispense with those *Tests* that deprive Him of the Subject's Service, He may as well Dispense with the Parliamentary Tests too, and bring into either House whom He please, even such men as will make Poenal Laws against Protestants.[8] I deny this, I deny that there is such Connection between the Dispensing Power in the one case, and the other, that the Recognizing the One necessarily, should infer a Power to Grant the Other. The men that insinuate thus much, give the King a Higher Prerogative than He desires; for it's Notorious, that in the one Instance the King can Dispense, and if He might as well do it in the other, What should hinder His Majesty to Dispense immediately with the Parliamentary Tests, and do His Work?

But you see the King claims no such Prerogative, and, Why should He be suspected to do it hereafter? There is more Reason for it at this time than there can be after the Poenal Laws are removed; for it's not to be doubted, but that it's more on the Heart of the King to set men of His own religion at *Ease,* than to *Ruine* and Destroy others. And if He cannot Dispense with this Parliamentary Test, He can no more Dispense with another such Test. And notwithstanding anything the Objector urges, I must persist, there is a manifest difference between Dispensing with such Test Laws as Rob the King of his Subjects' Service, and those Test Laws that exclude some men out of the Legislation. Though no Act can bind the King from any Prerogative that is sole and inseparable to His Person, but that He may Dispense with it by a *Non Obstante,* as a Soveraign's Power to Command his Subjects to Serve him: Yet in things that are not solely and

---

8. The first Test Act, that of 1673, excluded Catholics from public office while the Parliamentary Test prevented Catholics from sitting in either House of Parliament. See 25 Car. II, ch. 2 (1673) and 30 Car. II, st. 2, ch. 1 (1678).

Inseparably Incident to the Person of the King, but belong to every Subject, an Act of Parliament there (as Sir *Edward Coke* has it) may Absolutely bind the King. And it's well known, that though the Service of the Subject belongs solely to the Person of the King, yet the Legislative Power is not solely Incident to his Person, for the people have a share in it, which is enough to shew a difference between Case and Case, and that the holding, That His Majesty has a Power to dispense with the One kind of Tests, doth not infer a Power to Dispense with the other.

Nothing doth more nearly concern the Subject, than an Interest in the Legislation, for by a Concurrence of the Two Houses with the King, Liberty and Property may be made a most precarious thing. The King, with His Parliament, may dispose of them as They please. For, as the Commons are the King's Subjects, so they are the People's Representatives and *Trustees,* and by what they do, every Subject is determined. What Laws therefore are made, shewing the Qualifications, those persons must have, to whom the People commit so great a Trust, must be Indispensable, or the People cannot have that full Security of Liberty and Property, which by the Ancient Constitution of our Government is their Right. And on this account a Dispensation in the present Case is with the Subjects' Right, and is a Wrong unto them, and not within the King's Power to Grant.

"The King cannot *Dispense* in any Case, but with his own Right, and not with the Right of any other."

"To Violate men's Properties is never Lawful; but a *Malum per se,* as that Book is of *2 Hen. 7.* and according to that of *Bracton.*"

"*Rex non poterit gratiam cum Injuria & damno aliorum. Quod autem alienum est, dare non potest per suam gratiam.*"[9]

"On this ground it is that some Poenal Laws, punishable at the King's Suit by *Indictment* or *Presentment,* the transgressing of which,

---

9. The King shall not dispense grace when it comes to the injury or loss to others. But what belongs to another he cannot grant by his own grace.

is the Immediate wrong of *Particular Persons,* for which the Laws give them Special Actions, with which the King Cannot *Dispense.* As He cannot Licence a man to Commit Maintenance, to make a forcible Entry, &c."

"If in a Law all the King's Subjects have an Interest, the King Cannot Dispense with it, any more than with the Common Law. And a *Disability* in this Case cannot be dispensed with; as was adjudged in Sir *Arthur Ingram's* Case."

"Likewise by the Statutes of *5 Eliz.* Every Person, which shall be Elected a Knight, Citizen, Burgess, or Baron of the Cinque Ports for any Parliament, before he shall enter into Parliament House, shall take the Oath of Supremacy, appointed by the Act of 1. Eliz. and that he that entereth into the Parliament, without taking the said Oath, shall be deemed no Knight, Citizen, Burgess, or Baron, nor shall have any choice, but shall be as if he had been never Returned or Elected. Here be Words (saith Sir *Edward Coke*) that amount to a Disability, and therefore, that according to the former Resolutions, the King cannot Dispense with the same."

This I must stand upon, as what plainly Appears from the *Reason* of the Thing, and also from the Opinion of our Judges, that there is a very great difference between the King's Dispensing with the Laws, that Deprive Him of His Subjects' Service, and those that Secure His People's Rights, and that although the one is within the King's Power to Dispense, the other is not.

On the Whole it's clear.

I. That it belongs to the King's Prerogative to Dispense with all those Poenal Laws, that are a Grievance to the Subject, or Deprive His Majesty of His Subjects' Service.

A Prince had never a more fair Occasion to exercise the Dispensing Power, than our King has, who by it hath Saved a Nation from Ruine, and given that Ease to Conscience, which renders unto Thousands the greatest Satisfaction imaginable. For which cause it cannot but surprize the Impartial and Unbiassed, to find those Gentlemen denying the Dispensing Power to belong to the King, that for many years together have boldly affirmed, the sole Legislative Power to lie in His Breast: Especially considering, that the Prerogative has been no less Exalted by them to the Vexation of the Dissenter, than at this time Deprest, when exercised only for the Relief of the Oppressed; which sufficiently demonstrates that our High-Church-men are for the Prerogative, if by the Help thereof they may Establish their own Domination and Grandeur; but will be against it if His Majesty exercises it for the Benefit of the Dissenter, which is a thing that cannot (as some do foolishly insinuate) be for the Honour of the Protestant Religion.

II. That those to whom a Dispensation is given, may in Obedience to the King's Command, safely enter on places of Trust and Profit, anything in the Test Laws notwithstanding.

For, [without insisting on a Consideration that hath its weight too, *viz.* That the Conviction must be at the King's Suit, by Indictment or Information before the Penalties be incurred, or the Person disabled by the said Act, in which His Majesty can at pleasure *Non Pros,* or Pardon and thereby secure him from Danger, although he had no Dispensation]. I have from the Nature of a Dispensation Evinced, That those Dispensed with do not Transgress the Laws; They incurr not on the Poenalty, and therefore are in no danger, especially considering, that very Lately the Judges have, in a Judicial way, determined it; for hereby had the Judges' Resolution been Contrary to Law, yet the Gentry, and others, who must Govern themselves by the Judges' Resolutions, run no hazard by entering on places of Trust, with a *Non Obstante* the Act of Parliament: How much less than where the Case for many hundred years together has been cleared?

The Result of which is, That it's much more Safe for Dissenters to take a Dispensation, than Contrary to their Conscience submit unto the *Abjuring* of *Sacramental Tests.* The Case is plain. Take a Dispensation, and you run no hazard in this World, or that which is to come: But if you Abjure the Covenant, or take the Sacrament, according to the usage of the Church of *England,* contrary to the plain and manifest Convictions of Conscience, you may be miserable here and hereafter too.

III. That the King's Exercising this Dispensing Power cannot in the least hinder the settling Liberty of Conscience on such just and Equal Foundations as to put it out of the Power of any King to Alter it by Prerogative.

Let the Persecuting of any man, upon the Account meerly of his Conscience, be declared *Malum in se,* in such an Act as passes for Liberty, and that Act must thereby be rendered *Indispensable.*

FINIS.

Published with Allowance.

London Printed, and Sold by *R. Janeway* in *Queens-Head Alley* in *Pater-Noster-Row.*

Anonymous

THE
Clergy's late Carriage
TO THE
KING,
CONSIDERED.

In a Letter to a Friend.

Allowed to be Published this 2d Day of July, 1688.

*T*his anonymous tract in the form of a letter appeared three days after the trial and acquittal of the Archbishop of Canterbury and six other bishops for seditious libel. The bishops had been cited for their petition to James questioning his dispensing power in ecclesiastical matters and refusing to order his Declaration of Indulgence to be read from the pulpit as he had commanded.

On 27 April 1688 James had reissued his Declaration of Indulgence for religious toleration with its suspension of the penal laws. While the king claimed he would present the Declaration to the next Parliament for its approval, he issued it on the strength of his prerogative powers alone. Unlike his earlier declaration, this time the king ordered that it be read on two consecutive Sundays in every Anglican church. On 18 May the Archbishop of Canterbury and six other bishops presented a petition to James asking that the order be withdrawn. They pointed out that they had an obligation to defend the Act of Uniformity and that in 1663 and again in 1673 Parliament had rejected the use of the suspending power in such cases. Their petition was published the next day whereupon the seven bishops were charged with seditious libel and clapped in the Tower. Their trial took place on 29 June.

The trial was distinguished by the eminence of all concerned—the accused, the defense counsel who included a former lord chief justice, a former judge, and two former attorneys- and solicitors-general. While the chief justice claimed the suspending power was not at issue he allowed it to be discussed. Indeed, two of the puisne judges argued against the suspending power and for acquittal. To great public jubilation the jury returned a verdict of not guilty. The next day James dismissed the two outspoken judges from the bench.

"The Clergy's Late Carriage to the King" defends James and presents arguments in support of his suspension of penal laws. Beyond this it points out the embarrassing inconsistency in the attitude of Anglican clergy who always professed themselves believers in divine right monarchy, but were prepared to oppose their king when they disliked his orders. The charge was true enough, although passive resistance, as preached by the Church of England, permitted loyal subjects to refrain from obeying illegal commands so long as they passively suffered any necessary punishment. At any rate the charge of inconsistency highlights the difficult situation in which divine right clergy found themselves and their solution in extremis. The tract appeared in a single edition.

SIR,

Perhaps I am in the wrong, but I beg your Pardon if I can't think so, when I don't know it. On the contrary, I grow more assured in my Opinion, since the other Night, by all the Reflections I could make upon what past between us. It seems, I say unaccountable to Good Sense, Duty, Modesty, and everything that becomes a dutiful Subject (to say nothing of the Christian) that the *King* was not only not obeyed by the *Clergy*, where it was no Sin to do it, but where the Obedience was purely *Ministerial*. Had it been to *renounce* their own Religion, or to *receive* His, it had been *something;* but when it was to *secure* every Religion from Violence and Persecution: Nay, when it was a Declaration of *His* Mind about a good Work, and not of *Theirs:* No new Declaration of *Liberty of Conscience*, but a Publication of what He had done last Year; and that what was New in it, was only the *King's Resolution to have a Parliament next Winter*, in order to have that past into a Law, which the *Bishops* seemed only to dislike for want of being done by Law and Still to resist their King and Head, I say, this is something surprizing. In short, the Declaration was in its first part meerly *Historical*, what the King had done *April* 1687,[1] the last part what He would do, to wit, have a Parliament in *November* next at farthest to Establish this *Liberty of Conscience*. And as this was in truth the Business of the Declaration, the other but the Preface to it, so with trouble I say it, that this makes their Disobedience the more suspected, and unreasonable; for they refuse to tell the World, the *King* would have a *Parliament* to confirm the Liberty, which yet they profess to be for, in Parliament. I say, this looks with an ill Air, and carries too great a contradiction for Men of their Function and Learning; and yet so it must be, or they are insincere in their Petition. But this is not all; The Reverence these Gentlemen have always

1. Reference is to James II's Declaration of Indulgence of 4 April 1687 granting liberty of conscience to all his English subjects.

profest for the *Monarchy,* Their Opinion of the mighty Power of it, The Character they have fixt on those that have been scrupulous to obey it, in Cases less clear than this, is an aggravation of their Misfortune; for at this rate no *inferiour Minister* is so much as obliged to report the Act of a Superiour, if it is not suitable to his own Judgment. *A Clark of a Court* may refuse to read an Inditement, because he thinks the Man Innocent that is impeached at the Bar by it. No *Sheriff* ought to read a Proclamation, or execute an Offender unless his Judgment concur with that of the *Prince* or the *Judge.* It carries (whatever they think of it) the power of *Questioning* the Commands of Superiours into all the capacities and relations of Life, even where it is no matter of Faith. If I bid my Servant go tell a Man I deal with, He has used me very dishonestly, at this rate he may refuse for this reason, *That truly he has a better opinion of him,* and therefore won't go of my Errand. *Had the King set up for Lawmaking, or intended finally to abrogate Laws, or suspend Laws made against anything that was evil in itself, or Laws that preserve Property instead of those that take it away; or that it had touched upon matters of Faith, or the Worship of God, or intrenched upon any Priviledge that belongs to the* Church of England; *or if He had required them to read the Opinion of the Judges about the Dispencing Power, or a Treatise in defence of it, in order to Endoctrinate the People,* they might have had room for some Exception, and yet in this latter Case perhaps they had been little more than Ministerial too. But when it was only to tell his Subjects, in the most effectual way (more going to *Church than to Market*) that whereas He did emit a Declaration in 1687 for *Liberty of Conscience,* (the Historical part) *He resolved in* November *next, at farthest, to hold a Parliament for the Confirmation of it:* Give me leave to say, without offence, It looks as if the Exception were a *Cavil* and not a *Scruple.*

By whom else should the *Ecclesiastical Head* speak to the *Ecclesiastical Body?* for it therefore seems to me reasonable that they should have read it in their *Churches,* because they are the State *Meeting-*

Houses, and the *Clergy* the State *Mouthes.* Will they claim their Legal Priviledges, and not bate an Ace of being the *Church of England* as by Law Established, and yet refuse to let the Head speak by them the Mouth, His mind to the People, his Ecclesiastical Body? Can this consist with Ecclesiastical Headship and Obedience? where no Assent or Consent was exacted from them, nor were they to require it of the People; but as I said before, a meer *Report* of the *King's* Mind, referring to a publick *future Act,* of which the People's Information was requisite for their own Benefit and Content, as well as the *King's* Service. I say, for the *Clergy* to refuse their *Head,* and this *Head* too, that they so generally and earnestly desire to wear upon their Shoulders, and at this time of Day, and about a thing they say they have a due tenderness to, has an appearance as if they would widen Breaches and highten Animosities, ay, ripen and head them, too, instead of suppressing them. I say, it looks so, for I would fain have a better opinion of their Loyalty and Conscience than to think they meant it. However this Conduct goes *too far,* thus to *strive* and *chicane* with their *Prince,* and by popular pretences to raise themselves upon the breath of the Rabble above the duty they owe Him, this is at least *the appearance of Evil,* and unbecomes *Men of Peace and Religion,* to be sure such as pretend to be the *Successors* of the *Apostles,* that command Obedience for Conscience' sake, where Conscience was not imposed upon, and has been pleaded by this very *Clergy* against *Dissenters,* to urge their Conformity where matters of Faith and Worship to God were concerned.

Though this, I say, and not Religion, be the Case, yet such is the Malice of the World, as to say it, and such has been their Weakness, as to give occasion for it. I confess that has been the uneasiest part to me, that they have acted, I mean their *Mock Martyrdom,* to force Suffering and act it to a Farce. What else can be their Blessing People ten deep of a side, with *Have a care of your Religion, be faithful to your Religion, the Lord strengthen you &c.* and whilst not one *tittle* of their Religion, but the Liberty of other Men's was the Case: What shall an honest Man think of this? when the plain English of the matter was that they went to the Tower for not reading a Declaration for settling of Liberty *of Conscience* by Law, to hinder them from ever making Martyrs of other Men anymore for Conscience' sake. This is the Point before God and Man, after all the bustle their Nonresisting Principle has suffered them to make; and 'tis this I am scandalized at, to see a jest acted so much in Earnest, and Religion made one, and profained too, by such forced pretences. God give them Repentance and confirm the *King* in his wise course of Moderation: For the Liberty when settled will shame its Enemies, and save and encrease the number of its Friends, for whatever is suggested by ill Men, 'tis *Liberty of Conscience* that is aimed at. Liberty built upon a *Rock* and not a *Sand:* To be framed to exclude any one Party from the Power of endangering the rest: Can we honestly fear *Popery* should break this Liberty, when it even becomes a security against the more refined *Popery* of the *Church of England?* What will prevent the less cannot admit the greater. *The Net which will catch a little Fish, will not let a greater pass.* How unjust therefore are the Jealousies of those, and how impudent their Words that prejudge that matter, and will not leave it to the only place where the *Trial* of the sincerity of all Parties can be made? I mean a *Parliament.* To that time I refer the whole Controversy, and do beg all Parties to prepare to make the Session happy in trying not how to divide, but unite upon this great *Point;* where if the *Bishops* shew their conversion to Liberty, by a tenderness truly due to Conscience in every Party, I shall heartily change the opinion, their contrary practise, for so many Years past, has constrained me to entertain about them, but till then I have greater reason to count their present Zeal *A fit of Art,* than they have to suspect the Court of insincerity in the business of the present Declaration: A thought that Seven Years ago would have been with them *Insufferable* in a Dissenter, especially about any Act of power in the *Clergy's favour.* What then can one call Their crime, that in the name of *Religion, and Law,* can bring themselves to contest their *King's* command, upon his Judges' Opinions, in a case of so much mercy and goodness? For such an one this is, and the effect of it Heaven hath already blest. It is what might have become the greatest, and best of *Princes* of former Ages, but it looks as if it had been reserved for the glory of him that now Sways the *English Scepter;* and I confess I can't refrain hoping this goodness of his, will give Example, even where his power can't give Law.

London, *Printed for* H. L. and I. K. *and Sold by most Booksellers in* London *and* Westminster.

Revolution and Allegiance

[Gilbert Burnet, 1643–1715]

AN
ENQUIRY

Into the Measures of

SUBMISSION
TO THE
SUPREAM AUTHORITY:

And of the *Grounds* upon which it may be *Lawful* or necessary
for *Subjects*, to defend their *Religion, Lives* and *Liberties*.

*G*ilbert Burnet was an extraordinary individual. He was a bishop, an active politician, a prolific pamphleteer, and a historian. His tract, reprinted here, played a key role in smoothing the way for William and Mary to ascend the throne of England.

Burnet was born in Edinburgh. His father was an attorney and free thinker who criticized bishops but nevertheless refused to take the Presbyterian Covenant. Consequently he contrived to live as quietly as possible until the Restoration. He was then made one of the Lords of the Session. Gilbert was broadly educated and attended Aberdeen University where, to please his father, he studied to become a clergyman. He entered the Scots church while it was under Presbyterian control, although episcopacy was restored soon after. Burnet had a religious tolerance rare for his era. Indeed, both Anglicans and Presbyterians would later become annoyed at his moderation. During a visit to the English universities Burnet joined the Royal Society. On his return to Scotland he accepted a living at Saltoun in East Lothian, which he held until 1669 when he became professor of divinity at Glasgow. He was actively involved in public affairs and on familiar and surprisingly frank terms with both Charles II and James. For a time he was one of Charles's chaplains. In 1671 he was named bishop of Edinburgh.

Burnet later settled in England where he defended the first Catholic victim of the popish plot scare. During the exclusion crisis he tried to moderate between the parties. Yet he was a close friend to leading Whigs. In 1683 his two dearest friends, Essex and Russell, were both implicated in the Rye House Plot and executed. Despite the personal dangers, Burnet attended Russell on the scaffold and appeared for the defence at Algernon Sidney's trial. After these deaths he *prudently left England. He returned in 1684, only to be stripped of some posts because of a vehement anti-Catholic sermon he gave. At James's accession Burnet again left for the Continent. There he witnessed the terrible religious frenzy caused in France by the king's abrupt revocation of the Edict of Nantes, which had protected the civil liberties of French Protestants. He also visited Calvinist Geneva and corresponded with Lutherans. Finally he accepted an invitation from William of Orange and Mary to reside at the Hague, where he became a confidant of them both.*

Burnet was deeply involved in William's plans to invade England and personally accompanied that expedition. It was he who translated William's declaration into English. In preparation for the campaign he had thousands of copies of the remarkable tract, reprinted below, prepared in Holland to be distributed upon their arrival. Dubbed the most radical piece Burnet ever wrote, this call to arms succinctly summarizes its author's view of the nature of civil society, supreme power, the duty of self-preservation, and the limits on divine delegation of power, all with a decidedly Whig slant. In it Burnet remarks: "In all the disputes between Power and Liberty, Power must always be proved, but Liberty proves itself." The tract appeared in at least six separate editions and in addition was reprinted in collections of tracts published in 1688 and 1689.

With the accession of William and Mary honors were heaped upon Burnet. It was he who preached the sermon at the coronation of William and Mary. He was named bishop of Salisbury. Burnet personally attended William at his deathbed. He lived to advise Queen Anne and died in 1715.

This *Enquiry* cannot be Regularly made, but by taking in the first place, a true and full view of the nature of *Civil Society,* and more particularly of the nature of *Supream power,* whether it is lodged in one or more persons?

I. It is certain, that the *Law of Nature* has put no difference or subordination among Men, except it be that of *Children* to *Parents,* or *Wives* to their *Husbands;* so that with Relation to the Law of Nature; all Men are born free: and this Liberty must still be supposed entire, unless so far as it is limited by Contracts, Provisions and Laws. For a Man can either bind himself to be a Servant, or sell himself to be a Slave, by which he becomes in the power of another, only so far as it was provided by the Contract: since all that Liberty which was not expresly given away, remains still entire: so that the plea for Liberty always proves itself, unless it appears that it is given up or limited by any special agreement.

II. It is no less certain, that as the light of nature has planted in all men a natural principle of the love of Life, and of a desire to preserve it; so the common principles of all religion agree in this, that God having set us in this World, we are bound to preserve that being, which he has given us, by all just and lawful ways. Now this duty of Self-preservation, is exerted in Instances of two sorts; the one are, in the resisting of Violent Aggressors; the other are the taking of just revenges of those, who have invaded us so secretly, that we could not prevent them, and so Violently that we could not resist them: in which cases the principle of self-preservation warrants us, both to recover what is our own, with just damages, and also to put such unjust persons out of a Capacity of doing the like Injuries any more, either to ourselves, or to any others. Now in these instances of self-preservation, this difference is to be observed; that the first cannot be limited, by any slow forms, since a pressing danger requires a vigorous repulse: and cannot admit of delays; whereas the second, of taking revenges, or reparations, is not of such hast, but that it may be brought under rules and forms.

III. The true and Original Notion of *Civil Society* and *Government* is, that it is a Compromise made by such a body of Men, by which they resign up the right of demanding reparations, either in the way of Justice, against one another, or in the way of War, against their neighbours; to such a single person, or to such a body of Men as they think fit to trust with this. And in the management of this *Civil Society,* great distinction is to be made; between the power of making Laws for the Regulating the Conduct of it, and the power of Executing those Laws. The *Supream Authority* must still be supposed to be lodged with those who have the *Legislative Power* reserved to them; but not with those who have only the *Executive;* which is plainly a *Trust,* when it is separated from the *Legislative* Power; and all *Trusts,* by their nature import, that those to whom they are given, are accountable, even though that it should not be expresly specified in the words of the *Trust* itself.

IV. It cannot be supposed, by the principles of Natural Religion, that God has Authorised any one *Form of Government,* any other way than as the general Rules of Order, and of Justice, oblige all Men not to subvert Constitutions, nor disturb the peace of Mankind, or invade those Rights with which the Law may have vested some persons; for it is certain, that as private Contracts lodge or translate private Rights; so the *Publick Laws* can likewise lodge such Rights, Prerogatives and Revenues, in those, under whose Protection they put themselves, and in such a manner that they may come to have as good a Title to these, as any private Person can have to his Property: so that it becomes an Act of high Injustice and Violence, to Invade these: which is so far a greater sin than any such actions would be, against a private Person, as the publick Peace and Order is preferrable to all private Considerations whatsoever. So that in truth, the principles of *Natural Religion*, given those that are in Authority, no power at all, but they do only secure them in the possession of that which is theirs by Law. And as no Considerations of Religion can bind me to pay another more than I indeed owe him, but do only bind me more strictly to pay what I owe; so the Considerations of Religion do indeed bring *Subjects* under stricter Obligations, to pay all due Allegiance and Submission to their *Princes*, but they do not at all extend that Allegiance further than the Law carries it. And though a Man has no divine right to his property, but has acquired it by human means, such as succession, or industry, yet he has a security for the enjoyment of it, from a Divine right; so though *Princes* have no immediate warrants from Heaven, either for their Original Titles, or for the extent of them, yet they are secured in the possession of them by the Principles and Rules of *Natural Religion*.

V. It is to be Considered, that as a private person, can bind himself to another Man's service, by different degrees, either as an Ordinary servant for wages, or as one appropriat for a longer time as an Apprentice, or by a total giving himself up to another, as in the case of Slavery: in all which cases the General name of *Master* may be equally used, yet the degrees of his power, are to be judged by the nature of the Contract; so likewise bodies of Men can give themselves up in different degrees, to the Conduct of others: and therefore though all those may carry the same name of *King*, yet every one's power is to be taken from the measures of that Authority which is lodged in him, and not from any general Speculations founded on some Equivocal terms, such a *King, Sovereign,* or *Supream*.

VI. It is certain, that God, as the Creator and Governour of the World, may set up whom he will, to rule over other men: But this declaration of his will, must be made evident by Prophets, or other Extraordinary Men sent of him, who have some manifest proofs of the Divine Authority that is committed to them, on such occasions, and upon such persons declaring the will of God, in favour of any others, that Declaration is to be submitted to, and obeyed. But this pretence of a divine Delegation, can be carried no further than to those who are thus expresly marked out, and is unjustly claimed by those who can prove no such Declaration to have been ever made in favour of them, or their families. Nor does it appear reasonable to conclude from their being in posession, that it is the will of God that it should be so, this justifies all Usurpers, when they are successful.

VII. The measures of *Power,* and by consequence of *Obedience,* must be taken from the express Laws of any State, or body of Men, from the Oaths that they swear, or from Immemorial Prescription, and a long Possession, which both give a Title, and in a long tract of time make a bad one become good, since Prescription when it passes the memory of Man, and is not disputed by any other Pretender, gives by the common sense of all Men a just and good Title. So upon the whole matter, the degrees of all Civil Authority, are to be taken either from express Laws, immemorial Customs, or from particular Oaths, which the Subjects swear to their Princes: this being still to be laid down for a Principle, that in all the disputes between *Power* and *Liberty, Power* must always be proved, but *Liberty* proves itself; the one being founded only upon positive Law, and the other upon the Law of Nature.

VIII. If from the general Principles of Human Society, and Natural Religion, we carry this matter to be examined by the Scriptures, it is clear that all the passages that are in the *Old Testament,* are not to be made use of in this matter, of neither side. For as the Land of *Canaan,* was given to the *Jews* by an immediate grant from Heaven, so God reserved still this to himself, and to the Declarations that he should make from time to time, either by his Prophets, or by the Answers that came from the Cloud of Glory that was between the Cherubims, to set up Judges or Kings over them, and to pull them down again as he thought fit. Here was an express Delegation made by God, and therefore all that was done in that Dispensation, either for or against Princes, is not to be made use of in any other State, that is founded on another bottom and Constitution, and all the expressions in the *Old Testament* relating to *Kings,* since they belong to persons that were immediately designed by God, are without any sort of reason applied to those, who can pretend to no such designation, neither for themselves nor for their Ancestors.

IX. As for the *New Testament,* it is plain, that there are no rules given in it, neither for *the forms of Government* in general, nor for the degrees of any one form in particular, but the general Rules of Justice, Order and Peace, being established in it upon higher motives, and more binding considerations, than ever they were in any other Religion whatsoever, we are most strictly bound by it, to observe the Constitution in which we are; and it is plain, that the Rules set us in the Gospel, can be carried no further. It is indeed clear from the *New Testament,* that the *Christian Religion* as such, gives us no grounds to defend or propagate it by force. It is a Doctrine of the Cross, and of Faith, and Patience under it: and if by the order of Divine Providence, and of any Constitution of Government, under which we are born, we are brought under sufferings, for our professing of it, we may indeed retire and fly out of any such Country, if we can; but if that is denied us, we must then according to this Religion, submit to those sufferings under which we may be brought, considering that God will be glorified by us in so doing, and that he will both support us under our sufferings, and gloriously reward us for them.

This was the state of the *Christian Religion,* during the three first *Centuries,* under Heathen *Emperors,* and a Constitution in which *Paganism* was established by Law. But if by the Laws of Government, the *Christian Religion,* or any form of it, is become a part of the Subject's *Property,* it then falls under another consideration, not as it is a *Religion,* but as it is become one of the principal rights of the *Subjects,* to believe and profess it: and then we must judge of the Invasions made on that, as we do of any other Invasion, that is made on our other *Rights*.

X. All the passages in the *New Testament* that relate to *Civil Government*, are to be Expounded as they were truly meant, in opposition to that false Notion of the *Jews*, who believed themselves to be so immediately under the Divine Authority, that they could not become the Subjects of any other Power; particularly of one that was not of their Nation, or of their Religion: therefore they thought, they could not be under the *Roman* Yoke, nor bound to pay Tribute to *Cesar*, but judged that they were only subject out of *fear*, by reason of the force that lay on them, but not *for Conscience' sake:* and so in all their dispersion, both at *Rome* and elsewhere, they thought they were *God's Freemen*, and made use of this pretended *liberty as a cloak of maliciousness*. In opposition to all which, since in a course of many years, they had asked the protection of the *Roman* Yoke, and were come under their Authority, our Saviour ordered them to continue in that, by his saying, *Render to Cesar that which is Cesar's;* and both St. *Paul* in his Epistle to the *Romans*, and St. *Peter* in his General *Epistle*, have very positively condemned that pernicious maxim; but without any formal Declarations made of the Rules or Measures of *Government*. And since both the *People* and *Senate* of *Rome* had acknowledged the power that *Augustus* had indeed violently Usurped, it became Legal when it was thus submitted to, and confirmed both the *Senate* and *People:* and it was established in his Family by a long Prescription, when those *Epistles* were writ: so that upon the whole matter, all that is in the *New Testament* upon this subject, imports no more, but that *all Christians* are bound to acquiesce in the *Government*, and submit to it, according to the Constitution that is settled by *Law*.

XI. We are then at last brought to the Constitution of our *English Government:* so that no General Considerations from speculations about *Soveraign Power*, nor from any passages either of the *Old* and

New Testament, ought to determin us in this matter; which must be fixed from the Laws and Regulations that have been made among us. It is then certain, that with Relation to the *Executive* part of the Government, the *Law* has lodged that singly in the *King;* so that the whole Administration of it is in him: but the *Legislative Power* is lodged between the *King* and the Two Houses of *Parliament;* so that the power of making and repealing *Laws,* is not singly in the *King,* but only so far as the *Two Houses* concur with him. It is also clear, that the *King* has such a determined extent of Prerogative, beyond which he has no Authority: as for instance, if he levies many of his people, without a Law impowering him to it, he goes beyond the limits of his Power, and asks that to which he has no right: so that there lies no obligation on the Subject to grant it. And if any in his Name use Violence for the obtaining it, they are to be looked on as so many Robbers, that Invade our Property, and they being Violent aggressours, the Principle of self-preservation seems here to take place, and to warrant as Violent a resistance.

XII. There is nothing more evident, than that *England* is a free Nation, that has its *Liberties* and *Properties* reserved to it, by many positive and express *Laws.* If then we have a right to our *Property,* we must likewise be supposed to have a right to preserve it: for those Rights are by the Law secured against the Invasions of the Prerogative, and by consequence we must have a right to preserve them against those Invasions. It is also evidently declared by our *Law,* that all Orders and Warrants, that are issued out in opposition to them, are null of themselves; and by consequence, any that pretend to have Commissions from the *King,* for those ends, are to be considered as if they had none at all: since those Commissions being void of themselves, are indeed no Commissions in the Construction of the *Law;* and therefore those who act in vertue of them, are still to be considered, as private persons who come to invade and disturb us. It is also to be observed, that there are some Points that are justly disputable and doubtful, and others that are so manifest, that it is plain that any Objections that can be made to them, are rather forced pretences, than so much as plausible colours. It is true, if the Case is doubtful, the Interest of the Publick Peace and Order, ought to carry it; but the Case is quite different when the Invasions that are made upon *Liberty* and *Property,* are plain and visible to all that consider them.

XIII. The main and great difficulty here, is, that tho our Government does indeed assert the *Liberty of the Subject,* yet there are many express *Laws* made, that lodge the *Militia* singly in the *King,* that make it plainly unlawful upon any pretence whatsoever to take Armes against the King, or any Commissioned by him. And these *Laws* have been put in the form of an *Oath,* which all that have born any Employment either in Church or State have sworn; and therefore those Laws, for the assuring our *Liberties,* do indeed bind the *King's* Conscience, and may affect his Ministers; yet since it is a Maxim of our Law, that the *King can do no wrong,* these cannot be carried so far as to justify our taking Armes against him, be the transgressions of Law ever so many and so manifest. And since this has been the constant *Doctrine* of the *Church of England,* it will be a very heavy Imputation on us, if it appears, that tho we held those Opinions, as long as the Court and the Crown have favoured us, yet as soon as the Court turns against us, we change our principles.

XIV. Here is the true Difficulty of this whole Matter, and therefore it ought to be exactly considered: *First,* All general Words, how large soever, are still supposed to have a tacit exception, and reserve in them, if the Matter seems to require it. Children are commanded to obey their Parents in *all things:* Wives are declared by the Scripture, to be subject to their Husbands *in all things, as the Church is unto Christ.* And yet how comprehensive soever these words may seem to be, there is still a reserve to be understood in them; and tho by our Form of Marriage, the Parties swear to one another *till Death them do part,* yet few doubt but that this Bond is dissolved by Adultery, tho it is not named; for odious things ought not to be suspected, and therefore not named upon such occasions: But when they fall out, they carry still their own force with them. 2. When there seems to be a Contradiction between two Articles in the Constitution, we ought to examine which of the two is the most Evident, and the most Important, and so we ought to fix upon it, and then we must give such an accommodating sense to that which seems to contradict it, that so we may reconcile those together. Here then are two seeming Contradictions in our Constitution: The one is the *Publick Liberty* of the Nation; the other is the Renouncing of all *Resistance*, in case that we're invaded. It is plain, that our *Liberty* is only a thing that we enjoy at the *King's* Discretion, and during his Pleasure, if the other against all Resistance is to be understood according to the utmost extent of the Words. Therefore since the chief Design of our whole Law, and of all the several Rules of our Constitution, is to secure and maintain our *Liberty*, we ought to lay that down for a Conclusion, that it is both the most plain and the most Important of the two: And therefore the other Articles against *Resistance* ought to be so softened, as that it do not destroy this. 3. Since it is by a Law that *Resistance* is condemned, we ought to understand it in such a sense as that it does not destroy all other Laws: And therefore the intent of this *Law*, must only relate to the *Executive Power*, which is in the *King*, and not to the *Legislative*, in which we cannot suppose that our Legislators, who made that Law, intended to give up that, which we plainly see they resolved still to preserve entire, according to the Ancient Constitution. So then, the not resisting the *King*, can only be applied to the *Executive Power*, that so upon no pretence of ill Administrations in the Execution of the Law, it should be lawful to resist him; but this cannot with any reason be extended to an Invasion of the *Legislative Power*, or to a total *Subversion of the Government*. For it being plain, that the *Law* did not design to lodge that Power in the *King*, it is also plain that it did not intend to secure him in it, in case he should set about it. 4. The Law mentioning the *King,* or those *Commissionated* by him, shews plainly, that it only designed to secure the *King* in the Executive Power: for the Word *Commission* necessarily imports this, since if it is not according to *Law,* it is no *Commission;* and by Consequence, those who act in Vertue of it, are not Commissionated by the *King* in the Sense of the *Law.* The *King* likewise Imports a Prince clothed by *Law* with the Regal Prerogative; but if he goes to *Subvert* the whole Foundation of the Government, he *Subverts* that by which he himself has his Power, and by consequence he annuls his own Power; and then he ceases to be *King,* having endeavoured to destroy that, upon which his own Authority is founded.

XV. It is acknowledged by the greatest Assertors of Monarchichal Power, that in some Cases a *King* may fall from his Power, and in other Cases that he may fall from the Exercise of it. His Deserting his People, his going about to enslave, or sell them to any other, or a furious going about to destroy them, are in the opinion of the most Monarchical Lawyers, such Abuses, that they naturally divest those that are guilty of them, of their whole Authority. *Infancy* or *Frenzy* do also put them under the Guardianship of others. All the Crowned Heads of *Europe* have, at least secretly, approved of the putting the late *King of Portugal* under a Guardianship, and the keeping him still Prisoner for a few Acts of Rage, that had been fatal to a very few Persons: And even our *Court* gave the first countenance to it, though of all others the *late King* had the most reason to have done it at least last of all; since it justified a younger Brother's supplanting the Elder; yet the Evidence of the thing carried it even against Interest. Therefore if a *King* goes about to subvert the Government, and to overturn the whole Constitution, he by this must be supposed either to fall from his Power, or at least from the Exercise of it, so far as that he ought to be put under Guardians; and according to the Case of *Portugal,* the next *Heir* falls naturally to be their *Guardian.*

XVI. The next thing to be considered, is to see in Fact whether the

Foundations of *this Government* have been struck at, and whether those Errors, that have been perhaps committed, are only such Maleversations, as ought to be imputed only to Human Frailty, and to the Ignorance, Inadvertencies, or Passions to which all Princes may be subject, as well as other men. But this will best appear if we consider what are the Fundamental Points of our *Government*, and the chief Securities that we have for our *Liberties*.

The Authority of the *Law* is indeed all in one Word, so that if the *King* pretends to a Power to *Dispense* with *Laws*, there is nothing left, upon which the *Subject* can depend; and yet as if *Dispensing Power* were not enough, if *Laws* are wholly suspended for all time coming, this is plainly a Repealing of them, when likewise the men, in whose hands the Administration of Justice is put by Law, such as *Judges* and *Sherriffs*, are allowed to tread all Laws under foot, even those that Infer an Incapacity on themselves if they violate them; this is such a breaking of the whole Constitution, that we can no more have the Administration of Justice, so that it is really a *Dissolution* of the *Government*; since all Trials, Sentences, and the Executions of them, are become so many unlawful Acts, that are null and void of themselves.

The next thing in our *Constitution*, which secures to us our *Laws* and *Liberties*, is a *free* and *Lawful Parliament*. Now not to mention the breach of the *Law* of *Triennial Parliaments*, it being above three years since we had a Session that enacted any Law; Methods have been taken, and are daily a taking, that render this Impossible. *Parliaments* ought to be chosen with an entire Liberty, and without either Force or Preingagements;[1] whereas if all men are required

---

1. During the fall of 1687 in preparation for the elections to Parliament in 1688, each lord lieutenant was to summon his deputy lieutenants and justices of the peace and ask them three questions. Their answers were to be recorded, and those giving unsatisfactory replies were to be removed from office. The questions asked whether, if they were elected to Parliament, they would be willing to remove the penal laws and tests, assist others to get elected who were in favor of this removal, and support James's Declaration of Indulgence.

beforehand to enter into *Engagements* how they will *Vote* if they are chosen themselves, or how they will give their Voices in the Electing of others? This is plainly such a preparation to a *Parliament*, as would indeed make it no *Parliament*, but a *Cabal*, if one were chosen, after all that Corruption of Persons, who had preingaged themselves; and after the Threatening and Turning out of all persons out of Imployments who had refused to do it; and if there are such daily Regulations made in the *Towns*, that it is plain those who manage them intend at last to put such a number of men in the *Corporations* as will certainly chuse the persons who are recommended to them. But above all, if there are such a number of *Sherriffs* and *Mayors* made, over *England*, by whom the Elections must be conducted and returned, who are now under an Incapacity by Law, and so are no Legal Officers, and by consequence those Elections that pass under their Authority are null and void: If, I say, it is clear that things are brought to this, then the *Government* is dissolved, because it is impossible to have a *Free and Legal Parliament* in this state of things. If then both the Authority of the *Law*, and the Constitution of the *Parliament* are struck at and dissolved, here is a plain Subversion of the whole Government. But if we enter next into the particular Branches of the *Government*, we will find the like Disorder among them all.

The *Protestant Religion*, and the *Church of England*, make a great Article of our Government, the latter being secured not only of old by *Magna Charta*, but by many special *Laws* made of late; and there are particular Laws made in K. *Charles* the First, and the late *King's* time, securing them from all *Commissions* that the *King* can raise for Judging or Censuring them: if then in opposition to this, a *Court* so condemned is erected, which proceeds to Judge and Censure the *Clergy*, and even to disseise them of their *Freeholds*, without so much as the form of a Trial, tho this is the most indispensable *Law* of all those that secures the Property of *England*; and if the *King* pretends that he can require the *Clergy* to publish all his Arbitrary *Declara-*

tions, and in particular one that strikes at their whole settlement,[2] and has ordered Process to be begun against all that disobeyed this illegal warrant, and has treated so great a number of the *Bishops* as Criminals, only for representing to him the reasons of their not obeying him; if likewise the *King* is not satisfied to profess his own *Religion* openly, tho even that is contrary to *Law*, but has sent *Ambassadors* to *Rome*, and received *Nuntios* from thence, which is plainly *Treason* by Law; if likewise many *Popish Churches* and *Chappels* have been publickly opened; if several *Colledges* of *Jesuits* have been set up in divers parts of the Nation, and *one* of the *Order* has been made *Privy Counsellor*, and a principal *Minister* of *State*; and if *Papists*, and even those who turn to that Religion, tho declared Traitors by Law, are brought into all the chief Imployments, both *Military* and *Civil*; then it is plain, That all the Rights of the *Church of England*, and the whole establishment of the *Protestant Religion* are struck at, and designed to be overturned; since all these things, as they are notoriously Illegal, so they evidently demonstrate, that the great design of them all, is the rooting out of this *Pestilent Heresie*, in their style, I mean the *Protestant Religion*.

In the next place, If in the whole course of Justice, it is visible, that there is a constant practising upon the *Judges*, that they are turned out upon their varying from the Intentions of the *Court*, and if men of no Reputation nor Abilities are put in their places; if an *Army* is kept up in time of peace, and men who withdraw from that illegal Service are hanged up as Criminals, without any colour of Law, which by consequence are so many Murders; and if the Souldiery are connived at and encouraged in the most enormous Crimes, that so they may be thereby prepared to commit greater ones, and from single rapes and murders proceed to a rape upon all our Liberties and a destruction of the Nation: if, I say, all these things are true in fact,

2. James II's Declaration of Indulgence of April 1688.

then it is plain, that there is such a dissolution of the *Government* made, that there is not any one part of it left sound and entire. And if all these things are done now, it is easy to imagine what may be expected, when *Arbitrary Power* that spares no man, and *Popery* that spares no Heretick, are finally established. Then we may look for nothing but Gabelles, Tailles, Impositions, Benevolences, and all sorts of Illegal Taxes, as from the other we may expect Burnings, Massacres and Inquisitions. In what is doing, in *Scotland* we may gather what is to be expected in *England;* where if the King has over and over again declared, that he is vested with an *Absolute Power,* to which all are bound to *Obey without Reserve,* and has upon that annulled almost all *Acts* of *Parliament* that passed in K. *James* the First's minority, though they were ratified by himself when he came to be of Age, and were confirmed by all the subsequent Kings, not excepting the present.[3] We must then conclude from thence, what is resolved on here in *England,* and what will be put in execution as soon as it is thought that the Times can bear it. When likewise the whole Settlement of *Ireland* is shaken, and the Army that was raised, and is maintained by Taxes, that were given for an Army of *English Protestants,* to secure them from a new *Massacre* by the *Irish Papists,* is now all filled with Irish Papists, as well as almost all the other Imployments; it is plain, That not only all the *British Protestants* inhabiting that Island, are in daily danger of being butchered a second time, but that the *Crown of England* is in danger of losing that Island, it being now put wholly into the hands and power of the Native *Irish,* who as they formerly offered themselves up sometimes to the Crown of *Spain,* sometimes to the *Pope,* and once to the Duke of *Lorrain,* so they are perhaps at this present treating with another *Court* for the Sale and Surrender of the *Island,* and for the Massacre of the *English* in it.

---

3. A Scots King when attaining his majority could annul acts passed during his minority. However, James II annulled acts passed during the minority of his grandfather, James I, even though these acts had been ratified by James when he came of age.

If thus all the several Branches of our Constitution are dissolved, it might be at least expected, that one part should be left entire, and that is the *Regal Dignity;* and yet even that is prostituted, when we see a *young Child* put in, the reversion of it, and pretended to be the *Prince of Wales;* concerning whose being born of the *Queen,* there appear to be not only no certain proofs, but there are all the presumptions that can possibly be imagined to the contrary. No proofs were ever given either to the *Princess of Denmark,* or to any other *Protestant Ladies,* in whom we ought to repose any Confidence that the *Queen* was ever with Child; that whole matter being managed with so much mysteriousness, that there were violent and publick Suspicions of it before the Birth. But the whole Contrivance of the Birth, the sending away the *Princess of Denmark,* the sudden shortening of the *Reckoning,* the *Queen's* sudden going to S. *James's,* her no less sudden pretended *delivery;* the hurrying the *Child* into another Room, without shewing it to those present, and without their hearing it cry; and the mysterious conduct of all since that time; no satisfaction being given to the *Princess of Denmark* upon her Return from the *Bath,* nor to any other *Protestant Ladies;* of the *Queen's* having been really brought to Bed. These are all such evident Indications of a base Imposture, in this matter, that as the *Nation* has the justest reason in the World to doubt of it, so they have all possible reason, to be at no quiet till they see a *Legal* and *Free Parliament* assembled; which may impartially, and without either Fear or Corruption, examine that whole matter.

If all these matters are true in fact, then I suppose no man will doubt, that the whole Foundations of this *Government,* and all the most sacred parts of it, are overturned. And as to the truth of all these Suppositions, that is left to every *Englishman's* Judgment and Sense.

FINIS.

A. B. and N. T.
[John Wildman, 1624–1693]

Some REMARKS upon

GOVERNMENT,

And particularly upon the ESTABLISHMENT

Of the *English* MONARCHY

Relating to this present Juncture.

In Two LETTERS,

Written by, and to a Member of the Great
CONVENTION, holden at *Westminster*
the 22d. of *January*, 1688/9.

This important Whig tract has only recently been attributed to John Wildman, a republican pamphleteer, a successful land speculator, and, until 1688, an unsuccessful plotter.

Wildman practiced law and at some point served in Parliament's army although possibly not until 1649. He came to prominence in 1647 along with the Levellers as a spokesman for a democratic republic during the New Model Army's debates at Putney. He was especially intrigued by constitutions, and his biographer claims that his "The Case of the Army" in 1647, which was broadened into the second "Agreement of the People," was the first democratic constitution known to the modern world. Wildman abandoned the Levellers in 1649.

As a republican he was hostile to the Protectorate. Wildman was imprisoned by Cromwell in 1655 for plotting his overthrow and released in 1656, perhaps on condition he become an informer. Wildman was more interested in constitutional than religious issues and during the Interregnum married a Roman Catholic. He was also something of an opportunist and made a small fortune as a land manager and property speculator during the 1650s. His seizure of Windsor Castle in 1659 from supporters of General John Lambert stood him in good stead at the Restoration. Nevertheless, in 1661 he was rounded up with other republicans and put in prison where he languished until 1667. In 1683 his involvement with the Whigs led to another arrest, this time in the wake of the Rye House Plot. He was released in 1684 when no evidence was found against him. He then went from the proverbial frying pan into the fire, serving as James, Duke of Monmouth's, chief agent in England and falling under suspicion of complicity in Monmouth's ill-fated rebellion of 1685. Wildman fled abroad and by 1688 had found his way to The Hague where he became one of William's chief propagandists. He accompanied the prince to Torbay. Wildman was subsequently elected to the Convention Parliament where he was one of the most active members and was named to the committee that drafted the Declaration of Rights and to 63 other committees.

"Some Remarks upon Government" appeared in a single edition in January 1689 amid a flurry of pamphlets offering advice to the Convention. Of these, Mark Goldie found it the most substantial of four anonymous pamphlets that constituted a commonwealth Whig manifesto. These did not dwell upon the usual concerns of popery, allegiance, or the succession. Instead "Some Remarks upon Government," for example, discusses the origins of government, the flaws in the English constitution, and the importance of change in such areas as the electoral system, revenue, and the appointment of judges. The impact of the recommendations would have been to strengthen the powers of Parliament. This essay has been called the only Harringtonian contribution to the Revolution debate.

SIR,

YOU *have been highly Obliging in the frequent Accounts you sent me of Affairs, in this Great and Extraordinary Revolution. I was once very diffident, and could scarcely conceive that the* States of Holland, *or* Prince of Orange, *could have attempted so Expensive, and so Hazardous an Undertaking out of pure Generosity, meerly for our Sakes, and for the Re-establishment of our* Laws *and* Religion, *which did both equally Labour under the Pressures of an Ill Administration, and seemed to draw towards their last* Periods. *I knew the* States *had the Character of preferring their own, before any other Interest whatsoever, and the* Prince *had the Reputation of setting a due Value upon* That *which creates and proportions the Value of all things else. The Enterprize I lookt upon, as very Expensive in its Methods, and Uncertain in its Accomplishment, which made me prone to believe that something more lay coucht in this Vast Undertaking, than was exprest in the* Prince's Declaration; *But since His arrival and coming to* London, *I perceive He has, upon all Occasions, carried Himself with that wonderful Modesty, with such an unparalelled Care and Tenderness of our* Laws, Liberties, *and* Religion, *and adheres so Resolutely to every Particular in His Declaration, that I cannot but esteem these to be His Noblest Trophies: And that which crowns those Successes which have crowned His Generous and Pious Undertakings. His persisting to referr all to the Impartial Decisions of a* Free Parliament, *to Do and Establish such Matters, either in His, their Own, or the King's behalf, as they shall think fit, even then, when Honor and Power spread their Perswasives before Him to do otherwise, is so great a Thing that it exceeds all His other Glories, and strikes the Beholders with nothing less than Amazement. I do more rejoice than wonder at the Unanimous Concurrence which has hitherto been maintained between the* Lords *and* Commons *Assembled in Councel, and indeed in the Wishes & Desires of all the People in General. It is what this Juncture does highly require, and what the* Prince's *Conduct does Oblige. We are very busie here in the Countrey in Electing Members for the Great Convention which is to sit in* January, *and I think the Lot will fall on me to serve for my Neighbouring Borough. You know I was never fond of Business or Trouble, and truly Age seems now to have signed my Writ of Ease. I also always cherisht some* Cynical Notions, *which made me very much slight and disregard the Honours and Flatulencies of a giddy World: But the thoughts of being one of the Great Planters of a Government which shall last for Ages, and perhaps till Time has run out its last Minutes, is no Ordinary thing. This thought alone has envigorated my Age and baffled my Philosophy, so that you may expect to see me in* London *about the 22d. of* January *next; and in the mean time, if you will favour me with your Thoughts and Opinion of Affairs, and what Understanding Men do think will, or ought to be the Issue and Consequence of this great Revolution, you will very considerably add to the many Kindnesses conferred upon*

SIR,
Your assured Friend and humble Servant
A. B.

The Answer.

Yours (though it bore an early Date, yet) came not to my hands till last *Friday.* I am very glad that my slender Services have proved upon any account acceptable to you. I never thought myself qualified to pry into the Recesses of Government, or the privacies of a King. What I acquainted you with, was little more than what was publickly discoursed of in Coffee-Houses: But indeed such was the Management of Affairs during our late King's[1] Supremacy, That his most private Councels proved generally the next day's Table-talk, for as they

---

1. The writer seems to be referring to James II here.

were shallow, so was the bottom of them discoverable to every common Eye. The *Prince* has perhaps with more Courage than Caution, and a greater Zeal for the Protestant Interest, than Care of His own particular Concerns, undertaken mighty Things for us, and run such Risques in the Accomplishing of them, which Story can scarcely paralell. But what the sequel of this will be, I must leave to *Astrology.* 'Tis true, the people seem to be Unanimous to a wonder, and yet there are a *Sett* of Men in this Nation whom nothing will satisfie but to Lord it over their Brethren. These do still labour under some Discomposures, and although, in no respect disobliged, yet fearing they may receive a Crush in this great *Turn*, do by their Sourness and Discontent rather assist and further their fate, than anticipate and prevent it. The Protestant Dissenters are not esteemed, by Computations which have been formerly made, to amount to more than a 25th part of the Nation, the Church of *England* receiving all the rest. This I do believe to be true, if the Church of *England* be taken in the most large and comprehensive Sense, by including all such as frequent the publick Service: But if we might suppose them in the same Circumstances that Dissenters were in, at the time of this Computation made, under the Frowns of the Court, and the power of the Laws, which like so many Billows, beat in against them; if thus we might be admitted to view them in Reverse, I do believe their Numbers would not exceed, or Scarcely equal those of the Dissenting party. There are but very few in the Nation would undergo Fines and Imprisonment for the sake of the *Surplice* or *Common-Prayer.* The prevailing Opinion now in *England* is, *Latitudinarian:* Most Men are so far improved in their Judgements, as to believe, that Heaven is not entailed upon any particular Opinion, and that either an Episcopal, or Presbyterial way of Worship, together with a due observation of the Rules of Morality, may serve well enough to carry them to Heaven, the only Biass which enclines them to the one side or the other, being the Laws. *Be Subject to the Higher Powers, not for Wrath, but Conscience,* sways the Scale and gives the casting Vote in such Things as are thought indifferent. This is it which crowds the Church, otherwise the Sarsnet Hood and Lawn Sleeves might be as destitute of Votaries, as the Long Cloak and Collar Band.

Which way the succeeding Government will lean, I dare not determine, but it is more than probable, That *Episcopacy,* in that strictness in which it has of late Years been exercised, owed its *Continuance,* as well as Originally its *Being,* to the King: His power and His purse, has been liberally imployed in favour of the Church, and they as plentifully requited His Kindness, by their Doctrines of *Jure Divino-ship,* and *Passive Obedience.* So long as the King continued thus their Servant, He was in all Causes Civil and Ecclesiastical, their Supreme Head and Governour: But when the King became of another Interest, and they themselves were likely to be squeezed by the pressures of their own Weighty Doctrines, then *the Case was* immediately *altered* and *Plowden's Hogs could be no longer Trespassers.*[2] They instantly changed their Note, and rang their Bells backward, for they were all on fire, and likely to be reduced to their original Dust in a moment. Fears of *Popery* was first the pretence of their dissatisfactions. This was very plausible, and seemed once to give them an interest in the people. But surely now these Dangers are Removed; the Protestant Interest is likely to settle upon firm Foundations, and the *Prince* seems well affected to their way of Worship, and signalizes His Approbations by Communicating with them according to the Rights and Ceremonies of the Church, and yet they seem dissatisfied, and are still apprehensive of Danger.

2. Edmund Plowden, a sixteenth-century English jurist and the author of *Commentaries,* was so generally respected and cited that his name was embodied in the popular aphorism "The case is altered, quoth Plowden." This saying appears to relate to an incident in which Plowden was asked by a neighbor what legal remedy there was against a man who allowed his pigs to stray into the neighbor's field and was assured the law would protect him. Whereupon the questioner replied the pigs were Plowden's. "Nay then, neighbour," quoth Plowden, "the case is altered." See Burton Stevenson, ed., *The Macmillan Book of Proverbs, Maxims, and Famous Phrases* (London, 1965), 291.

What then can be the reason that this bright Hemisphere should thus be wrapt up in Clouds and Darkness? It must needs be this, That they have lost, or are likely to lose the King and Court's good Service employed in all or most of the former Parliaments so freely in their behalf. This in truth was the chief Pillar of their Church: That which first built, and afterwards supported it. Though the *Prince* does sufficiently approve of this Establishment in His Own Judgment, yet He is resolved to call a *Free Parliament*, being the purport of His *Declaration*, backt with many subsequent Promises and Assurances in which the People shall have freedom to Elect such Persons as are for the True Interest of the Nation, and not for the upholding a particular Interest or Faction. There shall be no Elections either forced by Power, or bribed by Treats; No false Returns, no Committee of *Affections* to determine according to the Court or Church of *England* Interest; No Parliamentary Pensions, nor Treats with Guineas laid under their Plates to seduce them from their honest Principles and the Interest of their Country. The *Prince* abhors such irregularities. He desires such an Assembly may meet, as may truly represent the People, to Enact and Establish such Laws and such a Government as may secure their Religion, Liberties and Properties, with the best advantage and security to the Nation that can be proposed. And although the Church of *England* is hereby left destitute of that unfair and irregular advantage it firmly had from the King's power and assistance, yet I doubt not but this and succeeding Parliaments will Enact such an Establishment in the Church, as may very well agree with the honest desires of the more moderate and pious Church-men.

What the Civil Government will be, is more difficult to guess at, but I can tell you what it has been, and wherein it seems defective and requires some touches of your Legislative Skill to help it out. This I am confident of, That if the Consultations of this great Councel does but produce what the Necessities of the People, and the

Conveniencies which a well-setled State does require, the Alterations will be very considerable. 'Tis true, there is a Notion generally received by the Nobility and Gentry of *England* that a *Mixt Monarchy* (just such a one as ours is, and no other) must needs be the best of Governments, and that amongst all others, none could boast of those advantages as that of *England.* This fancy is so rivetted in the minds of the People (spread abroad and preacht up, only to keep the people in peace, and from endeavouring an Alteration, which could not be effected without the Inconveniencies of the Sword) that I do believe All things will again settle upon its old *Basis,* and the Government be rebuilt with all its irregularities. However, because I understand you are in election to be one of Those, from whom succeeding Ages must derive their Happiness or Misery, I will make use of the Liberty you have given me, to express my Sentiments in this mighty Affair, in order to which I will in the first place acquaint you with my Notions of Government in general, and afterwards will descend to Particulars; And to our present Case as it now lies:

Government is a Power whereby a Community of Men are kept in Order, and disposed to act comformably to their Natures, and to the common advantage of the whole Body Politick. This Power is sometimes placed in one single Person, and then it is *Monarchy:* Sometimes in a select number of the *Chiefs,* when it assumes the name of *Aristocracy;* And sometimes in the whole Body of the People, which is called *Democracy.* But of these three *Primatives,* there are several Derivatives, Compounds, and Variations.

The first, *Magestracy,* I do allow to be grounded in Nature, and the first *Magistrate* to be a *Genarcha,* or Patriarch, who ruled over Families of his own Extraction, and Citties of his natural Generation. It was in this sense that the Fifth Commandment was given; and it was from hence that Men grew up into Citties, Kingdoms, and Empires, and therefore the Laws to regulate them ought to be such as are apt and fit to govern Families, for the preservation of their *Peace, Liber-*

ties and *Properties*, not to bind them to perpetual Slavery and Vassalage. So also, the Submissions due from the People to the Supream Power, are in their nature filial, not servile, as proceeding rather from Love and Gratitude, for protection given, than for fear of the Rod hanging over their Backs, which ought to be exercised only to prevent a common Inconveniency. But this Patriarchal Government, continues no longer than the Patriarch holds a power over his Family, to punish such offences in particular persons, as might otherwise (if allowed of) obstruct the common Interest; and to protect the whole Body and every individual in their natural and acquired Rights, both from Domestick and Forreign Invaders. For when the natural power of one or more in Conjunction shall exceed that of the Patriarch, or Father of the Family, this sort of Government is so far dissolved, that if they please and find it convenient, they may reassume their natural Freedom, or again engage in the same Family, by Pact or promise, or else leave it, and by compact with others, submit to what Laws or Measures of Living together in a Community they think fit. He that will make the natural *Magistrate* more Sacred than this, may at last commit Idolatry, and fall down to worship.

But this is not the State of any Nation or People now under Heaven: We are all shufled and blended together, so that we stand not Originally associated to any Magistrate out of natural Duty, but out of mutual fear of each other, which to avoid, produced, these civil Compacts, by which the World is now Governed. Thus being seperated from our Families, each Man has a right by nature to defend himself, which supposes his primary Allegeance now due to himself. He has farther an equal right with all others to all things necessary for sustentation, & an absolute right in his own person; & having thus a *mutuum jus* in both, he is fitted for mutual Compact with others. 'Tis certain that Nature, though She did provide for Mankind in its tender helpless and unexperienced years, a natural Governour and Protector, yet being withdrawn from that Power and Subjection, it falls into a state of War, which was the Condition of the World in those Times, which Historians call Heroical: When *Nimrod* obtained the Character of the stoutest Hunter, and *Hercules* travelled to tame Monsters and Usurpers.

The Patriarchal Government being at an end, and the People being now left in a state of War, occasioned by the Universal Right that every man had to every thing, the Government that succeeded was accordingly Martial and Warlike, and their Governours were rather Generals than Kings, and like them, Arbitrary and Unlimited. In this state the Chief Magistrate was properly and Originally called *Tyrannus;* but Lust, Ambition, and Avarice being the usual attendants of absolute power, did too far prevail, to the prejudice of those in Subjection, that both the Person and Title of such Governours in time became odious and contemptible. It was for this reason that *Plutarch* in his life of *Timoleon,* affirms that over a Tyrant, every man is a Judge, and may be an Executioner; and *Plato* in his Commonwealth, delineates a Tyrant amongst his Subjects by a Woolf amongst the Flock, placed there rather to devour than preserve them.

But the World soon grew weary of this Course of Life, and by experience found that Compact was more apt for the Coalition of Societies than mere Power; which is the cause, That in the more civilized and cultivated parts of the Earth, this sort of Government is very rare and unusual, unless sent by the Supreme *Power* of Heaven and Earth for the punishment of a People for some Sins committed, that thereby they may be compelled like the mute Fish in the Gospel, to bring their Penny unto *Caesar,* and after pay their Lives for Contribution. And it is observable that it prevails principally, and is no where else willingly allowed of, but where Idolatry and Invincible Ignorance are the National Sins.

This Tyranical Government, or State of War, being found uneasie in many places, and more intollerable than the Patriarchal Government in which they were first engaged, and also finding that there is now no Father of the Country, in a natural Sense. The People as be-coming Orphans, choose *One* or *More* to be their Guardian, which in several Countries goes under several Denominations. Thus the Peo-ple are in a state of Pupillage, and as a *Miner* cannot make a Con-tract to his prejudice, so we may conclude, that the People may meliorate their Condition by Compact, but cannot make it worse; and therefore it may with much more reason be allowed, that such Concessions which are made by them, and which infringe or dero-gate from their natural Rights should be void, than that what a Prince grants to his People out of his Prerogative (though for their better Government and well Being, for which alone Prerogative was first given and intended) should be null and of no validity, which some Precedents in our present Establishment seem to countenance and abet. Thus all Governments in the same degrees that they differ from Patriarchal and Tyrannical must derive their Originals from Com-pact, and the Governour must necessarily derive his Power from and by, the mutual Consent of the People he governs; unless God does himself immediately appoint a Magistrate, and even then the Peo-ple have usually confirmed, as in the case of *Saul. I. Sam. 10.* So of *David, I Sam. 16. 2 Sam. 2.*

I cannot but with *Grotius* believe, that *Salus populi est Suprema Lex.* Nor did *Junius Brutus* err in affirming that, *Imperii finis unicus est populi Utilitas.*[3] But on the contrary to imagine the People to be made for their King, and that a Million of Souls should be Born Slaves and Vassals to the Lust and Tyranny of one Man, who by nature is no more than their fellow Creature, made of the same mold, and stand-ing upon the same level with themselves, is nonsense and directly contradictory to the true notion of Government itself. In all States and Kingdoms whose Government is by Compact, the King cannot be supposed to be anything more than an Officer, elected and ap-

---

3. The single end of command is the advantage of the people.

pointed by the People to preserve the Government, and therefore the People must necessarily be supposed to have still a Reserve of Power in extraordinary Exigences above the King. *Quicquid efficit Tale est magis tale.* Their Concessions cannot extend farther than for their own preservation, and when that ceases, the Grant determines Our General and Original Rights cannot totally be swallowed up by any Compact that can be made to settle Liberty and Property, neither is all that was Natural now made Civil; wherefore that old Law was but old Reason. *Quod populus postremum jubet id ratum esto.*[4] Upon this Account the People in notorious cases, do themselves become the Accuser, Judge, and Executioner; it being but reason that in such Cases they should be allowed this priviledge; for as every man is the best Judge of his own health, and how such and such Meats and Medicines assists and helps the health and vigor of his Body; so in the *Body Politick*, the People must be Judge how this or that Governour or Law agrees with their Constitution, and Contributes to their Health, Peace, and Welfare. In the 17th. of *Deut.* And the 14th. *v.* God leaves the Election of a King absolutely to the People, and puts it into their choice whether they will have a King or not, and whosoever they pleased to set over them (provided he were chosen from among their Brethren) should be their King. Thus before *David's* Inauguration, *The People made a league with him,* 2 Sam. 5. 3. v. And by this they restrained and bound him up as they thought fit. And he who in any settled legal Government, arrogates to himself any other Supremacy over all or any part of this Brethren, other than what is immediately appointed by God, or claimed from the People, breaks those Bonds and Limits which they have set; and is as Civilians distinguish, *Tyrannus exercitio,* though not *Titulo.*

A Supream, Absolute, and Arbitrary Power, is essentially necessary in all Governments whatsoever, whether *Monarchial, Aristocrat-*

4. Let that be legal which the people command last of all.

ical, or *Democratical*, in respect of which, these three distinct Species differ no otherwise than as a Guinea from twenty Shillings, or forty Sixpences, which put together are equivalent one to the other. Thus the Supream Acts of all Governments are the same, for no State can go higher (nor ought to descend lower) than 1st to be able to redress a grievance, by making or repealing a Law. 2ly to have the power of War and Peace, 3ly. to judge of Life and Death, and 4ly to fix all Appeals in itself. So also if a mixture be made of these three Governments, yet it makes no change as to the product of a Supream Act; for they who limit one another, are yet Copartners and do the same thing together which one alone doth Legislatively. And as the prudence and foresight of the first Founders of these various Constitutions, saw any advantage or inconveniency peculiar to the people, place, or time they lived in, so they accordingly made various and suitable provisions and Laws, to assist the Good and to divert the Evil. Upon this account there are few Governments but have some things woven into their Constitution peculiar to themselves. In *Poland* where the Monarchy is Elective, and the *Prince* bound to observe the Laws, any Gentleman may safely and freely accuse his Prince. In *Arragon* the Chief Justice has a Tribunition power. In *Venice* the Duke stirs not out of the City without leave, and is made so much greater than any of the rest, only to allay the growth of Ambition in any one besides. In the form of Transactions, Most do follow the Plurality of Sufferage, but in several ways: In the Senate of *Venice* in many Cases there must be a Concurrence of three parts of four. In the Conclave of *Rome* at the Election of the Pope, two parts of three must concur: In the Consistory the Pope alone carries it against all the Council or Cardinals. In the Convention in *Poland, Potior est Conditio Negantis*, One Negative hinders all proceedings in the most important Affairs. In *Holland* the States General of the Provinces have but seven Votes in all, and these obliging according to the Plurality of Sufferage, but the number of States sent to manage the Interest of their single and Provincial Votes are unlimitted; and as the respective Provinces please to Delegate; wherefore their Votes may be more properly termed local than personal; but with us in *England* Votes are merely personal; for as we represent not Provinces or Places distinctly Supream, but mixed together; so the odd Vote carries all; by which it may happen that one man may make or destroy the best Law that ever was. From these particulars you may collect the varieties that are in Government, instituted according to the different Notions of the first Founders, and the Circumstances and Temper of the People Governed.

Monarchy vested with the most absolute powers that either Concession or Conquest can create I esteem the best of Governments, but that only happens when it represents God more in his *Justice* than *Singularity;* and when Mercy is the Ornament as well as Power the supporters of his Throne. In such a Government under a Prince whose Goodness and Wisdom runs in equal paralells with his power and greatness, the people are happy and secure, whilst their Neighbours live in fear and subjection, His Councils are private, and the Execution of them sudden, without which no great enterprise can be successful. To such a King is applicable the Answer which was made to this Question upon *Pasquill* in *Rome, Quid est Prerogativa Regis:* The Reply being *in optimo Rege nihil nimis, in Malo Omne Nimium.*[5] But to take a view of this Government in its dark side, under a Child, Fool, or vitious Prince, nothing carries such an aspect of Horror and Misery to the poor Wretches who live under it: Wherefore if we consider that the generality of Men, when let loose to their natural, or rather corrupted Inclinations, are much more apt to lean towards Tyranny and Oppression, than to such Methods as may promote

---

5. In the best king nothing is in excess, in an evil one everything is too much.

their People's Happiness, I think this sort of Government by no means desirable. It does at the best but keep the State which is directed by it, in a fluctuating and unsetled condition. It sometimes in the Reign of a Warlike and Ambitious Prince, like the Sea in a Storm, rowls in with rage, and Fury upon a Neighbouring Shoar, and again under the Tuition of another who is of a weak and pusillanimous spirit, it moulders and gives way to the loss of all its former Acquisitions, so that the Ballance of the Kingdom is never at a stand, the Scale moving sometimes upwards, and anon down again, and the People consequently kept in a rowling, unsetled condition, poor, miserable, and uneasie.

Aristocracy is composed by a select number of the Chiefs of the People to Govern the Rest, and stands like a Moderatour between the Excesses of Kingly and Popular Power: But this Mixture often produces Monsters, and as the greatest Storms are formed in the Middle Religion, so the Bloodiest Commotions are raised in this State, though most Temperate.

Democracy does properly and naturally reduce all to equality, and most carefully consults the People's Liberty and Property, but withall, it obliges every Man to hold his Neighbour's hand, and when it falls, it does with great difficulty recover its feet again. 'Tis true, that Monarchies are more Quick and Expeditious in their Attempts, but Common-Wealths, as they are more slow, so they are more sure, and in regard that their Councils are more publick, so are they generally more Honest and justifiable. Common-wealths are not like Monarchies, subject to the inconveniencies of Evil Council or Corruption where the Prince's personal folly or ambition, the Commands of an Imperious Wife, or the Flatteries of a Fawning Courtezan, may in a minute overthrow a People and Kingdom. We have found it by sad Experience, practised at home, where a Chambermaid has prevailed with her Mistress, and she again by a Kiss or Smile with the

Monarch; and we also owe all our present Discomposures to the Directions of a Zealous Priest,[6] managed by the Mediation of a Commanding Queen.[7] We are also sufficiently sensible of the great Unhappiness that befalls a people living under a Monarchy, in having their Prince of a Religion different from themselves. But this Inconvenience can never befall a Common-wealth, it being impossible to change, alter, or introduce any new Religion by such a Government, but such as the greater part of the people embrace and are willing to receive. But in Monarchies the King being but one person, may in that respect be more easily and probably seduced, both to his own and his people's irreparable Injury.

The Eastern Countries which lie under the Course of the Sun, as *Persia, Turky, Africa, Peru,* and *Mexico,* are most disposed to Monarchies, in which latter Quarter of the World the people are better Governed by the *Spaniard,* who are by fits in the Excesses of Kindness and Cruelty, than by the *Dutch,* whose Government is of a more even Temper. But in *Europe* and nearer the Pole, the people are disposed more to Republicks, tempered by fundamental Laws. *Nec totam servitutem pati possunt nec, totam Libertatem.*[8] Sir *William Temple,* whose insight in the Constitutions of States and Kingdoms, may deservedly give him a decisive Vote, tells us, That *Monarchies do indeed seem most Natural, but Common-Wealths the more Artificial sorts of Government,*[9] which was but a modest way of giving his suffrage for the last, for Art always corrects the defects of Nature, and pollishes it up to a greater Lustre: But when all is done, we find it experimen-

---

6. The Jesuit, Father Edward Petre, clerk of the Royal Closet, was believed to have had considerable influence on James II.

7. Presumably James II's second wife, the Catholic Mary of Modena.

8. Neither can all suffer slavery nor all liberty.

9. Sir William Temple, "An Essay upon the Original and Nature of Government" (1672), in *The Works of Sir William Temple, Bart. Complete in Four Volumes,* ed. Jonathan Swift, 1814 (rpt. New York, 1968), 1:21.

tally true, that all Governments like all sublunary things besides, have their Defects. Nature in every part is sick, and therefore can find rest in no posture. Human Laws grow out of Vices, which gives to every Government a tincture of Corruption.

That the Government of *England* was originally and always under the same constitution that now, or of late it did appear to be, I cannot conceive, though Sir *Edward Coke*, and some others, do seem with much earnestness to contend for it. I am of opinion, that like *Epicurus* his World, it is grown by Chance and Time to what it now is or lately was, by various Concussions and Confluence of People, Interest, Factions, and Laws, like so many Attoms of different shapes and disposures, springing from meer Accident in several Ages; for where there are Men, there will be also Interests, which creates Factions and Parties, and these, as they prevail, or are supprest, produce Laws for or against them, which so far alters the former Government, as new Laws are introduced in the room and place of Government, as new Laws are introduced in the room and place of old ones which were thought fit to be Repealed and Abrogated.

Although some Governments seem to be built upon firmer and more unalterable Foundations than others, yet there is none but ought to adapt itself to the Circumstances and Disposition of the People Governed, and as these do daily change, so ought the Government to shift and tack with them, that it may the better fit with the Necessities and changing Circumstance of those for whom it was first instituted.

That Property is founded in Dominion, I look upon to be a most undeniable Truth, for Naturally in the same degree that a Man has a Right and possession in a thing, he must necessarily have the Power and Dominion over it; To argue or defend the contrary, is as great an absurdity in Nature, as to say the Fire must be hot, and yet not burn such Combustibles as are cast into it. It is upon this account that the

Grand Seignior[10] is so Despotick in his Government, for by the Constitutions of that State all Lands are in the Crown, none hold longer than during pleasure, or for Life, and then their Lands revert to him that gave them. For the same reason, in the days of *England's* Ignorance and Poverty, when Arts and Learning were strangers to the Land, and the people were scarcely removed from their primitive estate of Nature and War, when every man had a universal Right to all things, and no man could by a peculiar property pretend to a Possession longer than his Sword and Bow could maintain it; Then I say were our Governours like *Generals*, absolute and unlimitted. 'Tis true indeed, we have some dark shadows of Laws and Councils, then in use, which our Governours thought fit, as they saw occasion to make use of; and we also find the People sometimes dissatisfied, treating their Magistrate with much Roughness and ill Usage upon his Male Administration; yet this does not all argue that their Governours were limitted and bound up by Laws, as now they are. These things are all practiced in *France, Turky,* and the most Arbitrary Monarchies in the World. Without Laws and Methods, such as these, one Man is not able to govern Millions, and therefore *Moses,* who under *God,* was Absolute and Arbitrary, was necessitated to appoint certain Rules and Methods, and to admit of others into the Government with him, as Assistants, by their Councel and Advice, the Work being too great for one Man to discharge. It was from the King's absolute Property in the Lands of *England* (which in those Times none

---

10. The reference is to the Turkish ruler, the Grand Seignoir, frequently used by English authors as the paradigm of a despotic, all-powerful ruler. A seventeenth-century dictionary describes his government as "Monarchical, the Emperor absolute Master of the Life, Honour, and Goods of his Subjects: His Orders are above the Laws, which are but few, and those in Favour of Arms, and for the enlarging of the State. The Ottomans believe firmly, that the Sultan's Will is the Will of God.... He is the only Heir of all their Possessions, for their Children and Friends never enjoy them but by his Permission." See *The Great Historical, Geographical and Poetical Dictionary: Being a Curious Miscellany of Sacred and Prophane History,* by Several Learned Men (London, 1694), Turks, 2.

could pretend to but by and through him who held the Sword) as well as from his power over the Laws that our old Tenures sprung of Knight-service, Sergeantry, Escuage, Socage, Villenage, &c. Then were all Tenures, *servile,* and all Persons held mediately or immediately from the King, which our Law-Books tell us, we still do; but there was a vast difference between our then, and present Holdings, the first being by actual Services paid; these now being only Nominal and Titular. To hold in *Socage,* is by the service of the Plow, (as almost all persons are said to do). The Tenant was in old times actually bound to Plow the Lord's Lands, in consideration of which Service, he granted to his Plow-man, instead of Wages, to hold another piece of Land to his own proper use; but now, though the Tenure does nominally remain, yet the Service is absolute; every Man being now become, by the circular motions of Chance or Providence, his own Lord, and his own Plow-man. His Property and Possession makes him the Lord over those Glebes which his Necessity (derived from his Ancestor *Adam's* Transgression) makes him Till.

Those Governments which succeeded the *Patriarchal,* were all Military; all people being then left by Nature in a state of War; but some Countries ripening into Prudence and Knowledge sooner than others, they also sooner betook themselves to Compact, and to such Methods of living, as might be for their Common Advantage. Amongst these, *England* was none of the earliest Reformers, but continued long after *Greece* and *Rome,* in that Natural state that the first Fathers of Families left it: and there was reason for it in respect it was an Island, and (in those Times, when *Navigation* was in a great degree a stranger to the World) not so apt for Commerce or Correspondence with other Countries which were more civilized; they had then no Government but what conduced to War, and no other King but a General. *Caesar* in his Commentaries, tells us, that he found the *Brittains,* poor, ignorant, and destitute of Laws; but he also gives them the Character of a People disposed to War, *Brittannos in Bello promptos & in Armis expertes.* All things (as in the state of Nature) were in Common, even to their Wives and Children: But the *Romans* having given them a taste of the sweetness and advantage of Government, they soon after began (as *Tacitus* in his Annals acquaints us) to make Application to their General, to protect and defend them, by his Power and Strength, in the peaceable enjoyment of certain proportions and allotments of Land, against all Invaders; In lieu of which Protection to them and their Heirs, they promise and swear to him and his Heirs, certain Services, together with Homage and Fealty. With this Notion of *Tacitus, Bede* seems to concur in the 4th. Book of his History, where he says, That Generals and Kings were amongst the *Brittains* as Terms Univocal, for Kings were always out to Battle in times of War, and in Peace, exercised the Legislative power at home. And *Ammianus* in his 15th. Book, is more plain and positive, for he tells us, That *Brittanni nulla separati fruebantur possessione, nisi Principis concessu & potestate defendatur.*[11]

From hence it may be reasonably allowed, that *England* was first Governed by an absolute Power, not from the Election of the People, nor by Conquest, but from the Temper, Disposition, and Circumstances of that Age of the World in which most Countries lay under the same sort of Government, and more especially by their Ignorance of better methods, which continued longer in Islands by reason of the difficulty of Commerce, than in Continents where a Correspondence was then more easily maintained. It is undoubtedly from this bottom, that the People of *England* are still supposed to hold all their Lands mediately or immediately from the King, and 'tis perhaps from hence that so many Commons and Wasts still remain uninclosed, and that Waifs, Strays, Wrecks, and Wasts, and all other things, in which no man can lay a particular propriety, are reputed to be in the Crown.

11. That the British enjoyed no separate possession except that defended by the permission and power of the prince.

Upon these reasons I conclude, that the property of all the Lands here in *England* being originally in no particular person, must necessarily (as the Law still is in such Cases) rest in the King, and those that held from or by his power, neither had or could have any right against that power by which they held, but only against others that were in a level with themselves.

How many these Landed Men Originally were, or what seperate proportions were alloted to them, whether the quantity of a County, Hundred, or Tything, or whether their Allotments were according to the largness of their respective Families, or their Prince's favour, I cannot say. But these Proprietors were probably the *Pares Regni*, or such as afterwards, by the growth of Laws and the removal of Ignorance, became by a settled and uncontroulable right, the Peers and Nobles of the Land; and having by their Prince's permissive favour long enjoyed their Dignities and Possessions, they at last wrought them up to an Establishment by Law, insomuch that what was held before *ad voluntatem Domini*, is now made hereditary, performing only some small Services and Acknowlegments to their King or General, some wherof were payable in times of War, as Knight Service, Escuage, petty Serjeanty, and grand Serjeanty, others in times of Peace, such were Burgage, Villenage, Socage, Homage, and Fealty.[12]

Thus did a part of the People first twist themselves into a real Property in part of the Lands of the Kingdom, and as the Prince proved kind and liberal, so did the numbers of these Proprietors increase, and their Properties grew more strong and indefeasable, and

---

12. Knight service was the obligation of a knight to attend the king in his wars for forty days a year, or less if he held less land in knight's fee. Escuage, another variety of medieval knight's service, required attendance on the king in his wars for forty days at the tenant's own charge, or he could send a substitute. In later times this service was commuted for a specific sum of money. A tenant holding by petty serjeanty need only supply the king with a small implement of war—such as a bow or sword—annually; grand serjeanty required the performance of some honorary service to the king in person but did not require personal attendance in war.

Burgage, villenage, socage, homage, and fealty were varieties of medieval land tenure each of which obligated the holder to perform particular services to the landlord.

so consequently their Power and Dominions; but the Prince on the other hand grows proportionably poorer and weaker, Both resembling a Boat which rises and falls with the flowing Element that bears it up. After this manner the Lords grew daily richer and stronger, till they had in a great measure, by their acquisitions striped the Crown of its chiefest Embellishments, and invested themselves in much the better share of the Lands of *England*. And their Power grew with their Property to that degree, that they who were Originally but Servants to the Prince, became now Masters of the Nation. This, King *John* to his sorrow, was sufficiently sensible of in his Barons' War; and it was from the Power of the Nobility alone that King *Henry* the Seventh did receive his Chaplet as well as Crown. He was a wise Prince, and from hence took an occasion of Jealousy, that the same Powers which raised and placed him in the Throne, might pull him down again and lay his Glories in the Dust. To prevent therefore all Dangers which might arise from their growing Greatness, he first procures a Statute to be Enacted against Retainers, that the number of the Followers and Attendants of Noblemen might be retrenched, for they did so far indulge the Vanity of a large Retinue in those times, that their respective Trains were sufficient for a Soveraign Prince's Guard. In the next place he procures the Statute of Fines to pass both Houses; whereby the Nobility got a power (which by the Common Law had not) to cut off Entails, and thereby to sell their Estates to the best Purchaser. Before this Statute, an Estate in a Nobleman's hand, might in some respect be said to be in *Mortmain*, for by the Intail it was so bound up in the Family, that it grew almost irremoveable; and thus having a power to purchase but not to sell, their Possessions, and consequently their Power grew daily greater, without a possibility of Diminution. But these Entails, as they were injurious to Trade and Industry, so by their Consequences they were dangerous to Regal Authority, and therefore this Device was contrived to prevent both these Inconveniencies: and it did indeed prove very effectual in divesting the Nobility both of their Property and Power, but at the same time it opened a Door to the Commonalty, and gave them free access to that Property and Dominion which the Nobility did by degrees part with. Nor did they neglect to improve this advantage they had got by Diligence, Industry and Frugality, for in process of Time they wound themselves into the better share of those Possessions which were first derived from the King to his Nobles, and from them thus to the Commons of the Nation.

The Effect and Consequence of these Acquisitions, made by the Commonalty, were discovered and feared by King *James*, but not felt till the Reign of King *Charles* the First, who by an imprudent Contest with *This* Superior Power, was first deprived of his Crown, and afterwards of his Life. The yearly Rents of *England* (besides the accrewing benefit of Trade, which is altogether in the hands of the Commonalty) amounts to 14 Millions *per annum*. Of this the King and Nobility both together hold not above one Million at the most, the King's Revenue being principally made up by the Excise and Customs, not by the Rents of Crown Lands; so that there remains 13 Shares of 14 of the Lands of *England*, and consequently a proportionable share of the Power in the Commons. But the Constitutions of our Government, as it now stands, placing the Dominion in the King, whilst the Property is in the People, does in this commit a sort of Violence upon Nature, in seperating thus the Soul from the Body, the Power from the Possession. This it is which causes these frequent Distempers and Convulsions in the Body Politick; for Power is a sort of Volatile Spirit which cannot subsist without a proper Vehicle to give it a Body, and this must be Possession, from which if it be once separated, it immediately evaporates and disappears.

Having hitherto traced the Government of *England* in its Originals and Procedures, I will farther take the liberty to advert some Particulars as they seem now to stand in its present Constitution; and in the first place, I cannot think it so happy and well composed a

Government, and so aptly suited to the present condition of the People, as most Men endeavour to represent it, for it seems in its Frame and Nature to be *sett* to Factious Interests and Dissentions, and thus it has been ever since the disunion between Property and Power; the Court and Country Interests are no new nor unknown Terms to us, and have been managed and upheld by their respective Votaries (though in some Kings' Reigns with greater Spirit and Animosity than in others) ever since, and for some time before the Barons' Wars.[13] The people have got the Possession, and the King is entrusted with a power and prerogative over it, or at least with so much, as may prove prejudicial to it. This Naturally creates Fears and Jealousies, least at any time the Prince by his power, should invade their Properties and abridge their Liberties, upon which account his Prerogative is the *White* they level at, esteeming it rather their Terror than their Security for which it was at first given and intended; and therefore when the people find an opportunity, either by their Prince's weakness, folly, or other unhappy circumstances, they have usually made breaches upon this Bulwark of the Crown, and by such Sallies and Incursions have got ground and advantage towards the farther securing of those Liberties and Properties they with so much Diligence and Reason endeavoured to provide for. So on the other side is the Prince jealous of his people, and is always fearful that they should snatch this Rod which he holds over their Backs out of his hand; and to obviate this Evil, he is not without his Counter-designs also, and therefore spares neither Money nor Power in the Elections of Parliaments and Juries, to obtain such persons to be returned, as for a Mess of Porridge will sell their Birth-right, and by advancing his Prerogative and lengthening his Scourge, are willing to ruine and undo their Country. And so it generally falls out, that when this *power* happens to fall into the management of an haughty daring

13. The Barons' Wars are the wars in the thirteenth century between the barons and kings John and Henry III.

Spirit, it breaks in upon the people, and endeavours to get again by Force, what his Ancestors had given away by Flattery. Thus there is always a Tide of Ebb or Flow, the Scales rarely or never standing even between the King and his People; and indeed the Constitution of our Government is such, that Murmuring and Dissentions do naturally spring from it: the *Ground* is disposed to produce such Weeds, we are always engaged in a sort of Civil War, and in this respect continue still in the same state in which Nature left us. *An House divided against itself cannot stand;* every Man has enough to do to defend his *own* from Domestick Invaders, and whilst this *Root* of Division is suffered to grow at Home, it's impossible to do anything that's Great abroad; every Design is poisoned with a Jealousie in its Cradle, and it is enough to make the people suspect it a Snake (though the Skin and Flowers in which it lies be never so plausible and pleasing) if the King does but hand it to them. From hence it is that our Government always tottered, twice fell down, and now lies in its primitive undigested *Chaos,* and he must be a greater Architect, than Perhaps our Nation can afford, to warrant its standing above three ordinary Reigns, if it be rebuilt upon its old Foundations. An Expedient to prevent this Inconvenience, will be a proper Subject for this Great Convention.

Another thing not well consistent with the Policy and Government of *England,* is the exceeding largeness of the Revenue of the Crown. In *France* indeed it is six times greater, that King being reputed to have 12 Millions, and the King of *England* but two: But we see the miserable Effects of it, in the extreme Poverty and Vassallage of his people. 'Tis true, the Kings of *England* once had more, for they had in effect all, but then the people were but one remove from the state of Nature, and the possessions are now got into the hands of the people, which they will be loath to part from, so that the Case is much altered. Whatsoever the Government of Heaven may be, yet on Earth in one State there cannot be two Equals, One must submit and the other must Govern, or else there will be a constant War; and while the King has so great a Revenue as to be able to maintain a Standing Army, there still remains so much of this Equality as will promote and maintain such Differences as ought by no means to be allowed of in a well constituted Government. But moreover, the people by the present Constitution, are Sharers with the Prince in the Supreme and Legislative Power in Parliament, and 'tis by them that Grievances must be redrest. It ought therefore in every Well-Constituted Government to be provided for, that this Supreme and Legislative Power may frequently, if not always, be in a capacity to Enact and Order such things as tend to the People's Benefit and Security; but in this, our Government is defective, it being in the Prince's power (as our Lawyers have generally determined) to keep off Parliaments as long as he pleases. And how is this defect remedied? Only by another, which on the other side they subject the Prince to, which is, by keeping him poor, that so his poverty may necessitate him to call frequent Parliaments. Thus by a mutual lameness or infirmity on both sides, the Prince and People are become equal Matches, Both Cripples, not able to go forward in any great Enterprizes abroad, but to lie struggling with each other at home. King *Henry* the Fifth, had but £.56,000 *per annum*, and Queen *Elizabeth's* whole Revenue was but £.160,000. But some kind Parliaments (and such they usually are to excess, upon the first accession of a King to the Throne) either bribed by Smiles, or flattered by Hopes of private Gain, have thought fit to fetter the Nation by advancing the Revenue to about two Millions *per annum;* so that now there is little hopes of meeting with those advantages and opportunities of tacking their Grievances to a Money Bill, which formerly they use to do; though in truth, even then the State was in a dangerous condition, that could not have a Remedy at hand upon every Disturbance and

Malady which should happen. This I think may not improperly be
esteemed a thing worthy of Your Thoughts to find a proper Expedient to redress it.

Another Particular which I take to be one of the greatest Solecisms
in Government imaginable is where the most Absolute and Supreme
power is yet without a Power to Remedy and Redress the People's
Grievances: Thus it has been for many years adjudged to be by the
Interpreters of our Laws and Government, the Judges. And to illus-
trate this by an Instance. Suppose the people are agrieved, and want
a Law to set them Right; The King has no power to make it of himself, and till he thinks fit to call a Parliament, the people must still
continue subject to their Government. But perhaps the King's Interest (which is unhappily divided from the people's) forbids this Expedient; What shall be done? Why then let them stay and be ruined,
till the King wants Money, which as the present Establishment is,
will never be. But suppose a Parliament is called, and they in their
proceedings happen to fret upon the King's Prerogative, a Favourite
evil Councellor, or some other Interest that the King has a mind to
promote and protect, though never so opposite to that of the Nation's, why then their Supreme and Legislative power is not worth a
Rush, for the King, though he has no absolute power himself, yet has
a power above this, to destroy it by a Dissolution or Prorogation
when he pleases, and so like the Cat in the Manger, can neither eat
Hay himself, nor suffer the Horse to eat to whom it belongs. This
seems contrary to all the Rules of Art and Nature, and more Unintelligible than the Doctrine of the *Trinity*, or *Transubstantiation*, for
here the Supreme power is subject to an Inferior, and the King who
is *Minor Universis*, yet is also *Major* and Superior to them; That
Power which was given for the Protection of the People is their Destroyer, and the great and weighty Affairs of the Nation becomes subject to the passions and humours of a single Person. This I think I

may safely affirm, That all Governments are built upon wrong bottoms, where there is not a Supreme and Absolute Power, which may without Controll, and upon any sudden Occasion or Emergency, alter, create, or repeal such Laws as shall be thought by them necessary for the People's Good.

Another thing that has been very incongruous and disagreeable in our Establishment is, That the Election of the Judges, and consequently the pronouncing of the Law, should be in the King's Power. If indeed he were a Third Person unconcerned in point of Interest, this Method would be more tolerable; but being *One* that so often sets up an Interest different from that of his People, and is subject to be seduced by the evil Councels of a Confessor, Miss or Favourite, and the People's Rights hanging wholly upon the Lips of these twelve men in Scarlet, it is most fit they should be chosen by Them who are chiefly concerned, and for whose benefit and protection both the King and Laws were first made and intended, otherwise that very Prerogative, which was given to the King only for the better enabling him to act for the benefit of the People, may be (and often is) set up against them. It is contrary to all Rule, that in any Controversie a Man should be Judge in his own Case; But he in effect is so who has power to make or unmake the Judge at pleasure: nor can this defect be well remedied by granting their Commissions *quam diu se bene gesserint*.[14] This will only oblige a greater care in the first choice, that they may be such as in their Principles will stand firm to the King's Interest. The Honour and Income of a Judge to one that knows not how other ways to live is a violent Provocative; it is a sort of lawful Bribery upon him to pursue his *Maker* and *Destroyer's* Commands though against all the Rules of Justice and Equity; *self Preservation* is his Warrant, binds him to a Compliance, and makes him think it

14. During good behavior.

more allowable to break his Oath than to destroy his Honour and the Interest of a young Favourite who makes hay with great diligence whilst his Sun shines.

I have often wondered at the unjust Censures of some in saying that our late King so often and so notoriously broke his word and promises to his People in not Governing them according to *Law*. For Instances, they urge His Dispensing with Statutes, and his hard Usage of the Gentlemen in *Maudlin* Colledge,[15] in both which I conceive he committed no breach of his Word or Promises if they be taken strictly and in a literal sense. This I think may easily be granted if it be considered, That the present Laws and Constitutions of *England* are such as do undoubtedly give the King a Power to make the Judge, and to the Judge a power to pronounce the Law. What he does judicially affirm is Law, and becomes from thenceforth the strongest Precedent, the last Judgement being always esteemed the surest and best Rule to go by. Now the King in both these transactions neither made or turned out any Judges but in such methods that former Judges had pronounced Lawful, nor did he do afterwards any thing either in the case of *Maudlin* Colledge or the Dispensing Power, but with the Opinion and Concurrence of his Judges being the Method that our Establishment and Laws in such Cases does direct.

There is also a great Cry against the late Judges, for giving their Opinions, and pronouncing Judgments contrary to the Laws of the Land, and no other Fate must be their reward, but that of *Tresilian* and *Belknap*.[16] It does, I must confess, seem very reasonable, that Men, who by their Honour, Oaths and Rewards, were bound indis-

15. As part of his campaign to place Catholics in the Anglican educational establishment, in 1687 James ordered the fellows of Magdalen College, Oxford, to elect a reputed Catholic, Anthony Farmer, their president. The fellows conceded the king's right to make the nomination, but—on the claim that the nominee was not of good character and not eligible under the college statutes—they elected one of their number instead. The dispute ultimately led to the king ejecting most of the fellows and replacing them with Catholics.

16. Sir Robert Tresilian, chief-justice of King's Bench and an advisor of Richard II, was hanged for treason in 1388. Sir Robert Belknap, chief-justice of Commons Pleas during the

tinguishably to administer Justice, should smart for those Delinquencies by which so many Hundreds have been ruined and undone. But in the first place, let me know how a Judge can give his opinion contrary to Law, whose very Opinion judicially given, by the Constitutions of our Government, is Law itself, and shall be deemed a stronger Precedent in the point, than any other formerly given. And Secondly, If Judges must suffer for giving Sentence contrary to former Judgments, there is scarcely a *Term* passes even in the best of Times, but there are Offences committed by them of this kind. How ordinary is it for a Judge to give his Opinion in common Cases contrary to his Brethren on the same Bench, and for one Court to reverse the Judgments of another? And how full are the Law Books of Judgments and Opinions directly contrary to each other? The Law is not Mathematically demonstrable, it is a Science which depends upon the Judgment and Opinion only of those that are Learned therein, which we often find various and uncertain. Is not a Judge Sworn to act and determine according to his Opinion only, and who can pretend a power to direct and rectifie it, or to judge whether the Sentence given, was not according to his real judgment, since none can know his heart and thoughts but *God*. And suppose it could be proved by Demonstration, that his Sentence or Opinion was not Law, this may proceed as well from his want of Knowledge as Honesty, and what Law is there to punish a Judge's ignorance or mistake? 'Tis hard that Men should be deemed guilty of a Transgression where there is no Law, or condemned to punishment where there is no Transgression. No, no, Though our King was misguided, and our Judges were corrupt, yet it is not at their doors, we must lay our Misfortunes but to the weakness of our Government, which gives a *Loose* to these Inconveniencies, and which pitts the Justice of the Nation

---

same reign, was exiled to Ireland for giving an opinion against Parliament's impeachment of Michael de la Pole. He was recalled in 1397.

upon the Frailties of a single Man in so Arbitrary a manner. Opportunity makes a Thief, and these Meshes in the Government, tempts the Ministers thereof to slip through sometimes when a Bait lies on the other side to invite them to it. It is from this Root that all our late Miscarriages sprung; We suffered much, and yet it was all but little, if compared to that which was likely to befall us, had not Providence snatcht us by a Miracle from the Jaws of Misery; and as it has delivered us from the Evil Administration of *Law*, so in some things I wish it would rescue us from the *Law* itself, and so far change it, that for the future it may be no more subject to such Shams and Delusions, nor in a capacity thus to become an Accessory to its own Death.

It seems farther very incongruous, That where Government is made up of two different Interests as here it is, the absolute power of Peace and War should be only in the King, whilst the power of maintaining it, continues in the People: For if the King should be led aside by a private Interest, and should refuse to make War in a time when perhaps the Safety and Honour of the Nation did wholly depend upon it; What a condition must the People then be in? Put the case, that before this our late but seasonable Deliverance, the King, in whom this Power did reside, should have opened the Gates of the Kingdom, our Harbours and Strengths (which are to protect us from Forreign Invaders) to a *French*, or *Irish* Army; Who durst lift a hand to stop this inundation of Tyranny, without incurring the penalty of a Traitor: Nay they must farther be called Friends and Allies, even whilst they pillage our Houses, and hold their Knives to our Throats. This Branch of our Laws serves to *cover* the Landing of a Foreign Power, and so long to cherish and keep it warm, till like the Serpent in the Fable, it at last stings the improvident Benefactor to death.

Another thing which highly requires Your Regulation, is the Elections for Parliament. 'Tis a great Blemish to our Government, that such whose Place gives them the Title of *Founders* of our Laws, and

Preservers of our Liberties; and whose Reputation for Principles of Honour, Honesty & Prudence should be beyond assault or censure, must yet be exposed to a Necessity of doing such things as are really mean and scandalous as well as expensive, before they can get into a Capacity of doing their Country service: for if such things be not done, some Pensioner from Court bids higher, jostles him out and gets thereby into a Power to put to Sale both the Laws and Liberties of his Country which he is willing to barter for the hopes of some Court Preferment, and the *Euge* of his great *Master*. In old times no person had an Electing Vote in the Shire, who had not a Freehold of *40 s. per Ann.* but I could easily demonstrate 40 s then, to be Equivalent in value to £.40 now, for by the discovery of the Western World, Gold and Silver is to that degree increased. Now if the number of Electors were reduced to those only having Freeholds of £.*40 per An.* these lavish Expences would certainly cease, and the Electors, though fewer in number, would be less apt to be led aside by such low and indirect means. There are also great irregularities in the Corporations and Burroughs Electing as well as in the Electors. I can see no reason why *Cornwall* a poor and barren County should return 43 Members for Parliament, and yet *Cheshire* together with the City of *Chester* should return in all but 3, and why old *Sarum* which has but 2 Houses, and those under the Commands of one Landlord, should send 2 Representatives to Parliament, whilst many other Towns which might deserve the Title and Priviledges of Cities send no Representatives at all. I can scarcely think a Parliament thus Constituted can truly and fairly represent the People, the Majority and Richest of them being by such inequallities excluded from an Electing Vote. The same inconvenience springs from the Constitutions of the Boroughs which Elect, not by vertue of their Wealth, Dignity, or Number of Inhabitants, but by the Burrough Houses in which they live, These only, (which perhaps are the most inconsiderable part of the Burrough) having in them the Electing power exclusive of the rest.

This Qualification makes such Houses sell better to a purchaser than any others in the Town, and it is customary for Gentlemen who are desirous of a Seat in Parliament, to lay out their Mony in such Bargains, and though it costs them dear, yet if it be possible, they will be Landlords of a sufficient number of these Borough Houses, (in the purchase whereof some Friend's Name is mostly made use of in Trust) that thereby they may Command an Election either for themselves or their Assigns at pleasure. What is this less than buying of Votes with Money? A Crime which has been always lookt upon with a severe brow, and yet Licensed by this old Usage. Nor can I discern why this Electing-power should be thus fixt to the Freehold in being, restrained to a small and inconsiderable number of Houses, as if Wood and Stone had a Rational faculty, and must be made use of to build and repair the Government.

The Methods of Electing in these Boroughs are various, Titles to Elect are also different, and very often dubious and uncertain. This necessitates double Elections, and countenances false Returns, which are often made ill use of; for the King having a power to nominate the Sheriff, and he to make a Return, it may happen that the true and rightful Members shall continue Petitioners only, whilst such as came in by unjust Returns, pass an Act to give the King Money for the maintainance of a Standing Army. This Artifice was of much use in the last Parliament at *Westminster,* and became so notorious from the great Number of Petitioners, that a Gentleman being asked, whether the House of Commons sate that day in the *Parliament;* No, (replied he) It stood in the *Lobby.*

It is Customary in the Borough of *Limmington* in *Hampshire,* to Elect by the *Ballot.* The manner is to give to every Electing Burgess (their number being limitted and known) a different Coloured *Ball* for every *Competitor,* each Colour being respectively appropriated to the several Competitors: As suppose there should be three Candidates, each Elector has three several Balls given him, which he so manages as to keep only that in his hand, which by its Colour belongs to the person he intends to chuse; this being inclosed in his hand, he puts it into a close Box made for that purpose, leaving no possibility to any one to detect what coloured *Ball* he put into it. Thus each having put in his *Ball* according to his Vote, the Balls of one Colour are separated from those of another colour, and so according to the Majority of Balls of one Colour, the Return is made. This Method I know to be of great advantage where it is made use of; It prevents Animosities and Distaste, and very much assists that freedom which ought to be in Elections. No man in this way need fear the disobliging of his Landlord, Customer, or Benefactor; for it can by no means be discovered how he gave his Vote, if he will but keep his own counsel. If this or some such Device were appointed to be made use of in every Borough over all the Kingdom, I am perswaded it would abundantly answer expectation, in the many Advantages which would attend it. And perhaps it would be of equal Benefit in all other Elections, as well as in those, for Members of Parliament, if the Government were so disposed as to fill up all Vacancies, whether in Church or State, by the plurality of Votes appointed to elect. And I am apt to believe that succeeding Ages may reduce it into a Law, that Privy Councellors shall be chosen by the Lords, Judges by the Gentlemen at the Bar, Bishops by their Dean and Chapters, Ministers by their Parishioners, Fellows and Masters of Colledges by the Graduates of the same Colledge, Sheriffs by the Gentry of the County, Officers of Trust in the State and in the Army by the Parliament, the Parliament by Freeholders of *£.40 per annum*, and all by the *Ballott*.

'*Tis much easier* (I know) *to find Faults than to mend them*; and I could mention many other things of the same nature, the Redress whereof, I hope will be thought of in this great *Convention*, before They proceed to dispose of the Crown. 'Tis an easier matter for a People to make ten *Kings*, than to unmake *One*, and to deck a Crown

with the highest Prerogatives, than to deprive it, when they are Confered, of the least of them. If the *Crown* be given again with the same
Qualifications that Other *Heads* wore it, It will then be exalted above
the People's reach, without some such assisting Miracle as was lately
shewn in favour of them. *Now,* to reform its Redundancies is natural, easie, and prudent, the Government being escheated to the People by the King's deserting it; But to offer at any such Attempts
afterwards, will be both unkind and imprudent, and will signifie no
more than the chatterings of a parcel of Magpies about an *Owl* in her
Majesty.

Some Men have espoused an odd and unwarrantable Notion, that
the King's Desertion of the Government amounts to a *Demise,* or
Civil *Death.* If this be so, the next Heir ought immediately to be Proclaimed, and must Inherit the *Crown* with the same inseperable Prerogatives that heretofore belonged to it, and all Laws or Acts of
Parliament made to limit and abridge them, (if Lawyers speak truth)
are void and null. But if the *Departure* of the King amounts to such a
desertion as dissolves the *Government,* then the Power must necessarily revert and vest in the People, who may Erect a new *One,* either
according to the old *Modell,* if they like it so well, or any other that
they like and approve of better.

Were such a mighty Thing to be determined by my single Vote,
the *Government* should be *Monarchy,* and this *Monarchy* should be
Absolute and Arbitrary, and the *Prince*[17] should be my King. 'Tis He
alone who is *The* Man in *Christendom* in respect of Courage and an
innate Disposition to delight in the Happiness of his People, with
whom I could freely and securely intrust my *All.* But the *Honour* I
have for Him, runs not to His *Posterity,* for as a good Man may
notwithstanding, get a Profligate Son, so I should be loath to Repose
such a Trust at a venture in the hands of any one whom I do not

17. William, Prince of Orange.

know. You have a great Work to do, and 'tis from Your Councels, that after Ages must date their Happiness or Misery, and it therefore Obliges Your most Serious Thoughts.

I hope, Sir, you will excuse the Liberties I have taken, in giving you so large a Diversion from better Notions of your own, which I know are of an higher flight and swifter wing than what I can pretend to: *Mine* I do not impose, but submit, as becomes,

SIR,
Your Obliged humble Servant
N. T.

[Samuel Masters, 1646?–1693]

THE

CASE

OF

ALLEGIANCE

IN OUR

Present Circumstances

CONSIDER'D.

In a LETTER from a Minister in
the City, to a Minister in the Country.

Rom. 4.22. *Happy is he that condemneth not himself in
that thing which he alloweth.*

LONDON.
Printed for *Ric. Chiswell* at the *Rose* and *Crown* in
St. *Paul's Church Yard*. MDCLXXXIX.

This tract in the form of a letter has been attributed to the clergy-man Samuel Masters. It was among the first of some eighty tracts on the crucial issue of allegiance that were published in the year of the Glorious Revolution.

Samuel Masters, a gentleman's son, was born in Salisbury the year Charles I surrendered. He attended Wadham College, Oxford, and was a fellow of Exeter College. His career as a minister began when he was appointed preacher at Stanton Harcourt and South Ley in Oxfordshire. He later became prebendary of Saint Paul's and Lichfield, chaplain to the earl of Radnor, and preacher to the hospital and precinct of Bridewell near London. Although the earl of Radnor's son, Francis, was a Tory member of the Convention Parliament, Masters seems to have been a moderate Whig in his sympathies.

"The Case of Allegiance" was licensed on 21 March before the Convention Parliament agreed that all holders of civil and ecclesiastical

office must take a new oath of allegiance to William and Mary by 1 August. The tract provides an excellent review of the Whig theory of English government at that significant point. What the author considers widely accepted errors about the subject's obligation to his king are discussed as well as the limits on loyalty oaths. Masters argues strongly for the propriety of switching allegiance from James II to William and Mary. He points to the contractual nature of the coronation oath and insists allegiance is sworn to the office of king, not to the person of the monarch.

The tract appeared in two variations. A reply, also anonymous, entitled "Reflections upon a Late Book, Entitled, The Case of Allegiance Considered, . . ." appeared in May. "The Case of Allegiance" was reprinted in State Tracts, *a collection of important pamphlets published in 1692–93.*

The Case of Allegiance Consider'd.

Reverend Sir,

You having thought fit to consult my Judgement about the lawfulness of *transferring* our *Allegiance* from the *late* to the *present KING;* I shall not mispend time in blaming the ill choice of so incompetent a *Casuist,* for so important a *Case;* but according to the Laws of that *Friendship* which have been for some time observed between us, I shall endeavour to approve my *readiness,* if not my *ability* in serving you.

I must not dissent from you, in professing a very tender and awful regard of *Conscience,* whose Authority I acknowledg to be sacred and inviolable, and in the neglect of which I expect no peace in my own mind, nor any confidence toward God: and I think it necessary to add, That we ought to take as much care to *inform* our *Consciences,* as to *follow* them; that we provide them all possible helps and advantages; that we place Truths in the fairest light, and view them with a steddy unprejudiced Eye: And we who are *Ministers* are more especially concerned to do so, who being appointed Guides, not only to ourselves, but also to others, must beware of the double guilt of *misleading* our Flock, by going ourselves *astray* before them.

You may believe me, Sir, as far as I can know myself, that I have no *Antimonarchical* Principles, or secret disgust to the Person of the late King, to alienate my mind from him: Neither am I conscious of any angry resentments of *former* Suffereings, or of any discontent with my *present* Station, or of any ambitious design, or hope of a *future* advancement, to bend my Inclinations to a concurrence with the present *Revolution;* for I solemnly protest, That if the late *KING* would have thought fit to continue his Government over us, though with many *tolerable* Inconveniences to the *Publick,* and though with any *intolerable* Prejudices to my *private* Interest, I would never have retracted my *Reverence* and *Submission* to his *Authority*, nor have desisted to intercede with Heaven for blessings on his *Person* and *Government*. Whatever *change* therefore it made on my mind, it did not, I assure you, proceed from any *design* or *choice* of my own, but was necessarily induced from a *change* without, and from those new Circumstances into which the late *King* unexpectedly cast us.

It is indeed very *difficult*, as you complain, to determine the present Case with a satisfactory *clearness* and *certitude*, because it is *complicated* of a great *variety* of things, some of which are *foreign* to our *faculty*, and which for the most part require a great niceness of thought to apprehend and distinguish them; because also we are yet scarce got out of the *amazement* into which so great a *Revolution* hath surprized us, and must have time to *recollect* and *compose* our thoughts, ere we can consider so *exactly*, or deliberate so *steddily* as such an Affair deserves; but chiefly because we have of late years imbibed some false *Maxims* and Notions, which unhappily *intangle* our *Consciences*, and *prejudice* our minds against that *truth*, which it is now become our interest to discover and acknowledg; and have had those *Notions* inculcated upon us with so much *force* and *importunity*, that through a *slavish fear* of those who have been a long time *practising* upon us, we have almost lost our liberty of *thinking freely*, and *judging impartially* of these matters. Yet these *difficulties* are not *insuperable* to an *honest inquisitive* mind; they may indeed prompt us to excuse candidly the *Errors* of others, and to seek more earnestly for *Wisdom*, to him that hath promised to *give* it to those that *lack*, without *upbraiding*; but should rather *animate* than *discourage* our industry in the researches of a Truth wherein our *Consciences* are so much concerned.

These things being premised, I will now set close to my Work; and upon a general view of the Design before me, I find it necessary for me to do these three things.

1. To discover and remove some *false Principles* about Govern-

ment and Obedience, whence the *obscurities* and *difficulties* in the present Case do chiefly arise.

2. To resolve the chief *difficulties* in the Case propounded.

3. To prove that *Resolution* to be consistent with all the Obligations that can affect a good *Conscience*.

1. It will be necessary in the first place to detect and discard those false principles of Government and Obedience which have been in this last Age too earnestly obtruded, and too easily entertained among us; and which are as a false biass on our minds to mislead their Considerations, and betray them into Error.

And if we find such Principles do rather *inslave* than *oblige* our *Consciences*, and are as inconsistent with *Truth*, as they are with the present *Revolution*, we must take the honest courage, to break off those bands, and assert our Liberty. Of this kind are chiefly these three.

1. That a *Monarchical* form of Government, and the appropriation of it to a particular Person or Family, is *jure Divino*, or by a *Divine Right*. How boldly this Principle hath been asserted by some men, you and I cannot be ignorant; upon which so great a stress hath been laid, that to alter the *Government* in the *State*, hath been thought as lewd an impiety as to alter either of the *Holy Sacraments* in the *Church*; to *divert* the Succession, as unlawful as to *pervert* the very Course of Nature; and to oppose a King, though in the most illegal extravagancies, or barbarous outrages, to be no less than fighting against God. If indeed such a *Divine Right* did appear, it must be acknowledged indisputable and inviolable, whatever sad consequences attend it; but upon examination we shall find that God hath nowhere instituted such a *Right,* but some men have with too bold a fraud, made use of his Name to advance and support their unreasonable pretensions. If by such a *Divine Right,* no more were intended than God's *permission* and *allowance,* it would have no Opponents; for we know of no *Law* that doth forbid a *Monarchical* form of Govern-

ment, or exclude *any* particular *person* or *family* from the Administration of it: But then the pretence so interpreted, will not be sufficient to render an *alteration* in the *Government* or *Succession,* a sin against God, as the assertors of this notion have sometimes pretended. They therefore who plead this Argument, must be thought to assert, That God hath by some Law or Constitution appointed *Monarchy* to be the *specific* form of Civil Government; and that the Crown should be entailed on such particular persons succeeding in the same Family, whereby the one cannot be changed, or the other debared without transgressing a Divine Institution. This being a matter of great importance, and of common continual concernment to mankind, we may reasonably expect, that if God hath made any such *Law,* it is somewhere *promulged* to the World with *sufficient* evidence and certainty; but though many have been for some years most sollicitously seeking after it, yet they are not agreed among themselves in the *discovery,* nor can direct us where we may certainly meet with it. I know but of two sort of *Laws* which God hath given to mankind, Either *Moral,* impressed on the human Nature; or *Positive,* revealed in the Holy *Scriptures;* but the *jus divinum* in dispute is a stranger to *both.* God hath indeed by *both,* instituted *Government,* or *Civil Authority* for the welfare and security of men in their Civil Societies; He hath also commanded, that *Superiors* govern *justly* and *mercifully,* and that *Inferiors* honour them with *duty* and *submission.* But I nowhere find that God hath commanded all nations, or ours in particular, to be under that form of *Government,* which in contradistinction to other forms is called *Monarchy;* or under some particular Person and Family in contradistinction to all others. The *Law* of *Nature* doth indeed erect a *Monarchy* in *Families,* over those who are naturally descended from him that is to Govern; but there being not the same *natural reason* in our *Civil Societies,* there is not the same *Law* of *Nature* to prescribe the same *Government:* And if some plead a *likeness,* or *analogie* between them, That can serve only for a *rhetor-*

ical illustration, but not for any *Logical proof,* such as the present case requires. From the Holy *Scriptures* we learn that God did once institute a *Monarchy* for the people of *Israel,* and appointed particularly that *David* should be their *King,* and also *intailed* the Crown upon his Posterity; but as God had particular Reasons for that institution, respecting the *Messiah,* so we have no Reason to think that God intended by that institution, to oblige any other Nation but the *Jews* only. In the *New Testament* we find *Civil* government supposed, and the *moral* Duties to be discharged both by superiors and inferiors, described and inforced, beyond what they are in any other institutions; but we nowhere find *Christ* and his *Apostles* prescribing the particular form of *Civil Government,* or preferring *Monarchy,* or condemning an *Aristocratic* or *Democratic* state; and much less determining the particular persons or families on whom the *Regal Dignity* shall descend. Some indeed have inferred from St. *Paul's* assertions, *Rom.* 13.1. that the particular forms of Government, and the particular persons which administer it, are by a *Divine Institution;* but however they countenance this mistake from our *English* translation, which says, *There is no power but of God, the powers that are, are ordained of God;* yet the Text is incapable of such a sense, if we read and render it exactly according to the Original.

St. *Paul's* words are Ὀυ γὰρ ἔστιν ἐξουσία εἰ μὴ ὑπὸ θεοῦ, αἱ δὲ οὖσαι ἐξουσίαι ὑπὸ τοῦ θεοῦ τεταγμέναι εἰσὶν, which in an exact Translation would run thus; *There is no Authority, if not of God; and the Authorities which are* (of God's Institution) *are ordered under God.* The plain Doctrine of which Text can be only this, That no man can have an Authority over other men, who are his Fellow-creatures, except it be derived to him from God, who is the Lord of all, and that whatever Power is derived to any Superiors over Inferiors, it must be subordinated to God, from whom it was derived. And as the Apostle doth infer from the former Assertion, That *Every soul should be sub-*

ject to, and not resist, this Authority, even for *Conscience-sake,* because derived from God; so he infers from the latter, That the Superior, who useth this *Authority,* must administer it as the Minister of God, for the good of men, in protecting Virtue, and discouraging Vice, because his Authority is subordinated to God, the Supreme and Absolute Lord of all Mankind.

And that the Apostle doth speak of *Authority* according to its general *nature* and *institution,* and not the *particular persons* by whom, or *forms* in which it was then exercised, is evident from the excellent properties and ends of this *Authority* which he enumerates; which do belong indeed to that *Authority* which God hath instituted, but cannot certainly be ascribed to the Government of *Nero* the present, and the worst of Emperors. And to make this more plain and unquestionable, it may be observed, that as Saint *Paul,* speaking of *Authority* in the general, calls it ἡ τοῦ θεοῦ διαταγὴ the *Ordinance of God;* so Saint *Peter* speaking of the persons by whom this *Authority* is administered, calls them ἡ ἀνθρωπίνη κτίσις, the *Ordinance of man,* whether it be the *King, as supreme, or inferior Magistrates commissioned by him.*

After all, I am ready to acknowledg, that the *Law of God* doth secure *Princes,* yea, and the *meanest* of their *Subjects* in the quiet possession of those *Rights* which they have justly acquired; but the *Rights* themselves are not founded on a *Divine* but *Human* Constitution; for though the Law of God doth prohibit us to defraud a *private person* of any part of his just possessions, yet we do not think that any *Law of God* did *antecedently entitle* him to such a posession, or doth *necessarily intail* it on his Family; but that his *Right* is grounded on the Laws and Constitutions of the Country in which he lives. So, though *Kings* have the Law of God to maintain and protect them in the use of that *Authority* to which they have a *just Right;* yet that *Right* is not to be measured by any Law of God, but the Constitutions of the Realm, and may be acquired or alienated without committing any sin against God, as they who assert a *Jus Divinum* would pretend.

2. Another false principle to be dismissed, is a wide mistake of the Nature of that Government under which we live, which asserts the *English Monarchy* to be *absolute* and *unlimited*, at least that in its *Original* and *Essential* Constitution it is so, and cannot be otherwise. We cannot but reflect on the *ill design*, or *ill conduct* of some who in their Discourses on this Subject, have transcribed out of their *common places* all the *great things* which any *Princes* have *asserted* to themselves, or have been *ascribed* to them by ambitious flatterers, or have been *acquired* by them in overreaching Compacts, or by a violent force; and have without any *restriction* or *exception*, applied them to the *Monarch* of our *Island*, as if there could be but one sort of *Government* in the world, or that *ours* did eminently include all the Prerogatives that can be conceived in speculation, or can be found to be ascribed to any King or Emperor in any Part, or Age of the World.

Upon this Principle they have exalted the *English* Monarch into as *Absolute* and *Arbitrary* a *Sovereign*, as any Emperour of *Rome* or *Constantinople;* they make his *Will* the sole spring of our Government, from which it is originally derived, and into which it must be ultimately resolved: they allow to an *English Parliament* no more power than to give some inauthoritative Advice, which the King may use or neglect as he thinks fit. They think a *Coronation Oath*, whatever it may be with respect to *God*, yet with respect to the *People*, is only a customary Ceremony, or insignificant Formality. They suppose all legal limitations of the Government to be but the King's arbitrary and temporary Condescentions, which he may retract without doing any Injury to the People; and, in a word, that all our Laws are entirely dependent on His Pleasure for their *Being, Continuance*, and *Influence;* but his *Will* is in all Cases unaccountable and irresistible. Such Maxims as these quite alter the Frame of our *En-*

glish Government, raise up our *King* into a *Tyrant,* and depress his Subjects into Slaves, and serve only to render the *King odious,* and his *People miserable;* and therefore, as no wise Man can forbear wishing that they may not be true, so upon enquiry we shall find that they have been advanced either by the *Fondness* of some, who frame Schemes of *Government* in their own imagination; or by the *Ignorance* of others, who are deceived with the sound of the aequivocal Name of *King,* or by the *Craft* of those who make a Trade of *advancing* the *Prerogative,* in order to their own *Advancement.* Indeed if the preceding Principle had proved true, That *Monarchy is a Divine Institution,* it would be necessary for us to grant, that no other Form of Government could be mixed with it, or *That* be restrained by any Limitations, because it cannot be lawful for Man to adulterate or infringe the Ordinance of God: But seeing the *Jus Divinum* doth not appear, we have reason to suppose that our *English Government* is built on the Topical Constitutions of this Countrey, and may differ from the Government of other Countreys, as much as our Tempers, Interests, and Circumstances do. For, if the Supreme Governor of the World hath not thought fit to prescribe *One Form of Government* to be everywhere observed, he hath permitted to every Nation a Liberty of framing to themselves such a Constitution as may be most useful and agreeable; and as it is *inconceivable* that all Nations should conspire in the same Platform of *Governments;* so it is most *unreasonable* to seek in *Judea, Italy,* or *France,* for the Measures or Properties of the *English* Government, which was made, and is therefore to be found only *at Home,* and should be described rather from its own *Laws* and *Constitutions,* than any fine *Notions* we can conceive of what it might or should be. And if we contemplate the Government itself, we may easily discover what its essential Forms and Properties are; for surely a Government that hath been publickly transacted through so many Ages, and hath made so great a Figure in the world, cannot remain an imperceptible Secret, or an unintelligible Mystery;

and I cannot forbear suspecting those, who disguise it with so many Uncertainties and Obscurities, that they design to mislead us into a mistake of that which they will not allow us to understand. A little skill in our *English* History will suffice to inform us, That the *Saxons* and *English*, from whom this Nation is chiefly descended, did first introduce the Form of our *English* Government, and that it was the same they had been inured to in *Germany;* where, as *Tacitus* observes, *Regibus nec infinita aut libera potestas:* Kings *had not an Absolute or Unlimited Power.* And from the ancient Records of those early Times we are assured, That the *Consent* of the People in a *Convention* or *Parliament*, did always concur to the making of *Laws;* and also their *Consent* in a *Jury* of Peers was always admitted in the Execution of *Them:* Whence the People of *England* have been always acknowledged to be *Free-men.* And though we read that the *Saxons* were subdued by the *Danes,* yet we find not that their Government was changed, but that, after a short Interruption, the Government and Country returned entirely into the Hands of the *Saxons.* The Duke of *Normandy,* whom we call the *Conqueror,* was *such* only with respect to *Harold,* who usurped the Crown, but not with respect to the Kingdom, which he claimed as Successor to King *Edward,* to whom he was related, by whom he was adopted, and from whom he had received a solemn Promise of the next Reversion; and accordingly we find, that though he made some external Changes in the Government, yet he made no essential Alteration in the Form of it; and the same kind of Government hath been transmitted by succeeding Kings to the present Age, with some *accidental Improvements,* as our Ancestors grew wiser by Experience, or the Necessities and Interests of the Nation did require. Now, inasmuch as our *English* Government was at first transplanted out of another Countrey, and hath been ripened into a Perfection by several degrees through a long tract of Time, it would be very *fanciful* to suppose one solemn time when the *Original Compact* between the King and People was first made, or to ask after a Book in which it is in a certain Form recorded; that Compact being nothing else than a tacit Agreement between the *King* and *Subjects* to observe such common Usages and Practices, as by an immemorial Prescription are become the *Common-Law* of our Government. And to understand these, so far as our present Case requires, there is no necessity that we should read over all the *Records* in the *Tower*, or all the *Volumes* of our *English History*, there being several ancient *Forms* and *Customs* among us, which fall under easie Observation, that are sufficient to inform us of the Nature of our *English* Government. For when at a *Coronation* we see a *King* presented to the People, and their Consent solemnly asked and given, what can we reasonably infer from thence, but that anciently *Kings* were advanced to their Thrones by the Consent and Agreement of the People? When we hear the King solemnly *Promise* and *Swear* to maintain to the People their *Rights* and *Liberties*, to conserve the *Laws*, and cause them to be observed; must we not conclude from thence, that there are *Rights* and *Liberties* reserved to the People; that the Will of the *King* is limited by the *Law* of the Realm: and that he is bound by *His Oath* to *conserve* the Laws, as we are by *Ours* to *observe* them? When we are taught to call the King our *Leige-Sovereign*, and ourselves his *Leige-Subjects;* do not those Terms import, that he is bound to protect Us in *All our Rights*, as we are bound to obey Him in *All his Laws?* When we read in the Preamble of every Statute, That it is enacted not only by the Authority of the *King's most Excellent Majesty*, but also by the Authority of the *Lords Spiritual and Temporal, and of the Commons assembled in Parliament;* is it not very evident from hence, that the *Parliament* hath a share in the *Legislative Power*, which is an eminent Branch of the *Supreme Authority* in this Kingdom? From these, and other such easie Observations, any impartial unprejudiced person will certainly conclude, that our *English* Government, according to its *Essential Constitution*, is a mixture of Three Forms of Government; for he observes a *Monarchy* in the *King*, an

Aristocracy in the *Peers*, and a *Democracy* in the *Commons;* all which share in *that Part* of the Sovereignty which consists in making Laws. And though our Government be called a *Monarchy*, because That Kind is *predominant* in the Constitution, according to the known Rule, That the *Denomination is to be taken from the Excelling Part*, the King having not only a share in the *Nomothetick* Power, but also the whole *Executive Power* committed to Him; yet we cannot but conclude, from the foregoing Observations, That our *Monarchy* is not *Absolute* and *Unlimited;* that the *Law* is the stated Rule and Measure of our Government; and that the *Law* cannot be made, altered, or annulled, by the sole Pleasure of the King: but as it is the first determinate Rule by which the King is to Govern, and the People to Obey, so it is to be made or changed only by the Consent of *Both* in a Parliament. I might confirm all this, by transcribing out of Books several Testimonies which occur in the Declarations of *Parliaments*, in the Writings of *Judges*, and others *Learned* in the *Law:* but as these would make a Letter too tedious, so they are unnecessary to an unprejudiced Considerer, and by others would be suspected of partiality to the People of whom they are a part. I shall therefore only add the Testimony of King *Charles* the I. who of all men had most reason to study, understand, and assert the Rights of the *English* Monarchy. He freely declares, in his *Answer* to the *Nineteen Propositions*,[1] p. 96, "That there being Three Kinds of Government among Men, *Absolute Monarchy, Aristocracy*, and *Democracy;* and all these having their particular Conveniences and Inconveniences: the Experience and Wisdom of our Ancestors hath so moulded *This* out of a mixture of *These*, as to give to this Kingdom (as far as Human Prudence can provide) the Conveniences of *all Three*, without the Inconveniences of *any One*." He also, in the same Answer, affirms, "That in this Kingdom the Laws are jointly made by a King, by a

---

1. See volume 1, 154.

House of Peers, and by a House of Commons." He likewise affirms in his Declaration from *Newmarket*,[2] "That the Law is the Measure of his Power." And in another Declaration to the Ministers and Free-holders of the County of *York*,[3] he acknowledgeth, "That his Prerogatives are built upon the Law of the Land."

From these and other such Passages which frequently occur in the Writings of the *King*, who so earnestly disputed for the *Rights* of the *Crown*, we may be abundantly convinced that the *English Monarchy* is not *unmixt*, or *unlimited;* and cannot therefore enough admire the lewd presumption of others, who have dared to attempt a change in our *English Government*, who prefer the extremes of *Tyranny* and *Slavery* to the just *temperament* of our *English Constitution;* who have laboured to tempt our *Kings* into an affectation of *absolute* and *arbitrary Power*, and have miserably overlayed the *Consciences* of their *Fellow-subjects* with a *boundless unlimited dread* of a *boundless unlimited Power.*

3. There are also great mistakes about the *measures* of our *Obedience* and *Submission*, which are necessary to be removed before our Consciences can make a free and impartial determination of the Case before us. We have been told it often, and with great earnestness, that we are bound in Conscience to yield an *active Obedience* to the *King* in all cases not countermanded by God, and to resist him in no case whatsoever. If indeed the two foregoing Errors had stood the proof, this would have followed by necessary consequence: for if a *Monarch* be *jure Divino*, he must be *absolute;* and if he be so, there is no case, not excepted by God, in which we must not *obey* him, and none at all in which we may *resist* him; but then we may make this advantage from the connexion which these Errors have one to an-

2. Charles I, "His Majesties Declaration to Parliament, in answer to that presented to him at Newmarket the ninth of March, 1641" (London, 9 March 1641/2), Wing C2801.

3. Charles I, "His Majesties Declaration to the Ministers, Free-holders, etc. of the county of York, assembled at Heworth Moore" (York, and reprinted at London, 3 June 1642), Wing C2280.

other, That if one of them be refuted, the rest must necessarily fall with it: and if according to the *English Principles* premised, our Government be founded on the *Constitutions* of this Country, and according to those *Constitutions* be mixt and limited, then there may be some cases in which it may be lawful for us not to obey the King, and not unlawful to resist him.

For though it may be true, that we are bound to *obey actively* whatever is commanded by the *Legislative Power* of the Kingdom, and is not repugnant to any Law of God; yet we cannot assert so much with respect to the *King only,* because he having not the whole *Legislative Power,* an Act of his *private Will* is destitute of that *Authority* which can derive an obligation upon Conscience: although therefore a King may require things not *inconsistent* with the Law *of God,* yet if they are beyond that *Authority* which the *Constitutions* of *England* have assigned to him, his Subjects are not bound in *conscience* to *obey* those *Commands;* and though in *some cases* they may *comply* by a *voluntary Concession,* yet they are obliged to *condemn* and *withstand* such proceedings if they increase so far as to threaten a fatal subversion of the *Government.* But how can we defend ourselves against any exorbitant Acts of the *King's* private Will, if disarmed and fettered by the Doctrines of *passive Obedience* and *Nonresistance?* what may not a King do, and a People suffer, if no defence may be used? I do not here forget to consider what *submission* God hath required to that *Supreme Authority* which he hath instituted, or what *honour* and *reverence* we are to pay to those *Governors* who sustain and administer it; nor how *impatient* men ordinarily are of the yoak of *Government,* and how apt to inlarge their *liberty* into *licentiousness;* nor how *pernicious* disorder and confusion must needs be to any Society; and therefore I use the utmost Caution I can to steer aright amidst the Rocks on the one hand, and the Sands on the other, that I may not make shipwrack of a good Conscience. I therefore premise and sincerely acknowledg, as I have learned from St. *Paul,* that *Every soul must be subject to the*

Supreme Authority which God hath instituted, and that if he resist, he is worthy of condemnation: and according to St. *Jude,* that we must not *despise dominions, or speak evil of dignities;* and that those untameable Spirits which are impatient of Government, are like *wild Beasts made to be destroyed.* I have also learned from St. *Peter, to submit to every ordinance of men for the Lord's sake, whether to the King as supreme, or to Governors sent by him,* so as not to *disobey* or *resist* them in the use of that *Authority* which the *Constitutions* of the Kingdom have *assigned* to them. I have from the same *Apostle* learned farther to be *subject with all fear, not only to the good and gentle, but also to the froward:* so that if a King in the administration of his Government should be too *sparing* in his *Rewards,* and over *severe* in his *Justice;* if too hard to be pleased, and as hard to be propitiated, I must be contented; if he injure me in my *private interests,* I must rather *submit* than oppose a *private* to a *publick* good; or if the *publick* Affairs of the Kingdom sustain any detriment or mischief from his Maleadministration, yet if it be such as will consist with the *being* of the Government and the *Safety* of the People, it should rather be born *patiently,* than redressed by a *violent* opposition. I acknowledge also that in all cases not certain and notorious, the Subject ought to presume the *Right* to be rather on his *Prince's* side than on his *own;* and never to think any oppressions *intolerable* till they are *evidently* such, or to call for a *violent* redress, till they appear otherwise *irremediable,* I must acknowledge also that I can see no Right the Subject hath from the *Law* of God or Man, to use any other resistance against a *King* than what is *defensive,* or to proceed *judicially* against him, or to inflict any punishment on his Person for any defaults of *Government,* because there can be no *Authority* in our Kingdom superior to that with which the King is invested. Yet after all these concessions it must be confessed that the *Regal* Power being in its Constitution *limited,* and in its Exercise liable to be *abused,* there may such cases happen wherein *defensive resistance* may be not only *lawful,* but a *necessary Duty.* And if we may not *lie for God,* much less may we do it in *flattery* to any *Man;* and if Subjects may not be defrauded of their *Estates,* no more should they be of their *Liberties,* to prevent their *abuse* of them. Wherefore to speak out plainly, and honestly in a case wherein *Conscience* is so much concerned, I must add, that we are not bound in Conscience to yield *Passive Obedience* to the King any farther than that *Regal Authority* extends, which the *Constitutions* of this Kingdom have invested him with; and that those *Constitutions* do not *impower* him to *treat* his *Subjects* according to his own *private Will,* but according to the *publick* rule of the *Law;* and by consequence, whatever grievance is *without* or *contrary* to *Law,* the Subject is not bound in Conscience to bear it, with respect to the *King* who had no *authority* to impose it, though he may *be* sometimes, with respect to the publick Peace; and if *Officers* be appointed by the King to *oppress* his Subjects *contrary* to Law, their *Commissions* being *illegal,* must be without *authority:* and therefore the Subject is not bound in Conscience to submit to them, but may *resist* their *injust assaults,* if he cannot otherwise *evade* them, and do not disturb the *Publick Peace* by the defence of his *private Interests.* And if we may suppose a case *so* sad, as that a King through ill *counsel* or some strong *temptation* should be changed from a *Father* into the *Enemy* of his Country; and should with an immoveable obstinancy ingage himself in such *illegal* designs, as plainly and inevitably tend to the *Subversion* of the *Government* and the *Destruction* of the People; his Subjects in such *unhappy circumstances* will be *excusable* before God, if they use so much *defensive resistance* as he hath made necessary for preserving the *Government* and *themselves.* For if in Nature a People is presupposed to Government, and Rulers are intended by God for the welfare of a People, and not a People for the pleasure of their Rulers, it will be most reasonable to infer, that when the End and the Means become inconsistent, the End should be preferred, and those Means prevented or rejected, which would destroy the End they should promote.

But these things are so easily anticipated by the common *sense* and *reason* of mankind, that there needs no long discourse about them; and they are indeed too *irksom* to an ingenuous mind to dwell long upon them: and though our *extraordinary case* at present hath made it *necessary* to say so *much*, yet I hope a like *case* will never happen again, to give occasion to Subjects to consider so *minutely*, the limits of the *Regal* Power, and of their own *submission*.

2. Having now rescued our *Consciences* from the prejudices of the foregoing *Errors*, we may be capable of making an impartial judgment of the case propounded, *Whether we can with a good Conscience transfer our Allegiance from the late to the present King? Allegiance* in its primary general sense signifies, being *obliged* or *bound*; in its political sense it imports that kind of *relation* which refers a *Subject* to his *Prince*, and by consequence it connotes the *duties* which result from that *relation*. And taking the word in its fullest latitude, there will arise these two difficulties to be distinctly resolved.

1. Whether our *Consciences* are *discharged* from *Allegiance* to the *late King?*

2. Whether we can with a good Conscience transfer our *Allegiance* to the *present King*, though not the immediate *Heir* of the Crown?

1. In resolving the former enquiry it will be necessary to premise, that our *Allegiance* to *James* the Second was not to his Person *absolutely*, but *respectively*, as he sustained the Character of *King*; and therefore as we owed no *Allegiance* to him before he was *King*, so neither can we owe him any now, if he *cease* to be so; and I think it too plain to need any proof, that it is possible that a person may cease to be King, though he still survive; and that a relation ceaseth when one of its Terms is lost. If therefore it appears, That *James* the Second doth cease to be our *King*, though he be still alive, our *Allegiance* to

him will be sufficiently discharged; and that he doth cease to be our
King, may, I suppose, be evinced from the following Considerations.

1. If *James* the Second did with an *immoveable obstinacy* ingage
himself in such *illegal* and *pernicious* designs as were *notoriously sub-*
versive of the *Government*, and *destructive* of the *People*, he did
thereby cease *de jure* to be our King, and our *Allegiance* to him is by
consequence discharged. The Title of *King* includes both an *Office* to
be discharged, and an *Estate* to be injoyed, but the latter is an *appen-*
dant to the former; when therefore he ceaseth to *govern* and *protect*
his People according to the Laws of this Kingdom, his *Right* must so
far cease to that *Power, Dignity,* or *Revenue,* which were assigned to
him for that end, except we can imagine some things to have a *moral*
power of *subsisting,* when the reason of them is gone. And as the
Office of the *King* is directed by the publick rule of the *Law,* so the
right which any person can have to the *Regal Estate,* must be founded
on the *Constitutions* of the *Realm;* and these *Constitutions* must either invest him with an *absolute Right* irrespective to his Office, and
then he would be an *absolute Monarch,* which is before disproved; or
else it must be a conditional Right, respecting the *Office* he is to discharge, and then the *Right* in *Equity* must cease, upon the non-
performance of the condition. Supposing also that a Person's *Right* to
the *Real* Estate be founded on the *Civil Constitutions* of our *Govern-*
ment, if he will set himself to *subvert* those *Constitutions,* he cannot
thereby but *Undermine* and *Destroy* his own *Right* which was *super-*
structed on them. And if he obstinately refuse to discharge the *Regal*
Office according to the proper fixt rule of the Law, though he still
usurp the title of *King,* yet he is become quite *another thing,* such as
our *English* Constitutions assign no *Authority* to, and to which we
are not supposed to owe any *Allegiance,* and which we cannot *recog-*
nize without becoming *Accessaries* to the most illegal practices, and
deriving on ourselves the heinous guilt of contributing to the ruine of
the Government and our Selves.

And as such a determination of the Case is most consonant to reason, so it is most agreeable to the antient principles and practices of *England.* By a Law made in King *Edward* the *Confessor's* time, it is declared, *That if a King doth not perform his Office, he shall not retain so much as the name of a King.* We read also that *Sigebert* King of the *West-Saxons,* being *incorrigibly Proud and Wicked, he was, in the beginning of the second year of his Reign, by the Nobles, and the People of the whole Kingdom assembled together, upon mature deliberation, and by unanimous consent of them, all driven out of his Kingdom.*

Thus also *King John* having broken his *Coronation-Oath,* and endeavoured by many ways to inslave both the *Church* and the *Realm,* after many applications, and a defensive War waged by the Barons against him, it was at last *agreed,* that *if he did again return to his former wicked Courses, the Barons should be forever released from all Allegiance to him; and when he afterward relapsed into the same courses, they in a general Assembly with the approbation of all the Realm, adjudged him unworthy to be King.*

We find also that King *Edward* the Second for following Evil Counsel, and refusing to hearken to good counsel, for his pride and arrogance, for breaking his Coronation Oath, for wasting his Kingdom, and being found incorrigible and past all hopes of amendment, was by *advice and assent of all the Prelates, Earles and Barons, and of the whole communitie of the Kingdom deposed from the Government.* I shall add only one instance more of King *Richard* the Second, to whom his Parliament sent Messengers to declare to him, among other things, *that they find in an antient Statute, and it hath been done in fact not long ago, that if the King through any evil counsel, or foolish contumacy, or out of Scorn, or some petulant wilfulness, or any other irregular way shall alienate himself from his people, and shall refuse to be governed and guided by the Laws of the Realm, and the Statutes, and laudable Ordinances thereof, together with the wholsome advice of the Lords and great Men of his Realm, but persisting headstrong in his own mad coun-*

sels, shall petulantly prosecute his own private humour, that then it shall be lawfull for them with the common assent and consent of the people of the Realm, to depose that same King from his Regal Throne, and to set up some other of the Royal Family in his place.

These Testimonies which I met with in a late *Pamphlet,* and which I am assured from an able hand to be *faithfully* recited, and of an *unsuspected credit,* I have *abridged* and *transcribed,* to confirm that *truth* on which the *Argument* is built, that according to our *English Constitutions,* a person may *forfeit* his *Regal Rights,* and cease *de jure* to be *King;* and that according to the *antient Statutes* and *irreprovable Usages* of this Country, the *Nobles* and *Commons* of *England* may *remove* such a person from the *Government,* when *necessary* to prevent a *general* ruine otherwise *inevitable.* Now that the *Late King* had brought matters to so great an extremity, as is in the *Argument* supposed, is evident from many instances so recent and notorious, that it was lately acknowledged by all of us in the lowdest Complaints. We saw him attempting to subvert our Parliaments, by *corrupting* their *Elections* with the meanest arts, and using his power to *pervert* or *frustrate* their counsels. We heard those high strains in which he claimed an absolute and arbitrary Power, our *Laws* were trampled on in *illegal dispensations,* and the most *partial Execution;* Some were disseised of their *Freehold* without a trial, and *levies* of Mony were made *without* and *against* Law; Our *Religion* and *Church,* which are the best of all those interests which are secured to us by a legal Establishment, were so boldly threatened and attacked, that we seemed to enjoy them but precariously, and to be in danger of seeing them speedily ravished from us. And when we consider that the *late King* was *instigated* and conducted in these exorbitant courses by the *Jesuits* and the *French King* who have long since convinced the World, that they dare to perpetrate any mischief or wickedness that will advance their glory, and promote their interests: When also we consider that he proceeded in these courses with so *obstinate* a *resolution,* that when his

Peers indeavoured to *reclaim* him by *advice,* they only thereby lost his *favour* and all their *Preferments;* and when some of his *Bishops peti-tioned* him in the *humblest* manner, they were answered only with *fury* and *imprisonment.* When lastly, we consider how *far* he had advanced in this *way,* that we already began to *despair,* and our Enemies to *tri-umph;* and if our *Glorious Deliverer* had not timely intervened, we might have been, in a few months, past all hopes of Recovery; We may surely upon these considerations be allowed to conclude, That *England* could not be in more danger, or any *Prince* lie under juster exceptions, or a people be more disobliged from their *Allegiance.* There are some who say, that if the *League* with *France,* the *Imposture* of a *young Prince,* the *Murder* of the *Earl* of *Essex, &c.* were clearly proved, they should not be able to contain themselves from re-nouncing all *Allegiance* to him; But though these may perchance be proved in due time, yet if they never are, there is certainly enough and too much besides to satisfy any reasonable Man.

2. If *James* the Second *deserted* the Kingdom without any *necessity* but what he induced on himself, and if he made no provision for the administration of the *Government* in his absence, but by taking away the publick *Seals* and cancelling the *Writs* of *Parliament,* designed to obstruct all regular proceedings; and if also he hath put himself into the hands of the *French King* the greatest Enemy of our Religion and Country,[4] *without whom* he cannot *return* to us, and with *whom* he cannot *return* without apparent *ruine* to his *Kingdom,* he doth thereby cease *de facto* to be our *King,* and we become discharged from all further *Allegiance* to him. I suppose few would hesitate in granting such a conclusion, if the *Late King* had by a *writing* under his *hand* and *seal* solemnly *abdicated* the *Government;* but I know not what

---

4. Louis XIV was regarded as a great enemy to Protestants when in 1685 he revoked the Edict of Nantes, which guaranteed the "irrevocable" right of French Huguenots to freedom of conscience. Louis proceeded to enact draconian measures to force them and their children to convert to Catholicism.

mighty force there is in a *form* of *Words* for *renouncing* the *Government*, that it may not be as effectually performed by a *proper* and *notorious* fact; or that a *King* may not as well *renounce* his *Crown* by *doing* it, as by *saying* it; and it is the thing itself and not the way of *expressing* it, which is the ground on which the relation between a *King* and his *Subjects* is *dissolved;* and therefore if a *King* doth actually desert his People, his Government and their Obedience must thereupon *actually* cease. You would perchance easily allow the argument, if the King had withdrawn *deliberately* and of *choice*, but it is said that he was rather hurried out of his *Kingdom*, by force and fear. It will be therefore necessary to relate to you the History of that transaction, which according to the truest account that I can meet with, is this: When the *King* went hence the first time, the *Prince* and his *Armie* were at a great distance, and a Treaty between them was *pretended*, but he left the City before his *Commissioners* could return with an *Answer* to his *Demands;* and it is certain that the Treaty was but a delusive Pretence, and that his Departure was resolved on some Days before; for he himself declared to a Person of Credit, that the *Queen* had obtained from him a Solemn *Oath* upon the *Sacrament*, on the *Sunday*, that if she went away for *France* on *Monday*, he would not fail to follow her on *Tuesday;* Which he accordingly attempted, and we are very well assured, that though his *Subjects* used some *Force* to *hinder* his *Flight*,[5] yet they used none to *compel* him to it. When he left this *City* the second time, he received a Message from the *Prince*, which desired him to withdraw some few Miles from *London*, lest the *Army* coming thither, and *Whitehall* being thronged with *Papists*, some Disorders might thence arise, not consistent with the *Publick Peace* or the *King's Safety;* but we are sure that it was altogether of his own *Choice* that he went first to *Rochester*, and thence out of the Kingdom.

5. James attempted to flee on 11 December 1688 but was intercepted and brought back. However, on reflection it seemed preferable to allow him to escape again.

If you reply that the *late King* being *deserted* by his Subjects, and exposed naked to the *Prince's Power*, was brought under a necessity of *flying*. I must answer, that that *Necessity* was not *absolute*, but *conditional:* For the *Prince* (to whom he lately allowed the *Character* of being always *Just* to his *Word*) had assured him in his *Declaration*, that if he would suffer the *Grievances* of his People to be redressed in a Free *Parliament*, his *Army* should peaceably depart. And not a few of his *Nobles*, and *others*, did earnestly beseech him to comply with those Terms, and solemnly *assure* him that in such a Compliance, they would faithfully adhere to him. If therefore the *late* King would have returned to the *English Government*, he need not have left the *Kingdom:* but if he *chose* rather to *depose* and *banish* himself, than *acknowledg* and *correct* the *Errors* of his *Government*, or let fall those *glorious Projects* of advancing *Popery* and an *Arbitrary Power* in *England*, we have no Reason to think such a *wilful Necessity* which he imposed upon himself, a sufficient Excuse for *deserting* his *Kingdom;* but rather to conclude, that if he would rather leave us, than leave off to oppress us, we are happily released from our *Allegiance* and *Oppression* together. Yet if we should impute his *Flight* rather to the *weakness* of his *Fear*, than to the *obstinacy* of his *Resolution;* I do not see how the same Conclusion can be avoided. For if he leave off to administer the *Government* himself, and rather *hinder* than *promote* its *Administration* by *others*, the course of the *Government* is thereby stoped, and either this Nation must *disband* into *Confusion*, or we are necessitated to seek out and employ some other *Expedient*. If you think that he might in short time *overcome his Fears*, and *return* to his *People* and *Government*, even this *Hope* is fatally precluded, by his making himself a *Royal Prisoner* to the *French King*, from whom he can expect only, to be *used* and *managed* as will most contribute to the *Designs* and *Interests* of that Haughty *Monarch;* insomuch that we cannot conceive his *Return possible*, without the *Consent* and *Conduct* of *Him* whom he hath made his *Patron*, and without the dread-

ful attendance of a *French Army*, and the dismal Consequence of utter
Ruine to our Church and Nation. And surely that *Prince* who can
forsake his People, and abandon them out of his Care, and make it
impossible to return, except as an Enemy to vanquish and destroy
them, may very well be thought to cease *de facto* to be a *King*, and his
Subjects to owe any *Allegiance* to him.

3. If the *Lords Spiritual* and *Temporal* and the *Commons* of *England* assembled in the late *Convention*, have upon mature Deliberation resolved and declared, that *James* the 2d hath *abdicated* the
Government and *vacated* the *Throne;* we may be satisfactorily confirmed from their *Authority* and *Judgment*, that he ceaseth to be our
King, and we to be his *Subjects*. That they have fully and expresly asserted so much, I need not prove; and their Testimony is so *proper*
and *authentick* in the present case, that we may with good Reason
suffer ourselves to be concluded by it. For the matter of the Enquiry
consists of several ancient Laws and customary Usages of this Kingdom, of which the two Houses are the most competent *Judges;* and
they representing the whole Nation, and being by our *Choice* commissioned to *consider* and *determine* this *Case* for us, we cannot with
any *Modesty* or *Equity reject* their *Determination*. If also we consider,
that in all Cases of a like Nature, the *Nobles* and *People* of *England* by
their Representatives, have *usually* and *finally* determined them; and
that upon the late King's withdrawing, the chief Power of the Nation
could reside nowhere rather than in the two Houses, it seems according to our *English Constitutions*, to be the *Duty* of *private* Men to
submit to such a *publick* Judgment. And indeed, if such a solemn *Assembly* of the three *Estates* of the *Kingdom*, after a long and serious
Consultation upon the Case, shall not be thought sufficient to *determine* it, I wonder who can, or may do it? For as particular Persons are
less capable of making so exact a Judgment, so if every one should
undertake to decide it, we must be reduced thereby into a helpless
state of utter Confusion.

Secondly, The other Difficulty in the present Case to be considered, is, Whether we may *lawfully* transfer our *Allegiance* to the present *King,* he being not the *next immediate Heir?* I may here presuppose that our *present King* is *acknowledged* by the *World* to be so eminently indued with all *Royal Virtues* and *Abilities,* and to have obliged the *Gratitude* of this *Nation* with so *glorious* and *happy* a Deliverance; that every *wise* and *good* Man among us cannot but be ready to address an hearty *Allegiance* to him, if it can appear *lawful* for him to do so; and where the *Heart* is so well inclined, it will not be difficult to convince the *Judgment,* if we consider these few Particulars.

1. That according to our *English Constitutions* it is not necessary that the next *immediate Heir* should succeed. For if we review in *History* the ancient *Usages* and *Practices* of our Country, which are the *Common Law* of our *Government,* we shall find, that, though the *Crown* hath been usually appropriated to the *Royal Family,* and in that Latitude is said to be Hereditary; yet it hath very frequently passed over the next *Heir* to some other Branch of the Family, which was thought more capable of promoting the publick Ends of the *Government* in its present Circumstances. And we find no publick Censure ever passed upon such a King, or his *Authority* and *Government* in the least disabled thereby. And to make this matter unquestionably *evident* to any Man who is not far gone in the *Conceit,* that the *Inheritance* or *Succession* of the *Crown* is *Jure divino,* I add that the *Kings* of *England* have been allowed by the whole *Legislative Power* of this Nation to dispose of the Crown by their Nomination, which, as it *may* suppose that they would not give it out of the *Royal Family,* so it must suppose that it was not necessary it should descend to the immediate *Heir;* for he being determined by *Nature,* could receive no Advantage from such a Nomination. Thus particularly it was allowed to *Henry* the Eighth, and he, according to the Statute in that behalf, setled the Crown on his Son *Edward,* and the Remainder on his Daughters *Mary* and *Elizabeth,* both which could not be

Heirs. And we find it also enacted in the 13th of *Elizabeth* that whoever should maintain in her Time that *she* and her *Parliament* might not limit the Descent of the Crown, should incur the Guilt of High-Treason, and after her Life, the Forfeiture of his Goods. From which Authentick Testimonies we cannot conclude less, than that it is not necessary that the next *immediate Heir* should always succeed.

2. Let us consider that our *Allegiance* being removed from the late *King*, it must be referred to some other Person, and we can think of none for whose sake we may justly deny it to the present King. The pretended *Prince* of *Wales* lying under such a general and vehement suspicion of being an Impostor, and being at present under the Conduct and disposal of the *King* of *France*, we see in him more Reasons to *dissuade* than *invite* our *Allegiance*. Our present *Queen*, who is the next *immediate Heir*, is not pretermitted; and though she hath a *Consort* in the Royal Dignity, yet he is such as was by *Marriage* become one with her, and who was admitted to the *Partnership*, not without her *Advice* and *Consent*. And the *King* himself being a Branch of the *Royal Family*, not far removed in the Succession, and who by the late *glorious Enterprize* hath retrieved the *Right* of both the *Royal Sisters*, and secured the *Government* itself from *Subversion*, it cannot but seem very *indecent* and *unjust* to *overlook* him in our *Allegiance*. If, lastly, we consider that the *Protestant Interest* in *Christendom*, and the *Civil* Interests of our own *Nation*, and of some of our best *Neighbours* are at present in most *imminent* and *extraordinary* Danger, which in Human Probability is not to be *avoided* but by the *Prowess* and *Conduct* of this *Illustrious Prince*, whom God hath by a *Special Providence* raised up among us; we cannot but conclude, that the *Series* of *Providence*, and the *Necessity* of *Affairs*, have determined our *Allegiance* to His *Majesty;* and that they seem to be unreasonably nice, who can sacrifice such *great Interests* to an *empty Formality*.

3. The great Council of the Nation having *actually* invested our

King with the *Royal Dignity*, he hath thereby a *Right* to our *Allegiance*, and according to the *Laws* of this *Realm*, we become *punishable* in refusing it, and are *indemnified* in performing it, although his antecedent Title to the *Crown* may not be such as to exclude all Exception. So great an *Article of State* as this can be fit to be decided only by the Wisdom of the Nation in the most Solemn *Assembly;* and when so decided, *ought* to be submitted to by all *private Persons*, or all *Settlement* must be an *impracticable* thing: and if our *Laws* should not be *executed* according to such an *authentick* Determination, the *Government* seems to be at a stop, beyond all hopes of reviving into Motion. I wish that they who *pretend* or *perplex* their *Consciences* about such Affairs, would consider seriously whether they are *proper* or *capable Judges* of such Matters, and whether their *Consciences* may not be better *conducted* by the Resolution of *such* as *are;* whether they behave themselves as becomes *private Persons*, who *oppose* their *Sentiments* to the *publick Judgment*, or whether any *Government* can subsist if such a *Presumption* be not restrained? For my own part I am verily persuaded, that in all *Civil* Cases, decided by their *proper Judges*, my Conscience ought to acquiesce, and if I may be thereby misled into any *Error*, it will be without *Guilt* before God. And I am also *informed* that by a Statute made 11 *Hen*. 7. we are legally *indemnified* in paying our *Allegiance* to the *King* in *being;* if we continue *faithful* therein, however infirm his Title may afterwards appear; and therefore I cannot see what *Danger* can *affright* us from our *Allegiance*, or with what *Safety* we can refuse it.

Thirdly, I have now given you my *Resolution* of the chief *Difficulties* in the Case propounded, and the *Reasons* on which it is built; and I can think of nothing more requisite to your Satisfaction, except to shew how this *Resolution* doth consist with all the Obligations which may affect a *good Conscience* in the present Case; which are, I suppose, chiefly these three, *viz.* the Prescriptions of that *Holy Religion* we profess; the Solemn *Oaths* we have taken, or the *Declaration* we have subscribed; and the avowed *Principles* and *Doctrines* of this *Church* in whose Communion we live.

1. As to the first. The *Rule* of our *Religion* being the Holy *Scriptures*, nothing can be *inconsistent* with one, which is not *repugnant* to the other; and according to the best of my Understanding, the principles I have proceeded upon, do not disagree with any Sacred Text, rightly interpreted. The first King of *Israel* we meet with in the Old Testament is *Saul*, who was advanced to the Throne as well by God's *Institution*, as the People's *Election*, and who was according to the People's desire, an *absolute Monarch*, like the other *Kings* in those *Eastern Countries:* But this, thanks be to God, is not our Case, who live under a *mixt Government*, and a *Monarchy* limited by the fundamental Constitutions of this Realm. And yet I cannot but observe how *David* (who is usually prescribed as an eminent Pattern of Loyalty) thought it lawful to raise a band of Souldiers for a *defensive Resistance* against the *unjust Persecutions* of *Saul*, though an *absolute Prince;* and surely we may conclude *a minori ad majus*, that such a *defensive Resistance* cannot be less *lawful*, when apparently *necessary* to preserve a *whole People* from *imminent* Ruine. I remember our Lord's determination, that his *Kingdom is not of this World:* and as I think we rightly infer from thence, that there is no *secular Force* belonging to his *Kingdom* for *inlarging* its Borders, or *securing* its Interests; so I can see nothing in these words to hinder, but that when any of the *Kingdoms* of this World is become the *Kingdom* of *Christ*, by incorporating his Religion among its civil Constitutions, then we may use any Expedients for the defence of our *Religion* which we might use in defending any other *Priviledges* of our *Civil* Establishment. Our Lord hath taught us, *to render unto* Cesar *the things that are* Cesar's; and his Apostle, that *we must render to all Men their Dues, Tribute to whom Tribute is due, Custom to whom Custom, Fear to whom Fear, and Honour to whom Honour;* but they have left us to the Constitutions of

our Country to determine, what the things of *Cesar* are, what *Custom* and *Tribute* is due, and when to be paid. I have already had occasion to consider the Doctrine of St. *Paul* and St. *Peter* concerning our duty of Submission to the *Supreme Authority*, and to those who administer it; And upon the general review of the whole, he seems to me to do the part of a *good Christian* as well as of a *good Englishman*, who hath on his Mind an awful regard for the *Supreme Authority* which is of divine Institution, who will not refuse an *Active Obedience* to the Laws of our Legislators, if consistent with the Laws of God; who can readily submit to the *King*, and to those that are *commissioned* by him, in the *Execution* of those *Laws*; who pays the highest *Civil Honour* to the *King* as the *Supreme Magistrate* of the *Kingdom*; who makes the most candid and honourable Constructions He can of all his *Prince's* Actions; who can quietly submit to any acts of Government, though they seem very unjust and grievous to his private Interests; and who never thinks a *defensive Resistance* lawful but when apparently *necessary* to save a *Kingdom* from utter Ruin. He that can do all this, is a good Proficient in his *Religion*, for he will find it not very easy to Flesh and Blood to go so far. But they who are not content with any Notion of Religion which will not expose to ruin the Kingdom that embraceth it, do but *traduce* our Holy *Religion*, and expose it to the *Contempt* and *Hatred* of the World.

2. Let us next consider how the *Resolution* I have given, will consist with the *Oaths* we have taken, and the *Declaration* we have Subscribed. You will here give me leave to premise that the *Forms* we have *sworn* or subscribed, are not to be taken carelessly according to the *meer sound* of words, but are to be understood according to the *Sense* which they plainly express, and which appears to be intended by our *Superiors* in imposing them. And if we consider our *Oaths* and Declaration according to this *Rule*, we shall discover that they have brought upon us no new degree of *Allegiance* or *Subjection*, which was not always due according to the ancient Fundamental Constitutions

of this Kingdom; that we have hereby lost none of our English Rights and Liberties; nor the *King* enlarged his *Prerogative* beyond what it always was and ought to be; and therefore if according to the ancient *Constitutions* of this *Kingdom,* the Government is mixt and the Monarchy *limited,* so it continues. If the Freemen of *England* were before these *Oaths* bound to no *Active* or *Passive* Obedience beyond what the Law of the Land prescribes, they are bound to no more since; and if it was formerly *lawful* for the People of *England* in an extreme necessity, to remove a *King* whose *Government* was became inconsistent with the Publick-Weal, and to set up another by whom the publick Interest may be secured, it is as *lawful* still notwithstanding these *Oaths* we have taken, or the *Declaration* we have subscribed. And to evince this more satisfactorily, let us descend to Particulars.

1. The *Oath* of *Supremacy* prescribed 1. *Eliz.* doth plainly appear from the *Preamble* and *Body* of the *Act,* and from all the parts of the *Oath* itself, to be intended only for asserting to the Queen a *Supremacy* over *Ecclesiastical* Persons, and in *Ecclesiastical* Causes, in opposition to the pretentions of the *Pope* and *Court* of *Rome.* When therefore it speaks of bearing *Faith* and true *Allegiance* to the *Queen,* and her *Heirs,* and lawful *Successors,* it is in opposition to all *Foreign* Jurisdictions, Powers, Superiorities and Authorities; and when it speaks of our assisting and defending her *Jurisdictions, Preheminencies* and *Authorities,* it is only of such as have been *parted* or *belonging,* or *united* and *annexed* to the Imperial *Crown* of this *Realm.* And that no new Power was hereby given to the *Queen* is evident, for when she was informed that this was by some pretended, she caused a Paper to be printed, called *An Admonition to simple Men deceived by the Malicious,* in which she declares,

> That she would have all her loving Subjects understand, that nothing was, is, or shall be meant, or intended by the same Oath, to have any other Duty, Allegiance or Bond required by

the same Oath, than was acknowledged to be due to *Henry* 8. And *Edward* 6.———and that her Majesty neither doth nor ever will challenge any other *Authority* than what was challenged and lately used by the said Noble King of Famous Memory, which is and was of ancient Times due to the Imperial Crown of this Realm; that is, under God to have the Sovereignty and Rule over all manner of Persons born within these Realms, Dominions and Countries, of what Estate either Ecclesiastical or Temporal soever they be; so as no other Foreign Power shall or ought to have any Superiority over them.

And to render this Exposition of the *Queen* more Authentick, we find it confirmed by an Act of *Parliament 5 Eliz.* wherein is this *Proviso;*

> Provided also, That the Oath expressed in the said *Act,* made in the said First Year, shall be taken and expounded in such Form, as is set forth in an Admonition annexed to the *Queen's Majestie's* Injunctions, published in the First Year of her Majesty's Reign; That is to say, to confess and acknowledg in her Majesty, her Heirs and Successors, none other Authority than that was challenged and lately used by the Noble King *Henry* 8. and *Edward* 6. as in the said Admonition more plainly may appear.

I think we may be abundantly satisfied from so express a Testimony both of the *Queen* and *Parliament,* that the Oath of *Supremacy* hath asserted no *new Power* to the Crown, nor derived any *new Allegiance* on the Subject, but hath only ingaged him to pay that Fealty, which an *Englishman* did always owe to his Prince; and if that be all, it doth no way contradict the Positions above asserted.

2. The Oath of *Allegiance* appointed by an Act 3. *Jacob.* 1. doth manifestly appear in the Body of the Act, and of the Oath itself, to be intended, not for making any new *kind* or *degree* of *Allegiance,* but only for asserting the old *Allegiance* of an *Englishman* against the

novel Doctrines and Practices of the *Pope* or *Court* of *Rome,* which pretended to a Power of *Excommunicating* and *Deposing* Kings, and of *releasing* Subjects from their *Allegiance,* and of *bestowing* this Kingdome on some other *Prince* at the *Pope's* pleasure. And that this *Oath was* intended only to assert our *Allegiance* in opposition to such *Popish* pretences, is evident from hence, that the *Oath* was at first *appointed,* and for some years was required, *only* of *known* or *suspected Papists.* And an *Act* of *Parliament* following 7. *Jac.* 1. declares concerning this *Oath,* that it is *limited and prescribed, tending only to the Declaration of such Duty, as every true and well affected Subject, not only by bond of Allegiance, but also by the Commandment of Almighty God, ought to bear to the King his Heirs and Successors.* We find also that King *James* doth professedly assert and defend no more in his Apology for this Oath, and in the *Act* of *Parliament* just before cited, that *Apology* is approved and commended. And it being in that very *Act* required that this *Oath* should be *Administered* not only to *Papists,* but also to all others his *Majesty's* Subjects, we cannot conceive that our Legislators *understood,* or *intended* it in any other, than that *limited* and *prescribed* sense they had before acknowledged. From hence therefore we may infer, that this *Oath* doth secure the *King* against all *Popish pretensions,* but not against the *English* Constitutions; and that the *Allegiance* we have sworn is no more than was *antecedently necessary* from those constitutions, and by consequence that if according to those *Constitutions* a King may be *removed* from the *Government,* and his people be *released* from their *Allegiance,* so they may be still, notwithstanding anything *expressed,* or *intended* in the Form of this Oath. But now if some among us (which I fear is the case of many) do mistake the matter of this Oath, and think they have Sworn to another *kind,* or higher *degree* of *Allegiance* than our Legislators intended, they cannot but thereby *inthrall* their *Consciences* with great perplexities; and can no other way find Ease, than by stating the *Obligation* of their *Oath,* according to the intention of those Superiours who imposed it; and this may relieve them, for I suppose that though a Man may through mistake suppose his Obligation to be greater than it is, yet that a *promissory Oath* doth really oblige him no farther, than the party by whom the form of his *Oath* was prescribed, and he to whom it was made, may be reasonably supposed to intend and require. Thus for instance, if a Man thinks he hath sworn *Allegiance* to the *person* of him that is *King,* so as to be bound to him, whether he Administer the *English Government,* or set up another quite *contrary* to it; or that it obligeth him to obey the Acts of a *King's private Will,* though without and contrary to *Law;* or that his *Allegiance* is not *terminable* but by death, although the person to whom he Swore, may long before cease *de jure,* or *de facto* to be *King;* and to mention only one case more, which I observe to be somewhat common, if any thinks, he hath sworn such an *Allegiance* to the *King's Heirs,* and *lawful Successors,* as obligeth him in *Conscience* to find out who is the *next immediate Heir,* to assist him in acquiring the Crown, and to pay subjection to him and to no other; although the great *Council,* or the whole *Legislative power* of the Nation should see reason to determine otherwise; In these and other such Cases, it is plain that our *Consciences* are intangled, not with the *real Obligations* which are upon them, but with our *mistakes* about them; that we conceit an *Allegiance* which our Ancestors never knew, and our *English Constitutions* do not require or allow.

3. The *Declaration* we have subscribed according to the Act in 14 C. 2. is in these Words, *That it is not lawful upon any pretence whatsoever to take Arms against the King; and that I do abhor that traiterous position, of taking Arms by his Authority against his Person, or against those that are Commissioned by him.* Which *Declaration* may be considered, in the present case, either as it expresseth our *own* judgment, or as it expresseth the judgment of our *Legislators,* who required it. As it is *our Declaration,* it can only import, that when we subscribed it, our judgment was really such, as we then thought this form of words

did properly express, but we did not hereby declare that we should never change that judgment, if convinced by sufficient Arguments, and therefore cannot be bound in *Conscience* never to think, or act contrary to that *Declaration*. But an Argument from this *Declaration* is of more force as it pleads the judgment and determination of our *Legislators,* which will therefore deserve to be more attentively considered. I acknowledg that this *Form* was intended, in direct *opposition* to the *Rebellious principles* and *practices* of thc times immediately preceding, and must conclude that according to the judgment of this *Parliament, King Charles* the I. did never *de jure* fall from his *Regal Right,* and that consequently the War his Subjects waged against him was a *Rebellion,* and the *positions* on which they proceeded were *traiterous;* and that it is not lawful upon pretence of his *Authority,* or any other pretence whatsoever to take Arms against his person, who continues to be *de jure King.* In all which the Parliament doth declare no *defensive Resistance* to be *unlawful,* which was not *always* so, nor condemn any *positions* which are not in themselves antecedently *traiterous;* and whoever thinks that they intended more, must suppose that that *Parliament* altered the Constitutions of our *English Government,* and did by apparent consequence, expose the Nation to utter Destruction. And if any of us in subscribing the Declaration, had any other apprehensions of it; we may, and I think we should renounce and condemn them.

4.[6] Let us in the last place consider how this resolution will agree with the received *Principles* and *Doctrines* of the *Church* of *England.* We need not, I know, profess so high a regard for our *Church,* as to think any doctrine upon her sole *Authority,* to be a Sufficient rule of our *Faith* or *Conscience;* and yet it cannot misbecome us to pay so great a deference to her Judgment, as never to depart from it without great *regret.* But upon second thoughts I find we shall be under no

---

6. In the original this was incorrectly numbered 3.

necessity of doing so; for though there have been for some time, a *party* among us who have appropriated to themselves the *Church* of *England* exclusive of their brethren; yet if we extend her Arms wide enough to embrace all her *genuine* children since the Reformation, we shall find enough on our side to justifie *our doctrines* to be consistent with her *principles.* Her Homilies nowhere, that I know of, assert the Errors I have here condemned, or condemn any of the positions I have here asserted. The Homilies of *Obedience* teach us to *Submit to lawful Authority and to know our bounden duties to common Authority,* but they teach us no *loyalty,* beside or contrary to law. The Homilies against Rebellion are particularly designed against the Papists, whose Rebellion was the occasion upon which they were written, and though they teach us not to resist our Prince if his Government be *legal,* however contrary to our *Religion* or any other interests, yet they nowhere forbid, a defensive resistance against *illegal* oppressions which threaten an inevitable ruin to our Country; for they describe the Rebellion they condemn to be no other than resisting or withstanding common Authority. And that the principles of loyalty which obtained in the Church at that time were no other than I have been now asserting, we may easily satisfie ourselves from that form of *Prayer* they are charged with by the Parliament, in Queen *Mary's* reign, *that God would turn her heart from Idolatry to the true Faith, or else shorten her dayes and take her quickly out of the way.* Also from the Reasons which the Bishops presented to *Queen Elizabeth* to prove that she ought to take away the life of *Mary Queen* of *Scots* because an Enemy to their *Religion* and *Country,* though the next Heiress of the Crown; as *Constantine* did of *Licinius* his fellow *Emperour* because he was an Enemy of the *Empire* and of the Christian Religion; And to such as might object against their Reasons and advice they thus reply, *If our danger be joined with the danger of our Gracious Soveraign and natural Country, we see not how we can be accounted godly Bishops or faithful Subjects if in common peril we should not cry out & give warning: Or on the other hand how they can be thought to have true hearts toward God and toward their Prince and Country that will mislike our so doing, and seek thereby to discredit us.* We may also know their principles in the present case from the *Subsidies* which the *Clergy* gave to the *Queen* in *several* Convocations in the fifth, thirty-fifth, and forty-third years of her Reign, for her maintaining and assisting the *Scotch, French,* and *Dutch* in their defence of their *Liberties* and *Religion* against the injust oppressions of their Princes, as may be collected out of the preambles of those Subsidy Acts. And if it were not too tedious, this might be fully attested out of the writings of such Bishops as were most eminent in those times.

Bishop *Jewel* speaking of *Luther, Melancthon &c.* hath these words *They do not teach the people to rebel against their Prince, but only to defend themselves by all lawful means against oppression; as did David against King Saul, and so do the Nobles in France at this day. They seek not to kill, but to save their own lives, as they have openly protested by publick writing to the world.* Bishop *Bilson* in his book of the *true difference between Christian subjection* and *Unchristian Rebellion,* dedicated to *Queen Elizabeth,* thus gives his Judgment concerning that defensive Resistance which the *Hugonots* used against the injust oppressions of their King. *I will not,* Saith he, *rashly pronounce all that resist to be Rebels: Cases may fall out in Christian Kingdoms, where the people may plead their Right against the Prince and not be charged with Rebellion. As for example, if a Prince should go about to subject his Kingdom to a forreign Realm, or change the form of the Commonwealth from Empire to Tyranny, or neglect the Laws established by common consent of Prince and People, to execute his own pleasure. In these and other cases, which might be named, if the Nobles and Commons join together to defend their Ancient and accustomed Liberty, Regiment and Laws, they may not well be counted Rebels.* In the next Reign, we have the judgment of *Abbot* Bishop of *Salisbury,* that *the Case of the Primitive Christians and of us differs in this, that they had no legal Right for their Religion, but were subject to the meer pleasure of the Government. And*

while it was so, Christians did suffer themselves to be killed, and killed none in their own defence; but when under Constantine *the Emperour they had the Laws on their side,* [Non tam caedebantur quam caedebant] *they did not so much yield up themselves to be killed, as allow themselves to kill others in their just defence.* Such were the principles of the Church of *England* in the Reign of Queen *Elizabeth,* and King *James;* but indeed in the next Reign, when *Popish* and *French* Councils found admission at our Court, then arose *together* the New Principles of *superconformity* in the Church, and of *Super Loyalty* in the State; which like a preternatural ferment, have ever since disturbed the peace of both, and must be again cast out, if we ever recover a true *English* Temper, or a peaceful settlement. If then we frame our Character of the *Church* of *England* from the first and purest half of her Age, before she was secretly practised upon, by the Arts of her subtle Adversary, we shall easily discover, that her principles of *Conformity* and *Loyalty* are far more *moderate* and *intelligible* than those, which since that time, have been most industriously and impetuously recommended under her *Venerable* Name. And I wish that every one who professeth an Honourable and kind regard for our *Church,* would no longer ascribe to her such Principles and Doctrines, which she for many years was ignorant of; wherewith the *Church* hath given great advantage to her Enemies, and received nothing but Scorn and Contempts, and by which she may oblige the present *Government* to treat her with less kindness, than she might otherwise expect. But I forget that I am writing a Letter, and how much pardon I already need for running it into so great a length; but I thought it better to give you so long a trouble in reading, than to leave any trouble on your mind unremoved. I beseech you to excuse candidly the mistakes I may have committed; and to accept the Services of
Reverend Sir

Your Affectionate Brother and Faithful Friend, &c.
London March 1688/9

Anonymous

A Friendly

CONFERENCE

Concerning the New

Oath of Allegiance

TO

K. *WILLIAM*, and Q. *MARY*,

WHEREIN

The Objections against taking the Oaths are
impartially Examined.

AND

The Reasons of Obedience Confirm'd, from
the Writings of the profound Bishop *Sanderson,*

And proved to agree to
The Principles of the *Church of England*, and
the Laws of the Land.

By a Divine of that Church.

Licens'd, April 19. 1689.

James Fraser.

LONDON:
Printed for *Samuel Smith*, at the *Princes Arms* in
St. Paul's Church-yard. 1689.

*T*his anonymous tract, licensed for publication on 19 April 1689, directly addresses the new requirement that office holders, both civil and ecclesiastical, must subscribe to an oath of loyalty to King William and Queen Mary.

To ease the consciences of the scrupulous, the new oath asked only for loyalty. It deftly sidestepped the issue of legitimacy and read: "I do sincerely promise and swear that I will be faithful and bear true allegiance to their majesties King William and Queen Mary." Nevertheless with King James still alive many individuals with troubled consciences were unclear what obligation they still owed King James. They were anxious not to violate their sworn oath to him and wondered whether William and Mary were usurpers like Cromwell. Office holders had six months during which to swear to the oath or lose their posts.

"A Friendly Conference" is in the form of a dialogue. The author is an Anglican clergyman and a Tory. He claims he had been a nonjuror with grave objections to taking the oath. But having closely examined the writings of Bishop Robert Sanderson, he says he became convinced it was his duty to take it. Sanderson wrote extensively on obligation and oaths from 1649 and the execution of Charles I through the 1670s. The arguments in the dialogue provide a full discussion of the various aspects of the controversy. The author refers to the de facto act of Henry VII, the laws on allegiance, and tries to distinguish allegiance to King William from allegiance to "that usurper," Oliver Cromwell. The tract appeared in a single edition.

A Dialogue Concerning the New Oath of Allegiance.

C. SIR, I am very happily fallen into your company, which, though I always loved, yet now I covet it upon an extraordinary occasion; and that, like a friend, I may apply myself without ceremony to you, I shall inform you, that I have lately met with the *New Oath of Allegiance,* which, is said, to be required of all persons in Office, about which I have some scruples; for though I am very willing to serve my Country, yet I would also as willingly salve my Conscience.

W. It were great pity, that persons of your worth and integrity, should at this time desert your publick stations, while you may in such a *critical* conjuncture be instruments of much good to both *Church* and *State;* and I know, that nothing but just reasons could incline you to refuse to act, as becomes you.

C. Perhaps both myself, and others, might easily be continued in our Offices, and a series of good men put into publick Employments for the future, if it were thought fit not to press so earnestly the taking of the *New Oath.*

W. But what security can *the King* have of the fidelity of his Subjects, unless they bind themselves to obey him by an *Oath of Allegiance?* since an Oath is the strongest obligation to duty.

C. And I wish, that Oaths could, and did bind all, that take them; and that I myself could be satisfied of the lawfulness of this.

W. Though I suspect my own Abilities, yet I will for this time sacrifice my Discretion to my Zeal, and if I fail in my Argument, I am sure, I shall not fail in my Intentions to serve you.

C. I desire you, without any Apologies, to address yourself to this task.

W. And that I shall chearfully, and readily, when you have told me your Scruples, that hinder your taking the Oath.

C. Two things I fear very much, should I take it, *viz. (1.) Lest I should be Hanged;* And, *(2.) Lest I should be Damned,* for doing it.

W. These are great Fears indeed: but I hope you only *fear where no fear is, (i.e.)* when you have no just cause for it. For, what reason can you have to fear *Hanging* on this account?

C. What reason, do you ask? Is it not Treason in the highest nature that can be, to swear Allegiance to a new King, when my old and true King is alive? and is not Treason a Capital Crime?

W. Not so fast, my good old Friend. For I believe you'd find yourself mistaken, and that, in the present circumstances, it is neither *Treason,* nor *Capital,* to swear Allegiance to King *William* and Queen *Mary,* according to the Laws now in force in the Nation.

C. What Laws (I pray you) are there, that can excuse me from Treason, if I should take this new Oath? You would highly oblige me, (Sir) if you will shew me them.

W. I cannot but think (however other things may have at present put it out of your head) that you have heard of such a Maxim of Law as this, *Corona tollit omnes defectus.*

C. Yes, that I have; the Lawyers found it upon *Henry the Seventh's* enjoying the Crown, notwithstanding an Attainder of High Treason, that stood unrepealed against him; and they did not think it worth the while to repeal it, because of that legal Maxim, *That the Crown takes away all manner of defects.*

W. If this be a true Maxim of our Law, then how can any man be guilty of Treason for obeying such Laws as are made by *the King in possession, and his Parliament?*

C. I'll tell you, Sir, why he is still guilty of Treason, *viz.* because that Maxim is only understood of defects *in the person of the King, not in his title to the Crown, (i.e.)* the possession of the Crown takes off the guilt of any capital Crime, as Murder, Treason, *&c.* from the person of the King, so that he cannot by his Subjects (because they are then his Subjects) be brought to any legal trial, or arraigned for them; but it does not give him a just right or title to the Crown, if he had it not before.

W. But Subjects are not bound to examine the Titles of Kings; their *Rights* are above our reach.

C. But here the *right* of the Crown is so evidently in another, that no man can doubt, to whom it belongs.

W. Let me ask you (Sir) one Question, *viz. Was not the Right and Title to the Crown apparently in* Henry *the Seventh his Wife, and not in him?*

C. I must (indeed Sir) own, that she was *of the House of* York, *who had the undoubted right and title to the Crown,* and that she was the undoubted Heiress of that Family; and that *Henry the Seventh* derived his Title only from his Ancestors of *the House of* Lancaster, *who were originally meer Usurpers of the Right of that other Family.*

W. Very well, Sir: *And do you not own, that our Laws are the best Interpreters of all legal Maxims?*

C. Yes, Sir, this I think is most reasonable to be acknowledged.

W. Then I need not ask any more. For have not our Laws made such an interpretation of the Maxim before urged, *viz. That the possession of the Crown doth so far take off all defects of title, as that the Subject shall be indempnified in his obedience?* Now though this Law cannot render a King safe *in foro interno,* but that if he hath unjustly taken another man's right, he must answer it before God; yet surely it secures both him and his Subjects *in foro externo;* so that neither he for commanding things necessary for the support of the Government, nor they for obeying him in such things, can be called to any account, or punished by men.

C. This I must grant: but (I pray Sir) where is there any such Law?

W. If you please to look in *Keeble's Statute-Book,*[1] p. 318. *(undecimo Henrici 7. c. 1.)* there you may see it.

C. I pray Sir, read the words to me.

---

1. Joseph Keble, *An Assistance to Justices of Peace* (London, 1683), Wing K114.

W. That I shall most readily do. In the Preface to the Act it is acknowledged, THAT IT IS NOT REASONABLE, BUT AGAINST ALL LAW, REASON, AND GOOD CONSCIENCE, THAT THE SUBJECTS GOING WITH THEIR SOVERAIGN IN WAR, &c. SHOULD LOSE OR FORFEIT ANY THING FOR DOING THEIR TRUE DUTY AND SERVICE OF ALLEGIANCE.

This is the very reason and ground of the Law, as appears by the following words of the Statute, which are these: *It be therefore ordained, enacted, and established by the King our soveraign Lord, by the advice and assent of the Lord's Spiritual, and Temporal, and the Commons in this present Parliament assembled, and by authority of the same, that from henceforth no manner of person or persons whatsoever he or they be,* THAT ATTEND UPON THE KING, AND SOVERAIGN LORD OF THIS LAND FOR THE TIME BEING, *in his person, and do him true and faithful service of Allegiance in the same, or be in other places by his command in his Wars within this Land or without: that for the said deed, and true duty of Allegiance, he or they be in no wise convict or attaint of High-Treason, nor of other offences for that cause, by Act of Parliament, or otherwise, by any process of Law, whereby he, or any of them shall lose or forfeit Life, Lands, Tenements, Rents, Possessions, Hereditaments, Goods, Chattels, or any other things: but to be for that deed, or service, utterly discharged of any vexation, trouble, or loss. And if any Act or Acts, or other process of Law hereafter thereupon, for the same happen to be made contrary to this Ordinance, that then that Act or Acts, or other process of the Law, whatsoever they shall be, stand and be utterly void.*

C. This I think is plain and full enough. For if I may lawfully perform any Act of Allegiance *to any King for the time being*, then certainly I may, without any danger, promise or swear such Allegiance to *any King in fact*, though he be not a *King of right.* But may not this

Law be made in respect of *Henry* the Seventh's right of Conquest, by which he held the Crown, and doth not this very much alter the case from our present state of affairs?

W. The Act expresseth no such thing, but the quite contrary; for the reason of it is this, because *it is contrary to all Law, and good Conscience, that the Subject should suffer or lose anything for doing service to his King.* And as for the right of Conquest,[2] though our *present King* doth not pretend to it, yet I can see no reason, but he hath as good a right that way, as ever *Henry* the 7th had, or could pretend to.

C. What that of Conquest? I cannot but smile to think you should imagine that there can be any Conquest without so much as a Sword drawn: *Henry the 7th* fought a famous Battle and was Victor therein, but King *William* never so much as struck a stroke for it.

W. Your smiling, Sir, will not alter my Opinion, no more than the reason you give; for may not a Victory be yielded without fighting? May not a Nation be Conquered by a major party within itself? Nay, was *England* ever conquered otherways?

C. I remember indeed, a saying of the wise and great *Cecil's*, viz. that *England is a Vivacious Animal, that can never be destroyed, but by itself:* And our own People were the Conquerors under *Henry the 7th;* nay, I think neither the *Romans, Saxons,* or *Normans* ever could have conquered us, but by our own Assistance, and consent of the majority amongst ourselves. But would not this incence the Nation against the *present King,* to set up a Title of Conquest for him?

W. I cannot see any reason for it, truly Sir, for hath he not already limited his right of Conquest, by referring himself wholly to his People, and accepting the Crown upon such terms as *their Representatives in Convention* thought expedient for the good of the Publick? And is not the agreement still firm (notwithstanding his right of

---

2. Traditionally a conqueror had no obligation to grant those he conquered their customary rights or, indeed, any rights at all. For the application to English constitutional theory, see J. G. A. Pocock, *The Ancient Constitution and the Feudal Law,* 2d ed. (Cambridge, 1987).

Conquest) that was made with the *Kentish men,* by *William* the *Norman Conqueror,* and have they not constantly enjoyed their native Rights, Laws, and Customs?

C. All this is very true: So that till I see further, I cannot but own that we may as lawfully swear Allegiance to King *William,* as *Henry the 7th* his Subjects could do to him, and are in no more danger of Treason, than they were in so doing. But yet there is one thing that makes me think our danger greater than theirs, *viz.* that if King *James* the 2d. should return by force (as he, that seen these last Revolutions can think nothing of that kind impossible) those that take this new Oath would be in most apparent danger to be utterly ruined by him.

W. Suppose all that you fear; yet according to Law we can be in no danger of ruin by him, for swearing Allegiance to the present King, because the Law doth indemnifie us for it. But if we refuse to take the Oath of Allegiance to him, that is in the possession of the Crown, doth not the Law itself put it into his power to take away our Estates and Liberties?

C. Yes, Sir, I am sensible that the Refusers (if it be tendered to them) are punishable by Law *with Premunire's,*[3] and *Imprisonment without Bail or Main-prize.*

W. You would do well then to consider, who is safest, he, who suffers for obeying, or who suffers for breaking the Law? And if King *James* return and resolve to punish contrary to Law, no other *Protestant* would be more safe, than those who have taken the Oaths.

C. My second objection is, *The fear of being damned, if I should take this new Oath of Allegiance.*

---

3. The offense of "praemunire" was developed to protect the royal rights of jurisdiction, especially against foreign powers, in particular, the pretensions of the pope. In that context it was applied to those who gave obedience to the papal process which belonged to the king alone. The summarizing statute, passed in 1393 in the reign of Richard II, punished offenders with loss of property and imprisonment at the king's will.

W. This is indeed infinitely a greater fear than the former, and therefore the objection ought to be answered with all the care that can be; and I doubt, will take up much more time in the due Examination of the Reasons for it, which I pray propose to me without further delay.

C. You cannot certainly be ignorant of the Reason, *viz. That it is a wicked Oath; and therefore it must be a damnable Sin in me to take it.*

W. But why (I pray) is it a wicked Oath?

C. First, from the matter of it, considered either in itself, or in respect of me who have reason to think that I am by right subject to another Person.

Secondly, from the Authority that imposed it, which I do not think is a lawful and sufficient power to ordain such an Oath. Now I know that in these Cases Bishop *Sanderson*[4] (the best and most impartial Casuist that I know, or ever heard of) tells me an Oath is altogether unlawful.

W. No man hath a greater Reverence for his Judgment, than myself; and no man hath, or can give me greater satisfaction than that Right Reverend and Judicious Bishop in the very point now in debate betwixt us.

C. Say you so Sir? No man's determination can have a greater influence upon me, than his, for certainly no man ever determined any Cases of Conscience more fully and clearly than he doth.

W. Why then Sir, I think we are agreed to submit the whole to his Determination.

C. Only where I think there is any just exception, give me leave to propose it for my fuller satisfaction.

W. With all my Heart, Sir.

C. Doth he not then in the plainest manner condemn any Oath,

---

4. Robert Sanderson, Bishop of Lincoln, wrote numerous essays on oaths. Among these see "De juramento, Seven lectures concerning the obligation of promisory oathes" (1655), Wing S589 and Wing S629.

where the matter of it is unlawful, of which you may see his Judgment in his third *Lect. de Juramenti obligatione,* Sect. 7. pag. 57.

W. Yes, Sir, in the plainest terms that can be. His words are these: *Rem illicitam dico, quae sine peccato fieri non potest. Est autem hoc genus juramenti adeo illicitum, ut non solum is peccat qui sic jurat, sed & is quoque, qui alium ad sic jurandum auctoritate, consilio, aut alio quocunque modo impellit, inducitve. That thing I call unlawful which cannot be done without Sin: But such a kind of Oath is so utterly unlawful, that not only he sins that takes it, but he also that by his Authority, or Advice, or any other way, doth compel, or perswade a man to swear to any such thing.*

C. Well, Sir, have a care then how you endeavour to perswade me to any such Oath; for if you please to read on, he gives you a full, and satisfactory Reason why a man that takes such an Oath must necessarily commit a Sin. For saith he, *Peccat qui sic jurat, sive intendat facere quod juravit, sive non intendat. Si intendat, peccat volendo rem illicitam, & sic non jurat non justitia: Si non intendat, peccat mentiendo, & sic non jurat in veritate. He who swears so (i.e.* to any unlawful matter*) sinneth whether he intends to perform it, or doth not intend it: If he doth intend it, he sins by designing an unjust thing, and so swears not in Righteousness: If he doth not intend it, he sins by lying, and so swears not in Truth.* And this latter is certainly a very great Sin; for he that swears, and doth not intend to perform his Oath, especially in any matter of Promise (as this of *Allegiance* is) *not only lies to Man but to God;* and affronts the Divine Majesty in the highest manner, by calling God to be a Witness to the truth of that which he knows to be a lie; and to punish him if he breaks his Oath, and yet resolves beforehand not to observe it.

W. 'Tis very true, for what can be a greater Affront to God's infinite Wisdom, or contempt, and mockery of his infinite Power? So that did I not think the matter of this Oath lawful, I must own myself guilty of the greatest fault to perswade you to take it.

C. Nay, Sir, I am very confident that you have satisfied yourself in it, and therefore wish you would do the same to me.

W. To proceed then; I pray you (Sir) tell me *what the matter of this Oath is?*

C. To bear true and faithful Allegiance to King William &c.

W. And do you not think it is lawful to pay him *true and faithful obedience, so long as he is in fact the King?*

C. That is the very thing I would be satisfied in.

W. Had you lived in the days of the late *Usurper,*[5] whose Actions need neither comment, nor censure, would you not have thought it a great breach of the Laws of Obedience, to have submitted to that *Usurper?*

C. I did live in his time, but I never voluntarily submitted to any of his Commands; and what I did out of necessity, and by compulsion, I hope, God will forgive me.

W. I question not but he will forgive it; and your old friend, Bishop *Sanderson,* puts it out of all question. Let me therefore ask you one Question more. *Do you think it more unlawful to pay true Allegiance to King* William, *than it was to pay it to that Usurper?*

C. No truly, there can be no reason to think so.

W. Very good. Yet Bishop *Sanderson* will tell you, that it is lawful, nay, a Duty to obey him.

C. Say you so, Sir? whereabout I pray you?

W. If you please to look in his Book, *De Oblig. Conscient. p. 176. Praelect. 5. Sect. 16.* you will find it most plainly asserted.

C. Oh, Sir! I long to hear the words.

W. The words are these, which I will now read to you: *Caeterum ubi quis pulso vi & armis legitimo principe, regnique haerede eo tamen adhuc superstite, imperii habenas accipit, & se pro Rege gerit,* &c. In

---

5. Oliver Cromwell.

English thus: *But when any man by Force and Arms hath driven away the lawful Prince, and Heir of the Kingdom, he being still alive, and hath got the power of the Realm into his own hands, and believes himself as King, when he is more truly an Invader of the Kingdom, than a King; so that there is no doubt, but that the right Heir hath manifest injury done him: If you inquire, what I think is to be done in this case by a good Sub-ject, who hath sworn Allegiance to his lawful Prince, or if he hath not sworn, yet oweth him as much allegiance as though he had? I answer, it seems to me, that it is not only lawful for a good Subject to obey those Laws, that are made by him who possesseth the Supreme Power in fact, though not by right, and to execute all other his Commands (if he com-mands nothing that is in itself dishonourable, or unjust); but also the ne-cessity of affairs may and do most frequently so require it, that if he doth it not, he is to be thought to be wanting to his own duty.*

C. The Case (I confess) he hath put so home, as if he meant it of the late Usurper, though the Lectures were read *Anno* 1647, but his determination seems so very strange to me, that I cannot be fully satisfied with his opinion, till I see some sufficient reasons for it.

W. No man was better able to give reasons for his own opinion, than himself. I shall therefore produce them to you (in the first place) which he builds upon, and after that, I suppose (Sir) you will need no other for your full satisfaction.

C. I pray you (Sir) proceed. For why, a good Subject should be wanting to his duty, if he doth not obey an Usurper's commands I cannot yet see, nor from whence that duty can arise.

W. This that right Reverend Author will soon tell you, *(ibid. p. 177. ad fin.) Oritur ergo ista obligatio, &c. This duty ariseth from two other duties, 1. That which every man owes himself. 2. That which he owes to his Countrey.*

C. As to the first; the duty that every man owes to himself, is to preserve himself, his Estate, and his Family, and to endeavour by all lawful means to live in peace with all men, and not to offend his present Governors, because he knows all that he hath, as well as his own life, is in their power.

W. And therefore the Bishop argues, *(ibid. p. 178. lin. 10.) That from hence the first necessity of obedience doth arise. Quam propterea non tam urget Apostolus, quam supponit, &c. Which necessity therefore the Apostle* (Rom. 13. 5.) *doth not so much urge, as suppose,* when he saith, *we must needs be subject, not only for wrath,* &c. *as though a sence of this was natural to every man; as if he was a mad man, that would rashly provoke him to wrath, who hath the power of the sword: and* (as he proceeds) *would by his contumacy incur his displeasure, when no necessity doth require it.* And as he concludes that 17th *Section* of his fifth Lecture; *Therefore it behoveth every man, as the shortest way for his own happiness. (Quod sine peccato fieri potest)* ταῖς οὔσαις ἐξουσίας ὑποτάσσεσθαι, *so far as he can without sin, to obey the present Governours that are set over him, and to submit to their Laws; and so by wellbearing that yoak which he cannot shake off, to make it something more light, easie, and tolerable.*

C. This is a good Rule in Prudence; but I don't apprehend, that it ought much to sway in conscience, for *worldly wisdom* is commonly the greatest enemy to our true (*i.e.*) our eternal interest.

W. Certainly, Sir, if (as St. *Paul* saith, *1 Tim. 5. 8.*) *He that provides not for himself, and especially those of his own Family, hath denied the faith,* (*i.e.* in his works) *and is worse than an infidel;* what words can express his crime, who for not doing that which is in itself lawful, in obedience to *the Powers that are set over him,* shall thereby forfeit or lose what God hath lent him for the maintenance of himself, and his Family? for not only prudence, but conscience; not only my temporal, but my eternal interest binds me to this duty, which I owe to myself, and those under my care.

C. The light of Nature binds me to it; and therefore much more the light of Scripture being superadded. For certainly our blessed

Saviour intended to *perfect*, not to cancel the laws of Nature by the laws of his Religion: and the design of the holy Scriptures was to make us *wise unto salvation*, not fools to ourselves and our posterities.

W. The Bishop tells us his next reason is *stronger* than the former, *and doth more immediately touch the conscience. Ibid. Sect. 18. p. 178.*

C. I pray you, Sir, let me hear it.

W. His second Reason is taken from the law of Gratitude, which he well calls, *optima aequi boni Lex, the best Law of right and equity. Ib. p. 180. lin. 12.*

C. How doth he argue from thence? For indeed nothing can be a more free and generous Argument, than Gratitude, and nothing more becoming a Gentleman's consideration: and on the contrary, nothing more mean, vile, and base, than Ingratitude.

W. In the same place (*p. 180. lin. 5.*) you'll find him arguing most demonstratively from that Topick, in these words: *Cum itaq; quod rerum nostrarum Domini sumus, &c. Since therefore we owe it to the Supreme Powers, that we possess, and are Masters of those things, which are our own; that we live safe from Rapine and Murder, nay, that we live at all, aequissima res est, ut pro tot, &c. it is the most equal and just thing in the World, that for so many, and so great Benefits, we should re-turn something to them.* And he concludes that eighteenth Section with these remarkable words: *Et profecto perversissimae mentis est, sub illius dominationis patrocinio velle vivere, cui parere nolis: & cujus pro-tectione gaudeas, ejus imperium detractare. And therefore it is the part of a most perverse mind to desire to live under the patronage of his Gov-ernment, whom you will not obey, and to detract from that Government, by which you enjoy protection.*

C. This Argument (I confess) is far more forcible upon us under our present circumstances, than ever it was, or indeed can be sup-posed to be. Were not our Laws, Liberties, Properties, nay our Reli-gion itself, apparently invaded by the late *Dispensing Power?* Did they not thereby aim at both our *Universities,* the very Fountains of

Religion and Learning? Were not our *Bishops* sent to the *Tower,* for keeping a good Conscience, and standing firm to the Laws of the Nation, and tried as the highest Criminals, only for doing their Duty as the best of Men? Were not all the honest Nobility, Gentry and Clergy of the *Church of England* struck at at once, who would not comply with their devices for ruining our Church and Nation? Nay, had not his present Majesty so freely and generously, with so much hazard, charge and trouble to himself, come in to our aid, it had been a great question long before this time, whether we should have had any Law, but that of the Sword; or any Religion, but that of *Popish Superstition and Idolatry;* or lastly, any Arguments to have inlightened our understandings, but those of Fire and Faggot, or the illuminations of Dragoons, those tender-hearted *booted-Apostles,* sent by the *Jesuits* to convert us, by beggering and destroying both us and our Families?

W. You see then, what great reason there was out of meer gratitude, to offer the Crown to him, who had so highly obliged us, and so apparently preserved us.

C. Yes, (Sir) and to keep it upon his head, by our due obedience to him, since the publick safety doth exact it from us. For what can we expect, but utter destruction, should things (by our disobedience to the present Government) be returned again into the former course, (*i.e.*) into their hands, whose very Religion binds them in the strictest obligations that can be to destroy us?

W. Now (Sir) you have brought me to the next reason that Bishop *Sanderson* urgeth, which he calls *tertia parendi necessitas,* &c. ibid. Sect. 19. *the third necessity of obeying the present power, by what right soever it is obtained; which* (he saith) *ariseth from hence, because no man is born for himself alone, but for the publick good of human kind;* from whence also he tells us *the manner and end of our obedience may be determined,* viz. *from the end and design of Civil Government.*

C. And in what doth he place the end of Civil Government?

W. His words are these *Civilis regiminis finis, &c. est humanae societatis salus, & tranquillitas,* ibid. p. 181. *The end of Civil Government, and of that obedience which is due to it, is the safety and tranquility of Mankind.*

C. So that whatsoever is necessary to the *safety of Mankind,* he saith we are bound *in conscience* to do, in obedience to any one, that hath the *Supreme Power in fact.*

W. Yes, Sir, you speak his full sence, and very near his very words; nay, in the same place, he reckons up three things in which we are particularly obliged to obey the present Powers, because they are absolutely necessary to the publick good.

C. I pray you, (Sir) what are they?

W. (1.) *Defensio Patriae, The defence of our Countrey against foreign Enemies:* and I think I may add against Seditions at home.

(2.) *Administratio Juris. The Execution of Laws, by which Rewards and Punishments are duly administered, as by Law established.* And these, Sir, you know are particularly your province: so that you cannot but see yourself bound in conscience to keep your *Commissions* both of the *Peace and Militia.*

(3.) *Commercii cura. The Preservation and Encouragement of Trade. For in these three things the welfare of Mankind doth so much consist, that without them it will be impossible but that all things must run to ruin, and all places be filled with Frauds, Injuries, Rapines, and Murders.*

C. But (as I remember, Sir), he hath one limitation at the end of this discourse, which seems to contradict all that he hath said before of this matter, *viz. de conscient. praelect. 5. p. 183. l. 2.*

W. It is this I believe, *Proinde Regni invasori sic praestandum est obsequium, ut fidelitas legitimi haeredi debita nulla tenius violetur, nec aliquid fiat in juris sui praejudicium. Moreover, Obedience is so to be paid to the Invader of a Kingdom, so as the Allegiance due to the lawful Heir be no way violated, nor any thing done to the prejudice of his Right.*

C. Yes, Sir, those are the very words: but (as it follows *Sect. 21. ibid.*) *how can this be done? For that which is pleasing to the Invader of a Kingdom, how can it but be most displeasing to the lawful Prince?*

W. This indeed appears a very forcible objection; but he hath (in the very same page) given so full and clear an answer to it, that it may pass for the fourth and last, and (as I think) the strongest reason for our Obedience to any Person whatsoever (even during the very life of the right Heir) that is in possession of the Crown.

C. This I imagine is the main difficulty, and therefore would be very glad to see it fully answered.

W. His words are these, *Respondeo rite subductis rationibus, non esse cur putemus legitimo principi sed extorri ingratum,* &c.

C. If the Quotation be long, I pray you, Sir, read it in *English,* for I know where to find it (*viz. pag. 183. l. 12. ibid.*) and so may if there be any occasion, compare the Translation with the Original.

W. Well, Sir, because you desire it, I shall hereafter always observe this method in discoursing with you.

C. Sir, you will extremely oblige me therein.

W. The Translation follows: *I answer, all things rightly considered, there is no reason to think that our Obedience to an unjust Possessor of the Crown, in the manner, and for the ends aforesaid, should be at all displeasing to the lawful Prince, though in banishment? but rather it is to be presumed, that our lawful Prince will consent to it, that Allegiance ought to be so paid to an Invader, since it is not to be thought so much for the advantage of him that unjustly hath the power, as of the whole Community; the safety of which, is far more the interest of the Right Heir, than of him who hath the Possession without Right.*

C. So one would rationally conclude.

W. Especially if we consider that instance of the two *Harlots,* who contended before *Solomon, 1 Kings 3. 26.* for the true Mother's Affections were so great towards her Child, that rather than it should be hurt, she condescended to part with her Right in it to the false Mother.

C. That very Example, (as I remember) the *Bishop* makes use of.

W. Yes Sir, and from thence seems to argue, *That the true Father of his Country,* cannot but have so much affection for it, that rather than it should be Destroyed, or his Subjects, (which may be rightly deemed his Children) should be Murthered, we cannot but think he will so far receed from his right at present, as to consent, nay, to desire, *that for their safety, they should rather modestly accommodate themselves to the present Affairs; than that by their unseasonable Resistance, they should bring upon themselves certain Destruction.*

C. Or if he have not such concern for them, I think we may conclude him to be a *very unnatural Father,* and not fit to exercise his *Paternal Power.*

W. Nay, I think, from hence, we may conclude that he gives *his tacit consent* for our Obedience to the present Governours, or else that he himself is not *compos mentis,* and so his consent is neither to be required nor regarded. But perhaps you have something to except against *the Lawfulness of the matter of the Oath* in Question.

C. I find nothing, at present against *the matter of the Oath in itself considered,* but many things that may render it *unlawful to me,* though it be never so *lawful in itself.*

W. This, I remember, is the second Objection against it. If you please to tell me what it is that you think may make it unlawful to you, I shall endeavour to answer as well as I can.

C. The first thing is this, that none of those Reasons you have given for Allegiance, do reach me in my Station, and therefore I am bound to decline such an Oath, and yet still to live quietly and peaceably under the Government.

W. But why are you hence bound to decline the Oath?

C. Because Bishop *Sanderson* saith, *Debere hominem pium,* &c.

That a Man of true Courage and Religion, ought as much as lies in him,
altogether to forbear taking all Oaths that are imposed by him that hath
not a lawful Authority. De Juram. oblig. pag. 97. line 16.

W. As to the Authority enjoining the Oath, we may have an occasion hereafter to discourse of it. But how if all those Reasons do most
fully concern you, and every honest Gentleman that I urged before,
will you not then conclude yourself bound in Conscience to take this
Oath.

C. But how can this be? For are there not Men enough that may
serve the King better than myself? or at least as well? why then doth
Gratitude to him, or the Concern for my private, or for the publick
Good, oblige me to take any other Office upon me, when both may
be better served without it? And may not I continue in a private Station without taking these Oaths, and provide well enough for myself
and my Family?

W. Consider (I beseech you, Sir) if every honest Gentleman in
England should argue as you do, and so quit all publick Employments
because they will not take the Oaths, how excellently would our
Church and *Nation* be governed, how securely would honest men be
protected, and how abundantly would the publick Safety be secured
by those that would be left in Office? *viz. By Men of neither Sence nor*
Honesty.

C. But why must every one argue so because I do?

W. May not every other man deduce the same Conclusion from
the same Premises, as well as you? Neither would you find yourself
and Family in a much better condition than the Community: For if
you should at this time of the day quit your publick station, and
refuse the Oaths, would you not thereby expose yourself to be looked
upon as a person disaffected to the present Government, and so be
exposed to the Anger of the Governors, and the Rigor of the Laws?

C. What Law, I pray, Sir? There is no Law can hurt me for refusing the Oath, as long as I keep myself in a private Station, and take no publick Office upon me.

W. This is the very same Mistake that I myself was liable to, till I took the pains to examine the *Statute-Book,* which hath convinced me of the contrary.

C. Let me beg the Favour (Sir) to shew me any *Statute* that compels every private person to take the Oath of *Allegiance.*

W. 'Tis very strange you should forget it. I pray you, Sir, look into the seventh year of King *James, cap. 6. Sect. 26. pag. 1046. Keeble's* Edition; where it is Enacted, *That it shall be lawful to and for any two Justices of the Peace (whereof one of the* Quorum) *to require any person or persons of the Age of Eighteen years, or above (under the degree of a Baron or Baroness) to take the said Oath.*

C. What Oath, I pray, Sir.

W. The very Title of the Act tells you, it is the *Oath of Allegiance,* and the Preface to it, refers to the third year of King *James, c. 4.* where the same Oath is particularly expressed and enacted.

C. But what if I will not take it when required by two Justices of the Peace?

W. Then you must take what follows, in the said Act of the 7th of King *James* viz. *That if any Person shall refuse the said Oaths, being of the Age of eighteen years or above, when it shall be duly tendered, then the persons authorized, shall or may commit the same Offender to the common Goal, there to remain without Bail or Mainprize, until the next Assizes, or General Quarter-Sessions.*

C. What of all this? An honest man may enjoy Quiet even in a Gaol, and his Family may be taken care of by some faithful friend.

W. But a man would not much care to chuse a Gaol to be at quiet in, when he may honestly be at liberty by taking the Oath.

C. No certainly unless he be mad; but however, if this be the worst of the Business, it is tolerable enough.

W. This is bad enough, but what is behind is ten times worse; for the same Act saith, That at the next Assizes or Quarter-Session, *If the said person of 18 years or above, shall refuse to take the said Oath, being there tendered to him by the Bench, every person so refusing shall incur the danger of PRAEMUNIRE mentioned in the Statute of 16 Richard 2.*

C. My Memory (I perceive, Sir) very much fails me: Wherefore I pray inform me what it saith concerning a *Praemunire.*

W. The Statute is in the 16th of *Richard 2. cap. 5.* The Words you have at the end of the second Section, *viz. They shall be put out of the King's Protection; and their Lands and Tenements, Goods and Chattels forfeit to our Lord the King; and that they be attached by their Bodies, if they may be found, or that Process be made against them by PRAEMU-NIRE FACIAS.*

C. This is a fine *Praemunire* indeed, to expose my Family to utter ruine; and myself not only to *perpetual Imprisonment,* but to have my Throat cut by every Villain, who may do it without any fear of punishment for it. But surely no Justice of the Peace can be so cruel to execute this Law upon me, whilst I may live peaceably, only because I cannot take the Oath.

W. If we of the *Church of England* refuse Offices on the account of the Oaths, we may be sure, that our Enemies will accept them; and surely it is but *ill trusting to our Enemies' kindness.*

C. Especially to such who watch all advantage against us, to be revenged of us for our late prosecution against them; and have been always ready to cry up *all Church of England Men* for *Papists in Masquerade,* and by consequence, for the worst Enemies to the present Governors and Government.

W. But they know well enough that the Principles of the *Church of England* teach us *Passive Obedience* and *Non resistance.* So that though we cannot pretend to make a King, yet we can and must obey him when he hath the Royal Authority, if we act as our Religion teacheth us; and can have no pretence to rebel against him: And how-ever our late Practice seem to have varied from this Rule, yet the Doctrine of our Church stands firm and unshaken, and is still the safest Rule for us to walk by.

C. However I know *none are so blind as they that will not see.* So that there is but little reason to expect any favour from them.

W. The best way then to prevent their power and malice is to take the Oath, since your own Casuist warrants it to be lawful; for Bishop *Sanderson* tells us (*de Juram.* pag. 97. l. 16) of Oaths that are only un-lawful, for want of due Authority. *At si praeter imperium vis, insuper adhibeatur,* &c. *But if besides the Command, Force be added, so that there be no refusing without the greatest danger, it is to be determined, that a truly Religious Man may admit of such an Oath.*

C. Aye, but is there not something follows that makes much more against it under our present Circumstances? *viz.* dummodo nihil contineat, *&c. If so, that the Oath contain no matter in itself Unlawful, or contrary to the publick Laws, or derogatory to the right of any third person; otherwise (I pray you observe carefully* what followeth*) he ought to refuse to take the Oath, even with the utmost danger of his Life.*

W. But how doth this make against the Oath in question? since I have (I think) already proved that there is nothing in the matter of it that is *in itself Unlawful;* nor anything *contrary to the Laws of the Land,* nay, that the Laws do particularly take care to indemnify all persons that pay true *Allegiance to the King for the time being,* and that all persons *above* 18 *years of Age,* are bound by Law, *under pain of a Praemunire,* not to refuse to take *the Oath of Allegiance.*

C. Yes Sir, I cannot deny but you have proved it: But the greatest difficulty is still behind, *viz.* The third condition of an Oath, without which we ought to refuse it, even with our utmost peril. For how can anything be more contrary to the right of a third person (who is so well known, that he need not be named) than this new Oath is to his right?

W. I shall waive all that discourse, that is common against *King James II.* by which some would perswade us he hath forfeited his right to our Allegiance; and all that might be said for the right of *our present King and Queen;* because I apprehend the *Titles to Crowns* are things so far above Subjects, that it is unbecoming them to make them their matter of Dispute; and because (of all things) I hate to speak anything of any *Crowned-Head* to his disparagement.

C. I am much of the Opinion; for I think *Titles to Crowns* are too high removed from us; and that *Crowned Heads* ought to be more Sacred than to have any Dirt thrown upon them. But how then will you give me any Satisfaction about this Matter?

W. Very easily, Sir, if I am not mistaken; for Sir, if you well consider the Matter of this Oath, *there is no such thing as the right of any person to our Obedience, either named or implied in it.* For we only swear *Obedience to the King and Queen,* without the least word concerning any person's right to be obeyed by us. So that the Matter of the Oath doth *no ways derogate from the right of any third person;* for it no ways medleth with it.

C. Sir, I do not well understand this Discourse; wherefore I pray be so kind as thoroughly to inform me in it.

W. If you will please to look into the former Oath of Allegiance made in King *James* the First his time, and used ever since, till this was made, you will see so apparent a difference as will be sufficient for your full Information in this Matter.

C. That I will do with all my heart, it is in *(3 Jacobi cap. 3. sec. 15.) viz. I do truly and sincerely acknowledge, profess, testifie, and declare in my Conscience before God and the World, that our Sovereign Lord King* James *is Lawful and Rightful King of this Realm, and all other his Majestie's Dominion, and Countries.*

W. Hold, Sir, you have read far enough. For is there any such thing in this new Oath, *as Declaring King* William *and Queen* Mary *to be Lawful and Rightful King and Queen.*

C. No Sir, there is not.

W. But there is in the former, is there not?

C. Oh! Now I see the difference very plain. In this Oath we only swear Obedience *to William and Mary King and Queen in Fact*; but in the former Oath of Allegiance we swore *to the Right of our Kings.* So that this last Oath (those Words *Lawful* and *Rightful*) being left out, doth no ways intermeddle with the Right of any King whatsoever.

W. You have hit right on it, Sir; so that we are hereby freed from swearing, to that which might not be so apparently true to all persons that are bound to take the Oath, and from medling with the Right and Title of our Supream Governors in swearing Obedience to them.

C. Yes Sir, I see we are freed thereby from great Snares that might have quite entangled the Consciences of all honest Men.

W. We owe it, as I have heard, to the Wisdom and Goodness of the *House of Lords,* and more especially to the *Earl of* Nottingham *and Earl* of *Danby*[6] whose Names ought always to be mentioned with Honour and Gratitude, for so signal a Service to our Church and Nation.

C. I fully concur with you in it, but yet do not think that this sufficiently answers the Objection I proposed. For was not our *Allegience* due to another *King by right,* and do we not swear to pay it to the present *King in Fact?* And is not this then an Unlawful Oath? Hear (I pray you) what Bishop *Sanderson* saith in this case *(De Jurament. praelect.4.§5.p.92.) Non licet ei, qui alterius potestati subest,* &c. *It is not lawful for him, that is subject to the Power of another Man, to determine anything of those matters in which he is subject, by an Oath, without the Express, or at least the tacit consent of his Superiour.*

---

6. Daniel Finch, second Earl of Nottingham, and Thomas Osborne, Earl of Danby, both former councillors of Charles II, were instrumental in persuading the Convention to reword the oaths of allegiance and supremacy. It was Danby who, in 1675, failed to get the nonresisting oath imposed on members of Parliament.

W. Read but the same Author (ibid pag. 94. lin. ult.) what a Tacit consent is, and that I think it will in a great measure solve the doubt.

C. I should be very glad to find it so; and therefore will read it in his own Language: *Consensum Tacitum intelligo, cum ex rei aequitate, vel alia probabili causa, verisimiliter praesumi potest Superiorem facto consensurum, vel saltum non contradicturum, si consuleretur.*

W. I pray you mind the words: *By a tacit consent I understand when by the equity of the thing, or by any other probable cause, it may be probably presumed, that the Superiour if he was consulted, would indeed consent, or at least not oppose.*

C. But Sir, can you think, that any King if he was asked, would consent, or not oppose, that his Subjects should swear *Allegiance* to any other Person, whilst he himself is alive, and ought to Reign over them?

W. Truly Sir, I think there is a very *probable cause* to believe it, *viz. The equity of the thing.*

C. I pray Sir, where lies that Equity?

W. It lies in this, that since the King which is supposed *de jure* cannot protect his Subject from utter Ruin and Destruction, for refusing the Oath of Allegience to the *King de facto,* he should give them leave to take it, (and so to preserve themselves) at least so long till he can retrieve his power to protect them.

C. This seems to be but Equity: Yet (methinks) it would be the ready way for a King never to recover his Power again.

W. We have seen the contrary in the Restauration of King *Charles II,* and I am sure, if the Subjects be destroyed for refusing Allegiance to the represent Powers, the King *de Jure,* can never recover his Subjects again.

C. That is certain; but (I cannot but think) the equity you talk of, would be more evident upon the Principles of *an Original Contract,* and the *reciprocation of Protection and Subjection.*

W. No doubt of it, if they were thoroughly proved; but I would argue with you according to your own Principles of the *Church of England.*

C. On my Reputation, Sir; you offer me as fair as I would desire.

W. You know the highest Monarchical-Men that ever were of our Church have founded *the Right of Kings over their Subjects, upon the Right of Parents over their Children.*

C. Yes Sir, but from this Principle I doubt you will scarce prove what you proposed.

W. I'll try Sir, if you please. Suppose then (as among the *Americans* it hath been) that the Government was only that of Families, and that a Father of a Family is forced (though never so unjustly) to flee from his House, and to leave his Children and Servants under the Power of another Person (who by their concurrence) hath forced him away; nay, that they have so far joined with the Invader, as by a Convention chosen out of their own Family, to yield up their Father's Authority to him, and to frame an Oath, which all of that Family should take, or else be put out of the Protection due to them as Members of it. Would it not be very hard, unequitable, and unnatural in the expelled Father (if his Consent was asked) to deny his consent than to submit to such an Oath, and rather to desire that they should be destroyed, and his Family utterly extinguished, than that they should take it?

C. I see no Reason to think otherwise.

W. Well, then (Sir, might they not justly presume of their Father's consent in this case) and so take the Oath?

C. On my Word, Sir, I think so; only I have one exception to make against taking this Oath, which I doubt will be very troublesome to you to satisfie me in. The objection is this, *viz.* in the Words of my old Friend so often before named: *Prior obligatio tollit posteriorem: A former Obligation taketh away the later;* nay, he comes home to our present Case (*de Juram. oblig. pag. 102.*) where he saith, That *a King having sworn that he will govern according to the Laws of the Land; and*

the Subjects having sworn to pay him due Fidelity and Obedience, utriq;
obligatur quod sui est officii fideliter facere: Both of them are bound faith-
fully to perform the duty they have sworn to.

W. But may not the King's male-administration of his Government, or the Subject's Disobedience, cancel this Oath?

C. No, Sir, for so he positively affirms, in the same place, in these
words, *Ita ut, neq; rex solutus est a suo juramento, si subditi debitum ob-*
sequium non praestiterint, nec subdita a suo si rex a justitiae tramite de-
flexerit. So that neither is the King freed from his Oath, though his
Subjects do not obey him as they ought; nor the Subjects from their Oath,
though the King doth not govern them according to justice.

W. But may not some other power dispence with this Oath?

C. In answer to your question, I refer you to the same Book, *prae-*
lect. 7. pag. 197. lin. 21. I pray, Sir, turn to it, and read the words.

W. Nec Papae, nec Senatui, nec ulli Synodo, &c. *Neither the Pope, nor*
the Parliament, nor any Council, nor any Governour Ecclesiastical or
Civil, hath the Power of Dispencing in Promises, Contracts or Oaths; or
of Absolving any one from the obligation he was under before the Dis-
pensation was made.

C. Nay, he further declares, that if such an Oath, as now we discourse about, should be taken, it would be absolutely void in itself; *ex*
irritatione legitimi Superioris, ibid. pag. 202. his words are very remarkable.

W. Therefore, Sir, I will not grudge the pains to read them: *Si quis*
alienae potestati subditus, &c. *If any that is subject to the Authority of*
another person, (as of his Master, his Father, or his Prince), shall either on
his own accord, or being moved by force and fear, take any Oath to which
he believes his Master, his Father, or his Prince, if he was present, would
not consent, he is bound not to keep that Oath, it being contrary to his
Duty, for the obligation of that Oath is dissolved by the contrary com-
mand of his lawful Superior.

C. Is not this clearly proved from the Sacred Scripture itself? See *Numbers, cap. 30. v. 3, 4, 5 & 6, 7, 8 & 9.*

W. The example there is very plain, *viz.* That if *a woman vow a vow, and her father, or her husband, disallow her, the vow which she vowed, and the oath which she uttereth with her lips, wherewith she bound her Soul, shall be of none effect.*

C. And the reason of the thing is no less apparent; for none can be *sui juris, i.e.* free to dispose of himself, in such matters wherein he is bound to another person, either by oath or promise, or natural subjection. Now when we are under an obligation of a former oath to our former King, which we cannot be freed from by his male-administration, which no power on Earth can dispence withal, and which makes void any subsequent oaths to any other King, Is it not a great affront to, and mockery of the Divine Majesty, to call God to witness, that I will perform an oath which I know is not in my power to perform; and to appeal to God to punish me if I do not keep my oath, when I know before I take it, that the oath is void in itself, and that by the same obligation I am bound not to keep it?

W. But suppose I have never taken the former Oath of Allegiance, how doth your objection concern me?

C. If you have taken the oath to any of King *James* his Predecessors, you must acknowledge yourself as much bound to him, as though you had taken it to himself; for so saith our most judicious Casuist *(de Jurament. pag. 105. lin. 6.) Si quis subditus,* &c. *If any Subject or Soldier, takes an Oath of Fidelity to his King, or to the General of an Army, he shall be thought to have taken that Oath, even to the Successors in the same Dignity:* Nay, the very words of the former Oath of Allegiance, do expressly bind us *to bear true Faith and Obedience to King James the First, his Heirs, and lawful Successors.*

W. But how if I have not taken it at all?

C. Yet still you cannot but be obliged by your natural subjection, being his natural born subject. Nay, the Laws of our Nation do oblige every subject from eighteen years old and upwards, (as is already proved from that Statute, *7 Jacobi cap. 6. Sect. 26.) under pain of being put out of the protection of the King's Laws, to take the Oath of Allegiance, when it shall be tendered* (according to Law) *by two Justices of the Peace, &c.* So that your having enjoyed the protection of the Laws, supposeth you have taken it, or at least that you was willing to take it; and by consequence, that you be as much obliged by that Oath, as though you had actually sworn it.

W. I will not put you to prove that consequence, for I think this evasion of your Objection signifies little; the greatest part of our Nobility, Gentry, and Clergy, having actually taken it.

C. Well then, why are they not still bound by it? And how come they to be loosed from the obligation of it?

W. You have asked me a question about this matter; I pray, Sir, give me leave to ask you one more, *viz.* How if it can be proved, that the Oath to the former King is (in our present circumstances) utterly void, and the obligation of it quite dissolved?

C. Then I think the objection would be fully answered.

W. First then I shall endeavour to prove, that the former Oath, during our present circumstances, is utterly void; and I need, I think, use no other Argument but only this, That the matter of the former Oath is (under our present circumstances) utterly impossible for us to perform. To this purpose, see Bishop *Sanderson, (de Juram praelect. 2. Sect. 12. p. 45.)* where he lays down this Maxim, *Rei impossibilis nulla est obligatio; there is no obligation to an impossible thing.* And he saith, *(ibid. lin. 7.) This is so evident in itself, that it is the very Rule of all Law, and needs no proof.*

C. I cannot but consent to the truth of this Maxim; but why is it impossible for me to perform Allegiance to King *James?*

W. Can a man serve two Masters? Is not all the power of the Nation actually in the hands of the present King? Have I not already proved that I am bound by the ties of Gratitude, of Duty to myself, my Family, and the Publick, to submit to the present Power? so that it is impossible both *impossibilitate facti, & juris;* for under our present circumstances, how can I know the commands of the former King? Or if I did know them, how can I obey them, at least, without an apparent hazard of my own life, and of the ruine of my Family, if not of the Nation? And you know the rule is, *id tantum possumus, quod jure possumus: That only we may do, which we can do by right; i.e.* which no ways contradicts any part of our duty.

C. But if I cannot act, I may suffer for him; that is not impossible.

W. Yes, you may so, Sir, if you please; but *cui bono,* to what purpose? What benefit would your present suffering be to the former King? Would he be anything the better for the ruine of his friends, and those who would pretend to be his subjects?

C. However if I cannot act for him, it is not impossible but I may keep myself from acting against him. If I cannot pay him Allegiance, can I not refrain from swearing Allegiance to his enemy?

W. Yes Sir, there is no impossibility in the thing (it may doubtless be done) but there is an impossibility with the respect to the Law.

C. I pray you Sir, make me understand that.

W. It is so plain in itself, that I wonder you should not apprehend it at the first hearing, *viz.* The thing itself, *i.e.* my refusing to take the Oath of Allegiance to King *William, &c.* is not impossible for me; but since I cannot refuse the Oath without ruining myself and my family (by incurring a *Praemunire* according to the Statute before mentioned, *7 Jacobi cap. 6.*) it becomes impossible for me, according to that duty which I owe both to myself, Relations and Dependants.

C. Still I need not take it, till the utmost extremity, *i.e.* till I have suffered Imprisonment; and that the Oath be tendered to me in open Court, either at Assizes or Sessions.

W. Since this delay would give a scandal and offence to the present Governours, especially in us of the *Church of England;* and probably, exasperate them against us and our Religion, since evil men, enemies to the Government, both of *Kings and Bishops,* might thereby get into our Offices of Power and Trust, both in Church and State. Nay, since (as I have already proved) there is nothing in the matter of the Oath, that is unlawful, but rather our duty in the present circumstances: And lastly, since we have no great reason to presume of the consent of the person concerned, *viz.* Of the former King, such a delay would be impossible for us, without being wanting to our Duty which we owe to our Nation; nay, to our Church, and to our most Sacred Religion. I shall proceed to another argument or two, to prove what I undertook, *viz.* that *the former Oath of Allegiance is actually void, and the obligation utterly ceased, during the present circumstances of Affairs.*

C. Sir, you will infinitely oblige me by it.

W. The second Argument I shall propose is this, *viz. The conditions that are necessarily understood in every Oath.*

C. I pray you, Sir, what are they?

W. The old Friend, our incomparable *Casuist,* will tell you Sir, *(de Juram praelect. 6. Sec. 12. pag. 177.) Si conditio nulla sit expressa in juramento,* &c. *If there be no condition expressed in the Oath, then all the conditions or exceptions ought to be understood, which by right, or common use, are implied in it,* viz. *Quoad potero, & licebit; rebus in eodem statu manentibus,* &c. namely *as far as I can, and it is lawful for me; things remaining in the same state,* and such like.

C. Very good; but how do you argue from thence?

W. I argue thus: In the *Oath of Allegiance* there is no condition expressed, therfore all those conditions and exceptions are understood before-mentioned; and no man can be bound by it beyond those necessary exceptions: So that when the state of affairs is so changed (as now it is) that it is not in my power, nor is it consistent with my duty to myself, my Family, and the Commonwealth, to keep my Oath which I made to King *James*, then I cannot be bound by my Oath to do it; but the obligation of that Oath must cease during the time of such an alteration.

C. The reason for that, good Sir.

W. My reason Sir, is, *No man can do more than he can do;* nor can a man be bound to do anything more, by any Oath or Obligation whatsoever.

C. But Sir, if you would please to be serious, I believe you can give me some parallel instance, that might more fully clear this point to me.

W. Suppose then, that I had sworn to yourself, that upon this day month, I will give you a Visit, and receive your Commands, at your own House, and that at that time I should be locked up Prisoner, so that I could not get out, unless I would venture to set the House on Fire, or to jump out of the Windows; do you think that I am bound by my Oath to hazard burning myself, or breaking my Neck to come to you? Or had you any such intention to bind me to such apparent dangers by Oath?

C. No, surely, God forbid.

W. Then I think I need say no more to enforce this argument; but (if you please) will go on to the next.

C. With all my Soul, Sir, you cannot oblige me more.

W. The third and last Argument is this, *viz.* that *the matter of the Oath is ceased, and therefore the Obligation must cease also.*

C. I pray, Sir, explain this a little to me, for my old eyes and understanding need a little more light to discern things clearly, than perhaps formerly they did.

W. Bishop *Sanderson* hath done it to my hand (*de Juram praelect. 7. Sect. 7. pag. 202.*) in these words, *fit Solutio juramenti obligationis ex Cessatione Materiae; aut per mutationem aliquam notabilem circa causam juramenti principalem: The obligation of an Oath is dissolved by the cessation of the matter of it; or by any remarkable change, about the principal cause of the Oath.*

C. Still, methinks, I am a little in the dark about it.

W. To enlighten you a little, I pray, Sir, answer me some few questions; as first, What is the matter of our Oath to King *James* the Second?

C. The matter of it is *to own him for our King, and to pay him Obedience as our King.*

W. Secondly, What was the principal cause of this Oath to him?

C. Because he was really our King both *in fact*, as well as *in right*.

W. Thirdly, Is there not now an alteration in the matter, so that we cannot pay our obedience to him with any safety to ourselves? And is there not a greater change in the principal cause of our Oath to him, *viz.* so that now he is not our King *in actu?*

C. Though he be not our King *in fact*, yet he may be in *right;* and therefore we are no less bound to obedience to him now than before.

W. Supposing he be so yet I may deny the consequence; even upon the Authority of the example given us in the same place (*ibid. pag. 203.*) by the same most profound Casuist so often named.

C. I pray Sir, what is that example?

W. It is this, *Si quis miles juret obsequium belli imperatori*, &c. *If any Souldier swears Obedience to the General of his Army, the War being ended, and he no longer General, the Souldier is no longer bound to obey him.*

C. I do not apprehend this reacheth our case.

W. But suppose that the General should out of fear leave his Souldiers, and that the Souldiers (though never so unjustly having frighted him away by their mutinies against him, or universal desertion from him) should choose another General; or that any other person should by force, or Conquest, or Consent, in his absence, be actually invested with the General's Office, Is not the Army (during this change) discharged from their Oath to their former General; and rather than suffer as Mutineers for refusing it, may they not lawfully swear Obedience to their present General in fact, though the other hath the right of the Office?

C. I have nothing at present to say against it; for it appears to me very reasonable, that when the root of an obligation is taken away, the obligation itself that springs from that root, must necessarily be taken away with it.

W. Now the root of an Army's obligation to obey their General, or of a Nation's Allegiance to their Prince, can be nothing else but his being in an actual capacity to command and protect them; whereso-ever therefore this actual capacity is changed (during the time the change remains) there the obligation to obedience must be changed also.

C. If so, then the former Oath *to King James,* doth no ways hinder me from taking this *to King William and Queen Mary.*

W. What else have you to except against this new Oath?

C. The next objection I have against it is this: That *this new Oath makes him that takes it, to call God to witness to a lie;* and what can be a greater, and more damnable sin than this? Is it not like the sin of *Ananias and Saphira, viz.* the *lying to the holy Ghost,* and *tempting the holy Spirit of God?*

W. This is (on my word) a most heavy charge, if it can be made out against it.

C. Why should you question it, is it not very visible? For do we not by this Oath own *William and Mary* to be *King and Queen,* and promise them obedience as such, whereas all the World knows that the Regal Authority is pretended to be another's Right?

W. No more haste than good speed, I beseech you, Sir; I believe a great part of the World is of another opinion. And supposing a man had a mind to assert King *William's* right of Conquest, possibly it would not be so easie a matter to refuse it.

C. No, Sir, it may be so, because it is not safe to dispute it.

W. Well, because I will not dispute the Titles of Kings, I will suppose the Right to the Crown to be in *King James;* and yet (pardon me if I say) I think your objection very easily answered.

C. I am so far from being angry at it, that I am very glad to hear you say so; and should be much more rejoiced to see it proved.

W. Do we assert anything in this Oath, to assert *King William* and *Queen Mary's* Right to the Crown?

C. Do we not assert them to be *King and Queen?*

W. But we do not swear to them *as lawful and rightful* King and Queen. Are not those two words *lawful and rightful* left out of the Oath, as it were on purpose to silence such objections as these are?

C. I wish I could see how this objection is answered by it.

W. May there not be one King in possession, though another King hath the Right? And is it a lie to own him King who is in possession?

C. I confess, I do not well understand it to be otherwise.

W. I will put you a parallel case by which it may be more apparent to you. Suppose a Tenant swears to his Landlord, that he will pay him his Rent, and own him as his Landlord; afterwards another gets the possession of the Estate (whether by right or wrong, that is not the question) and makes him swear to be a Tenant to him, and indemnifies him by Law for it; may he not take the latter Oath without telling a lie in swearing it?

C. No surely, if the Tenant knows that the first Landlord is still his right, and lawful Landlord.

W. Sir, you do not consider, that the Tenant doth not meddle with the right of the 2d Landlord's at all in his Oath, but leaves that to be determined by the higher powers; only he swears to turn Tenant to his New Landlord, and pay him his Rent so long as he is in possession of the Estate, and can indemnifie him by Law for so doing. How is this contradictory to his former Landlord's right; or how doth this give the lie to his own Conscience?

C. In that he knows in his Conscience, the former is in right, and according to justice, his true Landlord.

W. Why? hath he Sworn anything against the right and title of his former Landlord? but if he cannot defend his Tenant but that his family must be ruined if he does not own him, who hath the present possession, and pay him the Rent, who can blame him for promising to do so?

C. I pray Sir apply this to the present case.

W. I cannot but think it applies as readily as can be. For by my former Oath I own King *James* to be my King, and swear obedience to him; King *William* gets the possession of the Regal power, and commands me to swear Allegiance to him, the Laws of the Nation indemnifie me in doing it, and on the other hand I may be ruined if I do it not, and that by Law too; against which ruined my former King, though he may have the right, hath no power to preserve me. May I not then (during these circumstances) leave the dispute between the two Kings to God Almighty's determination, and prevent my own and my family's ruine by swearing Allegiance where I can do it with safety? nay, how do I lie by swearing him to be King in possession, when he really is so, though another may be King by right?

C. Oh! now I think I fully apprehend the thing: For as the Tenant, by taking such an Oath to the Landlord in possession, and paying his Rent to him, doth not swear or own that he hath a right to the Estate; so the Subject, by swearing or paying Allegiance to the King for the time being, doth not thereby swear or own his right to the Crown.

W. And to carry the parallel a little further, and more home to your present objection, As the Tenant by swearing to pay his Rent to his new Landlord, though he should know in his conscience that it is his former Landlord's right, yet doth not swear to anything that is false:

So the Subject that swears to pay Allegiance to King *William* &c. though he knows in his conscience the Allegiance is due to a former King, yet doth no ways lie against his conscience in so doing.

C. Give me one good reason for that, and I shall be satisfied fully as to this objection.

W. The reason is this; because neither the Tenant's nor the Subject's Oath doth any ways concern the right of the Landlord or the King: Nor is the Tenant, or the Subject in that case any ways a competent Judge about the matter of the right of a Prince or Landlord, or any ways required by either of their Oaths to own or determine anything about it.

C. After all the pains you have taken to satisfie my Conscience about this Oath, if I should still be in doubt about the matter, it would be thereby utterly unlawful for me to take it; for my old friend tells me (de Jurament. praelect. 7 sect. 14. p. 229.) Juramentum oblatum reluctante, vel dubitante conscientia non est suscipiendum; *An Oath imposed is not to be taken with a doubting or relucting Conscience.*

W. Before I return any answer to this objection, it will be very convenient to explain what is meant by a *doubting* and *relucting Conscience.*

C. Well Sir, first, then I pray tell me what is a doubting Conscience?

W. By a *doubting Conscience* I understand, when there appears no more reason on the one side of the question than on the other, to the Conscience of him that considers it: As to give you a plain similitude of a pair of Scales, which are so equally poized that they are at a full stand, so that the least grain of weight added to either Scale will weigh down the other: So when the Conscience is in such a perfect *aequilibreum* or suspence, that the least grain of Reason being added on either side of the question, will determine the matter, then it may be properly called a *doubting Conscience.*

C. Secondly What is a relucting Conscience?

W. By a *relucting Conscience* I understand, when the Conscience, though it doth not see any reason at present, yet fears or apprehends that there may be some reason which afterwards may appear, that may render the thing Unlawful concerning which it doubts at present.

C. Is it not Unlawful in either of these cases for me to act, whilest my Conscience hath any doubt about the matter, or any reluctancy against it?

W. First Sir, let me beg the favour of you to give me your reasons why you think so; and then I shall be better able to judge whether they reach the present question betwixt us.

C. The Bishop in the same place gives you two most evident reasons, the first is this; because *that which is not of Faith is sin* which is grounded on *Rom.* 14.23. The second reason is grounded on *Jeremy* 4.2. where we are commanded *to swear in judgement.* Now he that swears to anything concerning which he hath any doubt or reluctancy in his mind, acts contrary to his belief, and to his own judgement; and so is condemned by his own conscience.

W. I do not think that the Bishop laid down this rule for all cases, for I think he must be apparently mistaken if he did, for his Texts of Scripture will no ways bear him out in it.

C. Consider but the words of *St. Paul,* and surely nothing will be more evident than such a deduction from them, Rom. 14.22 & 23. *Thou hast faith, have it to thy self: Blessed is the man that condemneth not himself, in that which he alloweth. For he that doubteth is damned if he eats. For whatsoever is not of faith is sin.*

W. I have two reasons against any such universal consequence being deduced from these words, *viz.* first, *from the original Word,* that is rendered he *that doubts,* which I think is not rightly translated: Secondly, from the coherence of the words compared with the whole Chapter, supposing our translation to be herein authentick.

C. What is the exception to the translation?

W. The word in the Original is ὁ διακρινόμενος, which properly signifies quite contrary to *doubting,* viz. *thorowly-discerning,* and so it is rendered by the same Apostle in a place, which cannot possibly be otherwise interpreted, *viz.* I Corinth. 11.29. where giving the reason why he that receiveth the Sacrament unworthily *eateth and drinketh damnation to himself;* the cause he saith is this, μὴ διακρίνων τὸ σῶμα τοῦ κυρίου, *not discerning the Lord's body,* (i.e.) because he doth not *thorowly discern* the difference betwixt the Consecrated Bread and Wine at the *Lord's Table,* and common Bread and Wine at his *own Table;* but useth them both alike; for this is the grand fault that he chargeth them withal, v. 21. *that one of them was an hungry, and another was drunk* even at the Lord's Table; which they could not have been so wicked to have been guilty of, if they had thorowly understood what they were about.

C. If the word be so rendered, I must needs own there is no such consequence about a doubting conscience to be deduced from them. For then the Apostle's words are these, *He that is thoroughly convinced in his mind concerning eating, that it is not lawful for him to eat, is condemned* (for so the word κατακέκριται ought to be rendered) *if he doth eat. For whatsoever is done contrary to the clear conviction of a man's conscience is a great sin in him.*

W. But supposing the word be properly here rendered, *He that doubts,* yet the scope and coherence of the words compared with the whole Chapter, will not bear any such universal deduction as you urge from them.

C. That I would gladly be convinced of.

W. The Apostle in this Chapter speaks of nothing else but *means,* v. 2 & 3. and *days* and times, v. 5. as appears more fully by that general rule he lays down, *v. 14. I know and am perswaded, through the Lord Jesus, that there is nothing unclean in itself; but unto him that judgeth anything to be unclean to him it is unclean;* and urgeth, that therefore in these matters we should not judge one another, nor despise any one for them; but that *everyone should be fully perswaded in his own mind.* The reason of which discourse is apparent, *viz.* because some of the *Jewish* Converts to *Christianity,* were very strict in the observation of the Ceremonial Law concerning meats, and times; and others of the *Gentiles,* who believed the Ceremonial Law of the *Jews* to be abolished, were as strict and severe against any such observation, and did censure and contemn one another about these matters, concerning which there was no Law then in force, the *Jewish* Ceremonies being quite abrogated. The *Apostle* therefore concludes, *Thou hast faith have it to thyself, i.e.* thou rightly understandeth thy own liberty in these indifferent things, make use of this liberty so as not to censure, despise, or scandalize those that do not understand them so well as thyself: *Blessed is he that condemneth not himself in that which he alloweth.* Thou art in this happy that thou actest not in such things contrary to thy Conscience; and the reason of this happiness he gives in the following verse, *For he that doubteth is condemned if he eat.* For in these indifferent things, concerning which you have no command either of God or Man, if you do them with a doubting conscience, you shall be condemned in so doing, for that you might have let them alone; the reason of which he gives in this following Maxim, *For whatsoever is not of faith is sin; i.e.* for whatsoever things of this sort (which you have a liberty to do, or not to do) are done, whilst any doubt remains concerning them, are sins.

C. So that this Maxim *whatsoever is of Faith is Sin,* is to be understood of indifferent things, and no other.

W. This is evident by the example the Apostle gives, *viz. for he that doubteth is condemned, if he Eat.* For the Eating there, must be understood of the Eating such things as were unclean by the *Jewish Law,* which being abrogated by *Christ,* there was no Law that commanded Christians either to Eat them, or not to eat them. Wherefore a particular Example being given of a general rule, the rule itself must be understood of such things only which are *eiusdem generis* (i.e.) of the same sort with the example, and of no other, *i.e.* only of indifferent things.

C. So that it cannot be understood of things of any other nature, *i.e.* of such things as are either commanded, or forbidden by God, or the Magistrate. For in all such matters doubts and scruples are to be laid aside.

W. The matter then in debate betwixt us *(i.e.) the Oath of Allegiance,* being commanded by the present Authority, and necessary for the publick peace, and not to be omitted without the ruine of myself and Family, cannot be of that sort of things which may be done, or may be left undone; and by consequence ought to over-rule all doubts or reluctancy in me.

C. But will not the other reason urged by the Bishop from *Jerem. 4.2. Thou Shalt Swear, the Lord liveth, in truth, righteousness, and judgement,* reach our present case?

W. No I apprehend not, for all that is meant by that precept is this, Thou shalt Swear *truely, honestly, and seriously.*

C. But how can he that swears to a thing which he doubts of, swear *honestly, and seriously, or according to judgment,* when for all that he knows to the contrary the matter of his Oath may be unlawful?

W. If you remember what I told you a Doubting-Conscience that it is perfectly in an *Aequilibrium;* then the objection returns upon yourself. For why then should he not swear according to his own judgment, when for all that he knows to the contrary, the Oath may not only be Lawful, but necessary for him to take?

C. But supposing his Conscience be *relucting,* so as that he fears there may be something that may appear hereafter to be evil in the thing; what must he do in that case?

W. He may as well fear that something may hereafter appear to prove the thing to be his duty: So that this reluctancy as well as doubtfulness of Conscience (if a man will Act according to sound judgment) neither binds him to do, or not do such an action, about which he is *sui juris* that is wholly at his own disposal: but only to suspend Acting till he may be better satisfied.

C. But supposing the Command of any Authority makes the thing necessary to be done for the publick, or for his private safety, so that he is not *sui juris* in it; how then?

W. Why then, he must lay aside his doubtfulness, and reluctancy, because they ought not to take any place against his duty, whether it be private or publick. So that since I have proved that this Oath is in the matter of it lawful, and that we cannot refuse it without apparent damage to the publick welfare, and *incurring a praemunire,* by which we should destroy ourselves and Families, no doubts nor reluctancies of Conscience ought to hinder us from taking it.

C. This discourse was very necessary to inform me how great an errour it is to plead doubts and scruples, and reluctancies of Conscience, against the Commands of lawful Magistrates, about matters of decency and order, and such like; nay, since I think it hath prevented another objection, which I was about to make against this Oath.

W. I pray you, Sir, what is that?

C. It is this, That *the taking this Oath to King William* is very scandalous to many people, especially in us *Church-of-England-Men.*

W. This I am very sensible of; for there is nothing more common than to hear men talk at this rate. "It is a fine *Church and Religion* that teacheth men to turn their Coats, and to keep to no Principles of Loyalty, which before they so much boasted of. Do you not see what Weather-cocks these Church-men are, that will turn with any Wind that blows? They will swear, or forswear, backwards, or forwards, or any ways for their Interest; 'tis gain is their Godliness, *&c.*"

C. Ay, Sir, I have heard too much of such stuff: For even the *Plough-Jobbers* are apt to turn *Orators* against us; and their Rhetorick will be much more fluent, if we should generally take this new Oath which is so much contrary to the former.

C. Some creatures will *bark and snarl* because it is their nature to do so; but it is below any Wise man to take notice of them.

C. But however, no good Christian should give any just occasion of offence to anyone, for we know that our Saviour pronounceth *a Woe* and a dismal sentence against such *by whom offences come;* and saith, *That it is better for him that he had never been born, &c. Luke 17. 1 & 2.*

W. 'Tis very true, but when I do nothing but my duty, if any take offence at it, 'tis he that makes the scandal, and not I.

C. Yes, Sir, the reason of scandal I am sensible by the former discourse, is much the same with that of doubts, and takes place in no other things but such wherein I am wholly left to my own liberty.

W. Very true, Sir, for this is evident from the same 14th Chapter to the *Romans,* where the Apostle directs them, *v. 15.* not to scandalize their brother, because of such indifferent things as meals or days appointed by the Mosaick Law, which is now abolished; but where the supream Authority of the Nation commands us anything that is not unlawful, as this Oath of Allegiance; we are not to consider the offences that private persons may take at it, but are to take heed lest we offend those that are in Authority; and prejudice ourselves, or the Church and Nation of which we are members, by our disobedience to them.

C. Yes Sir, this hath always been the doctrine of the Church of *England;* and the reason of the thing doth plainly command it: or in such things private persons are not *sui juris* at their own disposal, but must be governed by their Superiours; so that the Law of avoiding Scandal cannot bind us in any such cases.

W. No Sir; for if it did, our Governours could command nothing (though never so good and necessary) which we could safely obey, but that some or other, either through ignorance, pride, or peevishness, might take offence at it.

C. But then it must be supposed that the Authority commanding be a lawful Authority: and this brings me to the last objection I shall make against this new Oath of Allegiance, *viz. That the Authority en-joyning it is unlawful, or at least not a sufficient and due Authority.*

W. I cannot deny that this is a good exception against such an Oath as we may avoid taking without prejudice to ourselves or the publick; but *where force is added to the Authority* our incomparable *Casuist* tells us, *(de juram p. 97 & 98.) a good man may take such an Oath, if so be that the matter of the Oath contains nothing in itself unlawful, or contrary to the publick Laws, or derogating from the right of any third person.*

C. Yes, Sir, I well remember the place, and that you have already proved all these three conditions to be contained in this Oath; and that therefore we may take it, though the Authority commanding it should be unlawful.

W. Nay Sir, the same Author is more direct and positive in this matter: For he saith (de Conscient. pag. 225.) Si lex injusta est ob defectum justitiae, quam legalem vocant, injusta ut sit, obligat tamen subditum. *If a law be unjust, for want of that which they call Legal Justice, though it be so unjust, nevertheless it binds the subject, and he gives a very good reason for it: Quia subditus non est legitimus & idoneus judex justitiae legalis; because the subject is not a lawful and fit judge of Legal Justice.* Nay, he further saith, *(ibid. p. 228.) Si ob apparentes utrinq; rationes subditus nesciat, &c. If upon the account of probable reasons on both sides, the Subject cannot know whether the law be just, or otherwise, the Subject is in that case bound to actual obedience; so that he sins if he does not obey, and if he does obey does not sin.* And this is not meerly *gratis dictum* his own bare assertion, but he gives us two substantial reasons for it; first, *because in doubtful cases, the condition of the possessor is rather to be chosen; that is of the Legislator, than of the Subject.* Second, *In a doubtful matter the safer part is to be chosen, but it is much safer that anyone should think himself bound who is free, than that he should think himself free when he is really bound.*

C. Now I believe it would be no difficult matter to prove that the Authority imposing this new Oath of Allegiance is at least very probable, since it is (all circumstances considered) the highest and best authority that could be had.

W. I have too long detained you from your rest to undertake that proof; and therefore shall conclude all at present with another saying of the same Right Reverend *Casuist* (de Conscien. pag. 221.) Lex injusta etsi fieri non debuit, facta tamen valet: *An unjust Law* (i.e. for want of Legal Justice, for of such a Law he speaks) *although it ought not to be made, yet it is valid when it is made.* And the reason he gives is sufficient to warrant our Obedience, *viz. For it may so come to pass, that what could not be commanded without sin, may yet be obeyed without sin.*

C. So that let the Legislators look to the Legality of their authority, it is nothing to me; it becomes me who am a Subject to remember that axiom on which he grounds all this discourse, *viz.* Vera obedientia non est disputatrix. *True obedience is not disputative.*

W. And for that reason have I, in obedience to your commands, betrayed my indiscretion, though, I hope, the authority and reasons of so learned, pious, and judicious a *Casuist* as Bishop *Sanderson* will not easily be thought contemptible. I therefore commit you to God's protection, and bid you a good night.

FINIS.

In the Wake of
Revolution

[Zachary Taylor, 1653–1705]

OBEDIENCE
AND
SUBMISSION
TO THE
Present Government,
DEMONSTRATED
FROM
Bishop Overall's
Convocation-Book

LONDON, Printed for *Robert Clavel* at the Sign of the *Peacock* in St. *Pauls-Church-Yard*, 1690.

Zachary Taylor, who has been characterized as a hard-headed Whig, is regarded as author of this pamphlet. The tract illustrates the ironic transposition of the views held by radical Whigs and extreme Tories on obedience and resistance after the Glorious Revolution reversed their political fortunes.

Taylor was the son of a Presbyterian minister who had held a preferment in Ireland and served as a chaplain in the royal army there. By 1649 the family had moved to Cheshire and two years later to Lancashire. With the imposition of religious conformity in 1662 the elder Taylor was ejected from his living and turned to teaching for a livelihood. His son, Zachary, was born in Lancashire. In due course he attended Jesus College, Cambridge, where he graduated B.A. in 1675 and received an M.A. in 1678. Like his father, the younger Taylor became a clergyman. In 1680 he was appointed vicar of Ormskirk in Lancashire and was still there ten years later when "Obedience and Submission to the Present Government" was published.

The tract was addressed to nonjurors and urged them to take the oath of allegiance to William and Mary. Taylor attempted to demonstrate the necessity for their pledge of loyalty by arguing from the tenets of Bishop John Overall's Convocation Book. This collection of canons adopted by Convocation in 1606 included a denial of the subject's right to resist an oppressive government or even a government that had been created by conquest or rebellion. Indeed, one of the reasons King James I had angrily rejected these canons was because of his vehement opposition to the teaching that any "thoroughly settled" government should be obeyed whatever its origins. Therefore, the canons of 1606 had never been formally approved. The Convocation Book was printed for the first time in 1690, more than eighty years later, when the Jacobites published it on the assumption it would help their cause. But Taylor turned its prescriptions against them by pointing to its stress on the necessity for obedience, not to the ousted king, but to de facto powers. He argues, as had the Tories before the Revolution, that government is not from the people but from God. He then concludes that the Glorious Revolution must be the will of God. In short he deftly turns Tory arguments against them. He defended the new government by their old theories, if not precisely the divine right of kings then the more traditional notion of the great sanctity of rulers and the necessity of obedience to authority.

"Obedience and Submission" appeared in two editions. Late in 1690 Thomas Wagstaffe published a tract that attacked it, and in the next year there appeared three essays, including one by Taylor, that defended its reasoning.

Obedience and Submission to the Present Government, &c.

THAT those of the Church of *England*, who have taken the Oaths to Their Majesties KING *William* and QUEEN *Mary*, have Deserted their Principles about Allegiance and Government, is the common Reflection cast upon them, by some, whom either Malice or Ignorance does Dispose to Reproach them: But since Bishop *Overall's* Convocation-Book[1] appeared, they now Plead Reason and Authority to Justify the Scandal, and pretend that they have got a whole Convocation of Unprejudiced and Learned Men, who have Unanimously Condemned the late Submission, and such, as being far removed from any Temptation, are the fittest and most fair Judges that we can be Determined by; (though their Proceedings not having the Royal Confirmation which is absolutely necessary for Canons,[2] does (as some think) very much, if not altogether invalidate their Authority, and makes them as insignificant as the last Convocation we heard of).[3] I thought therefore I might do some Service to the Church, and its Members, if I could in some Measure Vindicate It and Them, by proving that their Compliance with the present Settlement, has not

---

1. John Overall, *Bishop Overall's Convocation-Book MDCVI concerning the government of God's catholic church and the kingdoms of the whole world* (London, 1690). John Overall, bishop successively of Coventry and Lichfield and of Norwich and Regius Professor of Theology at Cambridge in the late sixteenth and early seventeenth century, took part in the Hampton Court conference of 1604. His Convocation Book, framed by the members of that meeting, was intended to discuss and settle the origin of both the civil and the ecclesiastical polities. James I took exception to some of the canons. The book was first published by William Sancroft, Archibishop of Canterbury, in 1690.

2. Because James I objected to several of the proposed canons the proceedings never were officially adopted.

3. Convocation agreed the courts of Star Chamber and High Commission, abolished in 1641, should remain suppressed, Laud's canons of 1640 were declared illegal and Convocation gave up its claim to tax the clergy. According to David Edwards in *Christian England* the result was that Convocations did not need to meet at all and were, in fact, suppressed from 1664 until 1689 and throughout most of the next century and a half. See Edwards, *Christian England* (London, 1983), 2:311.

in the least deviated from the Doctrine of the Church of *England*, as it was Professed and Taught in that Convocation.

I shall begin therefore with laying down the Doctrine about Government and Allegiance in Four Propositions extracted out of the Convocation-Book, to which may be Reduced, whatever almost can be pretended in this Controversy;

And they are these,

First, *That the Power of Kings was Originally Patriarchal, Derived from GOD and not from the People,* C. 2. 6, 13.

For though Kings are, or ought to be Bound up, and Limited in the Exercise of their Power by Laws, C. 15. yet that proceeds from GOD and Nature, who never intended Princes to be such *Leviathans*, whose wilful Pleasure should be Laws; but Parents of their Countrey, Impowered from Above to Maintain the Native Liberty and Property of their Subjects, as of their Children. For the Conceit of Absoluteness never did, or could prevail in any State, but where Superstition or Ignorance blinded Men's Reasons, as in *Turky*, and most of the *Eastern* Empires; or Parasitical Flattery, and the naked Sword Maintain the Arbitrary Usurpation, as it is in a Neighbouring Kingdom.

Second Proposition. *That Descent in Hereditary Kingdoms, is the ordinary Way whereby a Right and Title to the Crown is Claimable.*

I say, is the ordinary Way; For since Kings Rule by GOD, it is only, as the Convocation-Book saith, The Lord, who both may, and is able to overthrow Kings or Emperors, notwithstanding any Claim, Right, Title, or Interest which they can Challenge to their Countries, Kingdoms or Empires, *pag. 53.*

Third Proposition. *That no Violence is to be used to Kings from their own Subjects for any Irregularities that they commit,* C. 22.

For the Doctrine of Passive Obedience *to a Government Established by Law, whether the PRINCE be Limited and Sworn to Govern by*

Laws Chosen by the People, and Enacted with his Consent, or the PRINCE be Absolute, and his will sufficiently Declared, by the Law, is of absolute necessity to the Support of any Government; and they who deny that, can never clear themselves from the Suspicion of some Designs against this.

Fourth Proposition. *That having sworn Allegiance to a Prince, we cannot without the Dreadful Guilt of Perjury, transfer our Allegiance, whilst he continues to have an Authoritative Right and Title to the Crown,* C. 36.

I say an Authoritative Right and Title, because the Case may so happen, that these being separated, the Claim of Right without the Authority, cannot Challenge our Allegiance, as in the Case of the Kings of *Israel* and *Judah,* that were led Captive by the *Babylonians,* who they survived in *Babylon,* and some of them out of Confinement yet, (as it appears from *Jeremy's* calling for the People's Prayers, and Obedience to the *Babylonish* Kings) could lay no Claim to the Allegiance of their late Subjects. The Reason of which, is, Because it is the Authority, which is GOD's, that Commands our Allegiance; and though no Mortal can separate this Authority from the Person invested with it, yet GOD can, (of which more hereafter) and if he do transfer it to another, wherever it is placed, it calls for our Allegiance.

This is the Sum, I think, of what can be pretended in the present Controversie. To Reply to which, I will not Expatriate on what hath been abundantly offered by others, but Confine myself, as much as possible, to the Convocation-Book, that the Impartial Reader may judge which side, the Jurors or *Non-*Jurors, the Old Established Doctrine of the Church of *England* does countenance.

And as to the First Proposition, That Government in general, whether Monarchy, or any other Form, derives its Authority from GOD, the Author of Nature, and consequently of Human Society, and not from the People, (though their Consent be ordinarily necessary to the Constitution, both of the Form of Government, and the Persons Governing) is that which is to be the Ground-work of the whole Discourse, and therefore in the first Place to be admitted, which I the more Confirm, by observing from the Right Reverend the Author; First, That all Kingdoms are now (what was more peculiarly appropriated to the *Jewish* Nation in their First Constitution) in some sort *Theocracies,* wherein GOD according to His own Pleasure, takes away Kings, and setteth up Kings: For C. 35. P. 83. *GOD being the Universal Lord, and Ruler over all the World, the whole World is His Universal Kingdom; in the Government whereof, He useth the Ministry of Civil Magistrates, as well in other Countries, as amongst His own peculiar People* Israel, *without any Desert of theirs, but as in His Heavenly Providence, He thinks it most convenient,* p. 84. *Howbeit He does not leave them at Liberty to do what they list, but holds Himself the Helm of every Kingdom, and useth their Services in such sort, as be they Good or Bad, and their Designments Holy or Wicked; He ever makes them the Executioners of His own Just Judgments, Will, and Good Pleasure, according as He is minded to Punish any Kingdom, People, or Countrey.* And this He does by reserving to His Providence, the Prerogative of the Designation of the Person whom He intends for His Vice-Regent, and that even in Hereditary Kingdoms, as *Adoniah,* who was *Solomon's* Elder Brother, and Anointed by *Abiathar* to succeed his Father, so his great Disappointment may be an Instance. Nay, GOD sometimes for the only designed Usurpation of a Prince, whose Title, and that in an Hereditary, was altogether Indisputable, does deprive him of the Government in Part or Whole, and will not allow him so much as to Endeavour the re-gaining of it, which was the Case of *Rehoboam.* And how oft he has Extinguished the Line Royal, and Advanced to the Crown such as had no Relation to it, the History of the Kings of *Israel* does amply Testify. In all which Cases, since it was GOD's doing, the Dethroned Prince could have no Pretence unto the Subject's Allegiance. All that I will Note hence, is, *That the Line of Descent in an Hereditary Kingdom may be Interrupted, and yet the Law of Succession not Violated.*

Secondly, I Remark, That a Sovereign may be Devested of his Power which he received from GOD, and Decline into the Inferiour Condition of a Subject.

This is plain from the Kings of *Israel* and *Judah,* who of Independent Monarchs, became not only Tributary, but Subjects to the Kings of *Babylon,* and being Subjects, whatever other Duty might, yet Allegiance could no way be due unto them, that being in general, peculiar only to a Sovereign Prince, not Dependent on, or Tributary to, another. This is Confirmed and Improved from the Convocation-Book, which in the Case of *Jehu* intimates, That his former Prince became his Subject, *Ch. 25. p. 40.* and both he and *Ahud* are excused from Guilt in laying violent Hands upon their Liege-Lords, in that though they had been Subjects, yet before the Commission of the Fact, they were Advanced to be Judges, Princes, and Rulers of God's People, *C. 27. p. 53.* I will make no Corollary from hence, because of the Reverence that I bear to all such Heads as ever wore a Crown. I therefore hasten to the Last Observation; which is,

Thirdly, That when a Prince is thus Devested of his Power from GOD, and another Advanced to his Throne, our Legal Allegiance may justly be Claimed by the Possessor.

We have been told this from our Law-Books again, and again, and now you shall hear the Decision of it from the Convocation-Book, which taking Notice, *C. 28. p. 56.* of the strange Variations of Governments in its Forms, and Governours in their Persons, whether by Usurping *Nimrods,* or Traitorous *Phocas's,* gives hereunto this Satisfaction, *p. 57. That when either Ambitious Kings by bringing any Countrey into their Subjection, or Disloyal Subjects by their Rebellious Rising against their Natural Sovereign, have Established any Degenerate Form of Government, (viz.* Aristocratical, Democratical, *&c.) amongst their*

People; The Authority either so unjustly gotten, or wrung by Force from the True and Lawful Possessor, being always God's Authority (and therefore receiving no Impeachment by the Wickedness of those that have it) is ever (when any such Alterations are throughly Settled) to be Reverenced and Obeyed, and the People of all sorts (as well of the Clergy as of the Laity) are to be subject unto it, not only for Fear, but also for Conscience' sake.

Here you may see that upon a Revolution from the worst of Circumstances, Usurpation, and Rebellion, Obedience to the Establishment is acknowledged Due. And sure I am, That Malice itself cannot be so bitter as to think the present Settlement Parallel to this Representation: For,

First, Here was no Ambitious Monarch, but a Prince that had a Just Cause of War, on the Account of the Pretended Prince of *Wales,* which whether he was Real, or Supposititious, since he had not that Satisfaction which was but Equitable as he Demanded, he might Appeal to GOD to Decide the Truth and Justice of it by the Sword. And,

Secondly, As for those who did Desert King *James,* thus much may be said for them, That they could not with a Safe Conscience Assist him in that War, because they Esteemed it on his Side Unlawful, and therefore they were Obliged at the least to Lay down their Arms.

Thirdly, The Monarchy is not Degenerated into a baser Form. We have the same Constitution, the same Laws, the same Liberties, or Greater than we had before; and therefore if in want of all these we ought to yield (as the Book asserts) *Obedience;* in the Enjoyment of them, we ought to add unto it, *Thankfulness.*

All that can be moved hereupon, is, When a Government may be said to be Settled.

And with Submission, I cannot but conceive, That the Government is Settled, when the Crown with all its Dignities, Prerogatives, Administrations, Authorities, Revenues, *&c.* are generally Recognized, and Personally Enjoyed, which must be supposed to be, when all Places of Power and Trust, of Royalty and Importance, are in the Sovereign's Hands, and wholly at his Disposal. For to say, Because there are Foreign Wars, or Secret Plots, that the Crown is not in full Possession, since there always was, and always will be Discontented Parties at home, and Politick Machinations abroad, that either Actually do, or Craftily design to Disturb the Peace; so that we cannot but acknowledge that to be a Real Establishment, which hath the Countenance of Laws, and Parliament, to Own and Confirm it.

Thus since GOD hath been pleased to Devest the Late King *James* of that Authority which he had once Committed to him, and Transferred it into another's Hands; *both Clergy and Laity according to the Doctrine of the Church of* England, *ought to Reverence, Obey, and be Subject to it, not only for Wrath, but also for Conscience' sake.*

I have almost Flattered myself, so as to Believe the most moderate Persons will Subscribe what I have said, if I could but Produce any Moral Evidence that this was GOD's Doing: To Answer whose Expectations, I will Search after such Criterions, as may Evince the present Revolution to be the Will and Pleasure of Almighty GOD. I therefore before hand, declare my Aversion to such Doctrines (as have not long since been Censured by one of our flourishing Universities)[4] wherein, Success produced for an Argument of the Divine Aprobation of such Means, Methods, and Instruments, as are concerned in a Revolution.

But then I must assume, That GOD's Providence in permitting, is a sufficient Indication of his Will and Pleasure as to the Event; which

4. The campaign to exclude James from the throne and the discovery of the Rye House Plot of 1683 had raised the terrifying specter of civil war. The reaction of the Anglican church was a vigorous reaffirmation of nonresistance and insistence upon divine right monarchy. A convocation of the University of Oxford in July 1683 issued decrees against "certain pernicious books and damnable doctrines." The condemned books included works of Buchanan, Milton, Goodwin, and Hobbes. The damnable doctrines included the principle that authority is derived from the people, the compact theory of government, and the idea that a Christian can resist a lawless king.

whether He designs it that he may thereby Punish the Sins of his People, or that he may Protect the Peace of the Church, is above my Capacity to Determine. But since Prophecy hath ceased, sure I am, that nothing but his Providence is Vocal to us; and such strong Arguments may we produce from it (especially where we can find a Parity of GOD's Proceeding) as will not with Ease or Ridicule be Eluded.

I cannot therefore but observe, and that from this Convocation-Book, *C. 24. p. 47. That even the Success of Divine Benedictions are to be left to the Disposition of GOD's Heavenly Providence,* which is there ascribed to the very Reason, why *David,* though already Anointed King, was not Advanced to the promised Crown till *Saul's* Death. Whence since a Prediction, though Divine, is not sufficient Ground to proceed upon, until GOD's Providence does interfere; I cannot restrain my Pen from moving this Query, *viz.* Whether the manifest Interpositions of a Gracious Providence, that tends to the promotion of GOD's Honor, and the Establishment of his Church, (without which, Predictions themselves are not rashly to be Executed) be not to us (now that Prophecy is ceased) a Justifiable Ground for any Rational Man to Act upon, especially when it holds *Analogy* with those Proceedings, wherein GOD hath already Notified His Holy Will and Pleasure?

I think this will hardly be denied, and therefore all that remains, is to produce some Precedents wherein Royal Authority has been Translated, and GOD hath owned it for his immediate Doing. For if his Head was Interposed there, I see not how we can Exclude it here: Therefore,

First, When Kings have Illegally Oppressed their Subjects, and been too Arbitrary in their Imposition, GOD hath been pleased to Discharge them of their Trust: The Reason of which is, because they are GOD's Representatives, and therefore what they do by Implication is, and cannot but be Interpreted to be GOD's Work; and then as he saith of the Judges in the Execution of their Office, That they Judge not for Man, but for the LORD who is with them in the Judgment. The Wrong, if they do any, is an Injury to GOD, whose Judgement it is supposed to be; which Injury, he will not suffer to go unpunished. So the Usurpations of Princes, being Reflections upon GOD, whose Trustees they are, his Honor stands Engaged, (when our sins are sufficiently punished by such Scourges) to Vindicate its own Innocence, in Removing or otherwise Animadverting upon them that so abused his Trust. We have a notable Instance of this in *Rehoboam*, who being Rejected of the People, because of his Resolved Usurpations, and Endeavouring to Regain his Right by the Sword, is forbid by GOD; of which Prohibition, the Reason that is given by no mean Statesman, my Lord *Clarendon*,[5] is this, *Because he had been in the Fault himself.* The Application I leave to the Reader.

Secondly, The Instance of Time is another Mark of GOD's Interposition. For when His Church is on the Brink of Ruin, and the Designs against Her, have been so prevalent, that it is not in the Power of Man to overrule Them, than θεὸς ἀπὸ μηχανῆς,[6] He is a Present GOD in Trouble. This the Deliverance of the *Israelites* out of *Aegypt,* will Attest, who have made upon it, this Comfortable Observation; then, whenever the Tale of Bricks, *i.e.* The utmost Servitude is imposed; *Moses, i.e.* A Deliverer is near at hand. And the Methods prescribed by Father *Parsons,* for the Reduction of *England* to the *Roman* Yoak, found in the Closet of the Late King *James,*[7] and so re-

---

5. Edward Hyde, Earl of Clarendon.

6. The god from the machine (Greek for *deus ex machina*).

7. Robert Parsons was a prominent English Jesuit in the sixteenth century. He was a prolific and talented author and managed to publish scores of tracts under the noses of the Elizabethan authorities. He was particularly notorious, however, for his zealous promotion over the course of twenty years of a Spanish invasion of England. In 1690 Edward Gee published a tract purporting to contain extracts from a copy of Parsons' work that had been presented to James II. Gee's tract was entitled "A Jesuit Memorial for the intended reformation of England under their first Popish prince."

ligiously observed throughout his Reign, is too great an Evidence of our designed Extirpation for Impudence itself to deny.

Thirdly, The Way and Manner of this Revolution, which was without Bloodshed and Battles, *i.e.* Such as beseems the God of Peace, doth confirm the same. For not to enlarge on this, I desire any of the *Non*-Jurors to speak plainly, if they do not think the Peaceableness of the Restoration of King *Charles* to be an unanswerable Testimony of God's Work, and Interposition; for my part, I must confess I always did. And then I know not how to deny the Infatuation of his Brother's Desertion to intimate, that the same Hand that restored the One, was very much Consenting to the withdrawing of the Other.

I have done, and will provoke no Man by Reflections, but yet I earnestly intreat our *Non*-Juring Brethren, to Consider;

First, That the refusing of an Oath which may Lawfully be taken, as this in Controversie may, (if what these Canons say, be True) makes the Refusers Responsible for the Want of all that Good, which their Officiating in their Cures might have produced, together with all that Unsettledness in the STATE, which their Example hath encouraged.

Secondly, If what I have produced, be the Canonical Doctrine of the Church of *England*, let them be advised of the Mischief of that Fatal Division, which their Obstinacy will bring amongst us, and is already designed, if not begun, in a Form of Prayer pretended (though I think it smells too strong of Jesuite) to be theirs.

Therefore, for the Sake of Peace, whereof Christ is the Head, and his Doctrine is the Gospel: For the Sake of our Church threatened with a more Affecting and Pathetical Division than ever: For the Sake of the Reformation, which this Breach, above all things, will prejudice; and above all, for the Sake of GOD, Whose Truth and Worship, if another Revolution come, are, as far as we can see, to be extinguished. I entreat and beg of you seriously, to lay aside all Passion, Heat, and Peevishness, and whatever else may biass your Reason; and Consider, if what I have wrote be the Genuine Doctrine of the Church of *England.* For if it be not, I must Acknowledge my Mistake, and beg GOD Pardon for the Guilt, which by taking the New Oath I have incurred; which, till my Conscience be more enlightened, I am so far from suspecting, that I would not as my Conscience, for more Kingdoms than King *James* has lost, be in the same Guilt with those, who by refusing to take the Oaths, Contribute too much to the Designs of such, as will favour neither Them, nor Us, if our Sins should ever prevail with GOD to give them the Ascendency. Which GOD prevent for the Merits of His Son, the King of Peace and Truth. *Amen.*

FINIS.

[William Sherlock, 1641–1707]

THEIR

Present Majesties
GOVERNMENT

Proved to be

Throughly Settled,

AND

That we may Submit to it, without
Asserting the

Principles of Mr. Hobbs.

Shewing also,

That Allegiance was not Due to the
Usurpers after the late Civil War.

Occasion'd by some Late Pamphlets against the
Reverend Dr. Sherlock.

LONDON, Printed for *Robert Clavel*, at the *Peacock*
in St. *Pauls-Church-Yard*, 1691.

*T*his tract is generally attributed to William Sherlock, an Anglican divine. Sherlock was a prolific pamphleteer before the Glorious Revolution and a leading nonjuror after it. He explains in this tract why he abandoned that position and finally, if belatedly, swore allegiance to William and Mary.

William Sherlock was born in Southwark about 1641 and attended Peterhouse College, Cambridge. He graduated B.A. in 1660 and M.A. in 1663. Surprisingly it was not until 1669 that he obtained a preferment, an appointment to the rectory of St. George's in London. Once installed, however, he quickly gained fame as a preacher. Similarly, from his first publication in 1674 he gained celebrity as a writer. His quick temper and ready pen embroiled him in one acrimonious dispute with the Dissenters after another. One of Sherlock's favorite techniques, for example, was to ridicule the mystical aspects of Puritanism. In 1680 he became a doctor of divinity and with it other appointments followed—to the prebend of St. Pancras in St. Paul's Cathedral, to a lectureship, and, in 1685, to the post of Master of the Temple. It may have been no coincidence that shortly before this last appointment Sherlock wrote vigorously upholding the divine right of kings and insisting upon the subject's duty of passive obedience.

During the reign of James II Sherlock wrote against popery, a view he knew would annoy the new king, but he also continued to hew to his insistence upon passive obedience. Despite that stance in April 1687, when James commanded that the Declaration of Indulgence granting toleration to Catholics and dissenters be read from the pulpit, Sherlock was among those who refused.

After the Glorious Revolution Sherlock felt bound by his oath of loyalty to James and refused to take the oath of allegiance to William and Mary. He became one of the most prominent nonjurors. The day after he should have been deprived of his posts for failing to take the oath he publicly softened his stance when he preached praying for William and Mary as de facto monarchs. Nonetheless he would not take the oath of allegiance to them. It was not until August 1690—a year after the deadline for swearing—that Sherlock finally took the oath. He explained that a canon in Bishop Overall's Convocation Book had demonstrated the rightness of obeying de facto monarchs. For their part his enemies argued that pragmatism, not theory, had persuaded him. Sherlock had been convinced, they jibed, by William's victory over James in the battle of the Boyne a month before, and by his desire for office. In fact, promotion did follow his change of heart. A year after Sherlock took the oath, then published his reasons to a wondering world and called other nonjurors to follow, he was made dean of St. Paul's.

Sherlock had justified his conversion in a pamphlet entitled "The Case of Allegiance Due to Sovereign Powers," which became a best seller. It also drew numerous attacks. "Their Present Majesties Government Proved to Be Throughly Settled," reprinted below, was penned by Sherlock to defend his position against one reply in particular, a tract by Samuel Johnson, but it answered his other critics as well. In it Sherlock struggled to distinguish his theory from that of Hobbes and to explain why William was a legitimate ruler, but Oliver Cromwell was not. The argument he hit upon was this. Authority is from God but the people must consent to it. Allegiance rests upon the willing submission of the individual to a government. Sherlock found a new government to be thoroughly settled "when the new Prince has the full Administration of the Government and is owned as Soveraign by the Representatives of the people freely chosen." The interest in the subject and its author was so keen that this tract went into three editions, the first of which is reprinted here.

Their Present Majesties Government Proved to Be Throughly Settled, &c.

Having lately perused several Pamphlets, which the Authors' style, *Remarks on Dr.* Sherlock's *New Book about the Case of Allegiance due to Soveraign Powers*,[1] I find they pretend to Charge him with *Hobbism*. I presume, it may not be thought useless to give the True State of the Case, and thence to prove the Lawfulness of our Submission to Their Present MAJESTIES; and that without approaching or Bordering upon the Opinion of Mr. *Hobbs*, who I still think is much in the wrong, as I shall shew by and by. And this I shall the rather do, because it may help to remove the Prejudices of our Brethren, who have not yet owned the Government, being scandalized, that we seem to favour his Principles.

Having wiped off this Stain, I shall briefly shew, That those Principles, by which I am governed, are not dangerous to the Thrones of Princes: This I undertake to prove, Because, any Principle that shakes the Throne, would be a Stumbling-Block to all Loyal Men, and at least prejudice them against such Arguments as may be urged to prove our Submission Lawful. And it seems the more necessary to give this Argument its full Weight, because the Learned Dr. *Sherlock* has but touched upon that Point, and only ballances this Danger on the Prince's side, with the Doctrine of *Non-Resistance* on our Part; and indeed, it shews an excellent Providence, That God has so settled

---

1. A pamphlet with approximately this title was "Some Modest Remarks on Dr. Sherlocks New Book About the Case of Allegiance Due to Sovereign Powers, &c." (London, 1691), Wing S4526. Another had been published the previous year with an almost identical title, "Remarks upon Dr. Sherlock's Book, Intituled, the Case of Allegiance Due to Soveraign Princes, Stated and Resolved" (London, 1690), Wing S841. Sherlock's book "The Case of the Allegiance due to Soveraign Powers" excited an unprecedented number of replies, of which some thirty-four were attacks, twelve were defenses, and another six were satirical verse tracts. See Mark Goldie, "The Revolution of 1689 and the Structure of Political Argument," *Bulletin of Research in the Humanities* (winter 1980), 480.

the Governments of the World, as to establish an irresistible Power in each Government, to preserve the Peace of it, and yet lays a most considerable Restraint upon such Governours, by putting it into the Power of their oppressed Subjects, to be idle Spectators of this Danger in the day of Trial, and to transfer their Allegiance as soon as any prosperous Conquerour can get into their Thrones.

But I think we have something more to offer on this Subject, *viz.* That our Principles are not prejudicial to Princes, or dangerous to their Crowns; or at least, according to these Principles, all good Princes (as for such as are Arbitrary and Tyrannical, they must shift for themselves) may have great Hopes of Recovering their Dominions, if by the Misfortune of War, or any other Accident, they be driven from their Thrones; which seems not to be enough provided for, by the *Hypothesis* that our Learned Author has given us. For if as soon as any Usurper has got quiet Possession of the Throne, Submission be then peremptorily and absolutely required, as a Duty incumbent on all the Members of that Government, then the Case of a Good and a bad Prince, when they are once dispossesed, seem to be equally desperate, *viz.* Neither of them can with any Moral Assurance, promise themselves any Assistance at home, from such as were their Subjects. Whereas, I am concerned to see Princes, so unlike in themselves, to be set on the same foot in their Quarrels; and I am in pain, to say something, which may support the Hopes of injured Innocence; I presume I shall do it. If I fail in the Attempt, I hope the Reader will impute it to an honest Zeal, to protect Vertue and Innocence, that has blinded my Eyes.

And in prosecution of this design, I shall prove, That there was no Obligation to submit to the Usurpers after the late Civil War, and that though we should suppose them in the quiet Possession of the Government; I hope that I shall be able to make all this appear Reasonable, without denying the Doctrine taught in Bishop *Overal's*

Convocation-Book;[2] it may look somewhat like a Contradiction, but I must desire my Reader's Patience until I can come at it.

To contract this Discourse, as much as I can, I shall make this one Supposition, That Princes, who originally have no Right to their Thrones, when their Government is thoroughly settled, are invested with God's Authority, and must be obeyed by all the Members of that Government, in as full a Manner, as any other, the most Legal and Rightful Princes can challenge. This Principle is plainly taught in Bishop *Overal's* Convocation-Book, and I think fully cleared by the Learned Doctor *Sherlock;* and he is so able to maintain what he has advanced, that it would be great presumption in me, to endeavour to set it in a better Light.

Taking it then for granted, That all such Princes are to be reverenced and obeyed by their Subjects; our Enquiry is, When a Government may be said to be Thoroughly Settled?

This to me seems a very Knotty Question, and will require some thoughts to Resolve it; and I know not how to do it, but by looking back to the Original of all Soveraign Power, where we have been much in the dark; some saying, Lo it is here, and Lo it is there; some one thing and some another; one raising all Soveraignty from the natural Paternal Authority, and another founding it in Conquest, a third in Election; others again pretending, that the several Soveraignties of the World have had several Originals. But for my part, with submission to better Judgments, I shall assert, that all Soveraignty is founded in submission; and this shall be the Thread to my following discourse, which if I can maintain, I doubt not but to prove all that I have promised on this Point: For if it appears, that no Man is a Subject but upon his own submission, and that Conquest without this can give no Man Authority to Govern, and Command

2. John Overall, *Bishop Overall's Convocation-Book MDCVI concerning the Government of God's catholic church and the kingdoms of the whole world* (London, 1690). See above, Taylor, "Obedience and Submission," note 1.

me as his subject; then it plainly follows, that dominion is not founded in power; and that power, and a quiet possession, is no certain sign to us, that God has given the Soveraign Authority with it.

I Assert then, that all Civil Government, whether it be Elective, or Hereditary, Aristocracy, Democracy, or any other Form of Civil Government, it is all founded in submission; and I think there needs no other proof of this Doctrine, but to say, that a free man can never be made another's subject, but by his own consent, or submission, either in his own Person, or by his Representative. By the fortune of War, I may become another Man's Prisoner, but he must have my own consent to make me his subject; by the fortune of War, a Foreign Prince or a Rebellious Subject may get possession of our whole Kingdom, Usurp the Crown, and have the full and quiet Administration of the Government, and as it is usually done, Claim our Obedience as his Subjects. But in Truth, he has no true Title to it; indeed, if the War was just, all the whole property is his until we enter into Conditions; but the Obedience of Subjects is not due from us, until we have declared, and acknowledged him to be our Soveraign; and this I may call a Reciprocal Obligation, which either may refuse. Nor will it argue much bounty in the Conqueror to return us our Liberty and Property, in lieu of our Obedience; because without Obliging our Consciences, he can hope to reap but little fruit from all his Conquests; he can never be secure in his Throne, nor settled in his Government, until he has some Tie upon our Consciences; as we are his prisoners, he may Torment and Punish us; but all this while he has no hold upon our Consciences, all things are Lawful against him as against a publick Enemy, and we are free to draw our Swords against him, as soon as we can escape out of his hands; so that on these Occasions, a Conqueror is forct to stand Armed, or to bind our hands until he can bind our Consciences.

And this seems to be the key to understand those passages, quoted out of Bishop *Overal's* Convocation-book: The New Government is

then thoroughly settled, when the new Prince has the full Administration of the Government, and is owned as Soveraign by the Representatives of the people freely chose; we must then submit not only
for Wrath, but Conscience' sake, because it is the Ordinance of God.
Here therefore, I must presume to assert, that the right of Government is not derived from God, without the consent or submission of
the people; I do not say it is not derived from God, but the consent of
the people, together with the full Enjoyment of the Regal Power, is
our Visible Evidence, that such a Prince has received his Authority
from God; for till this be done, we cannot with any propriety of
speech, say that the Government is settled, nor is it called the Ordinance of God until it be settled. I say, Submission only makes a
Thorough Settlement, because, notwithstanding a quiet possession,
it is probable whole multitudes may wait an opportunity to overturn
it, unless the Nation has declared its willingness to Acquiesce by
Representatives, who are the mouth of the people, and impowered
to speak their minds.

I Would not have it thought, as if by this, I denied the Power of
God, to set an Usurping Tyrant over us against our wills; for God can
do it if he please, and make us the instruments of it; when he means
thus to afflict any Nation, or People, he can so incline their hearts,
as to make them receive him to be their King, who shall be their
Scourge; Or the Usurping Tyrant having them in his Power, may
make them willing to be his Subjects, on such Conditions as they can
get. And thus God can set a bad King over us in some sense against
our wills, and yet it is our own Act: For we owe him no Obedience,
and are not Obliged to Reverence, and Obey him on the score of
Conscience, until his Government be settled by our receiving him to
be our Soveraign, either in our own Persons, or by our Representatives.

I presume it will be sufficient to clear this Point, if I first prove,
that our Present Civil Governments could have no other Original;

and further, shew in what sense the Men of succeeding Ages, and our present Times, are not said to be Subjects, without their own consent or submission.

For the Reasons already given, I do suppose all Civil Governments must have their Original, either from Submission, or from the Paternal Authority. Now none of our present Princes can Claim their right from Paternal Authority, because it cannot be thought that any Prince now living, should be able to make good his Claim, as the direct Heir from *Noah;* though they want no flatterers, yet none of them are so vain as to give out, that they are the Heirs of this great Family; so that I shall take it for granted, that all pretences to Soveraign Authority from Paternal Power, are absolutely out of doors. And at present I can foresee nothing Material, that may be objected against this Hypothesis, unless it be what our Learned Author seems to object, *viz.* That as natural Authority is the most sacred, so no Man had Authority to give it away; that is, if I mistake not his meaning, a Father having Soveraign Authority over his Children, and Children's Children, &c. may not Transfer this Authority to any other Person.

Now to clear this doubt, Perhaps it would be no difficult Task.

First, To shew the Necessity of Transfering this Authority as families multiplied; for everything that is Absolutely necessary is Lawful, just as we say it was Lawful for *Cain* to Marry his own Sister.

Secondly, If it were Unlawful in the Original, a long Succession wipes off the Stain, as our Author plainly grants.

Thirdly, It being impossible to Govern the whole World by the care and inspection of one Man, and it being impossible to point out the direct Heir in each country, and again impossible to settle the Limits of his Government: I Conclude it was Lawful for every Parent to Transfer, so much of his Authority to some Single Person, as was necessary to preserve Peace in the Neighbourhood, reserving still so much to themselves as might preserve a Filial Obedience; and this might be done, as we see it is at this day amongst us, though a stranger to their blood, were invested with a Soveraign Authority over them.

But Lastly, though no Authority, be so Sacred as what is Natural, yet I conclude it Lawful, not only on Necessary, but Prudential accounts to Transfer it: If any denies it is *gratis dictum*, when they publish their Reasons, it will be time enough to put in our Answer.

So that in short, I suppose it Lawful for any body of Free Men, to invest any one of themselves, or a stranger, with a Soveraign Authority over them: And that all our Present Governments did begin in this manner, is more than probable, because none of them could have such Authority by any other means; the pretences from Paternal Authority are out of doors, Conquest will lay no Obligation to Obedience on Man's Conscience, and therefore nothing but Consent or Submission can do it.

It matters not whether this Submission was procured in gratitude for former Obligations, or by Flattery, or for fear of Rough Treatment; it may be sometimes a willing submission, and sometimes an Hard Choice, but one's own Submission only binds his Conscience; if he would brave his Adversary, and not yield to become his Subject, or Vassal, he would, as we say, be his own Man, as soon as he escaped his Adversarie's hands; whereas having once received him for his Soveraign, his Conscience is forever bound; and if I may so say, he carries his Chains with him to the Remotest Corners of the World. All Nations as far as I know being agreed, that no Subject can shake off his Obedience at his pleasure; and agreeable to this Principle they all Act, on occasion, calling any of them home, and proceeding against such as refuse to Obey their Summons, which you must confess ought never to be done by a bare Conquerour; I mean, who is not yet owned by the Estates: Or if such a Prince should pretend to Recall such as are Fled from his Usurped Government, though he has the Sword, and the whole Power in his hands, yet I suppose you will not say that such Refugies are obliged to return, and act the part of good subjects.

This therefore is a plain indication, that all our present Civil Governments were founded, and settled in the Consent, or Submission of our Ancestors; It remains now, to shew that their Posterity, and we of this Present Age, are not properly said to be subjects without our own submission: And it is Necessary to prove this, as well in Elective as Hereditary Governments; because the Government is not there Dissolved upon the Death of the Prince, nor would any Member of it be loose from his Obedience, though he should deny to Concur with them in the Election of a New King, and claim his Liberty at or before the Election.

I say then, as our Ancestors voluntarily submitted to be Subjects of this Hereditary Monarchy, so it is presumed to be our own Choice, they were as properly our Representatives, as those that we now Chuse in our own persons, and our Consent is as well presumed to the Enacting of their LAWS, as to those that are now made; and they transmitted no more Liberty to me, than they reserved to themselves. Nor is it any great Strain to presume our Consent in this Case; for, to give this Argument all the Force I can, I will suppose myself born in a very unhappy Government; but as a bad Government is better than none at all, so I should think it no foolish Choice, to Answer for my Off-spring, that they should be subject to the same Government, and might rationally suppose, that if they could now appear, they would ratify it in their own persons; because, all Civil Societies must soon be dissolved, if the Child be not born in the same Condition with his Parents; I mean, subject to the same Laws, and the same Government. Therefore, as my Ancestors did presume to Consent for me, that I should be subject to all the Laws which they Enacted, (for as yet I know no other Reason of my being subject to them); so amongst other things, they did Consent for me, that I should be subject to such a Government, to such and such a Prince. The Reason holds in both, by Vertue of their Act. I did as much Consent to be a Subject to the King of *England*, as I did Consent to any other Law which they Established. They thought it no Presumption to Consent for us, and we yet tread in their steps; for whatever Laws are now Enacted, will oblige our Posterity, as if it were their own Act; we Represent those that are yet unborn, and Choose for them; and as you find by what has been said, may rationally presume to do so.

Obj. *If it be Demanded, On what Account our Ancestors, Three or Four Hundred Years ago, should Choose a King for us?*

Ans. The Answer is very obvious, *viz.* They well understood the Conveniencies of Government, and therefore might well presume our Consent, to be Members of it, upon as good Terms as they could get; because, as I said before, a bad Government is better than none, since therefore they were to Choose for themselves, as well as their Posterity, and had an equal Interest in this great Affair, they might presume to Consent for us, seeing they consulted our Happiness and Security in the World; or if they acted foolishly and unfaithfully, yet since the thing must be done, or the World would become an *Acel-dama*,[3] they might on good Grounds presume our Consent, and Choose for us, as we yet do for our Posterity in other Cases; or indeed in the same Case, whenever we transfer any part of our Liberty, by enlarging the Prerogative of the Crown. We may Act wisely or foolishly, as it happens, but we Act not for ourselves alone, it affects our whole Posterity, whom we Represent, and who are supposed to Consent with us, for otherwise, I cannot see how it should oblige their Consciences.

Obj. *But it may further be Objected against this* Hypothesis, *That the Major Vote cannot include my Consent, unless I please.*

Ans. I grant it, if a New Government were now to be Erected, it could not; but where we could not Act in our own Persons, our An-

---

3. An Alceldama, a scene of slaughter.

cestors being our true Representatives, it was rational to presume on our Consent in what they did for us; and since we could not Choose for ourselves, our Consent is most rationally presumed to the Major Vote, as it is at this day, when any New Law is established; and since we cannot all act in our own persons, I suppose, every Wise Man would rather stand obliged by the Major Vote, than entrust his whole Property in the breast of those more peculiar Representatives, whom he elects himself, since it gives them so large a Power, and therefore is a Trust too great to be put into the hands of any one Man; and on this Account our Ancestors might well presume to Consent for us, that in these Cases we should be obliged by the Major Vote.

Indeed, at first sight it may seem somewhat hard, that our Ancestors should not reserve a Liberty to every particular Man to Choose for himself. We are naturally very fond of this Liberty, but in the main, it cannot be done, because no considerable Body of Men can be thus governed; and as it appears by the Event, they who have reserved most of this Liberty, have acted the most imprudently. Thus I suppose we are in some Measure sensible of the great Inconveniencies incident to an Elective Government in *Poland*, where, at their Diets, nothing is Enacted by a Major Vote, but only by a general Consent; the Wheel of Government moves so heavily, that that great People, who in their Persons are Valiant, in their Councils not inferiour to their Neighbours, and in their Numbers, as Considerable as any Nation in *Europe*, are become the Sport of Fortune, being miserably harrassed by every Puny Invader; and for want of giving away a little more Liberty, many of them frequently lose it all; Multitudes being daily carried into a miserable Captivity by their Enemies, by reason of those Dilatory Proceedings. So that our Ancestors might well presume to Consent for us, in passing away this Liberty; And indeed, with us there is such a true Temper observed, betwixt Liberty and Prerogative, that the whole Frame of our Laws, seem to be of our own inditing, being such as every Wise Man would Consent to, though we were to begin afresh. But this is more than needs be said; for if our Ancestors had Acted very Foolishly, and made our Condition much worse than it is, their Laws would have still Obliged us, they would have been lookt upon as our own Act, because they were our Representatives.

And now I hope it appears, I had some Reason to say, that no Man is a Subject without his own Consent, or Submission; but before I proceed to build upon this Principle, it may be neccessary to remove the scruples of one sort of men (for they are no Arguments) against what is advanced.

Object. *They may say, if Subjects give their Prince his Authority, they may take it away again, if they please.*

Ans. But we say, they give Him not his Authority, though he has it not without their Consent, or Submission; they are only the Pipes, or the Channels, whereby God Almighty conveys his Authority to him: For as I said before, to shorten my discourse, I take it for granted, that all Government is the Ordinance of God, and therefore though the subjects may Elect the Person, it is God that gives Him his Authority. It is a Woman's own Consent, that makes her Subject to the Law of her Husband; but yet Marriage being God's Ordinance, as well as Government, when it is done she cannot Recall, or Reassume her Liberty.

But only for Argument's sake, we will suppose all Authority derived from the People; yet then I say, it cannot be recalled, but by the Consent of all Parties concerned. And though our Representatives, may presume the Consent of the People, yet the King having a Negative Voice, nothing of this Nature, according to our Constitution, can be done without him, whilst he is able and willing to protect us. But if he abandons his People, and cannot, or will not come to protect us; and our Representatives, to prevent the utter ruin of the Common-wealth, do then agree, and declare the Soveraignty to be in the next Heir, that can protect us; and thus settle him in the full Administration of the Government, we must then submit, not upon Mr. *Hobbs* his base Principle, because dominion is founded in Power; but by Virtue of the Determination of our Representatives, which is lookt upon as the Act of the whole People, and includes the Consent of every Particular Person, which, as it appears by this discourse, is the only Visible means of conveighing a Soveraign Authority to any Person. And if this quiet possession, together with the free Consent of our Representatives, will not be thought a Thorough Settlement, I can think of nothing that can strengthen it, unless it be the Resignation of the Late King, which I presume, ought never to be expected, and would as much be wanted, upon the most Evident Conquest, as it is in this Case here before us. And therefore, I hope I may Conclude, that our Government is now Thoroughly Settled, and that we who submit to it cannot be charged with *Hobbism;* since we do not say that any Prince, who has quiet possession of the Throne, can Claim our Obedience, but only such as are Confirmed, and Settled in it by the Determination of our Representatives. This I think is a very Natural Explication of those Passages in Bishop *Overal's* Convocation-Book, which require our Obedience to a Government Thoroughly Settled; for that Government must needs be very Slippery and Tottering, which our Representatives, who are supposed to have the Hearts, and to be the Mouth of the People, will not Confirm.

And for as much as I was satisfied, that my own submission was both just and rational, without bordering upon Mr. *Hobbs* his base Principle, which I always detested: on this Occasion, I thought it Necessary to Recollect my thoughts on this subject, and commit them to writing, that I might the more closely examine, how well my Reasons Hung together. But I could not set them in a True Light, without spinning them out to this length, before I came to the matter in hand, which I chiefly designed, *viz.* To shew what a Vast Difference there is betwixt Mr. *Hobbs,* his Opinion of Government, and our own.

His comes from the Father of Lies; Ours I hope from the God of Truth; his is the dictate of self-interest, ours the Resolves of Reason and Conscience: He says all Soveraignty, or all dominion is Founded in Power, we say no such thing. The greatest Conqueror cannot Compel us to be his Subjects without our own submission; though he has Power over our Country, and our persons, yet he can lay no Obligation upon our Consciences to become his Subjects. This must be our own act, either in person, or by our Representatives: And if this Notion will bear the Light, there is no pretence to say as Mr. *Hobbs* does, that his having the Power of the Sword, makes us become his Subjects.

And as this *Hypothesis* does entirely Wipe off the Stain of *Hobbism,* so likewise is it a great support, or at least not dangerous to the Thrones of good Princes; for one would suspect that his thoughts were ill grounded, if they obliged him to maintain such Principles; and indeed, it is a Melancholy thing to think, that we should be obliged as good Subjects to pay Obedience to the first Conqueror, that shall get quiet possession of the Throne, as Mr. *Hobbs* has taught us.

But according to this *Hypothesis,* the Government of the New Prince is never Thoroughly Settled, until he has acquired the Consent of the People; there is no Obedience due to him, until they Confirm his Authority.

And this I call a great Security to all good Princes; for supposing it necessary to have their Consent to Confirm a Government, that began perhaps in Usurpation, and settle it, I know nothing more, that a Good, but Dispossessed Prince, can desire to maintain his Hopes of an happy Turn of Affairs, to Re-instate him in his Dominions. For Men may say what they will, and suggest, That every Body is ready to Adore the Rising Sun; and that the worst Title, provided it be prosperous, never wants hands to support and strengthen it; but for my part, I could never be Tempted, nor do I think we ever had reason to make such odious general Censures. And as I hope we now want not many honest Patriots, who would have supported the late King *James*, to the last drop of Blood, had his Government been so Legal, as to have merited such a Sacrifice; so even in this Age, to the Honour of our Holy Religion, we want not many Generous Instances of Men's Integrity to this rational Principle: For though *Cromwell* had as quiet Possession of the Three Kingdoms, as any Conqueror could hope for, though he had all our Persons naked and helpless, in his Power, and at one Time, no Armed Force against him, either at home or abroad; yet he could never compass the Consent of the People in a Free Convention or Parliament, as I shall shew you by and by.

This therefore may extreamly exalt the hopes of all good dispossesed Princes, who being just and innocent, may rationally expect, that the Free Representatives of the People, will not own the Usurped Power; and so long as this is not done, they may as rationally hope for Succour from their Subjects, on the first fair Occasion.

Obj. *But some may say, How can this be? Is it probable that an Usurper, in the quiet Possession of the Throne, should not, though with some Difficulty, procure an Acknowledgment of his Authority from our Free Chosen Representatives.*

Ans. I say it is probable, and this late Instance of a lasting Usurpation, where it could not be done, is a Convincing Proof, That it may be so again, if we should ever see the like unhappy Occasion.

I will grant that we live in a wicked Generation, and that the worst Tyrant will have many Followers, if it be but for Spoil and Plunder. He may be able to influence some by his Favours, others by his Threats; others again may go along with him out of pure Zeal, to reform such Grievances, as he shall please to Object against. But what is this towards influencing the Whole, or the Major part of the Nation? The Power of our Representatives is derived from so many Persons, that the Usurper's Bounty can reach but few of them; his Menaces, when they are so general, lose much of their Force, and as soon as he pretends to the Soveraignty, many of his most Zealous Followers prove his worst Enemies. If he should pretend to Corrupt the Representatives themselves, it is too considerable a Body to be awed by Menaces, too numerous for his Favours, generally of too great Integrity to accept his Bribes, and of better Fortunes than to need them; so that on this Score, a Dispossessed Good Prince might well promise himself an After-Game.

Obj. *But again it may be Objected, That if it be not Lawful to pay Allegiance to those Usurpers, whose Authority is not Confirmed by our Representatives, then our Condition at such Times, must needs be extreamly hazardous and desperate, being naked and destitute, and exposed to the Fury of those, who have all the Power in their hands.*

Ans. I cannot but say these are most unhappy Circumstances; but in a general Calamity, every good Man should be willing to bear his Share, and venture his Security, and even sacrifice his private Interest, to preserve the Ancient Government, and Royal Family.

Besides, in such Cases the Danger is not so great, as we generally presume it is: Indeed, it can hardly be thought, but the Usurpers will sacrifice some Worthy Patriots to their Ambition, as those did in the late Times; but when they find a good Title, cannot be attained without a Sea of Blood, and much present Danger to themselves, they generally sit down as contented as they can, only with a quiet Possession. And as for those Leading Men, whose Zeal may have exasperated the Usurper's Fury, they may live concealed, or generously follow their Unhappy Master into Exile, and there patiently wait the Happy Hour. Nor as the World goes with them, will they look upon this Honourable Banishment, as an hard Choice, since if it were just to submit to the Usurpers, they could not but expect to be lookt upon with an evil Eye, and perhaps to be Crushed at the first Opportunity.

And this, I hope, is sufficient to Convince any reasonable Man, That these Principles are not dangerous to the Thrones of Princes; for we do not Assert, with Mr. *Hobbs,* That as soon as any Prince or Rebel has got Possession of the Throne, we immediately thereby become his Subjects. Nay, though they should get, and keep quiet Possession of it, we yet say there is no Obedience due from us, until their Usurped Power be Settled, and Confirmed by our Representatives, whom we style the Fathers of our Country, who are the most knowing in these Affairs, and being at the Helm, can best judge, Whether things be come to that Extremity, or not. But, Morally speaking, this Recognition cannot be procured from them, but in the utmost Extremity; and in short, then only when they are entirely in the Power of a Conquerour, and sufficiently weary of their Dispossessed Prince, by reason of his Arbitrary and Illegal Proceedings.

Thus it literally happened after the late Civil War; for notwithstanding all the Endeavours that were used by the Usurpers, they could never procure an Acknowledgment of their Authority from our Free Chosen Representatives, as I shall now shew you by representing the true Matter of Fact, from Mr. *Whitlock's* Memoirs,[4] who must be allowed to speak as favourably to this Point, as the Case would bear.

And here, I suppose, it will not be necessary I should say anything of that part of the Parliament, commonly called the *Rump;* they indeed usurped the Government, but there was not so much as the Face of a general Consent in the Nation. Much less need I mention those 120 Persons, whom *Oliver,* as General of the Army, called together;[5] who at last devolved, what Authority they had on him. It was

---

4. Bulstrode Whitelocke, *Memorials of the English Affairs: 1625–60* (London, 1682).

5. After dismissing the Rump in April 1653, Oliver Cromwell ruled for several months as commander-in-chief. In that capacity he summoned a group of men to a "Nominated Assembly." The group of 140 men, 129 of whom were from England and Wales, met at Whitehall on 4 July 1653 and gave themselves the title of Parliament. They disbanded themselves on 12 December 1653.

never pretended they had any other Parliaments or Representative Body of the People to confirm their Power.

So that we are already come to *Cromwel's* Government, as Protector, in which alone, if anywhere this Settlement is to be found.

Now *Cromwel* had but Two Conventions or Parliaments, as he called them, both which we will consider, as also what they did towards Settling his Authority, by a free Parliamentary Submission, which we here presume to be necessary to make a Thorough Settlement.

His first Parliament was Summoned *June 9th. 1654* and there is very good Reason to suspect there could be no free Election, because there were such Restrictions and Limitations, which the Sheriff was to lay upon the People, ere they could be admitted to give their Votes.

Another Circumstance, which must necessarily prejudice the Freedom of this Parliament, was a strange Innovation made by the Protector, in admitting Thirty *Scotch*, and Thirty *Irish* Members into it: For, could we suppose all the *English* Members Freely Chosen, so great an Accession of Strangers must needs be a great Clog to the *English*. For if we may suppose these Sixty Strangers at the Protector's Devotion, they, with the Help of some Friends they were sure to find here, might probably do things in Favour of the Protector, against the Sense of the People of *England*, whose Opinions are best known by our own Members. And that these Sixty Strangers, were the Protector's Creatures, is no improbable Supposition; because, he would not otherwise have made this Innovation, or have fetched them so far for nothing. Besides, Five Sheriffdoms in *Scotland* returned, that not one fit to be a Representative, was to be found within their Liberty; which shews, That the Protector, and his States-men, were very nice in their Choice.

I might also Object against this Parliament, (and let it be Observed, That the former, and this Objection, lies also against his last Parliament) That it was not Free, because the Protector took upon him, to call only so many Persons as he pleased, augmenting the Number of Representatives in some places, and diminishing in others, according to his own Humour, without any Colour of Law; and having taken this Liberty, you may imagine he was careful to call most of the Representatives from those places, where he had most Creatures, as I might easily make it appear, if it were worth my Time.

But let us Consider what this Parliament did, when once they were come together.

After some few Preliminaries, we find them Entring on the Grand Debate, Concerning the Articles of the Protector's instrument of Government, and that in such a manner as made him jealous of their proceedings; and then he thought it High time, to impose a Recognition upon them, which they were to Sign, before they were suffered to sit again in the House. This Recognition (which may be seen in the *Memoirs*) can in no sense be called a Publick Act, since it was not first Voted in the House: And Effectually, upon this, many of them left that pretended Parliament, and they who did Sign it, presently Voted, that it should not be Construed to Comprehend the whole instrument, Consisting of Forty-two Articles; which was, as much as to say, they reserved still to themselves a Power to Break with him, in Case they could not Agree afterwards upon the said Articles.

And if we still Trace on their Proceedings, we find them always very Busy in their Debates, about the Government, and never able to come to any Conclusion about it, (unless I think upon Two Articles in Forty-two) till the Protector, being jealous of them, in great Heat Dissolved them.

His second Parliament Met *September 17. 1656.* And it must be confest, that this Parliament, did as far as they were able, Confirm his Usurped Authority: But nothing is more Evident, than that, this was a packt Number of his own Creatures; and as the Business was then Managed, it is Ridiculous to think, they could speak the People's sense in this matter.

For they were not only Crampt, as the former Parliament had been; but as our Author observes, none of them were suffered to enter the House, without a Certificate, that they were approved by the Protector's Council. And when almost an Hundred of the Members, who were Secluded upon that Account, demanded Entrance, it was slavishly voted by the rest, that they should make their Application to the Council, for their Approbation. This Produced a most Sharp Remonstrance, Signed with their own Hands, as may be seen at Large in the *Memoirs,* page 640. And if there were nothing more, this is enough to Void and Null all their Proceedings; This is sufficient to shew, that this was possibly, the most packt Assembly, that ever pretended to the Name of a Parliament; and that there is not the least Colour of Reason, to say, that what they did, could any ways be the Act of the People; Though this was the best Title the Protector had to his Government, as he himself thought, not being Solemnly Inaugurated before this pretended Submission, of the People in Parliament, as he called it.

I Should now proceed to Consider the Case of *Richard,* but there need not many words to Blow off his Title; since the only Parliament He Had, as its freedom was questionable on the former accounts, and because of the Exclusion of some Members, who it seems were unworthy, because they had been in Arms against the Rump Parliament; so they never came to any Conclusion, about the Recognition of his Authority.

And after all, if those pretended Parliaments had owned both *Oliver,* and his Son after Him, yet we could not call it the Consent of the Nation, because of the Violent Exclusion of the True House of Peers.

As for what followed, *Richard,* until the return of King *Charles,* everybody knows it was perfect Anarchy, and confusion. It is certain however, there never was any Parliament to Confirm the Authorities then in being: and since that is the only Legal way, to Testify the consent of a People, we may safely Conclude the Usurpation was never Settled.

I might proceed in this Argument, and at least make it probable, that if *Cromwel's* Government had been Confirmed, as far as the free Consent of our Representatives could have Settled it, yet it would not have been the duty of all Private Men, to own his Authority; which, though it be not at all necessary to maintain my opinion, I shall by way of Digression insist a little upon. Now this may seem a contradiction to what I have already Asserted, or at least Inconsistent with the Doctrine Taught in Bishop *Overal's* Convocation-Book, but I presume it is neither; and I only urge it, that the True State of the Controversy betwixt us, and some of our brethren, may the better be conceived, who insinuate, as if it were one and the same thing to pay Obedience to the present Government, or to that of the late Protector, or any other in his Circumstances. What has been said already, does sufficiently shew the Vanity of these Men; and therefore it must be observed, that if I fail in this attempt, it will not Prejudice those Principles I undertook to maintain; therefore, what I say on this head, must stand or fall alone, and I only propose it to the Consideration of Wiser Men.

What I have to say, Runs upon this Supposition, that an Usurpt Authority is not to be Obeyed, nor judged to be the Ordinance of God, until it be Thoroughly Settled?

It may be asked then, If there be quiet possession, and it be confirmed by our Representatives, what distinction can excuse us from paying Obedience to such Powers?

I Answer, our Representatives had no Authority to destroy the Monarchy: And therefore if they had thus Transgrest the Limits of their Power, it would not have Obliged those whom they Represented.

If it be Urged, that they have an Unlimited Power:

I Answer, it is True, but not unless, when they Act in their own Sphere, and in Conjunction with the King.

Obj. *But it may further be Objected, that at this rate our Representatives could not Transfer our Allegiance to their Majesties, since they could not make any binding Act without a King.*

Ans. I deny it. This they can do, as I shall shew you by and by; but it is an Exception from this Rule: They alone, can do no other Act, that can Oblige us: for instance, they cannot impose Taxes, or make Laws that shall Oblige us. In these, and in all other Cases, (except this instance now before us, of Confirming the Authority of a New King) it is our interest and security, that nothing should be Enacted, but by the Consent of the King, and our Representatives; and therefore, since we Commission them to Act only with the King, they can never Act without him.

Thus for instance, If a Conqueror has got the whole power into his hand, they may Transfer our Allegiance to him; Or if the Royal Family should be Extinct, they may proceed to a New Election. But if they pretend to Govern us themselves, without a King, this is more power, than we have given them; for we never Trusted the whole Legislative Authority in their hands; and I know not how they should come by it otherwise.

Obj. *But some will say, in such a Case it is Devolved to them.*

Ans. I deny it, they may have Power to dispose of the Crown as they please, but not to Assume the whole Soveraignty to themselves. By this means they will Lessen our Security; for whereas now we are Obliged only by Laws made by the King, and our Representatives, we should then be Obliged by Laws, made only by themselves; which I may say, is contrary to our Fundamental Law, *viz.* To be Governed by a King and our Representatives.

The Chain of my Discourse, hath led me into these untrodden

paths, I will Disentangle myself, as soon as I can, but all this was necessary to prove the thing I am aiming at. But to proceed,

Obj. Against this it may be Objected, that if the ROYAL FAMILY were Extinct, the whole Power would be Lodged in the Hands of our Representatives, and who may Resist them?

Ans. To prevent the Dissolving of the Government, it is Necessary, they should take the Sword into their Hands; but if they will not declare a New King, according to Custom, I cannot see why they may not be Compelled to it, since they have their Power only in Trust, not in their own Right: Thus in *Poland*, upon the Death of the King, if the Representatives of the People, who on that occasion are Entrusted with the whole Power, should pretend to be Lords *Paramount*, and would not proceed to a New Election; I know not why the People should not demand their Right, which is to be Governed by a King.

Now this would have been our Case, if our Representatives, in the late times, had patcht up a Government without a King: Though this had been done by our Representatives, it could not properly be called the Act of the People, because we never gave them such Authority. This you cannot but grant, unless you will presume, that we Commission them to destroy the Monarchy; which as you find can hardly be supposed in an Elective Kingdom, upon the Death of their King; but it is perfect Nonsense to suppose it, in an Hereditary Government, whilst the Royal Family is yet in being. It may be supposed, that we Commission them to Elect a King, in Case the Royal Line should Fail, or finding two pretenders, to declare who has the best Title, or to appoint a Protector, in Case of Infancy, or Lunacy; Or to receive a Conqueror into the Throne, in case our Natural Prince, be Fled out of His Kingdom, and incapacitated to protect us, and they in no condition to make opposition; or to invest the next Heir, with Royal Authority in case of Desertion, especially if the deserting

Prince, dare not, or cannot come to protect us; their enquiry not being, how he came into that condition, but whether he be in a Capacity to Protect us; and if he be not, they are then free to invest the next Heir with the Royal Authority. In all these Cases our Representatives may well presume on our Consent, though they Act without the King, because it is almost Absolutely necessary, these things should be done; and intolerable inconveniencies would ensue, perhaps to the utter Ruin of the Common-wealth, if they were not done. But to presume, that we give them Authority to take, and keep the whole Legislative Power in their own Hands, or to destroy the Monarchy, this is a strain beyond my comprehension, at least it is not Properly the Act of the People; and therefore they, whom they represent, must Ratify it in their own Persons, ere they can pretend a Thorough Settlement.

But then, if the People all the while shew great uneasiness under this Usurpation, if their cries be loud and clamorous, and many of them absolutely refuse to own the Authority; This has not the Face of a Settlement. Here is nothing, that looks like a general consent; and that though we should suppose our Representatives to have owned the Usurpt Authority; (for as by the Fundamental Laws of the Nation, we only Authorise them to act with the King); so whatever they shall do without a King, is not valid, unless it be in the Cases before mentioned, which both Necessity and Reason will allow; whereas, neither Necessity nor Reason can be pleaded in the former Instance.

But I do not pretend, that what I have said on this Point, will amount to anything like a Demonstration; a short-sighted Man may chance to find greater Flaws in it, than I am now aware of. Perhaps, my Zeal for Monarchy, has too much heated my Imagination; and I can only say, in my Excuse, That I have no pleasing Ideas of a Common-Wealth; and therefore, would willingly shut the door against it.

But if this will not stand the Test of a Judicious Reader, let this

Long *Parenthesis* pass for nothing, we need no such precarious Principles; our Case is good without it, as you may find in the other parts of this Discourse.

And now I have nothing more to trouble my Reader with, but only to Answer Two or Three Objections which could not so conveniently be considered in the Body of this Discourse; and then draw some Conclusions from it.

Obj. First then it may be Objected, That according to these Principles, we are now Settled upon a Legal and Rightful Government.

Ans. First, If this be well proved, so much the better; it is then no Argument against me.

Secondly, I can see no good Reason, Why we should not own it to be a Legal and Rightful Government, unless it be, that our Heads are perplexed with the nice Distinction of a King *de Jure*, and a King *de Facto*. By a King, *de Jure*, we commonly mean a Prince who has the Crown by Right of Inheritance; and it is thought, that any other Person can be, at best, but a King, *de Facto:* Upon this, many suppose, that His Present Majesty cannot be King, *de Jure*, at least, during the Life of King *James;* but yet may be obeyed, because the Law, made in the *11th.* of *Henry 7th.*[6] determines our Obedience to a King, *de Facto.* It is True, that Law indemnifies those who shall obey the King in the time being, as the Words of the Act run; that is, the King in possession, Whether he Claims the Crown by Right of Inheritance, or otherwise. But if Interpreters shall say, That he only is a King, *de Jure*, who Claims his Crown by Right of Inheritance, it is a visible Mistake; for all Mankind, as far as I know, are agreed, That a Conquerour, who makes a just War, upon the Submission of the Conquered Nation, becomes a King, *de Jure:* and if in this present Case, His Majesty is justly invested with the Royal Authority, he is so likewise, as I think I have proved. So that, you find this common Inter-

---

6. The so-called *De facto* Act, 11 Henry VII, cap. I (1495).

pretation is imperfect: a King, *de Jure*, should not so peremptorily be restrained to a King by Inheritance; but we run away with the Mistake; and without Considering, seem to yield the Point, as if His Present Majesty were only a King, *de Facto*.

I cannot say, Whether such as are skilled in the Laws, will allow of this Interpretation; but with submission, I presume it is agreeable to reason, and does not defeat the Design of the Law. To say, That a King, without a Title, is a King, *de Jure*, is a Contradiction; but to suppose, that he that originally wants a Title, does by an Act of Recognition, receive a Title; this we may suppose, without straining or forcing our Reason. I am sure it does not sound so harsh, as to require Obedience to an Illegal Government, for Conscience' sake. On other Occasions we make no Scruple to say, That a Sentence in a Court of Judicature, gives a Man a Title to an Estate; and upon this, the Tenants and Vassals, though it were procured corruptly, are to look upon him, and pay him Homage, as the Legal Possessor; and the like may be said in the Case before us, if our Representatives, without any good Reason, had placed His Majesty on the Throne, he had then been a King, *de Facto*, a Legal Possessor in the Eye of the Law; but if they acted according to Reason and Conscience, as I presume they did, he is then King, *de Jure*.

And if this were allowed for Sence, we should not be driven to say, That God Almighty requires our Obedience to Illegal Governments; which I cannot yet assent to, notwithstanding all the Authorities, which are brought to support this Doctrine. I acknowledge once for all, that *God removeth Kings, and setteth up Kings*, as He pleases; He is not bound by Human Laws, as we are; and when He has set up a New King, He must be obeyed; but an Usurpt Soveraignty must not be ascribed to God, or it does not appear to be His Act, until the New King gets quiet possession, together with an Act of Recognition; it is then soon enough to ascribe the Revolution to the Hand of God. When God means to carry things to this Length, He does by one means or other, dispose the People's Hearts, to receive such a Prince, and then he hath God's Authority.

Obj. *But it may be urged, That this Explication defeats the Design of the Law; which, as they say, was Enacted, to indemnify such as assisted* Henry *the* Seventh, *in case of a New Revolution; because, originally he had no good Title to the Crown; for if quiet Possession, and the Recognition of our Representatives, gives a Title, it may be said, there was no need of this Law.*

Ans. First, *Abundans Cautela non nocet;* They could never make themselves too secure; and therefore, lest their Enemies, as it was in the Fable, should say, that their Ears were Horns, they did wisely provide against it, fencing themselves with an Act of Parliament, though really there was little Occasion for it; but lest their Enemies might afterwards pretend, That *Henry* the *7th.* was not King, *de jure,* they declared it Lawful to Obey a King, de *Facto;* though at the time, there was no great Reason to Enact it barely on his Account.

And I presume, the rather, to make this Construction of it, because it is scarce credible, That *Henry* the *7th.* (who had so many Claims to the Crown, *viz.* Blood, Conquest, Marriage, and all strengthened by an Act of Recognition) should suffer his People to say, that he had no Rightful Title to the Crown; whereas it is said, he was the most suspicious Prince then living; and therefore, it is very improbable, he should own such a Blot in his Title, which must be, if he made himself thus a King, *de Facto,* only.

Secondly, If this be an empty groundless Surmise, His Majesty is yet a Legal King, because this Law supposes we may have such a King: And I may say, King *James* was no more; for though he had his Authority from God, the Law only was our Evidence of his Authority; just as we say, Marriage is the Ordinance of God; yet if a Man be not Married by the Form, which the Law prescribes, we presume to call it no Marriage. But after all, we are very unfortunate, if this Law, which was made to Govern and Direct us in our Obedience, should prove the main Foundation of all our Scruples; for perhaps, if our Fore-Fathers had not troubled us with this nice distinction of a King *de jure*, and King, *de facto*, we should not have coined it on this occasion, but have generally submitted to their Majesties, as Lawful and Rightful King and Queen.

Obj. But Secondly, against this Hypothesis may be Urged our Vulgar Maxim, That Conquest gives Right; for if there be any Truth in this saying, there is no need of our Consent.

Ans. This I have in part answered before, and if the Maxim be ill grounded, it must shift for itself.

Secondly, I allow there is some Truth in it, Conquest may give a Prince Right to the Conquered Dominions. When we are Conquered, we lose our Property. But I cannot conceive, that he should have Right to our Obedience, and our Persons, as so many Cattle, and Stock upon the Ground; and in short, if you would make this the sense of it, the condition of a Conquered People, would be most intolerable, since we thus bind their consciences without Reserving them any Property; it being agreed by all, that a Conqueror has the whole Property in the Conquered Country; and we only plead to have their consciences free, until they can make Terms for themselves, which I think ought not to be included in this Maxim; or it be, I had rather quit the Maxim, than lose my Liberty.

I Should now have done, only it may be convenient to draw some Conclusions from this Hypothesis, which may not be disagreeable to men of our Principles.

As first, If this be true, then it was not his Majestie's Sword, nor his Armies, that gave him his Authority over us, but our Representatives; in the Condition we were in, did justly Transfer our Allegiance to him, as I have already Demonstrated. This therefore must be great satisfaction to us all, that notwithstanding this great Revolution, things have run in the Right Channel, and that he did not get into the Throne, by Illegal means, which being supposed, we may the better hope for prosperity under his Government.

Secondly, If these Principles be True, then his Majesty was not Elected as some affirm; for in as much, as the Late King was not able, or willing to Protect us, the Crown Naturally Devolved on his Majesty, (for if Her Majesty, and Her Royal Highness the Princess of *Denmark* be pleased to postpone their Right, what is that to us) and if his Majesty upon the Late King's Leaving the Kingdom, did not presently take it, but left the doubt to be decided by our Representatives, it is no more than might be done upon a Descent, if there were two pretenders to the Royal Dignity; which being thus determined, I presume would not be Deemed an Election; their Act does not so much give the Crown, as determine, to whom it did belong. And I think this is much the same Case to that which is now before us; *viz.* The Consent of the Estates, to place his Majesty on the Throne, does no more Derogate from his Right, than the Act of Recognition,[7] past by King *James* the First, did suppose a Flaw in his Title.

Thirdly, Upon these Principles we may also Silence those Rash Men, who for Reasons best known to themselves, frequently tell us, that the Government was dissolved, when the Late King left us.

But surely these Men cannot see an inch before them, and I am almost ashamed to give them a serious answer. Let them tell me, if the Government did thereby Crumble into pieces, by what Right did our then Representatives, Erect another on the Ruins of it? If the Fountain of Honour failed, what Right had the Nobility to their Peerage, and why might not the meanest Peasant send his Representative, as well as any Landed Man, or free Burgher? These questions are too difficult to be resolved, unless it be upon the supposition, that the Old Government was then in being. They were at a loss indeed,

---

7. "A most joyfull and just Recognition of the immediate, lawfull, and undoubted Succession, Descent, and Right of the Crowne," 1 Jas I, cap. 1.

to know in whom the Government should be vested, and they came together to determine this great question, which they soon Wisely Resolved; And unless we quietly submit to what is done, by our Representatives in these Exigencies, we might as well say the Government was Dissolved, when the King Left us, if the remaining Powers might not Determine, where we should Pay our Obedience: For I suppose those Confusions, what by an unruly Rabble, and a Disbanded Army, did sufficiently shew the necessity of fixing somewhere; and I humbly suppose it is as evident to all Mankind, that the Late King would not, or could not come to Act his part in the Government.

But lastly, upon these Principles (if it were necessary to refute such vile Reproaches) we might secure our last Unhappy Prince, from being accounted the Grand Rebel, as he is styled in a late Scurrilous Pamphlet. For if it is only our own Consent, that makes us Subjects, we may at least be so favourable to the Ruins of Majesty, as to excuse him from being a Subject or a Rebel; since he cannot be the Head, he has not consented to be any other Member of the Government, not being here in Person, or any Deputed from him; though this cannot be said of any other Person, since they are Represented in our Estates, whether they will or not. Nor upon any other Hypothesis can I Conceive it Rational, to exclude the Late King himself from being a Member of this Present Government; but this way he is set at Liberty, and consequently, as free to Invade Their Majesty's Dominions, as any other Prince. If he molest us with an Unjust War, he must expect, at the Great and Dreadful Day, to give Account for all the Desolations and Blood-shed, that shall ensue upon it. If he is injured, he has a good God to Fight his Battles, and we a Merciful Creator, that I hope will Compassionate our Sins of Ignorance. I hope I may well call them so; for my part, my Conscience bears me Witness, That I think it my Duty to submit to Their Present Majesties' Government; and that I see nothing, that moves a Scruple in my Heart, but the contrary Example of some Worthy Men, who, I am perswaded, Act with great Sincerity. But since Example is no Argument, and if it were, is much stronger on our part; I dare not but follow the Dictates of my own Conscience.

FINIS.

[Sir Bartholomew Shower, 1658–1701]

REASONS

FOR A

New Bill of Rights:

Humbly submitted to the Consideration

OF THE

Ensuing Session

OF

PARLIAMENT.

LONDON:
Printed in the Year 1692.

*I*n many respects Sir Bartholomew Shower, an ardent Jacobite, seems an unlikely author for a tract urging the extension and refinement of the Bill of Rights. And yet there is little doubt that he wrote the essay.

Shower was the son of a prosperous Exeter merchant. He entered the Middle Temple in 1676 and was called to the bar in 1680. He rose quickly. In 1685 he was named deputy recorder of London, two years later he was knighted by James II, and in February 1688 he became the recorder of London, the chief legal adviser of England's greatest city. Shower's older brother, John, was a Presbyterian minister, and it may have been King James's tolerance of dissenters that strengthened Shower's attachment to the Crown and James's religious policy. At any rate he spoke for the Crown at the trial of the seven bishops in June. This clearly did not endear him to the city fathers, for in 1688, with the landing in England of William of Orange, Shower was replaced as recorder.

Shower opposed the new king and queen and was among those who published tracts attacking William Sherlock for his abandonment of the nonjuror position. He did manage to continue his legal practice, and this seems to have made him all the more conscious of the shortcomings of the recent Bill of Rights. He had initially opposed trial reform but by 1692, in a dramatically changed political climate, he was enthusiastically pressing for legal change, especially for change of the procedures used in treason trials. Those accused of treason, for example, were not given a copy of the charges against them or granted the right to be represented by counsel. A bill to modify the procedure in trials for treason was introduced into Parliament in 1690 but was not to become law until 1696. In the present tract Shower points out the haste with which the English Declaration of Rights was drafted and spells out a series of desired reforms that were neglected and in need of implementation. His essay appeared in a single edition.

Reasons for a New Bill of Rights, &c.

Considering the many impetuous and convulsive Struggles, which this Land hath so frequently groaned under, between the People and their Prince; and that some Persons of Honour, Sense and Sagacity, have always been engaged in those Convulsions; it must provoke an Agony of Wonder, that no more or better Provision is hitherto acquired, for the Ensurance of Men's Lives, Estates and Liberties.

The Defect can be ascribed to no other Original, than the sudden Cesser of violent and eager Essays for that purpose, which Violence is seldom durable, and therefore the Occasion of its own Disappointment; but now in the present Circumstances, when a Forreign War[1] hath employed the warmer and more sanguin part of Mankind, and an entire Calm overspread the Face of Domestick Counsels and Affairs, the Season perchance is arrived, for a mature and sedate, and consequently successful Consideration of sound, proper and true Methods, to secure Ourselves and Posterity in these Particulars.

However a provocative of this kind can never be unseasonable; though Provisions of Money in the approaching Parliament will be one thing, yet it cannot be the only one necessary, especially when a Flaw in our Title to any of these Ingredients of Bliss, destroys the necessity of that. It is therefore to be hoped, that the Courtier, Statesman and Officer will permit the Country Gentleman in some soft Degree, to attempt the Supply of his own as well as their Occasions; nor can the Proposal of the one obstruct the just Progress of the other; for it is the old fundamental Doctrine of a true *English* Parliament, that they should always concur, and now there's Reason and Opportunity for both.

1. The war begun by the League of Augsburg against Louis XIV lasted from 1689 until 1697. One of William of Orange's chief motives in pressing his wife's claims to the English throne was to bring England into this conflict.

To obviate Prejudice and Objection against a perusal or regard of the following Lines, it may not be amiss to premise, That the Author is neither Republican nor Enemy to the present Establishment; nor can the usual Artifice of Nicknaming a Proposition as Antimonarchical, render it the less acceptable to him that's concerned, as every *Englishman* formerly was, is today, or may be tomorrow, in this: It is too well known to have been an ancient as well as modern Court-trick, to advise Kings from encouraging, and the Commons from prosecuting of a full Security by just and rational means, with the terror and dread of a Commonwealth, as the unavoidable consequent of a true Liberty, though whosoever knows Men in *England*, must also know that Figure of Government here to be impracticable. But methinks since the Discovery of Priest-craft in Religions, and the Detection of Intreaguery in State Matters, Men should be wiser, than to slight or reject Endeavours for their own Happiness, because of Names, Titles or Epithets if of an harsh Sound, though improperly applied.

I am sensible of another Objection from the *Bill of Rights*, but surely that Scruple vanishes upon the first Reflection; for the nicety of the then Circumstances, the multitude of incurring Exigences both at home and from abroad, may well be agreed to have hindered a plenary or sufficient comprehensive Thought of all our then Grievances. It must be confessed, that the Instances there mentioned are considerable and great, and the Provisions made for them are useful and good, though too generally expressed, and perhaps obnoxious to some different Constructions, whensoever reduced or applied to particular Use; the Settlement of Religion and Church-men's Property by those *Items* is politick and happy; and in truth the *Bill* doth extend to little more than that, and the Health of Corporations; but the Acquirement of those Reliefs, was never intended to be exclusive of more, if more appeared necessary; the private Lay Gentlemen deserve some Consideration, for their Number exceeds both Clergy and Officers, though the latter are sufficiently numerous; nor is the Ballance of the Gentry inconsiderable in the Government.

Another Cavil is expected at these Papers as needless, because the Judges are fixed and free from Temptation, their Pattents are not now upon Pleasure, and those at present in *BR*.[2] (where the ensuing Queries do most frequently arise, and are most properly determinable) are Persons endued with Learning, Probity and Resolution.

Agreeing all this, and more, that they are, and so indeed they are, the Glory of the whole Revolution, it doth yet still remain worthy of a Thought that they are mortal, and another King may arise in *Israel*, that may make another Choice; and notwithstanding they should be more independent, through the certainty of their Office and Salaries, then formerly yet it may be of Men temptable by the accruer of a greater Pension, or the like; it cannot be forgot what some Ministers have rung in the Ears of former Princes, that Hearts not Heads, were necessary for that Court; that the Humour of the Man, and not his Knowledge in the Law, was the most considerable in the Election of a Judge: that Complaisance to Prerogative was a much better Quality than that of a judicious and crabbed, if stubborn Lawyer. But further, we should deserve the Pity of Fools, if after so much Treasure and Blood spilt for the Redemption of Liberty, the same should be ascertained by no better a Fund than the Life of three Men at the present in Power;[3] nor can their Preservation ensure *Englishmen* against Hardships in the subsequent Cases; for this Proposal evinces the Imperfection of our Laws as now received and practised, and the necessity of another Statute to explain or amend them. And therefore this Objection is an Argument rather to inforce than to discourage the Prosecution on it; for sure we are, these Judges will and must (as by Oath obliged) observe those Rules; and from thence springs the

2. An abbreviation for *Bancus Regis*, King's Bench.
3. King's Bench consisted of a chief justice and three puisne justices.

true Cause for new, but better Provision; nor do those Remarks aim at or import Reflection upon the present Practice, but meerly endeavour to demonstrate the necessity of a Law or two more; now new Laws do not always suppose Faults in *Fact*, but many times in *Posse*, they are as often made to obviate as to relieve against Grievance and Oppression; and were it otherwise, this is no more than every Act of Parliament past hath done; and therefore such new Law (as is here contended for) doth still appear necessary.

Now for PARTICULARS.

First, As to Life; the late Bill for regulating Trials in Cases of Treason[4] is a clear Evidence of the imperfect Defence which the Laws in being afford to Men's Lives; the Misfortune which attended that Bill doth call for a Reinforcement of that Design; the Opposal it met with (considering the Persons who made it) doth in a demonstrative manner declare its Conveniency and Necessity; and therefore the honest part of the Nation do hope that the next Session will pass that or another such; nor is there any Reason to despair on it, unless Men improve in their Fondness of Danger, even of Death; for no Person living can be undoubtedly secure, that he never shall become or be deemed a Malecontent, both which are one in point of Danger. As to the pretended Reasons against such Relief, a Line of Answer is more than they deserve; but however to propose some hints convictive of their Weakness may not be improper. It argues some Defect in thinking to pretend that the 25 of *Ed. 3*.[5] hath governed our Forefathers, and hitherto the present Age, and therefore we need no other Law; for might not this Objection have damned the Petition of Right, or

---

4. The procedures for treason trials were eventually reformed in 7 & 8 Will. III, cap. 3 (1696), The Trial of Treasons Act.

5. The 25 Edw. III, stat. 5, cap. 2, passed in 1350 was the main treason act and possibly the first to make it treason to levy war against the king in his realm.

any or every other Act of Parliament, because we had a *Magna Charta* before; besides Innovation and the dismal Consequences on it was always a Bugbear both in Church and State to prevent Alterations even for the better; but wise Men, if honest, have as often contemned the Pretence as ever 'twas objected, or otherwise we should have wanted that Pittance of Security which we have acquired already; but do hope to increase. It is manifest upon the First, Second, Third, and every Reading of that Statute, that 'tis a general, uncertain and obscure Provision, sufficient Confusion, Doubt and Contradiction hath there been in expounding it; the Chronicles and Reports of every Age since *Edward 3.* proves this, nor can our own Observations fail of furnishing us with Arguments of infinite Difficulties resulting from that Law, and many with Semblance of Reason and Authority on both sides; the late Paper skirmishes about the unhappy Lord *Russel's* Case do prove the need of a new explanatory, directive Act; as also the new Notions vented in the Earl of *Stafford* Case about Witnesses to several Facts or rather Circumstances which have precedented it almost to every subsequent Trial. Then in the Name of God, what Harm can accrue to the Publick in general, or to any Man in particular, that in Case of State Treason Councel should be allowed to the Accused, what Rule of Justice is there to warrant its Denial, when in a Civil Case of a Halfpenny Value the Party may plead either by himself or Advocate. That the Court is Councel for the Prisonner can be no effectual Reason, for so they ought to be in every Action, unto each Party, that Right may be done; but the *Frenchman's* Remark upon this Phantom, for 'tis no more hath sufficiently censured it, *That my Councel ask no good Questions for me, my Councel make no good Sign for me, me no like my Councel.* And it hath too often proved according to that poor Fellow's Observation; nothing but Practice, *No written Law excludes from Councel in any Case,* (says the great and late honest *Coke*) and there is the same pretence for denying a Copy of the Indictment, though that has been granted in case of Felony in one *Bothe's* Case, the which is in a Book called, *More's* Reports.

But some bold Whisperers do pretend, that the Times are, or may be dangerous, the Crown ought to have a Power to support itself, this will make Convictions difficult, the Government must sometimes have a Lift, there must be Methods to lop off an Enemy, or the Head of a Party now and then, and there is no better Convenience for it than a doubtful Law, and therefore no Explanation or Amendment is politick.

'Twas thought that these Principles had been abdicated with the late King, but since their renewal calls for an Answer, I'll briefly observe to those which vent them, that all Human Affairs are so unstable, and Courts under several, nay, under the same Sovereigns, do so often change Interests and Inclinations, and consequently Parties, that 'tis possible a malicious Chance may make the Enemy's Lot to become the Objector's; and so hath Fate most frequently doomed it in a most smart and Exemplary Form upon the Opponents of their Country's Liberty, that they have been lasht with that very Rod which they have refused to remove, have endured that very Oppression, which when in their Power, they denied to redress: *English* Story is too full of such Instances, and God forbid the increase of them again.

This Objection is absurd and subverts Fundamentals, for in such extraordinary Emergences of State and Consequence, the Parliament is, or ought to be at hand; the Use of that Assembly is not barely the Gift of Subsidies, but to help the King and People according to their respective Occasions, and there is the Crown's *Recipe*, Impeachments or Bills are his infallible Remedy; and our Constitution never intended any other Relief in case of such Difficulties, than that of a Parliament. Then if we consider the strict Rules of common natural Justice, 'twill appear, much more eligible, that sundry Offenders should escape, than one innocent should suffer, for that such Cases admit of no Restitution, the Reversal of an Attainder injuriously procured, cannot render a Satisfaction; the Head returns not to the Shoulders, nor Life to the Party, though the Title be restored to the Name, and the Estate to the Son of such a Martyr.

It is evident beyond contradiction, that within twelve Years past, many would have resigned the half of their Estates for the procurement of such a Law, as now (to the wonder of the Nation) themselves have opposed. The Fact admits of no Reason but Revenge or the Change of their Principles upon the Occasion of Power and Employments, each whereof is alike unmanly and therefore unwarrantable; but methinks they should consider that they are not certain of the stability and continuance of their present Settlements, much less of their Interests, and the same Occasion as formerly, may in future Ages revive, and then the Reviver of Complaints with their Suffering may be fruitless and vain, when the Opportunity of Relief is fled and gone; not good Hopes concerning future Administrations but good Laws only, that can give a Plerophory or full Assurance of Security. Now is the Season, if ever, for a Fixation of our Franchise from the Perils, from the actual endurance whereof we are but just delivered; it may be presumed, that the late turn of our *English* Affairs is not yet banished our Memory, nor the end of the Change buried in Oblivion, and the present Proposal was unquestionably one Design of the Revolution. The Convention of the Estates of the Realm in Eighty eight, eighty nine, intended somewhat more than the Ejection of Thirty or forty fat Officers, and the prefering as many other in their places, though of the more intelligent and honest Principles, for these are still Men, and liable at least, I will not say prone, to human Infirmities, and though not possibly equal, yet like to those of their Predecessors. The Purpose of the Nation's Wisdom was to gain a Security beyond the reach of Construction, Power or Craft to evade, and if the same be not hitherto accomplished (which whither it be or not, let the Reader be Judge). It is now therefore the Duty of all sincere and true *Britains,* to endeavour the Perfection of such their Security against every of their former or the like Mischiefs; the Necessity of the War summons a Parliament for Supplies, and this renews our Opportunity for to finish the intended Errant of the First Assembly after the Abdication. *This is the Time,* said a great Man upon a less Occasion, and every Man may say the same now, and with more Reason: Then as to the Second concerning our Estates.

It cannot be denied, that both Law and Equity do in their Practice need a Regulation; the Exorbitances of that Prerogative Court called *Chancery* do loudly cry for a Bridle, and that by an Act of Parliament. There 'tis that the single and sudden Thoughts of a Keeper are the only Rules for Justice, and the Power is but *Durante* (it must not be said) *secundum bene placit R.* and this may caveat the Rich and Bulky to promote some moderate Reformation of that Court, or else to resolve, that his Quarrel shall never be with a Courtier, and that he'll never incur the infortunate Character of dissaffected to the Government; for it hath been formerly, and may be hereafter very easy, with one of those Monosyllables Fraud and Trust (which have already almost devoured every other Title in the Law) to decree such a one a Beggar; Nickname his Purchase and his Estate doth instantly change its Owner; then if a Commoner prove his Adversary, whose Inheritance commands a *Borough,* the Wretch is remediless, and his Beggary everlasting; for there's no Appeal but in Parliament, and with his Hopes of Relief commences Priviledge, and then he must wait, at least till the Issue Male of the Family be extinct, and that is too long an Expectancy to be called a Relief. To expose the Dilatories and Expences of that Court is a Province much fitter for some Lawyer's Pen than mine. My only Remark is this, that that Court is too dependant upon another, that its Power is too Arbitrary, and its pretended Rules too uncertain; and although the Probity of the present Keepers do prevent Mischief at the present, yet future Reigns may use Creatures of a worse Kidney, and to worse Purposes, and then the Authority of the Seal as now in practice, will afford Opportunity to do Mischief more than sufficient. Then for the Law, it must be agreed to stand in the like need of a Purge too; but such Topicks would be proper to employ the Head of some Practitioner, whose Experience capacitates him to discover its blind side and corruptions; that which I observe is this, that there wants some Act to facilitate the Practice of Attaints, by allaying the severity of the Judgment therein, and then we might hope to see Corruption of standing Juries reformed, and the Consequences of that Corruption banished too, *viz* the forced Practice of granting New Trials, when the Verdict displeases the Judge, though the Fact be not within his Sphere; at our Assizes I have for several Years observed a great uncertainty in the Rules of Evidence, in the Gift of Actions, and in the Notions both of Titles of Land and Property in Goods, every Circuit perhaps differing from the last, but that seems ascribable to the great Latitude given to the sudden Opinion of a Judge by the predominant increase of General Issues, which leaves too much at the Discretion of a single Person. These and many more hints might be given of this kind, but of this enough, for they are Trifles to my last and chief Topick, because, concern but a few; for Men with Temper and Wisdom may easily prevent the Plague of Law Suits, and the want of one of them is generally the cause of Vexation either by Common Law or *Chancery;* but there's no Fence against Imprisonment, for the cast of a Man's Eye, the Smiles or Frowns of his Face, entire Silence or too much or too little Speech, as the Company pleases to interpret and represent, may raise Suspicions concerning Principles. If he keeps company he is judged by the Humour of that, if he keeps none he's thought reserved, and therefore the more dangerous; if a Maggot in his Head or a fanciful Thought in his Brain occasion a Laugh when ill News is arrived to the Court, or if the Distasters of his Personal or Family Concern, or a Pain in his Body provokes a sour Look upon the talk of a Victory or the like, these and a thousand more such are Badges of Malice to the Government, where Construction is at liberty, so that the following Doubts are of consequence to every one.

Thirdly, Liberty of Person; 'twould be Subject of Ridicule and Jest to attempt the Conviction of our Countrymen, that Liberty is pleasant, and to preserve it deserves our Care. It's one of our first Principles connatural to an *English* Heart, to be tender and jealous of its loss and Abridgment. The Contentions here both with Tongue, Pen and Sword for its continuance hath proved such a Theme needless; our *Magna Charta* places the contrary in equal rank with Disseizin and Exile, both which are sufficiently odious, the one depriving a Man of his Country, the other of his Fortune, and this debars him of the Pleasure, nay Use of both; it is pretended by all the Judges, that Liberty is the Darling of the Law, and Restraint the Badge of Bondmen and Vassals, but the Practice in almost all Ages hath given the Lie to such pretence; for nothing hath been so often and easily lost, to Peers and Commons, to the Grandees and the Peasant, upon very little or no Suspicion as personal Liberty. That particular Piques or private Malice of State Ministers or perchance that which is less cause; the insolent Humour of Commandments in Power, or the generous Behaviour of a Gentleman with its usual attendant Popularity, (which is always an Eye-sore at Court) or the Fears of Statesmen though resulting from their own Weakness when there's no Danger, or from their own false Steps in Government. Where there is these and such like Occasions, have frequently gaoled great Numbers of the best part of the Nation in all Ages. It must be impertinent to recollect Instances, since Members of Parliament have not been free even in Parliament time; as for the Oppressions of which Imprisonments, whosoever hath suffered them is sufficiently convinced, and he that hath not, may easily conjecture; for much the greater part of the Nation either by themselves or their Friends and

Acquaintance hath experimented the Pleasure of such forced Re-
tirement, within less space than Forty Years past, and therefore I'll
forbear to enlarge on it.

The Cause of this Grievance hath sprung from the Imperfection
or Uncertainty of our Laws concerning this Subject; the Questions
about it in *Charles I.* Time, were so fiercely debated, not only within
the Walls of the Commons House, but in the Press and Field too,
that their Notoriety recalls them to every Man's Remembrance; the
Opinions of Parliaments was always against indefinite, general, or
causless Commitments, but no Man imagined himself secure till the
late *Habeas Corpus* Act, which inflicted Penalties upon its Violators,
nor hath that accomplished the Design of ensuring a true Liberty, as
I shall now endeavour to demonstrate; that this Act was, and is a
wholsome Law, cannot be denied, and 'twas worth the Price it cost;
but yet another will deserve twice as much, for the former is deficient
to a great Degree. To convince that it is so, let it be considered that
31 Car. 2. did that Statute pass the Royal Assent, and since that time
Five hundred Persons to one have been committed more than ever
were tried, or so much as indicted. It is observable that every Year or
two, a dozen or twenty Lords are usually shopt, together with incredible Numbers of the greatest Commoners, over and besides the
small Fry of &c. Halls and Churches have been turned into Prisons
when the common Gaols were crowded even to danger of Infection;
and I am apt to believe that hundreds have been committed without
Oath, and consequently without just cause of Suspicion, for there
ought to be Oath of that Fact or Circumstance which rendered the
Party suspected. And this is the first Defect in the Statute, that it
doth not enjoin an Oath to be mentioned in the Warrant, which is
unquestionably consonant to Reason, that the Person and his Judges
may become privy to the true Reason of his Commitment; perhaps it
may not be for the Service of the Crown to name the Informant upon
the first Accusation, but that no Commitments ought to be without

Oath first made, is certainly Law; and an Injunction to mention an Oath in the Warrant, together with a Penalty for Imprisonment without Oath in Writing, will make the Ministers concerned more cautious in cases of Liberty; nor can any Reason be assigned in Nature why Priviledge should not be denied by Act of Parliament, in case of the Violation of the Subject's Freedom, which is and ought to be dear to us all. The end of frequent Parliaments is for Maintenance of Personal Liberty, and why such frequency should hinder Suit for Incroachments on that Liberty, the Reason is behind the Curtain. Another Fault is, That the cause of Commitment is not enjoined to be specially signified, charged for compassing the King's Death, or adhering to his Enemies, is in truth no more special or plain than to say for Treason, for there are a Thousand Acts and Ways of doing both these, and those dependant upon construction, so that a Man is not a whit the better informed to prepare for his Trial or Defence by the one than by the other; for when he considers of one Action obnoxious to strain, another, a third, or a hundredth may be trumpt to his Charge; the end of that Provision certainly was, to have the Fact known whereof the Party was accused. Again, Warrant to seize being charged for High Treason *in compassing or adhering, &c, and to bring before me to be examined,* and such Messenger to detain for Days, Weeks and Months, seems somewhat unreasonable, when the Party granting such Warrant expresses himself doubtful in his Judgment concerning the Charge, and the Fact indeed to need an Examination, yet this Case is not bailable; whether Secretary or Privy Councellor, not having actually taken the Oath of a Justice of Peace can commit for Felony or Treason, is no small Query, but the Ferments of latter times, and the supposed Necessity arising from thence hath answered that Problem by some Years' Practice, and therefore that Point is not to be stirred without doors, but surely they ought to be in the same State as other Justices, to answer Suits for unjust or wrongful Restraint of Men's Persons, and the Greatness or

Priviledges of these Officers ought not to exempt from common Actions, but the rather an Access to Relief against them, should be made more easy, since they monopolize that Trade, and consequently are more frequently liable to Mistakes wilful or by accident; the Method for such Relief is above my reach either to contrive or propose.

When the Cause is only Suspicion, Bail and that at Discretion of the Judge is now required, and this is all the Relief at present, and that is tantamount to none; for if the Judge or Minister pleases, such extravagant Sums and Estates may be required, as to render the Party remediless, and his Continuance in Gaol inevitable; here's no Measure prescribed, nor any Penalty imposed on the Judge if he be guilty of Excess in such his Demand. In case of an actual Breach of Peace, and the Complainant swears a Danger of his Life, the common Rate is £.40 Principle, £.20 a piece the Bail; but for Suspicions of Treason, or as generally disaffected to the Government, swinging Sureties for Bulk in their own Estates, and Sums in their Recognisance, have been and may be again exacted, and no Relief.

Commitments with the Clause of denying Pen, Ink and Paper, or Friend or Relation, are not provided against, nor yet in truth warranted by that or any other Law; for if the Party be not guilty of the Charge, or but suspected without Evidence sufficient, the Usage is not Humane or *English;* if he be guilty and there's Evidence for such Guilt, then Liberty of Access ought to be allowed to his Friends with the Use of Writing, that he may prepare for a Trial. For the Law never impowered a Secretary to commit a Man because thought dangerous to the Government, but because he is guilty of a Crime, and that he is only to secure him to be forthcoming to a Trial, not to punish him before his Trial, for till then it remains in doubt whether guilty or innocent.

Another Defect is this, Suppose a Man committed in *Trinity* Term for the Charge of Treason, and after the expiration of four or five

Months, and before the arrival of *Michaelmass*, the Secretary thinks fit that Bail be admitted, then though no Indictment or other Prosecution, this Bail may be continued from Day to Day, and from Term to Term, for seven Years together, and he can't help himself; within the Memory of Man this hath been practised for seven, nine, nay twelve Terms successively upon the same Recognizance; then it is an infinite Default, that if a Man be committed to a Country Gaol, and perhaps that may be, as it hath been, to *Hull* or *Canterbury*, this Man is remediless till an Assizes, and that sometimes not happening in several Years, and then this Wretch can't make his Prayer in *B.R.* he hath not Money to procure a Commission of *Gaol Delivery,* or *Oyer* and *Terminer*, and if he could, perhaps 'tis denied him, and no Provision made against such Denial. Now here is an indefinite Imprisonment, this Difficulty arises from a constructive Opnion upon that Law, that the Prayer may be either in B.R. or before *Oyer* and *Terminer*, as to be taken distributively and respectively, if here about Town in *B.R.* if in the Country then at the Assizes, though the Words are general, one or the other.

Further Remedy is, *If no Indictment the first Term, the Party is to be bailed, unless Oath be made that the King's Witnesses could not be produced that Term.* Now this needs an Explanation for the end of our Lawmakers unquestionably was, that he should be bailed, unless there was Evidence sufficient whereon to indict, and such Evidence could not be produced; whereas according to a litteral Construction of that Clause, any Man may be detained though not Evidence enough to found an Indictment, as if Oath be made that there is Evidence against *A. B.* and *C.* and every of them, that the Witnesses against them could not be produced, and no possibility to convict the Jurate of Perjury, for it may all be true in some Sense (and if true in any Sense it excuses from Perjury) and yet besides the Intent of the Law to have the Persons detained, there might be two Witnesses, one against one, and another against the other, and yet no Indictment could be on this for want of two Witnesses against each. Now 'tis plain when the Law says, *If he be not indicted he shall be bailed unless Oath be made that the Witnesses could not be produced*, it must be meant such Witnesses as could swear to the Indictment, which one alone could not, because the Statute requires two even upon the Bill, besides such litteral Construction renders the *Affadavit* Maker Judge of what is evidence, when perhaps he is ignorant of the thousandth part of the Difficulties and the Doubts upon that Subject; then for *could not be produced*, t'would be but reasonable that the Court should know and judge of the Reason of the *Nonproduce*, and not the Swearer; perhaps the Reason might not be sufficient in the Court's Opinion, but more than sufficient in the Swearer's; he might think an Horse-rase or Wedding, want of Pay or Recantation, or Forgetfulness of part of his Testimony, a Reason; nay, the Witness might be dead, and yet his Oath true, for there might be Evidence by Papers, and one Witness to prove them, and the other Witness departed, and so could not be produced; though these Thoughts are equivocal, yet they'll deliver him from the Charge of a wilful, false, corrupt and devilish Perjury; these short Notices are enough to shew an Occasion of an additional, explanatory Act.

Another Defect is this, That if committed to any Gaol in *Wales* as a dangerous Man, or upon Suspicion of Treason, he is remediless by this Law, unless he has Money to pay for a Journey to *London*, and that must be paid down before he shall be brought; for no Judge or other Authority there is bound to bail him, and then if he lies till their Session of *Gaol Delivery*, he can't be bailed upon the want of an Indictment, because the Treason is not specially signified; and then he is left as at Common Law, and how uncertain and merciless a Remedy that was before the making of this Act, we and our Forefathers have been sufficiently taught. A further Enemy to Liberty, is a Power still reserved to Judges of a Court, to commit upon pretence of Contempt to them, and this out of the Act, and such an Authority hath every little Petty Court of Record in the Nation, and Mistre's Experience tells us, every slight Matter makes a Contempt to them, and there's no examining the Cause, for the Court that commits is Judge of the Contempt, and further there's no Deliverance, till Submission and their Discharge.

Add to these Opponents of bodily Freedom, the new found Offices of a King's Sollicitor, &c. a Novelty never heard of till the latter end of *Charles II.* and the Subject has Reason to thank God that 'tis so late an Invention, for before that time the King had as few, and since hath had more Causes than any of his Subjects, 'tis from those Mutes that Characters are received, which extorts a bleeding in the Culprit's Pockets, for as that moves either open or shut, so doth the sign of a Shrug with the Shoulder, or a Wink tipt upon his superiour Officer, produce Hardships or Ease to the trembling Gaol-bird; perhaps the hint doth not take, and then there's a necessity of a secret Whisper, that the Bird in the Cage, is either a damned Tory or a confounded Republican, as the times respectively require; but if the Medicine requisite was duly applied, then with a Smile in the Face and the Hand on the Purse as the Cause, proceed these or the like Words, *He is an honest, harmless, fair-conditioned Fellow*; and an immediate Assent to the Partie's Bailment or Discharge is the certain consequent. In old time, the Ability of Bail was tried by Examination upon Oath in Court, but this new Office hath introduced a new Practise of giving Notes of the Names in order to Enquiry, and the Use and the Profit of such Practice is notoriously evident.

Lastly there's a Penalty on the Judge or Judges, if they deny any *Habeas Corpus,* but none if they refuse to bail or discharge, when and where they ought; then there's one thing more which ought to be considered, for it plainly spoils our Claim or Pretence of being a Free People, and that is the Power of our Lieutenancy as now established, for they are made and continued at the will of another, and they at their own wills may commit whom, and when, and for so long as they please; and as I am informed there's no relief, they sit and act when-soever they are bid, and composed in all places and times of some one predominate Party, for the Ballance can seldom be supposed exactly equal in such Assemblies, and by Consequence the lesser Party must expect their Mercy on every the least Occasion; now considering the Sides and Factions in *England* and their natural eagerness each against the other, and the small hopes there are of an Union, me-thinks true Policy should direct some measures and Rules of Re-straint, to prevent Oppressions and Hardships on either part; the Form of making such Provision must be submitted.

These are but few among many Instances, which might be pro-duced to evince the necessity of a new Law; nor is it convenient for a private Person to enumerate everything of this kind deserving Rem-edy; it suffices to offer such and so many *Items,* as may excite the Par-liament to consider of these and the other Mischiefs which need a Provision, and to continue Methods accordingly.

To conclude, a Word of Religion cannot be improper, the Act of Toleration hath exempted Dissenters from the Prosecution of the sanguinary and other Penal Laws; but that Exemption is imperfect, for that a Force still remains on their Consciences in respect of their Children, for though themselves are not constrained to frequent the Legal Church, yet absurdly enough they are constrained to educate their Children in Methods contrary to their own Opinions and Sen-timents, for no School is permitted them, though but to teach the *Assemblie's Catechism,* and this seems inconsistent in itself, that their Judgments may be freely persued in the one and yet restrained in the other, especially if a religious Reason induced the former, for if so the same obliges to the latter.

Now after all, the intent of these Lines is only to propose and not reflect, and surely thinking must convince Men, that such a Law would add to our Happiness, if procured; nay, it seems strange that any should oppose it, since that the want of it may prove any Man's

Misfortune, and no Man can be professedly desirous of Slavery, or dependance on another's Will for Liberty; but to the Shame of our Nation, there are too many in it, that are willing to be Slaves to a few, so as many may be Slaves to them; and from that corner we expect an Opposition; therefore to provoke an Appetite and Zeal for true Liberty, let us consider our Government and its Nature; 'tis a Monarchy Royal (as an Attorney General hath confessed) and not Seignoral, and by our Law the Subject hath an entire, absolute, independent and uncontroulable Interest both in Land and Goods; now yet without Freedom of Person, and that ascertained, we are not Freemen but Villains, and shall *Englishmen* content themselves to hold their Liberty upon Will? Let us consider the Examples of our Forefathers and follow them, let us read and recollect how the Patriots of the last Age, *Coke, Selden* and the rest, did esteem and value it, when they tugged it so nobly in their Conference with the Lords, *Anno Charles I. Quarto,* though the Argument then was against General Commitments, yet their Zeal and Courage was true and cordial for Liberty in general, and so ought ours to require an ample and compleat Security on it. If we conceive ourselves in person to be exempt from the Danger, because the Complaisance of our Principles may secure us from Hazard upon every Turn, let Generosity and a true *English* Good-nature raise a Concern for others, whose Discretion may prove defective upon such an Occasion; nay, the Inconstancy of Men and things may deceive even ourselves in some Events, and balk such our Confidence.

Let us be humane and pity the Miserable and Forlorn, that have been made so upon Suspicion only, during the Rage of other Men's Plots either real or sham, or that may become so hereafter upon the like Contingencies; to describe the Misfortunes of Patients in this kind, with their several Circumstances in particular and at large, would I am confident, melt the Soul of the most obdurate Reader, and to affect him there would need no use of Rhetorick; my Request is only, that he would once visit our common Prisons and view those Lodgings, which have at several times received the best of our *English* Worthies, and perhaps some of his own Acquaintance; if this be too nauseous a Task, let him but frame an Image in his Mind, that he saw the Body of a disturbed Citizen, hauled and dragged with Swords and Staves, from his House and Bed in the midst of Night; then consider him as bled by some Harpie of a Messenger for a certain Season, and withall listen to those insolent Huffs and Abuses of those insatiable Devourers of Coin and Liberty, during such his Bondage under their Dominion, then see him hurried to a Gaol or Dungeon, there loaded with Irons in abundance, disabling him to sit, or lie, or stand, without actual and continued Torment, excluded from the Benefit of Light or Friend, Pen or Ink, Paper or Book, Fire or Candle, or other Help of Nature, then consider the Fears and Anxiety of such a Captive, either for himself, or Family or other Relation, and that continued for Nights, Days, Weeks, Months; and invisible to any human Creature, except some griping Turnkey, whose Visits perhaps are followed with the approach of some devilish Tempter who comes to increase his Torture by the false Promises of Reward, if he will confess discover and evidence some unknown Story; or else unhuman Menaces of an infinite Misery and Death as its only end in case of Refusal; then review him as alone, his Soul wrackt, tortured and distracted between the dread of Dishonour and Gallows, and his Keeper's Usage changed (and that by Command of the tempting undertaker to facilitate his Design) and then the Wretch's Corpse is reloaded with a double Train of Artillery, and therewith removed to a nastier Sty, if such there be, and immediately the Nickhole of Light, if any, is stopt, and the Man left alone overwhelmed with Chains, Darkness and Stench, to which you may add the Disturbance of his Mind and Thoughts about the last Temptation, which is usually repeated while in this or the like condition; and here you may leave him a while to himself, and turn your Eye to his

Wife and Children with Tears and trembling Attendant at the Grate, after having by Pawns or Beggary got some Guineas wherewith to soften (if possible) the Gaoler's Heart, you may hear them begging and intreating for a sight of this their Relative though at a Distance, nay sometimes praying but a Notice and view of those exteriors of those Walls, within which such their Dearest lies thus intombed, and even this shall be denied with execrable Reproaches and Insults, and all under Pretence of express Orders.

Then follow those ambulatory Wretches and you'll find them making their Court to the Criminal, Agent, or his Deputy, for Leave to apply to the Secretary for Leave to see this *English* Slave, and this first Leave must be paid for too, or else there will arise an hope of Evidence with an Aggravation of his ill Character, and so an opposal of this their just and legal Right; but anon you'll meet them at *Whitehall*, where after four or five Days' Expence in Waiting, and a Curtesie dropt with a Crown to the Porter, and two of them with double the Sum to the Footman, my Lord's Clerk becomes visible; and when both are doubled again to him, at last the Secretary is seen, but then her first Address proves certainly abortive, and the second procures only an Adjournment for Inquiry and Recollection after the much no Evidence, which however to her Assurance of the Accused's Innocence yield some Hopes, and then it may be the Widow's Importunity extorts a Promise of Speech with King or Councel about the Matter, especially if the Dun be followed close. But then Business of Necessity enforces two or three more Excuses, and at last if the Woman's Patience, and Money can hold out to gain a frequent Access, so as to disturb his Lordship with repeated Cries and Tears, a Promise is made of an Order for Leave. Now to tire the Reader no longer with these Difficulties; upon Payment of expedition Money and the usual Fees, the Order is drawn and signed, and with Thanks and Joy received; notwithstanding all this Labour and Charge, this Order is not legible at the Prison, unless the Keeper's Spectacles be guilt, and when allowed 'tis worth but little, for the Keeper's Presence is commanded, and not a word must pass between Wife and Husband but in his Hearing, which frequently makes it a silent though mournful Meeting, for fear of Misrepresentation, and this dear bought Leave can serve but once, and its renewal in price comes little short of the first.

After all this, when the Man's Body hath contracted Distempers, and small Fortune is quite exhausted, and his Employment with his Credit lost, and consequently his Family undone, and his Children, if not himself consigned to Parish Care; then without Trial or Indictment *Ex mero motu,* of a sudden an Order issues for the Delivery or Bailment of this miserable Captive; and this called, and must be owned as Grace, though nothing but Suspicion did found the Commitment, or that the Man was thought of a Party, or had been in company with some that were thought so, and some of them perchance had been dabling at Treason or it may be only at true Politicks; and now what Reparation ever was, or ever can be made for such injurious Hardships. This hath been *English* Practice and the same may be possibly repeated. It is certainly therefore the Duty and Interest of our Senators to be wise, and consider and provide for their own and our Posterity now in this, their, and our Day.

Further consider Imprisonment as a possible and safe Instrument or means of Revenge even to Death, for there the Nod of a great Man may be an easie but effectual Guide to a Gaoler (I need not add here any Epithete or harder Name than his own) to provide unwholsome Lodging and worse Diet for his Enemy, especially if he be of a tender Constitution, and then 'tis finishing Work, without the useless Formality of a Challenge, or the ignoble Method of Hirelings and Assassinates, or the more base Fatigue of belabouring Witnesses and managing Juries, in all which there's somewhat of Danger and Hazard to the Avenger, and this hath been practised too in *England.*

When these particulars are duly considered, with the pretty tick-

ling Retirements of the Nobles and Rich of our Realm, and those repeated several times in one Age, and Year, and without Evidence
upon some of them, it may be justly expected, that such Consideration will create an Abhorrence of the least uncertainty or doubtfulness in the Laws of Liberty.

Some will object that these Proposals will embarrass the King's
Affairs in the next Session and therefore unseasonable; but this Objection doth answer itself, the Occasion for Supplies at present makes
our Relief probable in this Conjuncture, which upon another Meeting may find greater Opposition; and if the last Session counter-
mined part of this, a future may dam the whole, therefore now if ever
is the Attempt convenient. Besides a sound Zeal for the present Government, cannot be better testified, than by a cheerful Promotion of
such Laws, for that these Methods do conciliate and fix the Interests, Opinions and Affections of the People to the Crown, and a
Sense of present Ease, Safety and Liberty, with a certain Security of
its Continuance is the surest Preservative of Duty and Assistance
from the Subject; whereas an opposition hereto, must make the Government lose ground by narrowing of its bottom; for that which
crosses the Interest must alienate the Affections of the People, and
this hath been found true in Three Reigns already within our Memory. No Authority or Power can be so considerable and lasting, as
that which is founded on Love and Esteem, and those can never be
acquired with any great Certainty, but by the Allowance of such Concessions as the People need, or think that they need, or think that
they need, and do desire, or demand. Now the Miscarriages of former
Reigns with the Observation of the *French* and others' Tyranny,
which multiplies Commitments upon slight Fears or Suspicions, are
so continually in their Minds and Mouths, that their Belief of the
need of such Securities is not to be eradicated.

'Tis a gross Mistake to imagine, that an easie and full Power of
chopping Men in Pieces upon a Block, or confining them to *Newgate*

or other Gaoles, can add any Strength to the Crown, for *Englishmen* generally speaking are fond of a King, not only for his but their own sakes, and consequently such Fondness can be but of an equal Duration with their Ease and Liberty, and a Suretiship of its Permanency; for the Loss or Fear of the Loss of either, will quickly produce Aversion, and that Hatred, and that somewhat worse: upon which Account, 'tis incumbent upon all true Friends of their present Majesties, to promote this Prosecution of an Additional Security.

POSTSCRIPT.

At last it may be Queried, *What need of all this Bustle and Stir about Liberty, when Parliaments meet so often, that their Awe prevents all these and many more possible Oppressions;* to this I'll answer by another Query, *What new Security have we got, that if the War cease, we shall have a frequency of those Assemblies.*

ADIEU.

FINIS.

Index

Note: Pages in the front matter are indicated by the volume number followed by roman numeral page number(s) (e.g., I:xi–xii).

This book is set in 11 on 15 Adobe Caslon Semibold.
Caslon Old Face was designed in the early eighteenth century
by William Caslon. Caslon based his design on Dutch types
of the late seventeenth century.

This book is printed on paper that is acid-free and meets
the requirements of the American National Standard for Permanence
of Paper for Printed Library Materials, z39.48, 1992. ⊗

Designed by Betty Binns and Erin Kirk New
Typography by Brad Walrod, High Text Graphics, Inc.
Printed and bound by Worzalla Publishing Company,
Stevens Point, Wisconsin